MAPPING MODERN BEIJING

Mapping Modern Beijing

SPACE, EMOTION, LITERARY TOPOGRAPHY

Weijie Song

OXFORD
UNIVERSITY PRESS

OXFORD
UNIVERSITY PRESS

Oxford University Press is a department of the University of Oxford. It furthers
the University's objective of excellence in research, scholarship, and education
by publishing worldwide. Oxford is a registered trade mark of Oxford University
Press in the UK and certain other countries.

Published in the United States of America by Oxford University Press
198 Madison Avenue, New York, NY 10016, United States of America.

CIP data is on file at the Library of Congress
ISBN 978-0-19-020067-1

For Xiaojue Wang 王曉珏 *and Patrick Song* 宋昭齊

Contents

Acknowledgments

THIS BEIJING PROJECT was originally inspired by a 1997 conversation with Professor Chen Pingyuan when he returned to Peking University from a one-year visit to Columbia University sponsored by the Andrew W. Mellon Foundation. Since 1999, Professor David Der-wei Wang, my advisor and mentor, has encouraged me to continue the adventurous and long journey into the (in)visible Beijing with his unwavering support and wise guidance.

I would like to express my heartfelt gratitude to many other professors and teachers, including the late C. T. Hsia, Wei Shang, Ping-hui Liao, Wendy Swartz, Lening Liu, Paul Anderer, Andreas Huyssen, Carol Gluck, Gayatri Spivak, Hamid Dabashi, Elisabeth Bronfen, Michael Tsin, Robert Hymes, Haruo Shirane, Tomi Suzuki, Feng Li, Yunzhong Shu, Dorothy Ko, Leo Ou-fan Lee, Michelle Yeh, Xiaomei Chen, Ban Wang, Sheldon Lu, Kang-I Sun Chang, Haun Saussy, Ron Egan, Paul Kroll, Liu Zaifu, Yingjin Zhang, Xiaobing Tang, Kirk Denton, Michel Hockx, Tani Barlow, and Suisheng Zhao. I am also enormously grateful to Professors Yue Daiyun, Dai Jinhua, Wang Hui, Zhao Yuan, Wen Rumin, Yan Jiayan, Qian Liqun, Chen Yangu, Liu Huiying, Chen Sihe, Wang Ning, Cao Shunqing, K'o Ching-ming, Cheung Suk-hong, Mei Chia-ling, Cheng Yu-yu, Shen Dung, Hu Hsiao-chen, Li Hsiao-ti, and Kwok Kou Leonard Chan.

Parts of this Beijing book have been presented at different institutions. Friends, classmates, and colleagues deserve my deep appreciation: Carlos Rojas, Michael

ix

Berry, Jianmei Liu, Letty Chen, Robin Visser, Charles Laughlin, Ann Huss, Mingwei Song, Enhua Zhang, Christopher Rea, Michael Hill, I-Hsien Wu, Linda Feng, Hui-Lin Hsu, Lillian Ho, Andrew Schonebaum, Alexander Cook, Kerim Yasar, Eileen Chow, Jing Tsu, Chien-hsin Tsai, Jie Li, Andrea Bachner, Yomi Braester, Haiyan Lee, Haili Kong, John Lent, Shuang Shen, Nick Kaldis, Ko Chia cian, Woo Kam Loon, Liu Hsiu-Mei, Wong Nim Yan, Fan Sin Piu, Isaac Yue, Cao Weidong, Chen Xuguang, He Zhaotian, Zang Di, Li Meng, Qu Jingdong, Wu Fei, Li Kang, Shu Wei, He Guimei, Huang Yihan, Wu Xiaodong, Ji Jin, Pan Yao Ming, Lin Jianfa, Rongxiang Zhang, Richard Jandowitz, Alex Brown, James Cheng, Shu-mei Shih, Wendy Larson, Tze-lan Sang, Maram Epstein, Bryna Goodman, Ina Asim, Yugen Wang, Daisuke Miyao, Wei Hong, Daniel Hsieh, Paul Dixon, Charles Ross, Fenggang Yang, Juan Wang, Shaun Hughes, Beate I. Allert, Thomas Broden, Elena Coda, Atsushi Fukada, Patricia Hart, Kazumi Hatasa, Benjamin Lawton, Howard Mancing, Song No, Eiji Sekine, Marcia Stephenson, Dawn F. Stinchcomb, Mariko Moroishi Wei, Jennifer William, Alice Wang, Ai-Jen Wann, Victoria Beard, Michael Beard, Ellen Widmer, Yoshiko Yokochi Samuel, Stephen Angle, Xiaomiao Zhu, Terry Kawashima, Alexander Des Forges, Su Zheng, Mengjun Liu, Wei Su, Shizhe Huang, Paul Smith, Suzanne Spain, Azade Seyhan, Jingyuan Zhang, Philip Kafalis, Jordan Sand, Kevin Doak, Eleanor J. Hogan, Leo Shingchi Yip, Karen Beckman, David Brownlee, Siyen Fei, Suvir Kaul, Ania Loomba, Victor Mair, Ayako Kano, Thomas Moran, Robert Hegel, Zhao Ma, Chuck Wooldridge, Luca Gabbiani, Sujane Wu, Chen Xuechao, Hua-Yuan L. Mowry, Pamela Crossley, Sarah Allan, Wen Xing, Susan Blader, James Dorsey, Levi Gibbs, Leonard K. Cheng, Richard Davis, Cai Zong-qi, Sun Yifeng, Xu Zidong, Wang Chunhong, Kwong Yim-tze, Lau Yin-ping, Lee Hung-kai, Hsu Tzu-pin, Chan Wai-ying, Sitou Sau-ieng, and Wei Yan.

Rutgers University provides an extraordinarily supportive, motivating, and rewarding environment for my research and teaching. I must express my enormous gratitude to Ching-I Tu, Richard VanNess Simmons, Wendy Swartz, Jessey Choo, Dietrich Tschanz, Paul Schalow, Janet Walker, Senko Maynard, Young-mee Cho, Satoru Saito, Suzy Kim, Tao Jiang, Xun Liu, Louisa Schein, Tao Yang, Elin Diamond, Andrew Parker, Jorge Marcone, James Swenson, Ann Fabian, Doug Greenberg, and Peter March. Special thanks go to the generous support from the Department of Asian Languages and Cultures, the Confucius Institute of Rutgers University, Competitive Leave Fellowship Program, Rutgers Research Council Grants, the Chiang Ching-kuo Foundation for International Scholarly Exchange, L. C. Goodrich Fellowship, Weatherhead Fellowship, and President's Fellowship at Columbia University.

I feel extremely privileged and proud to work with Suzanne Ryan, Brendan O'Neill, Sarah Pirovitz, Abigail Johnson, and Alexa Marcon of Oxford University

Press, my copyeditor Henry Southgate, as well as Gayathree Sekar, Raj Suthan and the team of Newgen KnowledgeWorks, who have been tremendously supportive, understanding, and helpful while the manuscript was being prepared for publication. My heartfelt thanks also go to two anonymous reviewers for their insightful and instructive comments and suggestions. Chapter 3 appeared as "The Aesthetic versus the Political" in *Chinese Literature: Essays, Articles, Reviews* (*CLEAR*) 36 (2014); two portions of chapter 5 were respectively published as "Emotional Topography, Food Memory, and Bittersweet Aftertaste" in *Journal of Oriental Studies* 45, nos. 1–2 (2012), and "Positions of Sinophone Representation in Jin's Chivalric Topography" in *CLCWeb: Comparative Literature and Culture* 17, no. 1 (2015); "Epilogue" appeared as "Writing Cities" in Blackwell's *A Companion to Modern Chinese Literature* (2015) edited by Yingjin Zhang. I deeply appreciate Michelle Yeh, Cuncun Wu, Steven Tötösy de Zepetnek, and Emily Corkhill for the generous permission to reprint here. All versions have been revised for this work.

My parents, Song Wenmo and Sun Guangqin, and my parents-in-law, Wang Guangcai and Jia Fuxian, have offered invaluable and infinite support and help for the completion of this book and for the birth and growth of Patrick Song. My brother Song Weiguang also has provided constant help from Beijing in the different stages of this project. My deepest thank goes to Xiaojue Wang, my wife, classmate, and soul mate, who has always shared feelings and emotions with me in every step of my life since we first met at Peking University in 1995. Xiaojue is the extremely insightful and strict reader and critic of every chapter of my book. She is present in many ways in my thinking and writing. I dedicate this Beijing book to Xiaojue.

Weijie Song

The city is shown as at once a social fact and a human landscape. What is dramatized in it is a very complex structure of feeling.

—RAYMOND WILLIAMS

Emotion materializes as a moving topography.

—GIULIANA BRUNO

Introduction

AFFECTIVE MAPPING OF MODERN BEIJING

HOW DOES AN observer, whether a native, a stranger, a sojourner, a scholar, or a foreign traveler, look at, listen to, smell, taste, or touch the ancient yet modern Beijing?[1] Does one configure the material and spiritual life of the city as a living entity with mind and soul, with the help of scientific investigations or aesthetic imaginations? Or trace the long history of the capital by a positivist study of countless files and archives? Or analyze economic activities, social organizations, or collective mentalities of the metropolis by adopting the methodology of the *Annales* School? Or highlight Beijing's human characteristics, spatial diversity, political divisions, cultural inertia, or "affective turn" in the "realms of memories"?[2] As historians

---

[1] From 1928 to 1949, Beijing 北京 was named Beiping 北平 after the Nationalist government moved its capital to Nanjing. In 1937, the occupying Japanese imposed the name Beijing until the surrender of Japan in 1945. The Nationalist government restored the name Beiping until the end of the Chinese civil war between the Communists and the Nationalists. After the founding of the People's Republic of China in 1949, the city was chosen as the capital and renamed again as Beijing. The spelling Peking was used from 1949 to 1958. The *hanyu pinyin* Romanization, "Beijing," has been used within China since 1958. The American government continued to follow the Nationalist government in using Beiping until the late 1960s, but since 1979, "Beijing" has been gradually and widely adopted by governments, news organizations, and international agencies. For practical purposes, I use Beijing to call the city and capital in the major body of my book.

[2] See contemporary French historian Pierre Nora's summary of modern French history and historiography, and his reinterpretations of French characters by emphasizing the relations between history and memory, in "From Lieux de Mémoire to Realms of Memory" and "General Introduction: Between Memory and History," in *Realms of Memory* (New York: Columbia University Press, 1996), 1:xv–xxiv, 1–20. For classical documents on history and memory at the turn of the century and in the late twentieth century, see Friedrich Nietzsche, *On*

and social scientists have produced considerable scholarship on various aspects of urban planning and social movements, what insights can literature and literary studies provide to approach Beijing's spatial transformation, emotional vicissitudes, modern experiences, and urban narratives?

This book considers the relationship between Chinese and non-Chinese literature and the city of Beijing from the first half of the twentieth century. I aim to explore the literary topography of space and emotion, the (de)formation of modern subjectivity, individual desire and collective consciousness, political conflicts and historical violence, as well as nationalist sentiments and cultural memories centering around the ancient capital and modern city, which has framed the material infrastructures, human conditions, mental images, political regimes, cultural identities, and literary imaginations from the late Imperial and Republican periods to the Cold War era and after. Urban spaces are sociocultural constructs and always underlain by affective attachments. The city evokes emotional responses from inhabitants, sojourners, and visitors, and awaits never-ending writing and reading. The literary and artistic works on Beijing that I discuss in this book were composed by authors from mainland China, Taiwan, Hong Kong, Europe, America, and diasporic Sinophone communities.

ARTICULATING BEIJING IN MY HEART

Cities, like dreams, are made of desires and fears, even if the thread of their discourse is secret, their rules are absurd, their perspectives deceitful, and everything conceals something else.
—ITALO CALVINO

When reflecting on modern Beijing's accommodation of the past and the present, Lao Xiang 老向 (1901–1968), a native Beijing writer, noted in 1935, "I have lived in Beijing for thirty years, but I can't say that I have yet comprehended this city" (我在北平住了三十年了,但是我不能說已經認識北平).[3] The writer Xu Xu 徐訏 (1908–1980) stated with an ironic tone in 1934, "For those who missed and recalled Beijing with nostalgia, no one could express its special characteristics" (那些想念與留戀北平的人,是沒有一個能說出北平的好處的).[4] In his well-known essay "Missing Beijing" (*Xiang Beiping* 想北平, 1936), Lao She 老舍 (1899–1966), a

---

the *Advantage and Disadvantage of History for Life*, trans. Peter Preuss (Indianapolis: Hackett, 1980); Maurice Halbwachs, *The Collective Memory* (New York: Harper, 1980); Michel Foucault, *Language, Counter-Memory, Practice* (Ithaca, NY: Cornell University Press, 1922); and Nora, *Realms of Memory*.

[3] Lao Xiang, "Nan renshi de Beiping" 難認識的北平 [The unrecognizable Beijing], in *Beijing hu: xiandai zuojia bixia de Beijing, 1919–1949* 北京乎：现代作家笔下的北京 （一九一九─一九四九） [*Ah, Beijing: Beijing in modern Chinese writings, 1919–1949*], ed. Jiang Deming 姜德明 (Beijing: Sanlian shudian, 1992), 294. Unless otherwise indicated, the English translation is mine.

[4] Xu Xu, "Beiping de fengdu" 北平的風度 [Beijing's manners], in Jiang, *Beijing hu*, 375.

preeminent Beijing native writer, confessed, "There is a Beijing in my heart, but I can't articulate it" (我心中有個北平，可是我說不出來).[5] In "Captive Peiping Holds the Soul," published in *The New York Times* in 1937, the celebrated bilingual writer Lin Yutang 林語堂 (1895–1976) wrote, "Peiping is like a grand old tree, whose roots stretch deep into the earth and draw sustenance from it . . . . How can a Peiping resident describe Peiping, so old and so grand?"[6]

All these remarks are interestingly focused on the unspeakability and unrepresentability of the city in their minds and hearts. What is this indescribable quality of Beijing within and without the realms of feelings and emotions? These writers employ verbs such as "comprehend," "express," "articulate," or "describe" to address their relationship with the city, that of longing, remembering, learning, writing, understanding, or literary representation, dealing with the city in the same way they deal with a profound text open to endless encoding and decoding. What is illegible and inexpressible about the city, defying reading and deciphering? In *Sishi tongtang* 四世同堂 (Four generations under one roof, 1944–1950), a novel about occupied Beijing during the second Sino-Japanese war, Lao She portrays an Englishman, Mr. Goodrich, who lives in the city for thirty years and cherishes everything in this ancient capital: mandarin beads, opium sets, shoes for bound feet, official peacock feather insignia, and Chinese New Year woodcuts, among many others. Regarding himself as a living encyclopedia of Beijing lore and Beijing as his second hometown, Mr. Goodrich claims that he will write a masterpiece on Beijing. However, this promised manuscript of his idealized Beijing is never finished.

Centuries before Mr. Goodrich, Marco Polo (1254–1324) wrote about the compelling shock he felt upon first experiencing Beijing, the capital of the Yuan dynasty, and about the impossibility of describing the city's immensity and perfection:

The streets are so straight and wide that you can see right along them from end to end and from one gate to the other. And up and down the city there are beautiful palaces, and many great and fine hostelries, and fine houses in great numbers. [All the plots of ground on which the houses of the city are built are four-square, and laid out with straight lines; all the plots being occupied by great and spacious palaces, with courts and gardens of proportionate size. All these plots were assigned to different heads of families. Each square plot is encompassed by handsome streets for traffic; and thus the whole city

---

[5] Lao She, "Xiang Beiping" [Missing Beijing], in Jiang, *Beijing hu*, 409.

[6] Lin Yutang, "Captive Peiping Holds the Soul," *New York Times*, August 15, 1937. Another version is "Captive Peking," in Lin Yutang, *With Love and Irony* (New York: The John Day Company, 1940), 54–62.

is arranged in squares just like a chess-board, and disposed in a manner so perfect and masterly that it is impossible to give a description that should do it justice.][7]

In 1972, Italo Calvino (1923–1985), in a fictional version of Marco Polo's story, turns this mission impossible to learn and represent Beijing into a process of fluid and eloquent storytelling, in which Polo describes other cities he visited on his way to Beijing to an aged Kublai Khan, the ruler of this great city. Sensing the impeding crisis,

> that desperate moment when we discover that this empire, which had seemed to us the sum of all wonders, is an endless, formless ruin, . . . only in Marco Polo's accounts was Kublai Khan able to discern, through the walls and towers destined to crumble, the tracery of a pattern so subtle it could escape the termites gnawing.[8]

This "tracery of a pattern" that is so intangible and unable to be grasped, yet so durable as to survive the termites gnawing is precisely what literature of the city seeks to convey, yet simultaneously, is limited in its ability to represent.

Given the rich tradition of world literature about cities—Charles Baudelaire and Paris, Walter Benjamin and Berlin, Arthur Schnitzler or Hugo von Hofmannsthal and Vienna, Fyodor Dostoevsky or Andrei Bely and Saint Petersburg, James Joyce and Dublin, Charles Dickens and London, Saul Bellow and Chicago, Walt Whitman and New York, Jorge Luis Borges and Buenos Aires, Yasunari Kawabata and Kyoto, Lao She or Zhang Henshui 張恨水 and Beijing, Zhang Ailing (Eileen Chang) 張愛玲 or Wang Anyi 王安憶 and Shanghai, Jia Pingwa 賈平凹 and Xi'an, Ye Zhaoyan 葉兆言 and Nanjing, Xi Xi 西西 or Dung Kai-cheung (Dong Qizhang) 董啟章 and Hong Kong, Bai Xianyong 白先勇, Zhu Tianwen 朱天文 or Zhu Tianxin 朱天心 and Taipei—the city-text indeed invokes close reading of a wide array of generic varieties and differentiations. Richard Lehan observes,

> The rise of the city as inseparable from various kinds of literary movements— in particular the development of the novel and subsequent narrative modes: comic realism, romantic realism, naturalism, modernism, and postmodernism. These modes, in turn, contain subgenres like the utopian novel,

---

[7] Marco Polo, *Book of Ser Marco Polo*, ed. Henry Yule (New York: Scriber's, 1903), as quoted in Lin Yutang, *Imperial Peking: Seven Centuries of China* (London: Elek Books Limited, 1961), 35.

[8] Italo Calvino, *Invisible Cities*, trans. William Weaver (New York: Harcourt, 1974), 5.

the gothic novel, the detective story, the young-man-from-the-provinces novel, the novel of imperial adventure, the western, science fiction, and dystopian narrative.[9]

How to decode a city-text and chart a literary topography remains a challenge for literary storytellers and scholars.

I explore the intriguing relations between literature and the city of Beijing, from its final imperial years, to its Republican era, and to its socialist stage starting in 1949, when the People's Republic of China was founded. By charting the spatial trajectories of urban emotions in literary representations of modern Beijing, I address the following questions: How did the changing cityscapes in Beijing affect the formation and deformation of a modern subjectivity and generate new perception and apprehension, imagination and representation? And how did literary representations in turn capture and shape urban transformations and social constructions in the worlds of physical and emotional life? Literature takes as its task conveying the real and the imaginary, the material and the intangible of a city, and constructing in the reader's mind an urban imaginary that grounds the city in its multilayered lived spaces, historical temporalities, and emotional variations while resisting the limitations of its materiality.

EMOTION, *QING*, AND CHINESE URBAN NARRATIVE

In contemplating emotional life in any culturally specific setting, it seems important to note that emotions have a linguistic life and a public and political status that frequently engender formulaic modes of expression.

—ARJUN APPADURAI

Literary writers rely on imaginative forms of cities to explore what Georg Simmel (1858–1918) defined as "the state of mind,"[10] what Raymond Williams (1921–1988) regarded as a "structure of feeling,"[11] and what Harold Bloom (1930–) called "cities of the mind."[12] In his widely anthologized essay "Metropolis and Mental Life," Simmel suggests exploring the city by diagnosing "the state of mind" of city

---

[9] Richard Lehan, *The City in Literature: An Intellectual and Cultural History* (Berkeley: University of California Press, 1998), 1.

[10] Georg Simmel, "The Metropolis and Mental Life," in *On Individuality and Social Forms* (Chicago: University of Chicago Press, 1971), 324–339.

[11] Raymond Williams, *The Long Revolution* (London: Chatto & Windus, 1961), 64. See also his *The Country and the City* (New York: Oxford University Press, 1973), 158.

[12] Harold Bloom, "Introduction," in "Cities of the Mind," a series of literary places including New York, Paris, London, Rome, Dublin, and St. Petersburg; see *New York* (New York: Chelsea House Publishers, 2004), vii–xi.

inhabitants, in that "the psychological foundation, upon which the metropolitan individuality is erected, is the intensification of emotional life due to the swift and continuous shift of external and internal stimuli."[13] Williams proposes a way of describing "structure of feeling" in his early work *The Long Revolution*:

> The term I would suggest to describe it is structure of feeling: it is as firm and definite as "structure" suggests, yet it operates in the most delicate and least tangible parts of our activity. In one sense, this structure of feeling is the culture of a period: it is the particular living result of all the elements in the general organization. And it is in this respect that the arts of a period, taking these to include characteristic approaches and tones in argument, are of major importance. For here, if anywhere, this characteristic is likely to be expressed.[14]

In *Marxism and Literature*, Williams further defines structure of feeling as a set of collective sentiments in process that has not yet been formalized in fixed ideologies or values: "We are talking about characteristic elements of impulse, restraint, and tone; specifically affective elements of consciousness and relationships: not feeling against thought, but thought as felt and feeling as thought: practical consciousness of a present kind, in a living and inter-relating continuity."[15] The structure of feeling is related to new relationships and cultural forms and mediates those affective elements between the social and the personal. According to Williams, structure of feeling resides in personal interactions and relationships in everyday life and reveals itself in literature and arts of the time period.

The terms of "emotion," "feeling," "affect," "mind," "mood," and "sentiment," among others, have been used loosely and interchangeably. Categories, types, and meanings of emotions constitute one of the major issues in philosophical investigations. Ronald de Sousa succinctly states, "No aspect of our mental life is more important to the quality and meaning of our existence than emotions. They are what make life worth living, or sometimes ending. So it is not surprising that most of the great classical philosophers—Plato, Aristotle, Spinoza, Descartes, Hobbes, Hume— had recognizable theories of emotion, conceived as responses to certain sorts of events of concern to a subject, triggering bodily changes and typically motivating characteristic behavior." [16] Recent interdisciplinary studies seek to clarify the theoretical ambiguities of these keywords. Relying on Gilles Deleuze and Felix Guattari's

---

[13] Simmel, "The Metropolis and Mental Life," 325.

[14] Williams, *The Long Revolution*, 65.

[15] Raymond Williams, *Marxism and Literature* (Oxford: Oxford University Press, 1977), 132.

[16] Ronald de Sousa, "Emotion," in *The Stanford Encyclopedia of Philosophy*, first published Febuary 3, 2003, substantive revised January 21, 2013, http://plato.stanford.edu/archives/spr2014/entries/emotion/.

A Thousand Plateaus and Brian Massumi's translation notes, Eric Shouse delineates that "feelings are personal and biographical, emotions are social, and affects are pre-personal," and further elucidates that "an emotion is the projection/display of a feeling. Unlike feelings, the display of emotion can be either genuine or feigned . . . . We broadcast emotion to the world; sometimes that broadcast is an expression of our internal state and other times it is contrived in order to fulfill social expectations."[17] In this sense, emotion is interpersonal and social, combining individual and collective/public feelings.

Theoretical approaches from Sara Ahmed, Teresa Brennan, Patricia Ticineto Clough, Jean Halley, Melissa Gregg, and Gregory J. Seigworth, among others, attempt to "distinguish among emotion (as tied to a particular body or subject), feeling (the subjective response to emotion), and affect which is often imagined as a quality that escapes emotions and feelings because it does not belong to a particular body or subject but, rather, enables a bidirectional capacity to affect and be affected."[18] Stephanie Trigg also points out that, broadly, affect can be interchangeable with emotion, yet for contemporary theories, affect is pursuing the emphasis of poststructuralism and deconstruction on subjectivity, identity, and the body.[19] I would agree with Stephanie Trigg that emotion can serve as an inclusive and umbrella term for other keywords like affect, sentiment, feeling, and passion, and emotion is also more historical, in that it pays more attention to the dialectic of continuity and discontinuity among premodern, modern, and postmodern culture.

In the larger context of traditional Chinese language, literature, and philosophy, *qing* 情 carries double meanings and can alternatively refer to both emotion and situation, "both inner feeling and (actual or conceptual) circumstances."[20] With regard to *qing* as emotions or feelings, Confucius (551–479, BC) says, "What are human

---

[17] Eric Shouse, "Feeling, Emotion, Affect," *M/c journal* 8, no. 6 (2005), http://journal.media-culture.org.au/0512/03-shouse.php. See Gilles Deleuze and Felix Guattari, *A Thousand Plateaus*, trans. Brian Massumi (Minneapolis: University of Minnesota Press, 1987). Brian Massumi contends that it is necessary to make a distinction between affect and emotion; see his *Parables for the Virtual: Movement, Affect, Sensation* (Durham, NC: Duke University Press, 2002).

[18] Katharine Ann Jensen and Miriam L. Wallace, "Introduction—Facing Emotions," *PMLA* 130, no. 5 (2015): 1254. See Sara Ahmed, *The Cultural Politics of Emotion* (New York: Routledge, 2004); Teresa Brennan, *The Transmission of Affect* (Ithaca, NY: Cornell University Press, 2004); Patricia Ticineto Clough and Jean Halley, eds., *The Affective Turn* (Durham, NC: Duke University Press, 2007); and Melissa Gregg and Gregory J. Seigworth, eds., *The Affect Theory Reader* (Durham, NC: Duke University Press, 2010). See also Aaron Ben-Ze'ev, *The Subtlety of Emotions* (Cambridge, MA: MIT Press, 2000); and Jennifer Harding and E. Deidre Pribram, eds., *Emotions: A Cultural Studies Reader* (London: Routledge, 2009).

[19] Stephanie Trigg, "Introduction: Emotional Histories—Beyond the Personalization of the Past and the Abstraction of Affect Theory," *Exemplaria* 26, no. 1 (2014): 3–15.

[20] For a brief and extensive overview of traditional discourse of *qing*, see, for instance, David Der-wei Wang, *The Lyrical in Epic Time: Modern Chinese Intellectuals and Artists through the 1949 Crisis* (New York: Columbia University Press, 2015), 6–10, 23.

feelings of men? They are joy, anger, sadness, fear, love, disliking, and liking. These seven feelings belong to men without their learning them." (何謂人情？喜、怒、哀、懼、愛、惡、欲，七者弗學而能).[21] Tang Yijie 湯一介, the renowned modern scholar of Chinese philosophy, examines emotion in Pre-Qin Confucian moral philosophy, and points out,

> "*Qing*" typically refers to the "seven *qing*" (delight, anger, grief, fear, love, dislike, desire [*xi, nu, ai, ju, ai, wu, yu* 喜怒哀懼愛惡慾]), the "six *qing*" (delight, anger, grief, enjoyment [*le* 樂], fondnesss [*hao* 好], dislike), or the "five *qing*" (delight, anger, grief, enjoyment, resentment [*yuan* 怨]).[22]

Qing begins with *xing* 性 (human nature); this reminds of Deleuze, Guattari, and Massumi's recent characterization of affect as prepersonal. Martin W. Huang remarks that Mencius (ca. 372–289, BC) optimistically proposes, "[I]f you allow people to follow their *qing*, they will be able to do good" (乃若其情，則可以為善矣); by the Western Han dynasty (206 BC–9 AD), Dong Zhongshu 董仲舒 (c.a. 179–104 BC) was among the first to highlight the negative moral connotations of *qing*; in the Song (960–1279) Neo-Confucian scheme, especially in Zhu Xi's 朱熹 (1130–1200) thoughts, *qing* is possibly overflowing and morally suspect; nevertheless, Wang Yangming 王陽明 (1472–1529), a leading philosopher in the Ming (1368–1644) Neo-Confucian School, unprecedently emphasizes the significance of human subjectivity.[23] Wang Yangming's notions of "philosophy of mind" (心學), "consistency between words and deeds" (知行合一), and "attaining the supreme conscience" (致良知),[24] enlighten and propel Feng Menglong 馮夢龍 (1574–1646), a follower of Wang Yangming's School of Mind, to advocate a "cult of *qing*" (情教) in late Ming vernacular literature.[25]

David Der-wei Wang 王德威 further outlines the trajectories of *qing* from the late Ming to the late Qing periods:

> The late Ming saw the climax of the poetics of *qing*, represented by the works of Tang Xianzu 湯顯祖 (1550–1616) and fellow literati. In response to the

---

[21] Confucius et al., *The Book of Rites (Li Ji): English-Chinese Version*, ed. Dai Sheng, trans. James Legge (Beijing: Intercultural Press, 2013), 104.

[22] Tang Yijie, *Confucianism, Buddhism, Daoism, Christianity, and Chinese Culture* (Beijing: Foreign Language Teaching and Research Publishing Co., Ltd; Berlin: Springer-Verlag, 2015), 56–57.

[23] Martin W. Huang, *Desire and Fictional Narrative in Late Imperial China* (Cambridge, MA: Harvard University Asia Center, 2001), 25–28.

[24] Shi Changyu, "Wang Yangming's Neo-Confucian School of Mind and the Growth of Ancient Chinese Popular Novel," trans. Yao Zhenjun, *Frontiers of Literary Studies in China* 2, no. 3 (2009): 195–217.

[25] See Paolo Santangelo, "The Cult of Love in Some Texts of Ming and Qing Literature," *East and West* 50 (2000): 439–499.

moralistic interpretation of *shiyanzhi*, Tang argues that "intent is nothing but feeling" (志也者, 情也). While valorizing the innate, primordial power of *qing*, Tang and his contemporaries also recapitulated its multiple connotations. One thus sees a wide range of approaches to the meaning, function, and consequence of *qing* in the following centuries. For instance, Wang Fuzhi 王夫之 (1619–1692) contemplates the fusion of feeling and scenery; Huang Zongxi 黃宗羲 (1610–1695) differentiates *zhongqing* 眾情 (public feeling) and *yiqing* 一情 (individual feeling); Cao Xueqin 曹雪芹 (1724–1763) ponders the paradox of *qing* and *qing buqing* 情不情 (feeling nonfeeling); Gong Zizhen 龔自珍 (1792–1841) challenges the historical and intellectual strictures of *qing* (*youqing* 宥情); Liu E 劉鶚 (1857–1909) yearns for a nationhood nurtured on the cosmology of *qing*. With this spectrum of *qing* discourses, from amorous attachment to historical bearing, from transcendental thought to political awareness, Chinese moderns came to reformulate their lyrical/*shuqing* thought.[26]

Paolo Santangelo classifies emotions and states of mind based on Chinese literature and history (in particular the Ming-Qing dynasties), illustrates the closest "equivalent" English translations of the emotions or mood represented directly or indirectly in the Chinese source, and lists the following five families of emotions:

In each language emotions and states of mind may be grouped in terms of similarity and affinity under the larger umbrella terms of affective complexes, which presumably represent as many families of emotions including—for the sake of convenience—variants and intermediate phenomena. Such larger complexes of emotions are: 1. negative projections (Fear, suspicion, anxiety and surprise), 2. positive projections (love, affection, desire, hope), 3. satisfactory affections (joy, aesthetic/religious perception, pleasure, satisfaction), 4. aggressive emotions (anger, hatred, jealousy), 5. unsatisfactory affections (sorrow, depression, shame).[27]

---

[26] Wang, *The Lyrical in Epic Time*, English manuscript, and the first chapter "Introduction: Inventing the 'Lyrical Tradition,'" 1–38. For a representative anthology of modern scholarship on Chinese lyrical tradition and its modern interpretation, see Kwok Kou Leonard Chan 陳國球 and David Der-wei Wang, eds., *Shuqing zhi xiandaixing* 抒情之現代性 [The modernity of lyricism] (Beijing: Sanlian shudian, 2014).

[27] See his emotion database homepage, http://users.libero.it/p.santangelo/database.htm, and a more detailed and extensive explanation in his "Some Conclusive Remarks on the Examination of Different Sources: The Analysis of Non-literary Documents (Moralistic and Judicial Materials)," in *Love, Hatred, and Other Passions: Questions and Themes on Emotions in Chinese Civilization*, ed. Paolo Santangelo and Donatella Guida (Leiden: Brill, 2006), 404–408.

He also rightly notes that "emotions are inextricably linked to the inner life of the individual but also to his social life."[28]

In this book, I understand emotions—interpersonal, social, and historical—as a subtle typology rather than a sustained discourse. Literature, a paramount form of "emotion," "feeling," "affect," "sentiment," and "mind," serves as the significant vehicle through which the "atlas of emotions"[29] of a city can be outlined and illustrated. Therefore this book attempts to explore the multilayered and overlapping affective mapping of literary Beijing in terms of individual and personal "lived experiences" as well as the collective, social, political, and cultural "state of mind." Andreas Huyssen maintains that "literary techniques of reading historically, intertextually, constructively, and deconstructively at the same time can be woven into our understanding of urban spaces as lived spaces that shape collective imaginaries."[30] Literary authors' points of view, sensibilities, perceptions, representations, and imaginations investigate and describe the individual and collective emotions and "mental life," correlating and complementing what historical and social data and statistics reveal about the material reality of a city.

In Chinese studies, cities have seldom been the focal point. With the majority of the population being peasants, China has been considered a predominantly rural country, where the idea of "native land" allegorically represents the nation-state. Leo Ou-fan Lee points out that Chinese scholarship in Western academia was "preoccupied with rural villages."[31] Joseph W. Esherick also observes, "[I]n a nation of peasants, Chinese cities have not always received the attention they deserve."[32] Not until the 1980s did academic research on Chinese cities start to emerge in English-language scholarship as the history of Chinese cities and urban lives attracted increasing attention. Most of these studies were conducted in the fields of history and social sciences, which substantially help our understanding of the unique trajectories of Chinese urbanism.[33]

---

[28] Paolo Santangelo, "Introduction," in Santangelo and Guida, ed., *Love, Hatred, and Other Passions*, 2. The three-volume *Passion, Romance, and* Qing: *The World of Emotions and States of Mind in* Peony Pavilion (2014) edited by Tian Yuan Tan and Paolo Santangelo (in Brill's encyclopedic series, Emotions and States of Mind in East Asia) provides an extensive glossary of specific terms and expressions related to the representation of emotions and states of mind in *Peony Pavilion*, a famous drama written by Tang Xianzu in the late Ming dynasty.

[29] I am indebted to Giuliana Bruno's *Atlas of Emotion: Journeys in Art, Architecture, and Film* (London: Verso, 2002).

[30] Andreas Huyssen, *Present Pasts: Urban Palimpsests and the Politics of Memory* (Stanford, CA: Stanford University Press, 2003), 7.

[31] Leo Ou-fan Lee, *Shanghai Modern: The Flowering of a New Urban Culture in China, 1930–1945* (Cambridge, MA: Harvard University Press, 1999), xi.

[32] Joseph W. Esherick, ed., *Remaking the Chinese City: Modernity and National Identity, 1900–1950* (Stanford, CA: Stanford University Press, 2000), ix.

[33] G. William Skinner, *The City in Late Imperial China* (Stanford, CA: Stanford University Press, 1977); William Rowe, *Hankow: Commerce and Society in a Chinese City, 1796–1889* (Stanford, CA: Stanford University Press,

Since the 1990s, English-language literary studies of modern Chinese cities have grown apace. Yingjin Zhang calls attention to the recurrent city-country antithesis "deeply ingrained in the mentality of modern Chinese writers," and explores the spatial, temporal, and gender configurations and changes in modern Beijing and Shanghai.[34] Leo Ou-fan Lee examines Shanghai's literary sensibility, cultural cartography, modern consciousness, and cosmopolitan imagination. Recently, mainland Chinese scholars asserted that the discursive predominance of twentieth-century revolution and enlightenment defines and determines the nature of modern Chinese literature; that is, peasants and villagers become the dominant images, if not stereotypes, of modern Chinese literary narratives.[35] However, the ongoing modernization process, the rapid development of globalization, and the recent colossal growth of urbanization, particularly in mainland China since the 1990s, among other factors, have changed the ratio, size, and scope of rural and urban population as well as the relation between infrastructure and superstructure, and have therefore redefined the literary liaison between the country and the city, and entailed the booming of literature and literary studies of the cities at the turn of the twenty-first century.

It is worth noting that "*chengshi wenxue*" 城市文學 (urban literature) is a broad, loosely defined subgenre and literary keyword. The terms "*cheng*" 城 (city, wall), "*shi*" 市 (city, market), "*chengshi*" 城市 (city), and "*dushi*" 都市 (metropolis) refer to a set of multiple meanings ranging from county administrative centers, small market towns, midsized cities, and large capitals, to major metropolises (including treaty ports and commercial manufacturing centers) in terms of size, population, function, administration, and governance.[36] *Chengshi wenxue* has also been alternatively mixed with *dushi wenxue* in the heated debates on the rise of literary mappings of Chinese cities and metropolises since the 1990s. Furthermore, the Chinese

---

1984); and *Hankow: Conflict and Community in a Chinese City, 1796–1895* (Stanford, CA: Stanford University Press, 1989); Frederic E. Wakeman, *Policing Shanghai, 1927–1937* (Berkeley: University of California Press, 1995); Frederic E. Wakeman and Wen-hsin Yeh, eds., *Shanghai Sojourners* (Stanford, CA: Stanford University Press, 1992); David Strand, *Rickshaw Beijing: City People and Politics in the 1920s* (Berkeley: University of California Press, 1989); Susan Naquin, *Peking: Temples and City Life, 1400–1900* (Berkeley: University of California Press, 2000); Madeleine Yue Dong, *Republican Beijing: The City and Its Histories* (Berkeley: University of California Press, 2003); and Wu Hung, *Remaking Beijing: Tiananmen Square and the Creation of a Political Space* (Chicago: The University of Chicago Press, 2005).

[34] Yingjin Zhang, *The City in Modern Chinese Literature and Film: Configurations of Space, Time, and Gender* (Stanford, CA: Stanford University Press, 1996), xvii.

[35] See, for instance, Zhang Hongsheng 張鴻聲, "'Wenxue zhong de chengshi' yu 'chengshi xiangxiang' yanjiu" "文學中的城市" 與 "城市想象" 研究 ["The city in literature" and research of "urban imagination"], *Wenxue pinglun* 文學評論 1 (2007): 116–122; and Yang Jianlong 楊劍龍, "Lun Zhongguo dushi wenxue yu dushi wenxue yanjiu" 論中國都市文學與都市文學研究 [On Chinese urban literature and urban literary studies], *Jianghan luntan* 江漢論壇 [Jianghan forum] 3 (2013): 11–16.

[36] Zhang, *The City in Modern Chinese Literature and Film*, 6–7.

term "*chengshi wenxue*" vaguely indicates both "cities in literature" and "literature in cities," and the cities serve as geographical backgrounds, cultural settings, or the subject matter for literary imagination and aesthetical/political investigation. Scholarship of Chinese urban literature has focused on, among others, the relationship between the city and the people;[37] the rise and fall of literary schools and narrative modes;[38] the configurations of time, space, and gender in urban milieu;[39] the new urban culture and alternative modernity in wartime China;[40] urban imagination and cultural memory;[41] multimedia, urbanism, and global transformation in Maoist and post-Maoist China;[42] as well as emotions, feelings, affects, and literary topography.

FIVE METHODS OF IMAGINING BEIJING

> Work on a good piece of writing proceeds on three levels: a musical one, where it is composed; an architectural one, where it is constructed; and finally, a textile one, where it is woven.
>
> —WALTER BENJAMIN

Founded in 1045 BC, Beijing has been for more than 850 years the capital of China. Imperial Beijing with its palaces and city walls, its "preparatory divination," "cardinal axiality," and emphasis on north-south orientation was perceived as a belated implementation of China's ancient city ideal illustrated in *Zhouli* 周禮 (The rites of Zhou dynasty). According to *Zhouli*, the capital city was the culmination of "cosmic orders," which bespeak the authority of the empire. Arthur F. Wright sees in this cosmological order the essence of Chinese cities: "Throughout the long record

---

[37] Zhao Yuan 趙園, *Beijing: cheng yu ren* 北京: 城與人 [Beijing: the city and its residents] (Shanghai: Shanghai renmin chubanshe, 1991).

[38] Yan Jiayan 嚴家炎, *Zhongguo xiandai xiaoshuo liupai shi* 中國現代小說流派史 [A history of the schools of modern Chinese novel] (Beijing: Renmin wenxue chubanshe, 1989); Wu Fuhui 吳福輝, *Dushi xuanliu zhong de haipai xiaoshuo* 都市漩流中的海派小說 [Fiction of Shanghai school in urban vortex], (Changsha: Hunan jiaoyu chubanshe, 1995); Yang Yi 楊義, *Jingpai haipai zonglun* 京派海派綜論 [Beijing school and Shanghai school] (Beijing: Zhongguo shehui kexue chubanshe, 2003); and Wang Dewei 王德威, *Ruci fanhua* 如此繁華 [Urban splendor] (Shanghai: Shanghai shudian, 2006).

[39] Zhang, *The City in Modern Chinese Literature and Film*.

[40] Lee, *Shanghai Modern*; Shu-mei Shih, *The Lure of the Modern: Writing Modernism in Semicolonial China, 1917–1937* (Berkeley: University of California Press, 2001).

[41] Chen Pingyuan 陳平原, *Beijing jiyi yu jiyi Beijing* 北京記憶與記憶北京 [Beijing memories] (Beijing: Sanlian shudian, 2008).

[42] Luo Gang 羅崗, *Xiangxiang chengshi de fangshi* 想像城市的方式 [Ways of imagining cities] (Nanjing: Jiangsu renmin chubanshe, 2006); Yomi Braester, *Paint the City Red: Chinese Cinema and the Urban Contract* (Durham, NC: Duke University Press, 2010); and Robin Visser, *Cities Surround the Countryside* (Durham, NC: Duke University Press, 2010).

of Chinese city building we find an ancient and elaborate symbolism for the location and design of cities persisting in the midst of secular change."[43] Jeffrey F. Meyer
writes that Beijing exemplified "the earthly termination of the axis of the universe,
the center of the world, the pivot of the four quarters."[44] This cosmologically structured urban layout, which Marco Polo described as the epitome of perfection,
remained largely intact as the Chinese empire approached its end.

With regard to modern Beijing's distinctive spatiality, David Strand points out,
"early-twentieth-century Beijing, as a physical entity, remained a city stubbornly
defined by walls, walled enclosure, and gates," and was "composed of circles within
circles."[45] The spatial stability that seems to transcend the vicissitudes of time gives the
illusion that Beijing stayed static and eternal, with a quality of "positive, transcendent, and enduring antiquity."[46] The ostensibly fixed spatiality of Beijing obscures a
fundamental temporality manifested in various dynastic histories as well as the turbulent changes brought by modernization. From the looting of Beijing in 1860 to
larger-scale looting in 1900, from the moment when the city wall was dismantled to
make room for the first railway in Republican China to the complete destruction of
Beijing's city walls to materialize a socialist modernity, modern Beijing has appeared
in different spaces and in different temporalities.[47] Such a complex temporal and
spatial configuration of Beijing is precisely what my book sets out to explore.

With the rise of treaty port cities such as Shanghai and Canton since the second half
of the nineteenth century, this seemingly unchanging city took on another set of connotations. Often regarded as the antithesis of Shanghai, Beijing was considered authentically Chinese, cultural, and moral, rooted in tradition, elegant, serene, and grand. It
was everything Shanghai was not: an antiurban noncity. This binary rhetoric was at
the center of the cultural debates of "*Jingpai*" 京派 (Beijing school) versus "*Haipai*"
海派 (Shanghai school) in the 1920s and 1930s. Zhou Zuoren 周作人 (1885–1967)
mocks Shanghai culture as "fundamentally deprived of rationality and elegance."[48]

---

[43] Arthur F. Wright, "The Cosmology of the Chinese City," in Skinner, *The City in Late Imperial China*, 33.

[44] Jeffrey F. Meyer, *The Dragons of Tiananmen: Beijing as a Sacred City* (Columbia: University of South Carolina
Press, 1991), 1.

[45] Strand, *Rickshaw Beijing*, 1.

[46] Naquin, *Peking*, 699.

[47] If *Cheng* 城 (city) and *Qiang* 牆 (walls) cannot be separated in traditional definitions of Chinese cities, in which
a city can be called a city as long as it has walls within it (Sen-dou Chang, "The Morphology of Walled Capitals,"
in Skinner, *The City in Late Imperial China*, 75–100), then Beijing was confronted with the destiny of disappearance when the outer city walls were eventually dismantled in the dominant Maoist urban planning in the 1950s.
Liang Sicheng 梁思成 (1901–1972), son of the cultural giant Liang Qichao 梁啓超 (1873–1929) and a leading
architect in modern China, lamented with deep sorrow, "The rough opening on the wall is analogous to a fresh
wound." See Wang Jun 王軍, *Cheng ji* 城記 [Beijing record] (Beijing: Sanlian shudian, 2003).

[48] Zhou Zuoren, "Shanghai qi" 上海氣 [Shanghai spirit, 1927], in *Shanghai* 上海, ed. Ma Fengyang 馬逢洋
(Shanghai: Wenhui chubanshe, 1996), 62.

Even the non-*jingpai* writer Lin Yutang writes with a critical tone, "Shanghai is terrible in her strange mixture of Eastern and Western vulgarity, in her superficial refinements, in her naked and unmasked worship of Mammon, in her emptiness, commonness, and bad taste."[49] In his study of city literature, Yingjin Zhang argues that the Beijing-Shanghai opposition was marked by strong emotional attachments, which associated Beijing with a native land and cultural heritage and saw Shanghai as a trade and commercial center, a betrayal of ancestral roots.[50] Shu-mei Shih and Robin Visser further point out that this antiurban discourse entertained by May Fourth Chinese intellectuals was emphatically informed by their anti-imperial and anticolonial cultural standpoint.[51]

The Beijing-Shanghai binary rhetoric remained resilient through most of the twentieth century. For instance, in his 1960s study of the May Fourth Movement in Shanghai, Joseph T. Chen made a demarcation between two types of city in 1910s China, represented by Beijing and Shanghai:

> Historically, Peking was a museum city of old Chinese civilization, and an educational and political center. As the capital of China, traditionally it has always been identified with the North . . . . Shanghai, on the other hand, was a modern, urban, cosmopolitan, and Western-oriented treaty port city . . . . While the great Chinese heritage gave Peking its quality of simplicity, serenity, grandeur, and imperial stature, the nascent Western influence quickly transformed Shanghai into a lively, mobile, competitive, iconoclastic, and materialistic center.[52]

Shanghai modernity was measured by speed, height, brightness, as conveyed by the neon sign "light, heat, power," which illustrates Mao Dun's 茅盾 (1896–1981) leftist view of Shanghai's spectacle in his monumental novel *Ziye* 子夜 (*Midnight*, 1933). The imagery of Beijing, however, was shaped and defined by ancient city walls, gate towers, the imperial palaces, historical relics, idyllic scenes, and slow yet elegant manners, all together constituting tokens of harmony and tranquility unfolding in a timeless, horizontal capital.

---

[49] Lin Yutang, "A Hymn to Shanghai," in his *With Love and Irony* (New York: The John Day Company, 1940), 63–64.

[50] Zhang, *The City in Modern Chinese Literature and Film*, 15–16.

[51] Shih, *The Lure of the Modern*, 175–177; Robin Visser, *Cities Surround the Countryside: Urban Aesthetics in Post-Socialist China* (Durham, NC: Duke University Press, 2010), 12–13.

[52] Quoted in Rey Chow, *Woman and Chinese Modernity: The Politics of Reading Between West and East* (Minneapolis: University of Minnesota Press, 1991), 78–79.

This prevailing analytical framework pits Beijing against Shanghai, an authentic, traditional Chinese city against a Westernized modern treaty port, a pastoral, slow-paced, static, "antiurban" city situated in a "rural-city continuum" against a chaotic, fast-paced, volatile metropolis with a cosmopolitan, global orientation. Such a dichotomous discourse carries an inherent anxiety that Beijing did not follow the evolutionary path to converge with the type of modern city arising in the West and best embodied in China by Shanghai. Consequently, it disables further investigations of the diverse ways Beijing as a distinctive city has been perceived, illustrated, and imagined in literary and artistic representations.

In recent years, Beijing studies have gained increasing attention for historical and political reasons in the English academic sphere, but little attention has been paid to the urban experience—empirical and imaginary—that the "ancient capital" has undergone throughout the modern century, and even less to the affective registers arising from that experience. This book explores the emotional and geopoetic dynamics of Beijing as the city encountered the challenges of modern times. Drawing from a vast reservoir of written and visual sources ranging from literary canons to exotic narratives, modernist poetry to martial arts fantasy, and popular romance to urban planning, this book aims to construct new methods of understanding and conceptualizing the emotional topography of the urban transition and transformation "betwixt and between" the looting of Beijing in 1900 and the founding of a socialist capital in 1949 and beyond, against the great backdrop of the tumultuous twentieth century.

I consider five modes of creating a city-text that fashion Beijing:

(1) a warped hometown,
(2) a city of snapshots and manners,
(3) an aesthetic city,
(4) an imperial capital in comparative and cross-cultural perspective, and
(5) a displaced and relocated city on the Sinophone and diasporic postmemory.

These viewpoints highlight varied, interrelated dimensions of Beijing, which together constitute the dynamism of the city's imagery and fabricate an urban palimpsest of modern Beijing.

With regard to portraying one's native city, Walter Benjamin (1892–1940) writes, "The superficial inducement, the exotic, the picturesque has an effect only on the foreigner. To portray a city, a native must have other, deeper motives—motives of one who travels into the past instead of into the distance. A native's book about his city will always be related to memoirs; the writer has not spent his childhood there in vain."[53] Indeed, traveling into the past highlights the temporal dimension of a city in the minds of its natives, yet the spatial traces of Beijing, in particular the interior spaces unapproachable to strangers and foreigners, cannot be ignored. For modern Beijing's native sons and daughters, the "deeper motives," the memoir representations and the literary acts of traveling into the past, come across in factual and fictional, psychological and emotional, encyclopedic and fragmentary eulogies of Beijing's aesthetic and cultural charm. But a native writer cannot be blind to certain liminal, transitional, and traumatic moments in Beijing's passage into the modern era. First, in 1900, Beijing, the capital of the Qing dynasty, was looted and subsequently occupied by eight allied foreign powers, including England, Germany, Russia, France, America, Italy, Austria, and Japan, which forced open the ancient, celestial city and the Chinese Empire and inflicted a physical and psychological wound. Second, in 1928, Beijing was renamed and downgraded as Beiping after the Kuomintang 國民黨 (or KMT, Nationalist Party) moved its capital to Nanjing; thus the city lost its status as political center and its original distinction. Then, in 1937, Beijing was invaded and occupied by the Japanese troops during the Second Sino-Japanese War, marking yet another humiliating and distressing stage of the city's history. Finally, in 1949, the Gongchandang 共產黨 (Communist Party) reclaimed Beijing as its national capital, an event described as the peaceful liberation of the city by the Communist Party and as the fall and decline of the city by the Nationalist Party. From foreign invasion and looting to East Asian military violence, from dynastic crisis and domestic warlords' tyranny to the Chinese Civil War chaos and later the Cold War sociocultural transformation, these ongoing crises and transitions define and redefine the emotions and "structure of feeling" of native Beijing writers, who portray a victimized yet survived hometown shot through with pain and ordeals, brutality and agony, cataclysms and crisis, despair and hope, symbolic death and rebirth. They stand at the threshold of the traditional and the modern, drifting back and forth, wandering inside and outside, and hesitating at the crossroads, during a liminal journey from premodern empire into modern nation-state.

In chapter 1, I focus on Manchu writer Lao She, arguably Beijing's most representative native writer, and his major novels and dramas from prewar time via the Second Sino-Japanese war to the seventeen-year period of Socialist China (1930s to 1950s). Lao She's affective mapping of modern Beijing envisions his native city as a warped hometown swept by the advent, expansion, and menace of modernity as well as the whirlwind and whirlpool of political violence and historical change. From Lao She's point of view, Xiangzi 祥子, a rickshaw puller, lonely individual, frustrated

---

[53] Peter Szondi, "Walter Benjamin's City Portraits," in *On Walter Benjamin: Critical Essays and Recollections*, ed. Gary Smith (Cambridge, MA: MIT Press, 1988), 19.

orphan, and the protagonist of his critically acclaimed prewar novel *Luotuo Xiangzi* 駱駝祥子 (*Rickshaw Boy*, 1937), attempts to construct a body contact or corporeal linkage with his beloved Beijing, yet ends up as a walking beast and wandering ghost in the unfathomable darkness of the city. Beijing is such a gigantic space and hard to grasp; therefore, Xiangzi has to crystallize his urban fantasy into his obsession with the rickshaw, a material thing that constitutes his object of love and longing, the most intimate medium between his body and the lure of the city, and the possible capital or property that he wants to possess. Nevertheless, in the fetish-worship of the rickshaw, Xiangzi is also turned into an object and thus totally alienated by the reification of his humble wish. And deep beneath this fetishism lies the impulse and enticement of the city, or more precisely, the city itself becomes a huge apparatus. Like a wandering ghost, the rickshaw boy struggles and is trapped in the enormous machine through which social identity and fragmentary subjectivity are created and contested. He ultimately feels bound, exhausted, rejected, and ruined on the "mean streets" and in the labyrinth of the colossal city. As the poverty-stricken youngster strenuously attempts to survive under tough urban living conditions and to construct and materialize his fantasies, he suffers from his misunderstanding of safety exits and prison houses, and the enchanting and disenchanting city chronotopes. Beijing, the modern city, is configured as the locus of tears and laughter, attachment and detachment, as well as utopian dream and chronotopic rift. *Rickshaw Boy* deploys a realist metamorphosis to demonstrate the rise and fall of the symbolically homeless orphan who encounters a whole process of dream-making and dream-waking irony in the literary topography of urban desires.

In the first half of the twentieth century, violence in and toward Beijing was manifested in competing and conflicting modes: spectacular or ordinary, fast or slow, concentrated or scattered, detectable or disguised. Lao She's pivotal trilogy, *Bewilderment*, *Ignominy*, and *Famine*, combined into his wartime epic, *Four Generations under One Roof* (1944–1950), discloses an affective mapping of military violence, family degeneration, urban misery, and nation-state suffering in wartime Beijing, a warped and wounded city under Japanese occupation. I aim at charting the spatial trajectories of wartime emotions, such as nostalgia, mourning, shame, anger, and hatred, that mediate the new and modern interactions of family and city, self and society, individual and nation-state, and urban history and traumatic memory in Lao She's World War II atlas of emotions. The Little Sheepfold Lane, a representative alleyway in Beijing, and other real and fictional places and spaces, ranging from a small, clandestine room in a family house to the gigantic Tiananmen Square in the heart of the city, display the urban emotions and cultural memories shaped by war and violence and invoke a performative psychogeography of pain and catharsis, trauma and redemption, nostalgia and longing, loss and epiphany, and melancholy and hope: modern emotional negotiations between private obsession and public passion, personal desire and collective guilt, and quasi-loyalist affection and nationalist sentiment.

Right after the 1949 political divide, Lao She's three-act drama *Longxu gou* 龍鬚溝 (*Dragon Beard Ditch*, 1951) unveils an intriguing ideological chronotope of the great transformation from pre-Mao dystopia to Maoist paradise formed by socialist urban planning. As a hygienic dead corner and a figurative miniature of the underprivileged ghetto, the old Dragon Beard Ditch revealed the presocialist everyday life of a shabby and dirty compound occupied by many households east of the Bridge of Heaven, the southern part of Beijing. As soon as Beijing became a socialist capital, the haunting danger of contamination and the social sickness in the filthy ditch had been symbolically cleaned in the sense of hygienic sweeping and socialist/ideological purification. I would argue that *Dragon Beard Ditch* offers a salient, distorted, and imaginary example of the socialist production of space by physically and psychologically transforming an infamous stinking creek and slum into a new and neat socialist community. The socialist sun shines over Dragon Beard Ditch, where the inhabitants are endowed with new class consciousness and socialist sentiment, released from their hygienic and political morass, and warmly welcome baptism and redemption by the newly established Maoist regime. Although the ditch transformation project was not yet completed at the time of writing the drama, Lao She envisions a socialist space that stages a socialist illumination from the present and forges a new chronotope colored by an ideologized utopia and a utopianized ideology.

In socialist Beijing, the blooming of a hundred flowers and the contending of a hundred schools of thought, a short-lived period of liberalization in 1956 is unpredictably followed by the Anti-Rightist Campaign in 1957, and later the nationwide utopian and dystopian/disastrous mass mobilization of the Great Leap Forward, as well as the Great Proletarian Cultural Revolution. In the heyday of the Maoist political and cultural transition, Lao She's three-act play *Chaguan* 茶館 (*Teahouse*, 1957) scans and spans the decline of the Manchu Empire, the failure of the Warlord regime, and the downfall of the Nationalist government, recapitulating and condensing the fifty-year history and politics into a shrinking public space and a pessimistic miniature of old Beijing misery. I decode the Yutai Teahouse as a physical and psychological place and space, and a warped space-time continuum that presents the interactions between material deformations and emotional vicissitudes against the backdrop of political changes and historical violence. Anthony Vidler understands the spatial warping as concrete and conceptual, physical and psychological changes and transformations in urban scenes and multimedia artistic practices.[54]

---

[54] Anthony Vidler, *Warped Space: Art, Architecture, and Anxiety in Modern Culture* (Cambridge, MA: MIT Press, 2002).

My approach focuses on the constant rearrangement of material objects, such as tables, chairs, furniture, and ornaments, within the Yutai teahouse, and its consequent spatial deformation and warping under the gravity of urban transformation and political change. Meanwhile, I also chart the intriguing relations between the teahouse and the streets, between the interior and exterior spaces, and between nostalgic sympathy, sense of loss, and self-mourning that implode in the teahouse and urban horrors and darkness that extend and explode from within.

Different from the lyrical, artistic, and embellished tones adopted by native writers and Beijing experts (*Beijing tong* 北京通 or *Lao Beijing* 老北京) such as Qi Rushan 齊如山 (1875–1962) and Jin Shoushen 金壽申 (1906–1968), Lao She uses a deliberate oxymoron to capture a prevailing yet contradictory image of his hometown through the eyes of disenchanted rickshaw puller Xiangzi: "The city paid no attention to death, paid no attention to disaster, and paid no attention to poverty. It simply put forth its powers when the time came and hypnotized a million people, and they, as if in a dream, chanted poems in praise of its beauty. It was filthy, beautiful, decadent, bustling, chaotic, idle, lovable."[55] Although from time to time Lao She discloses his fond memories of his beloved city, his widespread and critically acclaimed Beijing narratives contribute to a long-sustained series of warped hometown images incarnated in his emotional topography of the mean streets, the besieged courtyard houses, the marginal and miserable street-corner society, and the damaged and distorted teahouse in the first half of the twentieth century.

Whereas the famous Manchu bannerman's affective mapping of a warped Beijing emerges as a vital theme of the native city, another mode of literary topography of modern Beijing, mostly fiction serialized in literature supplements of newspapers and later published as best-sellers in book form, captures the fleeting instants in Beijing's floating, ephemeral everyday life on the one hand, and on the other hand seizes the everlasting image of the city, its traditional charm and modern urbanism, as well as its flow of emotions and social manners. These Beijing stories became enormously popular between the 1920s and the 1930s, and created what I shall call in chapter 2 a modern Beijing in the narratives of snapshots and manners. The finest achievements of this kind are represented in Zhang Henshui's (pen name of Zhang Xinyuan, 1895–1967) popular romances—*Chunming waishi* 春明外史 (Unofficial history of Beijing, 1924–1929), *Jinfen shijia* 金粉世家 (Grand old family, 1926–1932), and *Tixiao yinyuan* 啼笑因緣 (Fate in tears and laughter, 1929–1930), among others. From the material culture of everyday life to the cultural debates of the time, from family sagas to street gossip, from warlords' cruelty

---

[55] Lao She, *Rickshaw: The Novel of Lo-t'o Hsiang Tzu* (Honolulu: University of Hawai'i Press, 1979), 240.

to chivalric assassination—all produce not only "fiction for comfort" and meet the needs of the literature market,[56] but also register both the transient and transitional symptoms and the long-lasting pains and pleasures in and about Republican Beijing.

Zhang Henshui's Beijing representations are marked by two conflicting modes of temporality: the condensation of time in news-style snapshot writings about palpably felt social changes and transformations and the extension of time involved in the observation and representation of manners, customs, and social mores. Whereas the former compresses time and concerns events that are consequential and need immediate attention, the latter deals with ways of life and being and registers a sense of time that is a stream, continuous and historically embedded. This contradiction between instantaneity and duration is significantly visible in Zhang's narrative structure, conditioning and simultaneously conditioned by two interrelated ways of observing, apprehending, and narrating the city. These two modes of temporality compete and converge and together constitute the very form of Zhang's novels.

When ongoing Beijing stories were written, published, distributed, and consumed serially in newspapers over time, the literary mapping produced a city image in time-lapse snapshots, unfolding in a series of instantaneous pictures of modern existence ranging from political events and social scandals to daily goings-on, as well as kaleidoscopic spaces and locations including theaters, restaurants, teahouses, province hostels, bathhouses, schools, and train stations, among others. The importance of snapshot narratives lies in momentariness, instanteity, and punctuality. Instantaneity refers to the brief exposure of time for the event to be captured by the writer and novelized into a segment of literary text, and the short turnaround time for this text to be published and distributed. When we define snapshot writing, it is insufficient to merely point out its rapidity. The short time duration also indicates the timeliness and liveness of the represented event.[57] Therefore, instantaneity is also conceived of as a consequence of the piece of writing: it deals with the moment, with the timely response to the reported event. Such news-style writings produce

---

[56] Perry Link, *Mandarin Ducks and Butterflies: Popular Fiction in Early Twentieth-Century Chinese Cities* (Berkeley: University of California Press, 1981), 9. Actually, Zhang's fiction is not only for comfort, but also for discomfort, because most of his works do not follow the popular model of a "happy ending." T. M. McClellan defines some of Zhang's novel as "oneiric romanticism," and correctly points out that the dreamlike quality contains enchanting daydreams but also haunting nightmares. See T. M. McClellan, "Change and Continuity in the Fiction of Zhang Henshui (1895–1967)," in *Modern Chinese Literature* 10, nos. 1–2 (1998): 113–134. See also Zhang Henshui, *Xiezuo shengya huiyi* 寫作生涯回憶 [Research materials on Zhang Henshui] [Memoirs of my writing career], in *Zhang Henshui yanjiu ziliao* 張恨水研究資料 [Research materials on Zhang Henshui], ed. Zhang Zhanguo 張佔國 and Wei Shouzhong 魏守忠 (Beijing: Zhishi chanquan chubanshe, 2009), 7–73; Chen Pingyuan, "Literature High and Low: 'Popular Fiction' in Twentieth-Century China," in *The Literary Field of Twentieth-Century China*, ed. Michel Hockx (Honolulu: University of Hawai'i Press, 1999), 113–133.

[57] See Philip Auslander, *Liveness: Performance in a Mediatized Culture* (London: Routledge, 1999).

a sense of immediacy and urgency and suggest the acutely felt social impact of the event, which strikes the reader with a piercing force.

The flip side of urgency is forgettability. The vignette narrative of social occurrences is not only momentary and responsive, but also short-lived and perishable. In this light, it comes close to what Walter Benjamin designated as information:

> The value of information does not survive the moment in which it was new. It lives only at that moment; it has to surrender to it completely and explain itself to it without losing any time. A story is different. It does not expend itself. It preserves and concentrates its strength and is capable of releasing it even after a long time ... retain[ing] their germinative power to this day.[58]

Benjamin's distinction between information and story is made with respect to their temporal capacities. Whereas information is a narrative of the moment, a story is characterized by its durability. The art of storytelling produces a type of narrative for what Benjamin called *Erfahrung*, a lived experience that requires a long duration of time, as opposed to *Erlebnis*, a consciousness triggered by a momentary shock or disruption in modern urban life.[59]

What literary form might be adequate to convey both the urgency prompted by inexorable changes in a modern city and the ethos of modern existence, something one can only experience by being there for a long duration? Such ambivalence is registered on the level of narrative form. Zhang Henshui's Beijing stories combine features of news-style, journalistic writing and observational social novels, with both perspectival, subjective and omniscient, omnipresent narration. Many critics see in such works a narrative inconsistency and deficiency. Fan Boqun 范伯群, for instance, criticizes "a mishmash of first- and third-person narration" in Zhang's *Unofficial History of Beijing*.[60] Eileen Chow, however, argues that such a mishmash might be precisely the reason for the novel's success: "the appeal of the novel lies in its quality of *bricolage* (mishmash, or *jiaocuo*, to use Fan Boqun's phrase) of genres, styles, temporalities, omniscient and subjective narration."[61] In the different context of modern Western urban popular culture, John Fiske regards "bricolage" as an

---

[58] Walter Benjamin, "The Storyteller," *Illuminations* (New York: Schocken Books, 1968), 90.

[59] Benjamin, "The Storyteller," 163.

[60] Fan Boqun, "Lun Zhang Henshui de jibu daibiaozuo" 論張恨水的幾部代表作 [A discussion of a few of Zhang Henshui's representative works], *Wenxue pinglun* 文學評論 [Literary review] 1 (1982): 53, quoted in Eileen Chow, "Serial Sightings: News, Novelties, and an *Unofficial History of the Old Capital*," in *Rethinking Chinese Popular Culture*, ed. Carlos Rojas and Eileen Chow (London: Routledge, 2009), 67.

[61] Eileen Chow, "Serial Sightings," 67. The difference between Eileen Chow's reading and my study is that Chow focuses on the urban snapshots in Zhang Henshui's *Unofficial History of Beijing*, yet my interpretation of Zhang's three major novels extends from the modern urban experiences (curiosity and shock) to Zhang's subtle

"everyday practice" that "creatively combine(s) materials and resources at hand to make objects, signs, or rituals that meet their immediate needs."[62] Whereas snapshot narratives register the shocks and anxieties experienced by city dwellers in modern times, the apprehension of human behaviors and social customs indexical of a collective mind requires a different type of narrative. For Zhang, the combination of these two narrative styles seems to provide the most compelling literary form to convey the treacherousness of modern urban existence. His Beijing stories create an epistemological and psychological mechanism for modern citizens to come to grips with reality, with a version of life that is more real than reality.

In describing domestic affairs, interpersonal relations, social customs, values, and mores, Zhang Henshui's *zhanghui* 章回 (chapter-linked) installment fiction has an anthropological bearing and a close affinity with the traditional genre of "*shiqing xiaoshuo*" 世情小說 (novel of manners), which was fully developed in the vernacular literature of Ming and Qing dynasties. In *Zhongguo xiaoshuo shilue* 中國小說史略 (*A Brief History of Chinese Fiction*), Lu Xun 魯迅 (1881–1936) designated *Jin ping mei* 金瓶梅 (*The Plum in the Golden Vase*) and *Honglou meng* 紅樓夢 (*The Dream of the Red Chamber*) as fictions about "*shiqing*" 世情 or "*renqing*" 人情 (human interest). In illustrating the former's narrative style, he notes,

> The writer shows the most profound understanding of the life of his time, his descriptions are clear yet subtle, penetrating yet highly suggestive, and for the sake of contrast he sometimes portrays two quite different aspects of life. His writing holds such a variety of human interest that no novel of that period could surpass it.[63]

Zhang Ailing made use of the English term "novel of manners" to categorize this group of literature and rendered it into Chinese as *shehui xiaoshuo* 社會小說 (society novels) or *shenghuo fangshi xiaoshuo* 生活方式小說 (novels of manners). In her discussion of Han Bangqing's 韓邦慶 (1856–1894) *Haishanghua liezhuan* 海上花列傳 (*Sing-song Girls of Shanghai*), which she regarded as the late Qing successor of Cao Xueqin's *The Story of the Stone* (also known by the title of *The Dream of the Red Chamber*), she maintained that authors of novels of manners are "most adept at

---

linkage of those experiences with his understanding of the "Chinese mind," or the everlasting manners and emotions, in traditional and modern Chinese chapter-linked romances.

[62] John Fiske, *Understanding Popular Culture* (London: Routledge, 1991), 150.

[63] *Lu Xun Quanji* 魯迅全集 [Complete works of Lu Xun] (Beijing: Renmin wenxue chubanshe, 1981), 9:180. English translation from Yang Xianyi and Gladys Yang, *Lu Hsun, A Brief History of Chinese Fiction* (Beijing: Foreign Language Press, 1959), chaps. 19–20.

capturing the nuanced differences in manners and behaviors between people of different social stratifications" (能體會到各階層的口吻行事微妙的差別).[64]

Writings in snapshots and writings of social manners both make truth claims. However, they appeal to two different types of veracity: snapshot-style narratives see the truth value in a reality engendered by photojournalism, a photographic referentiality Roland Barthes calls "*ça a été*" (that-has-been), a factual recording as opposed to imaginary fabrication;[65] novels of manners feature a type of realism in verisimilitude, which conveys a sample of life faithfully with the help of literary techniques and mediation. In her evaluation of the social novel between the 1920s and 1940s, with Zhang Henshui's work as its best representative, Zhang Ailing raised a sharp question—"What if the transformative era changes so drastically that fictional writings cannot follow the reality, and people feel curious about what really happened around them?" (是否因為過渡時代變動太劇烈, 虛構的小說跟不上事實, 大眾對周圍發生的事感到好奇?)—and attributed the quality of *pingdan jinzhen* 平淡近真 (as naturalistic as life) to its capability to retain the original, genuine flavor of life (*rensheng wei* 人生味).[66] The observational, realistic effect in Zhang Henshui's writings is indeed generated through his sophisticated depiction of life with no immoderate sentimentality or excessive emotionality, no unrestrained fantasy or extreme dramatization. These two modes of realism, temporality, and narration are imbricated in Zhang Henshui's work and create a unique vision of modern Beijing, a "true drama" or a "realm of emotional and spiritual reality."[67] For the male protagonists—whether they be flâneur, voyeur, detective, poet, modern youth, "old soul," or horse carriage driver—the visual pursuit of the evasive and conflicting aspects of Beijing is also personified in the figures of women, who are as evasive and conflicting as the city they inhabit, which formed their Weltanschauungen. From the courtesan house to the grand mansion, from zigzag alleyways to Heaven's Bridge (the entertainment district for the poor people), Zhang Henshui anchors diversified urban locales and cultural sites and maps the spatial traces of his literary characters' sentimental education in his urban images and imaginations, which amount to a subtle combination of realist depiction and romantic emplotment. In Zhang's

---

[64] Zhang Ailing (Eileen Chang), "Yi Hu Shizhi" 憶胡適之 [Remembering Hu Shih], in her *Zhang Kan* 張看 [Chang's view] (Taipei: Huangguan, 1991), 177.

[65] See Xiaojue Wang, "Memory, Photographic Seduction, and Allegorical Correspondence: Eileen Chang's *Mutual Reflections*," in *Rethinking Modern Chinese Popular Culture: Cannibalizations of the Canon*, ed. Carlos Rojas and Eileen Chow (London: Routledge, 2009), 194–195.

[66] Zhang Ailing, "Tan kanshu" 談看書 [On reading], in *Zhang Kan*, 188, 94; italics added.

[67] Peter Brooks, *The Melodramatic Imagination: Balzac, Henry James, Melodrama, and the Mode of Excess* (New Haven, CT: Yale University Press, 1976), 4.

Beijing narratives, "the eye's photographic registration of objects yields to the mind's effort to pierce surface, to interrogate appearance."[68]

Looking at Beijing in its final days of imperial grandeur from the privileged height of the city walls, Juliet Bredon, a British writer who was the only daughter of the late Sir Robert Bredon and the niece of the late Sir Robert Hart, and lived in Beijing for many years, wrote,

> Truly the Chinese understand better than we how to adapt their buildings to the surrounding landscape, the frame to the picture, and the picture to the frame. On our right lies the Chinese City. In summer when all the trees—of which almost every little courtyard contains one or two—are in leaf, it gives the impression not of a town but of a huge park dominated by the blue dome of the Temple of Heaven which rises like a graceful stone flower above the foliage.[69]

This highly quoted passage has often been used as a historical source document to describe the charm of Beijing before its transition from an imperial into a modern, Republican city, in a similar way as Hedda Morrison's (1908–1991) old Peking photographs were employed as firsthand visual representations of scenes and lives in Beijing. Largely overlooked is the British picturesque concept that Bredon adopts in her appreciation for Beijing. She portrays a cityscape as a vista, a "park," and a harmonious, "dignified unity" of buildings and landscapes, which are mutually compatible like a picture and a frame. In her emphasis on the relation between buildings and their natural or landscaped surroundings, there is an unmistakable element of the British Picturesque aesthetics formed first in British landscape painting in the late eighteenth century, which foregrounds aesthetic values in the pictorial integration of architecture and landscape, cultural and natural environments. In illustrating the picturesqueness of the past in Beijing at the outset of modernization, Bredon further observes, "What remains of the older civilization, however, is so picturesque that to look back on the days when its illusions were still unbroken must always be a pleasure to whoever has felt that illusion."[70] The incommensurability between an ancient, grandiose Chinese city and the rising Western-style buildings evokes a sense of intricacy and abruptness, or of a "strange, fascinating" past lingering in the present.[71]

---

[68] Brooks, *The Melodramatic Imagination*, 2.

[69] Juliet Bredon, *Peking: A Historical and Intimate Description of Its Chief Places of Interest* (Shanghai: Kelly & Walsh, 1922, second edition, revised and enlarged), 29.

[70] Bredon, *Peking*, 59.

[71] Ibid.

Such a picturesque portrayal of Beijing is one of many representations that employ diverse aesthetic discourses to convey the cityscape. In "Sugeladi tan Beiping suoxu" 蘇格拉底談北平所需 (Socrates talks about what Beijing needs), one of a series of letters composed by Shen Congwen 沈從文 (1902–1988) on the verge of the Communist takeover of Beijing, this key figure of the Beijing School envisions the city as a "Republic of Art" built on the principles of art, literature, and music.[72] In an article entitled *"Pingjiao jianzhu zalu"* 平郊建築雜錄 (Miscellaneous records of Peiping suburban architecture), Liang Sicheng and Lin Huiyin 林徽因 (1904–1955) proposed the concept of "architectural aesthetic" as a new principle to apply to Beijing and its ancient buildings. The article starts with the following observation:

All around the outskirts of Peking are numerous buildings dating from the last two or three hundred years. If you happen to go on an outing, everywhere you look you'll see ancient buildings rich in flavor.

(北平四郊近二三百年間建築物極多, 偶爾郊遊, 觸目都是饒有趣味的古建。)[73]

How to elucidate this flavor emanating from these architectural works of art? Liang and Lin maintain that the beauty of a piece of architecture may stimulate a distinctive sensibility—a pleasure of *"jianzhuyi"* 建築意 (an architectural flavor) apart from that of *"shiyi"* 詩意 and *"huayi"* 畫意 (a flavor suggestive of poetry or painting).[74] Through clever human work and the infiltration of time, natural materials developed into an integration of art, history, and geography, a construct of human intelligence and human life, which elicits a special fusion of *xing* 性 and *ling* 靈 (innate sensibility and mind), *shen* 神 and *zhi* 志 (spirit and intention) in the observer. They designate this multilayered fusion of materiality and emotionality, spatiality and historicity, secularity and sublimity, as an architectural aesthetics. In Liang and Lin's reflections on architectural beauty, it is not hard to see influences of both classical Chinese and Western philosophies, in particular, the Ming-dynasty Gongan School and the Kant's aesthetic theory.

---

[72] Shen Congwen, "Sugeladi tan Beiping suoxu" [Socrates talks about what Beijing needs], in *Shen Congwen quanji* 沈從文全集 [Complete works of Shen Congwen] (Taiyuan: Beiyue wenyi chubanshe, 2002), 14:370–381.

[73] Liang Sicheng and Lin Huiyin, "Pingjiao jianzhu zalu" [Miscellaneous records of Peiping suburban architecture]; see Wilma Fairbank, *Liang and Lin: Partners in Exploring China's Architectural Past* (Philadelphia: University of Pennsylvania Press, 1994), 181. For the Chinese version, see Liang Congjie 梁從誡, ed., *Lin Huiyin wenji—Jianzhu juan* 林徽因文集·建築卷 [Selected writings of Lin Huiyin: volume of architecture] (Tianjin: Baihua wenyi chubanshe, 1999), 16.

[74] Liang, *Lin Huiyin wenji*.

By perceiving Beijing as an aesthetic object, they do not intend to sever the city from its own history, its sociopolitical environment, or its everyday praxis. On the contrary, by claiming an aesthetic realm free from volatile real politics, by attending to the architectural aesthetics of the city, these intellectuals emphasize Beijing as a cultural and artistic entity, not merely a national allegory, a symbol of political power, or an encased specimen in what Joseph Levenson may call a "museumified" imperial China.[75] In establishing a cultural or aesthetic Beijing, they provide literary and artistic imaginations that essentially effect an entirely new appreciation, thus releasing the city from the dominant analytical frameworks of politics, empire, traditionalism, or nationalism. Whereas Chinese literature never lacks urban narratives ranging from personal *biji* 筆記 accounts (literary notes and sketches) to local gazetteers, an urban literary imagination that derives aesthetic pleasure from city experiences and regards the city as an aesthetic object was something newly emergent in the twentieth century.[76] Such a literary creation of an aesthetic Beijing is a crucial part of the formation of Chinese literary modernity.

Therefore, chapter 3 addresses how Lin Huiyin, a female poet and architect, carries out an aesthetic and impressionist mapping of Beijing's everyday objects, imperial relics, and socialist sites from the post–Warlord era to the high Cold War years. As a "renaissance woman," Lin Huiyin performs multiple roles as poet, essayist, short-story writer, famous salonnière, architectural historian, and cofounder of one of the earliest architecture departments in modern China. Lin's "Taitai de keting" 太太的客廳 (Madam's Salon), a seemingly apolitical literary public space in Beijing, especially when viewed regarding the formation of public opinion, played an important role as a literary arena where the project of Chinese enlightenment was conceived, new and modern knowledge was imported and disseminated, and the symbolic capital and its materialized form, that is, the literary anthology, was produced and reproduced. In addition to her literary perception and aesthetic imagination of Beijing, Lin goes beyond the interiority of the salon to physically investigate architectural buildings in the city and beyond in both scientific and aesthetic ways as an architect and architectural historian.[77] This chapter also examines Lin Huiyin as a key figure in the "Beijing School"

[75] Joseph R. Levenson, *Confucian China and Its Modern Fate: Volume I* (Berkeley: University of California Press, 1965), 82.

[76] See traditional literati's *biji* urban essays such as Meng Yuanlao 孟元老, *Dongjing menghua lu* 東京夢華錄 [*The eastern capital: A dream of splendor*] (Beijing: Zhonghua shuju, 1982). For a brief survey of literature related to Beijing in the Ming and Qing dynasties, see Dong, *Republican Beijing*, 248–252.

[77] I also explore Lin's way of seeing when I scrutinize her essay "Outside of the Window," which examines her own position of observation "Window" is significantly different from other two typical images: "balcony," a position of the bourgeois observer's gaze, and "flâneur," the one who is away from home and plays the role of a passionate explorer, curious spectator, amateur cartographer in urban landscape.

to inquire into that group's literary activities, its naming and utilization of the textualized and aestheticized city space, and its lyrical constructions of everyday life in Beijing. Lin's aesthetic and cultural planning and preservation of the ancient capital, her archaeological investigation of its urban space, and her unprecedented appearances in different places, including the roof of the Hall of Prayers for Good Harvest, significantly expand the topography of Beijing and contribute unique meanings to the landscape of the modern city. I would argue that in her literary writings of the 1930s and her failed project of urban planning of the socialist capital in the 1950s (against the Maoist and socialist propaganda), Lin deliberately juxtaposes the aesthetic versus the political, the pastoral versus the counterpastoral, in particular the lyrical and aesthetic urban items in everyday life and the threatening and disturbing images of modern industrial civilization. Imperial palaces and other grand buildings still dominate the urban landscape of Beijing. However, in Lin's poetics and politics of urban objects, the sensuous, superfluous, and aestheticized items constitute the cultural texture and material basis of the city, which outlive historical transformations and political turbulence and protect Beijing from the gust and dust of modern times.

In its long history as an imperial capital, Beijing has been the subject of abundant literature. In the Republican time, a large number of Ming and Qing writings about Beijing were reprinted, including both official gazetteers and personal accounts.[78] At the same time, confronted with Beijing's transformation into a Republican city since the start of modernization, a group of transitional scholars such as Yu Qichang 余棨昌 (1882–1949), Qi Rushan, and Jin Shoushen, among others, set out to record, narrate, and memorialize a vanishing imperial Beijing. Their anecdote-style accounts seek to construct an encyclopedia of imperial ways of life covering all aspects of everyday practice and take an inventory of the city, its history, and the lifestyle that was forced to disappear with the end of the Manchu Empire. Considering the continuous vitality of various local customs and manners, these mnemonic narratives can be regarded as participating in a newly emergent process of popularization of the imperial aristocratic lifestyle rather than merely dedicating a melancholic elegy to the vanishing empire. Madeleine Yue Dong further points out that whereas these writings contribute to the creation of a collective memory of an "old Beijing," this denotes in effect not just the imperial capital but also a living part of the present, the Republican Beijing.[79]

Chapter 4 examines a different type of literary representations of imperial Beijing, which operate in a comparative, cross-cultural, translingual, and even cosmopolitan way. I consider works by Lin Yutang, a bilingual literary giant; Princess

---

[78] See, for instance, Naquin, *Peking*, 699; and Dong, *Republican Beijing*, 248–252.
[79] Dong, *Republican Beijing*, 246–265.

Der Ling 德齡公主 (1886–1944), First Lady-in-Waiting to the Empress Dowager Cixi 慈禧太后 (1835–1908); and Victor Segalen 謝閣蘭 (1878–1919), an adventurous French writer and ethnographer, all of whom are well versed in both Eastern and Western cultures. Different from their contemporary chroniclers of the city's imperial history and material life, these authors place imperial Beijing in a fresh and comparative framework. In the years when Beijing began to remake itself into a modern city as a constituent part of China's modern nation-state, these writers endeavored to fabricate Beijing as an imperial capital. Whereas their imaginations respond to public interest in and curiosity about the forbidden, inaccessible core of the imperial sovereign, they entertain a different goal from making Beijing either an Orientalist spectacle or a museum of the past, a pitfall that Joseph Levenson warns would render the past only "historically significant," or at best "aesthetically significant—merely aesthetic, fragments of a vanquished, vanished whole."[80] These cross-cultural representations of an imperial Beijing reflect their authors' dual cultural position. By constructing a narrative subject that is situated in a new dynamism of the East and the West, the past and the present, these writers create a comparative and cosmopolitan perspective from which to perceive, understand, and imagine the city. Whereas Beijing stands for an ideal imperial polis planned and materialized in accordance with Chinese cosmology and universal humanity, it is also repositioned from the center of the cosmos into a new world order with various competing civilizations.

These writers' identities as both insiders and outsiders, Chinese and non-Chinese, and their multilingual capacity further confound the duality of the past and the present, China and beyond, in their works. In elucidating the taxonomy of intellectual attitudes toward Chinese modernity, Lin Yutang argues, "People with utmost intellect take modern culture as one that is shared by and belongs to the whole world, and their own culture as molded and blended into the world culture. Therefore, one's advantages can compensate for other's inadequacies" (上識之士，以現代文化為世界共享共有之文化，本國文化，亦不熔鑄為世界文化之一部，故能以己之長，補人之短).[81] Such a practical and cosmopolitan view is more or less shared by his contemporaries engaging with cross-cultural, comparative reflections on imperial Beijing. They regard themselves as both native and foreign to this city.

In attending to Beijing in a way marked by both intimacy and detachment, they facilitate a liberating force of comparison. This amounts to a critical faculty that

---

[80] Levenson, *Confucian China and Its Modern Fate*, 114.

[81] Lin Yutang, *Lin Yutang wenxuan* 林語堂文選 [Selected writings of Lin Yutang] (Beijing: Zhongguo guangbo dianshi chubanshe, 1990), 2:370.

Edward Said locates in humanism, which may bring about knowledge of other cultures in a way other than the essentializing, imperialist Orientalism. Such a cross-cultural framing also allows a new angle from which to comprehend one's own culture. In his discussion of humanism, Erich Auerbach (1892–1957) quotes from Hugo of St Victor's (1096–1141) *Didascalicon*: "The man who finds his homeland sweet is still a tender beginner; he to whom every soil is as his native one is already strong; but he is perfect to whom the entire world is as a foreign land."[82] Edward Said further elaborates on this passage, "The more one is able to leave one's cultural home, the more easily one is able to judge it, and the whole world as well, with the spiritual detachment and generosity necessary for true vision. The more easily, too, does one assess oneself and alien cultures with the same combination of intimacy and distance."[83] Lin Yutang's reflection a few decades ago seems to respond from afar to what Said proposes: "A good traveller is one who does not know where he is going to, and a perfect traveller does not know where he came from."[84] This ideal, cosmopolitan self who is both distanced from its native culture and intimate with others leaves some crucial aspects of transcultural practice unexplored. One key issue is the politics of language. All three writers used languages other than Chinese to narrate imperial Beijing. While Segalen used French, his mother tongue, Lin and Der Ling opted to write about Beijing in English. How did the fact that these writings were all in a language other than Chinese affect their Beijing imageries? Could these writers navigate between languages with the same ease and accuracy as between cultures? The circulation and popularity of the Beijing narratives and their translations among readers of the native or translated languages prompt one further question: would a bilingual or multilingual reinvention of Beijing facilitate the city's passage into cultural mobility and modernity?

I would argue that Lin Yutang, Princess Der Ling, and Victor Segalen envision their indigenous and exoticist urbanscape of Beijing, a factual and fictional imperial capital, viewed from near and afar—respectively from the perspective of a Universalist construction, a cross-cultural female expression and an "aesthetics of diversity." By presenting pleasant rather than painful, harmonious rather than contradictory images of an everyday and an imperial capital, Lin Yutang, "a bundle of contrasts" and a "world citizen," describes Beijing as an ideal, mythical, metaphorical, and semiotic city, a cultural code surviving barbarism, looting, conquest, and turbulence in modern times, particularly in his *Moment in Peking* (1939) and *Imperial Peking: Seven*

---

[82] See Edward W. Said, *Reflections on Exile and Other Essays* (Cambridge, MA: Harvard University Press, 2000), 185.

[83] Edward W. Said, *Orientalism* (New York: Vintage, 1978), 259.

[84] Lin Yutang, *The Importance of Living* (New York: The John Day Company, 1937), 332.

Centuries of China (1961).[85] Princess Der Ling articulates the inner voices in "the Great Within" (the Imperial Forbidden City), and the fierce confrontations and subtle negotiations between Manchu imperial politics and Western thought/technology inside the Forbidden City in her series of imperial Beijing books, including *Two Years in the Forbidden City* (1911), *Old Buddha* (1928), *Kowtow* (1929), *Jades and Dragons* (1932), *Golden Phoenix* (1932), *Imperial Incense* (1933), and *Son of Heaven* (1935). Her narratives unveil invisible people, places, and things, and stimulate the desire to consume insiders' stories of the "Great Within." Her dual identity as ethnographer and informant, and the narrative tension between official and unofficial history, interweave to depict both the grand narratives about the imperial capital and female perceptions and memories. Obsessed with pure difference and disparity, Victor Segalen embarked on his long journey from Hong Kong (which he finds characterized by a British style) to Shanghai (Americanized) and eventually to Beijing, where he finally settled down, called the imperial capital "my city," named his Beijing courtyard house "my palace," and labeled his study room as "my China." In his representative novel *René Leys* (written in Beijing between November 1, 1913 and January 31, 1914 and published in French in 1922, three years after his accidental death), Segalen creates a fictional, mythical, and treacherous city underneath the Forbidden City, to incarnate his exoticist ideal in the twilight of the Manchu Empire. His ideal city, mythical garden, "horizontal wells," exotic romances, and imagined abyss of the ancient capital shed new light on the mapping and (mis) understanding of Beijing as heterotopia by generations of foreign writers. All three writers dip into both Eastern and Western cultures and deploy a comparative vision to explore Beijing's liminality: their narratives are both outsiders' imagination, akin to anthropologists' investigations of foreign lands or exotic cities, and natives' reading and elucidation of the city that they inhabit and experience.

The looting of Beijing in 1900 left an open wound in the minds of its inhabitants and the Chinese people. How to account for, narrate, and work through these traumatic experiences would become a haunting task not only for individual victims and the nation but also for modern Chinese literature. Zeng Pu's 曾樸 (1872–1935) *Nie haihua* 孽海花 (A flower in the sea of sins, 1905), Li Boyuan's 李伯元 (1867–1906) *Gengzi guobian tanci* 庚子國變彈詞 (Tanci, on the Boxer Rebellion of 1900, 1902), and Lin Shu's 林紓 (1852–1924) *Jinghua bixue lu* 京華碧血錄 (Record of blood shed in righteous death in Beijing, 1913) are among the earliest works to address this traumatic incident. Whereas the 1900 looting of Beijing signified the excruciating pain at the advent of modernity, the 1949 Chinese division embodied yet another

---

[85] Lin Yutang, *Moment in Peking: A Novel of Contemporary Chinese Life* (New York: The John Day Company, 1939); and *Imperial Peking*.

moment of mutilation in the Chinese body politic. With the CCP's takeover of the mainland and the KMT's retreat to Taiwan, hundreds of millions of people were forced to relocated and uprooted from their hometowns. For diasporic Chinese who migrated to Sinophone regions outside of mainland China at the 1949 division,[86] any accounts of Beijing had to deal with the lived experiences of recent geopolitical diaspora and mental suffering. The emotions of bidding farewell to a lost city and a severed nation were so powerful and destructive that diasporic Chinese had to rethink, restructure, and reframe their memories—individual and national, urban and cultural—in order to rechart their routes, roots, belongings, and identities.

In her work on the Holocaust, memory, and family photographs, Marianne Hirsch coins the term "postmemory" to elucidate the relationship between the second generation and the traumatic experiences that took place before their birth yet were transmitted to them. She regards postmemory "as a structure of inter- and trans-generational transmission of traumatic knowledge and experience. It is a consequence of traumatic recall but (unlike posttraumatic stress disorder) at a generational remove."[87] The Beijing narratives by émigré writers in Taiwan and Hong Kong that I will consider are not about transmitted memory, inherited memory, or "absent memory"[88] of the generation after. Here, it is useful to recall Hirsch's clarification of multiple layers of connotations of the "post" in "postmemory." She observes that "post" points to both a temporal delay and a location in the aftermath, both a critical distance from and a troubling interrelation with the original memory. I regard these émigré Beijing recollections as an urban postmemory, with all the layerings of meanings that "post" carries. More important, these stories rarely address the 1949 trauma directly. Instead, they deal with these experiences vicariously and replace them with seemingly irrelevant, minor, or personal stories. Liang Shiqiu 梁實秋 (1903–1987) and Tang Lusun's 唐魯孫 (1908–1985) Beijing recollections paint a cuisine-oriented city; Lin Haiyin 林海音 (Lin Hai-yin, 1918–2001) romanticizes her childhood years

---

[86] See Shu-mei Shih, "Global Literature and the Technologies of Recognition," *PMLA* 119, no. 1 (January 2004): 16–30; David Der-wei Wang, *Hou yimin xiezuo: Shijian yu jiyi de zhengzhi xue* 後遺民寫作：時間與記憶的政治學 [Post-loyalist writing: The politics of time and memory] (Taipei: Maitian, 2007); Shu-mei Shih, *Visuality and Identity: Sinophone Articulation across the Pacific* (Berkeley: University of California Press, 2007); Jing Tsu and David Der-wei Wang, eds., *Global Chinese Literature: Critical Essays* (Leiden: Brill, 2010); Jing Tsu, *Sound and Script in Chinese Diaspora* (Cambridge, MA: Harvard University Press, 2010); Shu-mei Shih, "The Concept of the Sinophone," *PMLA* 126, no. 3 (2011): 709–718; Shu-mei Shih, Chien-hsin Tsai, and Brian Bernards, eds., *Sinophone Studies: A Critical Reader* (New York: Columbia University Press, 2013); and Xiaojue Wang, *Modernity with a Cold War Face: Reimagining the Nation in Chinese Literature across the 1949 Divide* (Cambridge, MA: Harvard University Asia Center, 2013).

[87] Marianne Hirsch, "The Generation of Postmemory," *Poetics Today* 29, no. 1 (Spring 2008): 106.

[88] Ellen S. Fine, "The Absent Memory: The Act of Writing in Post-Holocaust French Literature," *Writing and the Holocaust* (1988): 41–57.

in Beijing; and Zhong Lihe 鍾理和 (1915–1960) describes it as a disenchanted dystopia. Jin Yong's 金庸 (Louis Cha, 1924–) martial-arts narrative imagines an imperial capital of loyalty, betrayal, (in)justice, and dynastic changes and exiles in the Ming and Qing transition. As individual, communal, and national memories are projected onto, reframed, and displaced by other aspects of life or other historical times, as they are restructured, dislocated, and emanated from national peripheries, they turn into what I call postmemory, and Beijing into a displaced post-hometown.

Chapter 5 investigates how Sinophone writers in Taiwan and Hong Kong compose their diasporic stories and postmemory of Beijing during the Cold War era. I first center on Liang Shiqiu, a Beijing native, Taipei dweller, and sophisticated connoisseur of fine cuisine, and briefly address Tang Lusun, another Beijinger and erudite food essayist with a famous nickname, *chanren* 饞人 (the man with a craving for fine food). Both Liang and Tang moved to Taiwan before the People's Republic of China was founded, and published a large amount of reminiscent writings about Beijing and its life, in particular, its cuisine. Liang blends food memory and diasporic nostalgia in his depictions and recollections of the long-lasting flavors of Chinese food and the lingering aroma of Beijing dishes during his Taipei years. From 1949 to the 1980s, Liang's repetitive, regurgitative, and compulsive writings on Chinese cuisine, in particular Beijing food, reveal an intriguing dialectic between starvation and satisfaction, necessity and extravagance: the absent authentic hometown flavors can be symbolically replaced, yet also displaced by verbal composition and exhibition of the cuisine; and the yearning for a lost hometown can be gratified by spiritual consumption and emotional mapping of the lingering flavor and bittersweet aftertaste of "authentic" homeland food. Therefore, his culinary *xiaopin wen* 小品文 (little prose pieces) are presented to feed not only the starving body but also the diasporic mind craving an imagined homecoming to a distant, idealized Beijing. Liang channels his unquenchable nostalgia into lavish descriptions and verbal exhibitions of his obsession with the flavors of home. His gastronomic writing recollects and remaps Beijing and Chinese delicacies in terms of emotional affiliation and spatial rearrangements or "reunion," making the disappeared reappear in the gourmet kingdom and the "republic of letters." Liang's culinary aesthetics and little prose pieces about food and diet, and taste and aftertaste, constitute a symbolic trope of and an imaginary solution to the fundamental human hunger, the unique and universal *chan* 饞 or craving, and the everlasting homesickness and spiritual loss.

This chapter continues to explore the ways indigenous Taiwan writers Zhong Lihe and Lin Haiyin departed from Taiwan, resided in Beijing, eventually returned to Taipei, and projected their diasporic "state of mind" into their sojourning experiences and diversified memories about Republican Beijing. A famous Hakka writer inflicted by poverty and poor health, Zhong traveled from Taiwan to the Chinese mainland with a strong "*Yuanxiang*" 原鄉 (original home) complex, or Chinese consciousness. Based on his five-year stay in Beijing between 1941 and 1946, Zhong Lihe wrote a novella, "Jiazhutao" 夾竹桃 (Oleander, 1944), which provides a bleak portrait of Beijing's lower-class life and sharply criticizes its moral degeneration. He concentrates on a crowded and impoverished residential compound in a slum neighborhood, taking it as a lab to explore Beijing's urban milieu, Chinese nationhood, and national character from the point of view of an anthropologist or ethnographer, and depicts Beijing as a filthy and diseased city where the lower-class people are trapped in urban darkness and destitution. While Zhong's work is shot through with profound disillusionment about the old capital, Lin Haiyin, from a female viewpoint, presents a warm, beautified, and sentimental city image. Starting in the 1960s, Lin published a series of her Beijing memories, in particular her representative novel *Chengnan jiushi* 城南舊事 (*Memories of Peking: South Side Stories*), derived from her twenty-five years living in Beijing from 1923 to 1948. Lin Haiyin, a "Taiwan Girl in Beijing" who takes the city as her second hometown, contributes *petits récits* focusing on "personal feelings and daily minutiae"[89] against the backdrop of the May Fourth Movement and other historical events. She romanticizes her bittersweet memory, lived and imagined, of the south side of Beijing from an innocent girl's perspective.

The last part of the chapter deals with Jin Yong's Beijing fantasy and the Sinophone chivalric writing strategy of exclusive inclusion and inclusive exclusion. Written in the British Crown Colony of Hong Kong in the Cold War era, Jin Yong's topography of the imperial capital Beijing in the Ming–Qing dynastic transformation blends the real and the imagined, and envisions a dialect of absence and presence with an intriguing reference to premodern Beijing and modern Hong Kong. It charts a wide range of chivalric activities: intruding into the political center embodied by the Forbidden City (the "Great Within") and fleeing to peripheral regions such as Xinjiang's Islamic community, the overseas kingdom of Brunei in Southeast Asia, and an unknown place somewhere inside Yangzhou and later Dali City along the Southwestern border. I consider his three martial-arts novels, *Shujian enchou lu* 書劍恩仇錄 (*The Book and the Sword*, 1955–1956, 1975 revision), *Bixue jian* 碧血劍 (The sword stained with royal blood, 1956, 1975 revision), and *Luding ji* 鹿鼎記 (*The Deer and the Cauldron*, 1969–1972, 1981 revision). By emplotting political, ethnic, and cultural crises in dynastic transitions, Jin Yong explores various topics, including gratitude and revenge between Han and non-Han peoples,

---

[89] Peng Hsiao-yen, "Introduction: Lin Hai-yin's *Memories of Peking: South Side Stories*," trans. Steven K. Luk, in Lin Hai-yin, *Memories of Peking: South Side Stories*, trans. Nancy C. Ing and Chi Pang-yuan (Hong Kong: The Chinese University Press, 2002), xiv.

ambivalent individual identity, and imagined cultural memory against the backdrop of the 1949 Chinese division and the post-1949 migrations in Sinophone worlds. By intertwining literary topography and chivalric fantasy, Jin Yong's martial-arts narrative from the 1950s to the 1980s inscribes post-loyalist attachments and detachments into the imagery of Beijing, an imperial capital, and into Hong Kong, the birthplace of his chivalric geography, thus suggesting a frustrated yet flexible identity and a supplementary yet self-sufficient "republic of letters" in his remapping of Beijing's and China's past for contemporary Sinophone articulations.

For these Sinophone writers, Beijing becomes a shared platform of emotions and reminiscence, a revisited space of anxiety and desire, and an opening to articulate their poignant and shifting subjectivities. By challenging prevalent discourses of colonialism, nationalism, and cosmopolitanism, this chapter sheds new light on critical issues such as nostalgia and amnesia, disappearance and reappearance, replacement and dislocation, geopolitics and geopoetics in their domestic and diasporic trajectories and affective mapping of the old yet new Beijing.

These five chapters together constitute critical approaches to space, emotion, and literary topography of modern Beijing. "Topography," according to J. Hillis Miller, "is the product of a triple figurative transference. 'Topography' originally meant the creation of a metaphorical equivalent in words of a landscape. Then, by another transfer, it came to mean representation of a landscape according to the conventional signs of some system of mapping. Finally, by a third transfer, the name of the map was carried over to name what is mapped."[90] In defining topography, the key words include "lieu," "place," "landscape," "territory," "architecture," "geography," "mapping," "region," "realm," "area," "location," and "dwelling." For Miller, topography is "the act of mapping."[91] I would argue that literary topography, or literary act of mapping, is produced after a subjective, sentimental, and sometimes scientific journey, akin to the physical and psychological journey of a writer (or a cartographer with literary sense and sensibility) charting and exhibiting familiar or new terrains. And if exhibition is "a vehicle for the display of objects or a space for telling a story,"[92] then literary topography is done not only to chart spaces and stories, but also to create territories in which emotions, feelings, and meanings can be enciphered and deciphered. Literary mapping is also romancing, criticizing, exhibiting, familiarizing, and defamiliarizing, adding enchantment or disenchantment to the image of this literary space. In this sense, "literary topography" is also similar

---

[90] J. Hillis Miller, *Topographies* (Stanford, CA: Stanford University Press, 1995), 3–4.

[91] Ibid., 4.

[92] Ivan Karp and Steven D. Lavine, eds., *Exhibiting Cultures: The Poetics and Politics of Museum Display* (Washington, DC: Smithsonian Institution Press, 1991), 12.

to "literary Geography," which, according to Franco Moretti, refers to the study of *space in literature* (the dominant is a fictional one); or it may indicate the study of *literature in space*" (real historical space).[93] The two approaches are disparate but also overlapping.

Literary topography of modern Beijing indicates, therefore, a possibility, using Moretti's words, "to be the bridge between the old and the new, forging a symbolic compromise *between the indifferent world of modern knowledge, and the enchanted topography of magic storytelling.*"[94] The metamorphosis of Beijing's everyday places and spaces in Lao She's major novels and dramas unfolds the Manchu author's rhetoric of oxymoron and Beijing complex about his beloved yet warped native city. The tension and relation between Zhang Henshui's popular snapshots of fleeting urban shocks and everlasting sorrows illuminate his affective mapping of the social manners and urban transformation in Republican era. Female poet and architect Lin Huiyin captures the aesthetic dimension of Beijing vis-à-vis the political and ideological urban planning. The images of the imperial capital constructed in bilingual, transcultural, and comparative works by Lin Yutang, Princess Der Ling, and Victor Segalen highlight the pleasures and pitfalls of collecting local knowledge and presenting cosmopolitan visions. Along the Taiwan Strait, in the shadow of the Cold War ideology, a multilayered displaced Beijing appears and reappears in the Sinophone articulations of Beijing postmemory, and brings to light the mind and heart of diasporic Beijing natives Liang Shiqiu and Tang Lusun, Taiwan sojourners Zhong Lihe and Lin Haiyin, and Hong Kong émigré writer Jin Yong. Exploring the distinctive yet relational narrative modes of urban imagination and cultural memory, this book investigates and reveals the complex nexus of urban spaces, archives of emotions, and literary topography of Beijing in its long journey from imperial capital to Republican city and to socialist metropolis.

---

[93] Franco Moretti, *Atlas of the European Novel, 1800–1900* (London: Verso, 1998), 3.
[94] Ibid., 72.

The magnification of all the dimension of life, through emotional communication, rational communication, technological mastery, and above all, dramatic representation, has been the supreme office of the city in history.

—LEWIS MUMFORD

The structure of feeling of the memoirs is then significant and indispensable as a response to this specific social deformation.

—RAYMOND WILLIAMS

1

A Warped Hometown

LAO SHE AND THE BEIJING COMPLEX

1900, THE TWENTY-SIXTH year of Qing Emperor Guangxu's 光緒 (1871–1908) reign, witnessed a violent spectacle of foreign conquest and a traumatic wound on the mind of China when the Eight-Nation Alliance defeated both the Boxers and the Manchu Army and occupied the imperial capital, followed by a carnival-like looting of Beijing.[1] Empress Dowager Cixi and Emperor Guangxu were forced to flee helter-skelter from the Forbidden City, "the Great Within," to northwestern China. Under the shadow of this unprecedented imperial catastrophe and calamity, a poor Manchu bannerman/soldier named Shu Yongshou 舒永壽 died defending the fallen city. At this time of savage massacre, the death of a Manchu soldier might seem to have had little effect on the suffering city. However, the death of Shu Yongshou left a permanent scar in the mind of his son, Lao She (Lau Shaw or Lao Sheh), pseudonym of Shu Qingchun 舒慶春,[2] who was one year old when this tragedy of his family, city, empire, and dynasty took place. The Shu home was among countless houses in Beijing that were plundered by foreign troops. With a tone of humor and satire, Lao She recollected

---

[1] For a study of the looting of Beijing in 1900, see James Hevia, "Looting Beijing: 1860, 1900," in *Tokens of Exchange: The Problem of Translation in Global Circulations*, ed. Lydia H. Liu (Durham, NC: Duke University Press, 1999), 192–213.

[2] Like "Lu Xun" or "Mao Dun," "Lao She" is a pseudonym; unlike "Mao Dun," it is not a political pseudonym. Rather, "Lao She" indicates an "old house," or "hometown," from which we can come to grips with the man and his Beijing complex.

his near-death experience when foreign invaders broke in: "I was sleeping soundly when they entered our house. If I had awakened, they would have sliced me up with their swords, since they were angry not to find anything valuable in our home."[3]

Hu Jieqing 胡絜青 (1905–2001), Lao She's wife, recalled this incident in her postscript for Lao She's incomplete autobiographic work, which was posthumously published as *Zhenghongqi xia* 正紅旗下 (Beneath the red banner):

> His father died in a grain shop on the Southern Long Avenue, when the allied army of the imperialist powers entered Beijing. It was his cousin, also a Manchu soldier, who witnessed it . . . . Defeated in battle, [his cousin] went past the grain shop. As he walked in to look for some water to drink, he happened to see Lao She's father lying there dying. His body had received extensive burns when the gunpowder he was carrying was hit by an incendiary bomb and exploded. Fatally injured, he had crawled into the grain shop to await his death.[4]

A close examination of this tragic incident shows that the fatal wound was inflicted by both the modern weapons of the Western invaders and the outdated gunpowder used by the Qing army. Ironically, what this Manchu bannerman and hundreds of other soldiers sacrificed their lives to defend was an abandoned city, as the imperial rulers were already safely on their way to the ancient capital, Xi'an. How to negotiate emotionally between individual loss and national mourning, between violent or progressive modernities and meaningful or meaningless histories: all these questions inform and infuse Lao She's affective mapping of his native city. By reading four of his works, *Rickshaw Boy, Four Generations under One Roof, Dragon Beard Ditch*, and *Teahouse*, this chapter examines how Lao She's Beijing narratives envision a warped hometown as the locus of horror and courage, anticipation and disillusionment, attachment and detachment, and dream and nostalgia. This warped native city is not merely a sociohistorical setting against which the experiences of the modern are dramatized, but, more importantly, is depicted as what Raymond Williams calls "a human landscape" where a complex "structure of feeling" unrolls.[5] The great writer articulates

---

[3] Lao She's afterword (1961) to his drama *Shen Quan* 神拳 [Magical boxers, 1958], "Tu le yikou qi" 吐了一口氣 [Exhale freely], in *Lao She juzuo xuan* 老舍劇作選 [Selected dramas of Lao She] (Beijing: Renmin wenxue chubanshe, 1978), 369–373. See also David Der-wei Wang, *Fictional Realism in 20th Century China: Mao Dun, Lao She, Shen Congwen* (New York: Columbia University Press, 1993), 112.

[4] Hu Jieqing, "About *Beneath the Red Banner*," in Lao She, *Beneath the Red Banner* (Beijing: Panda Books, 1985), 214. See also Britt Towery, *Lao She, China's Master Storyteller* (Waco, TX: The Tao Foundation, 1999), esp. chap. 1.

[5] Williams, *The Country and the City*, 158.

a Beijing in his heart, embarking on an emotional journey to his beloved city with a literary map, which is not merely a virtual tour-guide map of geographical and historical sites, but an affective map with personal preferences and memories, alternative mapping of emotions and epiphanies, inerasable marks of pleasure and pain, unique cartography of fear and melancholy, hope and longing.

UTOPIANIST (DIS)ENCHANTMENT, MATERIALIZED DESIRE, AND URBAN DARKNESS

But the tigers come at night,

With their voices soft as thunder.

As they tear your hopes apart,

As they turn your dreams to shame.

—HERBERT KRETZMER

In his pioneering study *A History of Modern Chinese Fiction*, C. T. Hsia (1921–2013) regards Lao She's *Rickshaw Boy*, written on the eve of the second Sino-Japanese War, as "the finest modern Chinese novel up to that time."[6] The novel deploys both a "fictional realism" and a "psychological realism" to portray the fate and failure of rickshaw puller Xiangzi (Hsiang Tzu), an orphan in/of Beijing.[7] When the novel starts, Xiangzi is an orphan arriving in Beijing from nowhere. Having undergone all disillusionments after both his wife and his lover died and his humble dream of possessing a rickshaw of his own proved deluded, Xiangzi ends up a lonely and frustrated man, without home, property, or belonging. In this section, I aim to explore the following issues: first, utopianism or utopianist sensibility as noteworthy symptoms of individual wishes and collective urban desires; second, the rickshaw as the object of desire and the token of wrecked subjectivity; third, nights in Beijing as a symbol of urban darkness connected with the misperceptions of daytime and nighttime, labor and leisure; and fourth, streets, in particular mean streets, as the sites of

---

[6] C. T. Hsia, *A History of Modern Chinese Fiction*, with an introduction by David Der-wei Wang (Bloomington: Indiana University Press, 1999), 187. Four English versions of Lao She's *Luotuo Xiangzi* are available: Lau Shaw, *Rickshaw Boy*, trans. Evan King (New York: Reynal & Hitchcock, Inc., 1945); Lao She, *Rickshaw: The Novel of Lo-t'o Hsiang Tzu*, trans. Jean M. James (Honolulu: The University Press of Hawaii, 1979); Lao She, *Camel Xiangzi*, trans. Shi Xiaoqing (Beijing: Foreign Languages Press, 1981); and most recently, Lao She, *Rickshaw Boy*, trans. Howard Goldblatt (New York: Harper Perennial Modern Chinese Classics, 2010). In this section, I will use Jean M. James' translation, and borrow renditions from Howard Goldblatt and Evan King.

[7] For the fictional realism in Lao She's works, see Wang, *Fictional Realism in Twentieth-Century China*, chaps. 4 and 5; for the psychological realism in *Rickshaw Boy*, see Lydia H. Liu's *Translingual Practice: Literature, National Culture, and Translated Modernity—China, 1900–1937* (Stanford, CA: Stanford University Press, 1995), chap. 4.

pleasure and pain, daily circus and hostile playground, dreamland and dystopia, and physical performance and moral decline.

The impoverished rickshaw puller Xiangzi was once a contented urban dweller and invested a passionate love in the city that welcomed him. The city offers resources for ambitious individuals, a sense of homecoming and belonging, and meaning in life. As a genuine proletariat possessing nothing on earth that "he could call his own,"[8] Xiangzi's fantasy is nourished by his naïve belief that Beijing provides opportunities for wish fulfillment and solutions to life crises. Surviving his first pilgrimage ordeal of being robbed of his first and only property, a brand-new rickshaw, by ruthless, bandit-like army soldiers in warlord-controlled Beijing, he craves any sort of urban sight and recuperates by returning to his beloved city:

> Xiangzi wanted to kiss it, kiss that gray stinking dirt, adorable dirt, dirt that grew silver dollars! . . . The only friend he had was this ancient city. This city gave him everything. Even starving here was better than starving in the country. There were things to look at, sounds to listen to, color and voices everywhere. All you needed was to be willing to sell your strength. There was so much money here it couldn't be counted. There were ten thousand kinds of grand things here that would never be eaten up or worn out.[9]

For Xiangzi, the most reliable way to sustain his identity as a qualified urban inhabitant is to construct a bodily contact or a corporeal linkage with Beijing by kissing, seeing, hearing, smelling, and even treading on his dream kingdom, where even the stinking dirt turns out to be cherished and adorable. At this point, Beijing becomes a spiritual hometown and an overwhelmingly beloved and emotionally attached city, where a wanderer, an orphan, and a survivor like Xiangzi could settle down: "When he saw the bustle of people and horses, heard the ear-piercing racket, smelled the dry stink of the road, and trod on the powdery, churned-up gray dirt,"[10] Xiangzi just wanted to join the street crowds and kiss his treasured earth, which, to his mind, offered him access to potentials, possibilities, and pleasure.

Here, Xiangzi's affective mapping of Beijing can be diagnosed as a noteworthy symptom of "utopianism," a notion Richard Dyer defines as a sensuous feeling rather than a reality or true modes of utopia, the path to redemption and perfection. This kind of utopianism is, more or less, "the image of 'something better' to escape into,

---

[8] Lau Shaw, *Rickshaw Boy*, trans. Evan King, 38.
[9] Lao She, *Rickshaw*, trans. Jean M. James, 31.
[10] Ibid.

or something we want deeply that our day-to-day lives don't provide."[11] Therefore, what the narrator reveals is Xiangzi's resilient sense of a better world full of refreshing urban objects, colors, and sounds—all in all, the surreal materiality of his love and desire. Xiangzi prefers starving in Beijing with affection and satisfaction to living in the village he came from. Remarkably, the narrator speaks out Xiangzi's inner thoughts, which provide an overoptimistic vision of the city: "If you begged for your food on the street, you could still get soup with meat in it, while the best that the village had was cornmeal bread."[12] In Xiangzi's utopian sense of life in Beijing, "abundance" is everywhere and eliminates poverty in reality. Boundless "energy" radiates from Xiangzi's body and mind and becomes the only capital he can employ and claim. He surely takes "work and play" as synonyms, because, in his utopian illusions, the distinction between working time and leisure time utterly disappears. "Intensity" is evident in Xiangzi's ambition, an excitement and affectivity of living and longing. Last but not least, "transparency" is definitely Xiangzi's "state of mind," in that he carries out open, sincere, spontaneous, and trustworthy communications with his customers and patrons.[13]

Even the sound and fury of the city could turn out to be enjoyable and precious: "everything he saw was familiar and dear. If he were to die while sitting there, he'd be content."[14] This is a joyous construction of personal utopia and sense of belonging in modern Beijing's everyday life by the happy and gullible rickshaw boy, whose sparkling eyes warp and beautify the "street corner society" and whose enchanted heart develops a strong affective attachment to urban daily life:

The gateway tunnel was jammed with every kind of cart and all sorts of people. Everyone wanted to get through it quickly, but no one dared hurry. The cracking of whips, shouts, curses, honking of horns, ringing of bells, the laughter were blended into a continuous roaring by the megaphonelike tunnel, making a "weng weng." Hsiang Tzu's big feet cut forward and jumped backward while his hands fended off people to left and right. He pushed his way into the city like a great skinny fish that follows the waves and jumps for joy. He caught sight of Hsin Street; it was so broad and straight it made his eyes sparkle when they

---

[11] Richard Dyer, "Entertainment and Utopia," in *The Cultural Studies Reader*, 2nd ed., ed. Simon During (London: Routledge, 1999), 371–381; Dyer's article first appeared in *Movie* 24 (1977): 2–12. For a broad discussion of utopianism, see, for instance, Krishan Kumar, *Utopianism* (Milton Keynes: Open University Press, 1991); and Lyman Tower Sargent, *Utopianism: A Very Short Introduction* (New York: Oxford University Press, 2010).

[12] Lau Shaw, *Rickshaw Boy*, trans. Evan King, 45.

[13] Dyer, "Entertainment and Utopia," 376.

[14] Lao She, *Rickshaw*, trans. Jean M. James, 31.

saw it, just as brightly as the sunshine reflected off the roofs above him. He nodded his head.[15]

Since Beijing is such a gigantic city and thus difficult to grasp, Xiangzi's fantasy has been incarnated and materialized in his obsession with the rickshaw, the object of his love and longing, and the possible capital or property that he is eager to possess. For Karl Marx, capital must be conceived of as a process; it cannot be reified as a thing. Yet for Xiangzi, a country bumpkin, urban newcomer, and ignorant rickshaw puller, capital must be reified as a material object of desire, be it a rickshaw in his hand or the silver money in his pocket. Only then is he able to perceive the existence of capital, and more significantly, of his own being and belonging. "The owners of money," says David Harvey, "are free (within constraints) to choose how, when, where, and with whom to use that money to satisfy their needs, wants, and fancies."[16] Personal freedom and the pursuit of autonomy and pleasure can be connected with the ownership of money. Xiangzi is naively convinced that he can liberate himself from the contract bondage of the rickshaw guild and from the employer-employee relationship once he can afford to purchase his own rickshaw.

Xiangzi does not take the rickshaw as an inhuman machine, but as a part or an extension of his body. For him, the rickshaw is the most intimate medium between his body and the lure of the city. Xiangzi's relationship with the rickshaw nearly surpasses those with other human beings in the novel, even his wife, Tigress (Hu Niu 虎妞), or his true lover, "*Xiao Fuzi*" 小福子 (The Little Good Fortune), a low-rank prostitute with a heart of gold. He feels a harmonic combination between the modern instrument and himself:

How could a man so tall, pulling such a gorgeous rickshaw, his own rickshaw too, with such gently rebounding springs and shafts that barely wavered, such a gleaming body, such a white cushion, such a sonorous horn, face himself if he did not run hard? How could he face his rickshaw? This was not false pride. It seemed to be a kind of duty. He couldn't show off his strength and exhibit the excellence of his rickshaw to full capacity if he didn't fly. That rickshaw was really endearing. It seemed to understand everything and have feelings after he had pulled it for six months. It responded promptly when he turned or squatted or straightened up and gave him the most compatible kind of assistance. There was not the slightest separation or disharmony between them. When

---

[15] Ibid., 32.

[16] David Harvey, *Consciousness and the Urban Experience: Studies in the History and Theory of Capitalist Urbanization* (Baltimore, MD: Johns Hopkins University Press, 1985), 4.

he came to a flat stretch with little traffic, Hsiang Tzu might hold the shafts with only one hand and fly along sagely with the whisper of the rubber tires urging him on like a damp cool breeze. You could wring the sweat out of his clothes when he got to his destination. It was just as if they had come out of the washtub. He felt exhausted, but it was a happy, honorable exhaustion, like that following a long ride on a famous horse.[17]

The emotional topography of individual desire, pride, dignity, and obsession binds the proletariat Camel Xiangzi to his rickshaw, a transportation instrument or machine imported from Japan. The body language and politics, the individual's feelings and emotions, and the divisions of social formations across the city are vividly represented and mapped in Lao She's urban narrative.

Consequently, while the rickshaw is imagined as an extension of the pauper's body and a beloved instrument to make a living in the city, Xiangzi himself is turned into an object and thus totally alienated in his incurable and hopeless worship of the rickshaw. Not only does he fall into the trap of an-ungrudging fetishism, but he is also haunted and dominated by the material object. And deep underneath this fetishism lies the fatal encounter between an individual dream and the urban exploitation and manipulation where Xiangzi struggles like a small screw, being bound, exhausted, discarded, and ruined by the gigantic city.[18]

In this light, the second half of the novel shows utopia becoming its opposite, an antiutopia or dystopia, where Xiangzi's nonstop frustrations and failures indicate the moral decline and self-destruction of the once ambitious rickshaw puller. Joseph S. M. Lau argues that "[i]n [Xiangzi's] character, there is nothing to suggest that his downfall is his individual responsibility . . . . His defeat can only be explained in terms of the society in which he moves, which nullifies all his efforts towards independent and honest living."[19] From Lau's naturalist point of view, man becomes a victim of the society or the metropolis at large. The narrator discloses that a strong sense of breakdown and homelessness overwhelmingly occupies Xiangzi's mind, but he cannot figure out the exact reason and is entrapped by a strong sense of loss of direction—even though, as a rickshaw puller, he is a living map of the city: "Where should he go? He had no objective. Ordinarily, pulling a rickshaw, his legs went in

---

[17] Lao She, *Rickshaw*, trans. Jean M. James, 11–12. Howard Goldblatt uses "consciousness and emotion" (different from James' "feeling") in his translation, 15.

[18] The streets of the city are never a labyrinth, since he is a living map and is driven by customers to go back and forth, here and there. Nevertheless, when he steps out of the working time and into his own world and temporality, he does not know where to go.

[19] See Joseph Lau, "Naturalism in Chinese Fiction," *Literature East and West* 2 (1970): 150.

the direction set for them by the lips of his fare. Today, although his legs might take him where they chose—they were free—his heart was surprised and confused."[20]

Overdetermined by his class and social status, the rickshaw puller has lost his sense of direction and his own subjectivity in the city: "Everyone else had an out somewhere. Hsiang Tzu was the only one who couldn't get away because he was a rickshaw puller. Bran is what a rickshaw puller gets to eat and blood is what bursts out of him. He puts forth the greatest efforts and gets the least reward. He has to take the lowest place among men and wait for the blows from every person, every law, and every hardship."[21] And Xiangzi cannot locate the reason for his miserable destiny. In the following episode, Lao She captures Xiangzi's change of mind, when his marriage with Tigress and their new home turn out to be a trap:

Mixing the old furniture up with the new and putting it all in the same place within the same four walls made him recollect the things that had passed, the old things, and confronted him with uncertainty and anxiety about the future, with all the fears that new things bring. In everything he was allowing some other to do with him as that other pleased; he too was some kind of piece of furniture or ornament, some strange, queer thing that seemed at the same time to be completely new and to be identical with something out of the past; he did not know himself, was not sure of his own name and identity.[22]

Xiangzi has no place to hide, no destination. His body and will are no longer his own possessions. Now, when confronting the naked body that he was so proud of earlier, he even feels a strong embarrassment about his own physical existence: "He undressed himself and stood in his complete nakedness looking down at his body, feeling the deepest sensation of shame and mortification."[23]

The warped city reveals its dark face and shows its repressive and oppressive force, by which Xiangzi is brutally deprived of humanity, hope, drive, and desire in his once beloved city:

Hsiang Tzu remained in this "cultured" city, but he was being transformed into an animal. Not a bit of it was his own fault. He had stopped thinking and, therefore, the human being in him was destroyed. He bore no responsibility for that at all. He'd never hope again. He'd just sink blindly, stupidly, lower

---

[20] Lau Shaw, *Rickshaw Boy*, trans. Evan King, 223.
[21] Lao She, *Rickshaw*, trans. Jean M. James, 114.
[22] Lau Shaw, *Rickshaw Boy*, trans. Evan King, 219.
[23] Ibid., 223.

and lower, into a bottomless pit. He ate, he drank, he whored, he gambled, he cheated, and all because he had no heart left in him. Others had taken it from him. All that remained was his big frame, and now he waited for it to burst open like an abscess. He was getting ready for the potter's field.[24]

Moreover, the intimate interaction between Xiangzi and his rickshaw diminishes, and the man's passion and desire surrounding the machine becomes a "dead fire" that cannot be rekindled. Xiangzi's *telos* is missing and damaged, and his strong motives to survive in the tough urban atmosphere give way to an overwhelming mood of hopelessness and helplessness. "His hope, in the past, had lain solely in pulling a rickshaw. Now he detested pulling a rickshaw. Of course he couldn't cut his connections with rickshaw pulling all at once, but he certainly was not going to fumble with rickshaw shafts as long as he could find some other way of getting hold of three meals a day."[25] Meanwhile, Beijing itself has lost its status of national capital, and been haunted by a gloomy sense of loss and decline, and an untimely nostalgia of its glorious past and original excellences. David Der-wei Wang addresses the devastating loss of the city and the subsequent change of urban structure of feeling: "Beijing is shrouded with a ghostly veil of nostalgia . . . a phantom city thriving only in and for the past. No longer at the political center, the people of Beijing hang on to the past by observing obsolete customs, recalling old glories, and cultivating wistful airs."[26] The ritual respectability remains, but Xiangzi has lowered his "great expectations" and takes advantage of any tiny chances or byproducts of occasional street weddings and funerals: his "livelihood now depended primarily on these vestigial ceremonies and customs. He'd hold a flag or an umbrella when someone got married. He'd hold up a funeral scroll when someone was buried. He didn't rejoice, he didn't wail, he was there solely for the sake of ten or so pennies."[27] In this sense, Lao She's 1930s Beijing resembles Charles Dickens's literary London: "both lure and

---

[24] Lao She, *Rickshaw*, trans. Jean M. James, 233. Ling Zifeng's 凌子風 faithful cinematic adaptation *Rickshaw Boy* (1982) vividly captures the moments of Xiangzi as a living dead person and wandering ghost falling into the unfathomable darkness of the city.

[25] Lao She, *Rickshaw*, trans. Jean M. James, 236–237.

[26] Wang, *Fictional Realism in Twentieth-Century China*, 154. By capturing the details of bygone local specialties, Lao She presents a bleak image of the former capital: "After Peking was honored as a former capital, the things it was known for, its handicrafts, food, dialect, and police, had gradually spread outwards in all directions. That westernized Ch'ingtao had Peking-style 'rinsed lamb' too. You could hear the gloomy calls of street vendors selling noodles late at night in bustling Tientsin. Shanghai, Hankow, and Nanking all had policemen and official messengers who spoke in Peking dialect and ate sesame seed pancakes. Jasmine tea traveled from south to north, passed through a double smoking, and went south again. Even the pallbearers sometimes took the train to Tientsin or Nanking to carry the coffins of high officials." See Lao She, *Rickshaw*, trans. Jean M. James, 247.

[27] Lao She, *Rickshaw*, trans. Jean M. James, 248.

trap: a lure to those who are called to it as if by a magnet, because only the city offers the means of realizing a heightened conception of self; a trap in its workings, which lead to human destruction."[28]

In addition to Charles Dickens, Lao She also had a tremendous fondness for Joseph Conrad, and remarked, "'Nothing' often becomes the ending of Conrad's fiction. No matter how much will and vitality a man has, no matter how good or bad his personality is, once he steps into this realm of 'Nothing,' he is unable to free himself from the curse."[29] A disenchanted and dystopian façade in the remainder of the novel, Beijing betrays a significant and cruel "nothing" or "emptiness" and appears like a mythical demon or an invisible devil hand that manipulates Xiangzi's life-world and "state of mind" haunted by an unavoidable fatalism. The unspeakable living conditions push the depressed Xiangzi down into the horrific center of the city, like the lonely Marlow crying, "The horror, the horror" in Conrad's masterpiece, *Heart of Darkness*. Beijing has turned out to be Xiangzi's own "heart of darkness," and its warping power and entrapping urban milieu, his own antihero identity, and the whirlwind of modern times recall the devastating typhoons and swallowing "black hole" symbolically presented in Joseph Conrad's sea novel.[30]

Strikingly, nights affect the rickshaw puller's fate and feelings; nighttime also indicates the urban darkness and horrors in which Xiangzi is deeply trapped and eventually degenerates. The following five nights are worthy of attention. First, Xiangzi steals three camels in a night, indicating the first step of his moral decline and decay. Second, the night that Tigress seduces Xiangzi becomes another dark epiphany in which Xiangzi realizes the impossibility of controlling some inner desire in his body as he wishes and believes that she has completely destroyed the clear, fresh spirit he had brought from the village. This incident destroys his sense of masculine dignity and damages his self-righteousness. Third, the night when Tigress comes to Mr. Cao's house to tell Xiangzi that she is pregnant, it pushes Xiangzi into a helpless, if not yet desperate, situation. The fourth night, Xiangzi is robbed of all his savings for a second rickshaw. He is also forced to fall into Tigress's trap of marriage. However, a more terrible night awaits him. His wife, together with his son—his hope and future—dies in the darkness. The rickshaw boy ends up as a walking beast and wandering ghost. Those dark nights not only highlight the important moments in Xiangzi's life but also symbolize his final destiny: falling into the unfathomable

---

[28] Lehan, *The City in Literature*, 39–40.

[29] Lao She, *Lao She wenyi pinglun ji* 老舍文藝評論集 [Collection of Lao She's literary criticisms] (Hefei: Anhui renmin chubanshe, 1982), 9.

[30] See Wang Runhua 王潤華, *Lao She xiaoshuo xinlun* 老舍小說新論 [A new treatise on Lao She's novel] (Taipei: Dongda tushu gonsi, 1995).

urban darkness. At the story's end, after suffering from all kinds of desperation and crisis, Xiangzi remains an orphan, a lonely ghost, and a frustrated man wandering the streets.

In *Rickshaw Boy*, streets constitute the most significant chronotope "where the knots of narrative are tied and untied."[31] When addressing Dostoevsky's works, Bakhtin forcefully argues that "the threshold and related chronotopes—those of the staircase, the front hall and corridor, as well as the chronotopes of the street and square that extend those spaces into the open air—are the main places of action in his works, places where crisis events occur, the falls, resurrections, renewals, epiphanies, decisions that determine the whole life of a man."[32] The "chronotopes of the street," and even the street per se, stand as sites and signs of discipline and disorder, as well as symptoms and symbols, of modern urban experiences.

For Camel Xiangzi, a homeless youth from an outer province and a ground-zero orphan, Beijing's streets represent life opportunities and the lure of new possibilities, as well as traps leading to his bodily destruction and moral decline. He runs on the surface of the city and lives by employing his only property, his body, and pulling the rickshaw through avenues and streets, where people buy and sell, where body and labor are sold and bought. Furthermore, the street is not a monolithic and homogeneous space. During the rickshaw boys' break from work, the streets also constitute a space for their entertainment, where bodies are exhibited and recognized. In other words, it is exactly on the streets of Beijing that Xiangzi experiences the vicissitudes of life: here, he makes his living and exhibits his muscles and professional skills; he creates his daydreams of purchasing a rickshaw of his own and suffers from the disillusionment of his desire for an independent subjectivity; he stirs his economic/sexual/political urges and is at times defeated by an unnamable destiny and the invisible supremacies of the city. The phantasmal avenues and streets of Beijing happen to be spaces where lonely ghosts wander aimlessly, hunt futilely, and dream hopelessly. Xiangzi's desire to possess a rickshaw leads him to be possessed by a huge machine—the city per se. Ultimately, Xiangzi turns into one of the phantoms wandering in the urban wilderness.[33]

---

[31] Mikhail Bakhtin, *The Dialogic Imagination: Four Essays* (Austin: University of Texas Press, 1981), 250.

[32] Bakhtin, *The Dialogic Imagination*, 248.

[33] The street can be also connected with contingency and crisis in daily life. Siegfried Kracauer describes the affinity between *film* and the *street* as one based exactly on its chaos: "The affinity of film for haphazard contingencies is most strikingly demonstrated by its unwavering susceptibility to the 'street'—a term designed to cover not only the street, particularly the city street, in the literal sense, but also its various extensions, such as railway stations, dance and assembly halls, bars, hotel lobbies, airports, etc . . . . Within the present context the street, which has already been characterized as a center of fleeting impressions, is of interest as a region where the accidental prevails over the providential, and happenings in the nature of unexpected incidents are all but the rule." *Theory of Film: The Redemption of Physical Reality* (Princeton, NJ: Princeton University Press, 1997), 62.

In the dystopian part of the novel, Xiangzi is totally lost in the streets with which he was once so familiar. "When he reached the avenue there were only a few pass-ersby, and the brightness of the streetlights on this deserted thoroughfare made him feel even more completely swallowed up in his desolation."[34] The streets manipulate Xiangzi's body, use and abuse the rickshaw boy's ambition and hope. They also con-stitute the infrastructure of his life, structuring his daily performance, his irresistible yet unsatisfied desire, and the routes of his frustration and disorientation. The traces of his emotions are graphically and symbolically mapped out on Beijing's streets, thresholds, and houses.[35] And now, Xiangzi is like a moth, inevitably drawn to the flame of the city without knowing the potential danger in his dream of city life.

Modern literary critics and scholars of Beijing have highlighted the rickshaw puller as a moral model, in sharp contrast with the visible moral decline of the petit bourgeois intellectuals. In his famous story "An Incident," which has been included in middle-school textbooks in mainland China, Lu Xun described a typical image of a rickshaw puller. "His dusty, retreating figure seemed larger at that instant. Indeed, the further he walked the larger he loomed, until I had to look up to him. At the same time he seemed gradually to be exerting a pressure on me, which threatened to overpower the small self under my fur-lined gown."[36] Here, in the moment of epiphany, Lu Xun places this small incident of urban everyday life on a subliminal level higher than contemporary political events, and reconfigures the image of a man from the low part of society: "the military and political affairs of those years I have forgotten as completely as the classics I read in my childhood. Yet this incident keeps coming back to me, often more vivid than in actual life, teaching me shame, urging me to reform, and giving me fresh courage and hope."[37] Lin Yutang once pointed out that the "greatest charm of Peking is, however, the common people, not the saints and professors, but the rickshaw coolies" because they are optimistic, sincere, and can even tell their sad stories of "poverty and misfortunes with humor, refinement, and fatalistic good cheer."[38] What Lao She attempted to apprehend, however, is the absurdist and disenchanted moments in Xiangzi's hopeless struggle for "the order of things" and the meaning of life. In modern Chinese literature, Lao She contrib-utes a detailed portrait of a modern individual deeply obsessed with a rickshaw and frustrated within the urban milieu. In doing so, Lao She demonstrates a modernist

---

[34] Lao She, *Rickshaw*, trans. Jean M. James, 69.

[35] See Peter Stallybrass and Allon White, *The Politics and Poetics of Transgression* (Ithaca, NY: Cornell University Press, 1986), esp. chaps. 3 and 4.

[36] Lu Xun, *Selected Stories of Lu Hsun*, translated by Yang Hsien-yi and Gladys Yang (New York: Norton, 1972), 43.

[37] Lu Xun, "An Incident," 44.

[38] Lin, "Captive Peking," in *With Love and Irony*, 62.

sensibility of the deadening situation of the city, which leads to the decline and destruction of the subjectivity and morality of modern human beings.[39]

In his study of the history of the novel, Georg Lukács divides modern novels into two grand categories of "abstract idealism" and "romanticism of disillusionment." He observes, "the demonic character of the problematic individual" encounters failure "in the face of reality" and reveals "his inner problematic" on his "adventurous course," and "the demonism of the narrowing of the soul is the demonism of abstract realism . . . It is the mentality which chooses the direct, straight path towards the realism of the ideal; which, dazzled by the demon, forgets the existence of any distance between ideal and idea, between psyche and soul . . . ."[40] With regard to the second category, Lukács states, "(t)he romanticism of disillusionment not only followed abstract idealism in time and history, it was also conceptually its heir, the next historico-philosophical step in *a priori* utopianism."[41] If we view *Rickshaw Boy* from this critical approach, then, Xiangzi's utopianist fantasy and wishfully blind love of Beijing as the sole reality are evidently based on his fervent yet concrete obsession with the unpossessible rickshaw, a symptom of demonism of concrete and reified realism. On the other hand, the novel is a modern epic of an individual hero who sets out to encounter every high and low of reality and eventually ends up a frustrated and degenerate antihero. In this respect, Lao She's *Rickshaw Boy*, I would argue, presents a combination of a concrete idealism as well as a realism or naturalism of disillusionment.

ATLAS OF WARTIME EMOTIONS

To be homeless is much more a mental than a physical condition.
—PATRIZIA LOMBARDO

The outbreak of the second Sino-Japanese War (1937–1945) drastically changed Lao She's literary stance and style, which, at the early stage, were marked by his famous black humor and ironic laughter. Together with hundreds of thousands of other Beijing inhabitants, Lao She was forced into exile. Although he "had studiedly avoided all literary politics" during the prewar period, Lao She actively participated in the anti-Japanese cultural campaigns and later headed the Chinese Writers'

---

[39] Compared with modern Shanghai, modern Beijing seems to be a city in which everything lags behind. From the very beginning, the competition between Beijing and Shanghai was unequal because with the burden of history, Beijing started to step forward slowly. Even so, the rise of modern industrial civilization and capitalism also brought new technology, systems, states of mind, or grand transformation to Beijing, and Lao She sensitively and insightfully grabbed hold of the modern traces in the city.

[40] Georg Lukács, *The Theory of the Novel: A Historico-Philosophical Essay on the Forms of Great Epic Literature*, trans. Anna Bostock (Cambridge, MA: The MIT Press, 1971), 97.

[41] Lukács, *The Theory of the Novel*, 117.

Anti-Aggression Association.[42] In 1941, Lao She started to work on an ambitious and colossal trilogy, *Huanghuo* 惶惑 (Bewilderment), *Tousheng* 偷生 (Ignominy), and *Jihuang* 饑荒 (Famine); the novels first appeared as serial publications in Chongqing and were later published in book form in Shanghai, constituting his war epic, *Sishi tongtang* (Four generations under one roof, 1944–1950).[43] Between 1946 and 1950, he lived in the United States on a cultural grant at the invitation of the Department of State; there he finished *Four Generations*, which depicts the life in occupied Beijing under Japanese exploitation and coercion. Although Lao She himself did not live through the occupation, he based the trilogy on borrowed stories from his family members and friends and his deep understanding of the social mores of his native city.

Four Generations focuses on the wartime experiences and emotions of inhabitants in *Xiao yangjuan hutong* 小羊圈胡同 (the Little Sheepfold Lane), the birthplace of Lao She himself. An ordinary alley or lane that connects several quadrangular compounds in the northwestern district of Beijing, close to *Huguo si* 護國寺 (Temple of Guarding the Kingdom), the Little Sheepfold Lane forms a major chronotope and an allegorical microcosm of Republican Beijing under Japanese occupation. Imbricated with personal feelings and collective memories, urban sensibility and nationalist consciousness, Lao She's representation of the fallen Beijing and its rebirth traces the wartime emotions in relation to diversified urban places and spaces, and depicts the emergent and changing structures of feeling of people remaining in the assaulted and invaded city. Raymond Williams' concept of "structure of feeling" is helpful here in dealing with the relationship between literature and its evocation of everyday life experiences that are in the process of developing. In other words, "structure of feeling" offers a useful way of understanding Lao She's wartime Beijing narrative, addressing the shared military and political oppression, yet different emotional states of Beijing residents under the Japanese occupation. The "affective elements of consciousness and relationships"[44] provide transient, lived responses to the special social-political circumstances of the time in an abandoned city temporarily under Japanese rule.

The Little Sheepfold Lane consists of six households, and the novel focuses primarily on three of them: the Qis 祁, Guans 冠, and Qians 錢. Located at House Number 5, the Qis embody the Confucian family ideal of "four generations under

---

[42] Hsia, *A History of Modern Chinese Fiction*, 366.

[43] Ida Pruitt's abridged English translation *The Yellow Storm* appeared in 1951. For a recent study of Ida Pruitt, see Marjorie King, *China's American Daughter: Ida Pruitt (1888–1985)* (Hong Kong: Chinese University Press, 2006).

[44] Williams, *Marxism and Literature*, 132.

one roof," which was a safe haven and is now on the verge of destruction and collapse under Japanese domination. Old Man Qi was born in the 1860s and is depicted as a rigid yet respectful patriarch (grandfather). His son, Tianyou 天佑 (Tien Yiu), is an honest manager of a cotton goods store, who commits suicide after being framed and humiliated by the Japanese. The eldest grandson, Ruixuan 瑞宣 (Rey Shuan), is an English teacher with a liberal attitude, and he regrets his passive choice to stay in the fallen city. His wife, Yunmei, 韻梅 a virtuous and capable woman, is the backbone of the big family. The second grandson, Ruifeng 瑞豐 (Rey Feng), turns into a traitor and a collaborator with the Japanese invaders for his own interests. The youngest grandson, Ruiquan 瑞全 (Rey Tang), a college student, becomes a steadfast member of the anti-Japanese resistance army in the suburbs.

The Guan family is represented as the evil force in the Little Sheepfold Lane. Guan Xiaohe 冠曉荷 (Kuan the Morning Lotus) and his wife, Da Chibao 大赤包 (Big Red Pepper), take any chance to establish liaisons with the Japanese in order to gain power and status. In a farcical way, Lao She ridicules how Da Chibao is appointed as the Director of the Bureau for the Inspection of Beijing Prostitutes. While their eldest daughter, Gaodi, is portrayed as timid but decent, their second daughter, Zhaodi, ends as a spy for the Japanese secret agency.

In the Qian family, Qian Moyin 錢默吟, a poet who used to indulge in traditional Chinese poetry before the occupation, has been framed by his neighbor Guan and sent to prison. His eldest son was killed when Japanese soldiers arrested his father, and his second son sacrificed his life to drive a whole truck of Japanese soldiers into an abyss. With his family ruined and his cultural ideals shattered, Qian eventually becomes a determined patriot and anti-Japanese resister.

Through a thorough portrayal of the life experiences of these three families, the novel explores wartime violence, the Japanese occupation, and their physically and psychologically catastrophic aftermath. In the end, Japan is defeated, the wartime tragedy of humankind comes to an end, and the traitors and collaborators are punished in a restored Beijing. In his reading of *Four Generations*, David Der-wei Wang proposes three narrative modes of the real that are entangled in the novel. First, it is a patriotic and semiautobiographical story, told with a melodramatic tone. Second, the novel creates a lyrical nostalgic narrative "for acquaintance from different social strata, for local customs and street scenes, and even for his old residence." Third, it can be read as "an exposé novel in the tradition of the late Qing fiction of exposure, and provides a grotesque panorama of a society turned upside down," thus establishing a farcical discourse.[45] I would further argue that these three narrative modes—melodramatic, nostalgic, and farcical—are closely related to the author's

---

[45] Wang, *Fictional Realism in Twentieth-Century China*, 186.

investigation of different modes of urban structure of feeling during the Japanese occupation of Beijing. These disparate structures express collective emotions amid everyday life experiences, form senses of community, and provide emotional responses to the violence and destruction wrought by the occupation.

In dealing with a warped and wounded city under Japanese rule, the trilogy unfolds around a nexus of space, emotion, and violence. Violence is manifested in competing and conflicting modes: spectacular or ordinary, fast or slow, concentrated or scattered, detectable or disguised. The novel seeks to depict multiple forms of violence: military violence, secret policing and imprisonment, physical torture and mental oppression, family degeneration and betrayal, urban misery, and national calamity. Lao She approaches the constellation of places and spaces at micro- and macro-, and actual and fictional levels. The imagery of an ancient city of Beijing provides the essential backdrop for his atlas of wartime emotions.

A quick timeline would illustrate how modern China is marked and marred by war, violence, and calamities: 1894–1895, First Sino-Japanese War; 1900, Boxer Rebellion and the Looting of Beijing; 1911–1912, the Xinhai Revolution; 1915, the National Protection War; 1916–1928, Warlord Era; 1926–1927, Northern Expedition; 1927–1936, First Stage of the Chinese Civil War; 1937–1945, Second Sino-Japanese War; 1945–1949, the Chinese Civil War; . . . foreign looting, military invasion, warlords' tyranny, and civil war, all in all, have brought to the limelight a decades-long tumultuous history of pain and trauma, brutality and suffering, cataclysm and crisis.

The stable mind of Beijing or the city's well-balanced cultural mentality before the Japanese invasion is envisioned through the eyes of Old Man Qi, who represents the old generation of native inhabitants. Like a living fossil, Old Man Qi has experienced and survived major historical events since the looting of Beijing by the Eight-Nation Alliance. Remaining alive each historical incident, dynastic or republican, domestic or international, he witnessed changing scenes on the streets or around the city gates, listened to the shocking sounds of pistols and rifle fire, and observed the disparate flags, uniforms, and political faces of emperors, warlords, and presidents: "Suddenly the nine gates of the city would be closed and the sound of rifles and the sound of guns would not stop day or night. Suddenly the gates of the city would be opened and down the main streets the victorious warlords, with high carriages and big horses, would fly and run."[46] However, all this political, historical, and military turmoil can hardly shake Old Man Qi's fundamental belief in the stability of his city. He is ignorant of and nonchalant about any political ideologies. He defines and perceives time by celebrating each festival in the lunar calendar, and

---

[46] Lau Shaw (S. Y. Shu), *The Yellow Storm*, trans. Ida Pruitt (New York: Harcourt, Brace and Company, 1951), 3.

his main concern is to fulfill the basic everyday needs and maintain family ethics. Beijing is like a super-stable fortress where any wars, calamities, or grand transformations would only last a short while—in Old Man Qi's calendar, three months. For people of his generation, the city acts as their everlasting mother earth, which will stay intact and immune to political climate or historical vicissitudes. There might be "inevitable headaches and the little fevers"; however, these nuisances would soon pass and strengthen the immune system. Even after the Marco Polo Bridge Incident on July 7, 1937, when Beijing was quickly conquered by the Japanese, Old Man Qi's faith did not waver: "Looking at his own house, his own son and grandsons, and at the flowers and shrubs he had planted himself, Old Man Chi [Qi] felt that his work of a lifetime had not been in vain. The walls of Peiping were the eternal walls; his house was the house that would never decay."[47]

What supports this structure of feeling for a group of native Beijingers, including Lao She himself, is their profound emotional dedication to the city and its culture. In this critical moment, confronting the devastating catastrophe that would destroy the way of life in Beijing, Lao She, through his fictional figure, Old Man Qi, provides a lyrical portrayal of the beauty of Beijing's everyday life and pays nostalgic tribute to his native city. What constitutes the foundation of this emotional attachment is not only the city's glorious imperial past or its political significance, but its essential way of life as perceived by urban inhabitants in relation to spaces ranging from the courtyard to broader public areas. Although the Qi family cannot afford a pergola or canopy over the courtyard or ice boxes in their rooms, and has never tried luxurious dishes such as ice bowl or lotus leaf drink with the eight precious ingredients, they also have comfortable daily pleasures and enjoyment. For Old Man Qi, life in Beijing means the moment every morning when he pushes open his door and looks at blue, white, and red morning glories with the dew still on them, holding their tiny trumpets upward as if making music to glorify the Creator. In a highly lyrical and nostalgic tone, Lao She depicts a fair Beijing summer for ordinary city people in a peaceful year:

The summers of Beiping [Peking] were beautiful in peaceful years. Each summer—from the time the cherries of the Ming Tombs Valley were brought to market to the time the dates began to turn red—was an epic of the history of fruit . . . . Old Man Chi [Qi] did not have the habit of going to the public parks or to the Beihai Park, but after his noon nap he would walk slowly to the Temple of National Protection. There, in the Hall of the Heavenly Kings— when there was no temple fair—would be storytellers, and the old man would

---

47 Lau Shaw, *The Yellow Storm*, 11.

drink a cup of tea and listen to the stories. The hall was high and deep so there was always a gentle breeze which could give the old man a chance to get away from the heat. When the sun went to the west he would walk slowly back home. He would carry back two or three cantaloupes for Little Precious and Niu Niu. They would always be under the big locust trees, picking up the locust blossoms and waiting for their great-grandfather . . . . The evening meal would be eaten in the courtyard under the shadow of the walls. The old man would rest awhile after the meal, and then taking an earthen bowl and a sprinkler would water his flowers. When he had finished this work, the day would still not be dark, so he would sit under the eaves, and with the children watch the bats flying low or tell them a story that had been told countless times before. In this way the old man's day was done.[48]

Illustrating the minute, sensuous details of everyday life, Lao She's Beijing narrative is permeated by an innocent simplicity and a poignant nostalgia for the way things used to be. Jean Franco discusses how memory is constructed in relation to everyday life: memory is "intimately bound up with particularities—a gesture, a casual remark that sticks in the mind, some seemingly unimportant everyday activity."[49] Lao She's Beijing imagery is composed of a tangible and accessible atlas of objects, smells, sounds, sights, and colors, "with a tenderness that is not matched in any of his earlier works."[50] Ranbir Vohra observes as follows: "By so describing life as it used to be, the festivals and colors, the preparation of foods, the easy rhythm of life that blended with seasonal changes, and contrasting this with what happened during the Occupation, he graphically highlights the destruction wrought by wars on civilization and culture."[51] This overwhelming sense of nostalgia and the successive loss during the Japanese Occupation of Beijing serve as the emotive foundation for the emergent Wartime structure of feeling for Old Man Qi and other urban residents.

In a humorous way, as if humanity could be measured quantitatively, Lao She uses percentage calculations to evaluate old and new elements in his characters and to diagnose and distinguish the Qi family members in wartime Beijing. If the Old Man Qi represents 100 percent old China, then his son Tianyou is 70 percent old and 30 percent new, and the second grandson, Ruiquan, makes 70 percent new and 30 percent old. Ruixuan, the eldest grandson, caught between the generations, is 50 percent old and 50 percent new. Just as he can see

---

[48] Ibid., 210–212.

[49] Jean Franco, *The Decline and Fall of the Lettered City: Latin America in the Cold War* (Cambridge, MA: Harvard University Press, 2002), 255.

[50] Ranbir Vohra, *Lao She and the Chinese Revolution* (Cambridge, MA: Harvard University Press, 1974), 143.

[51] Ibid.

the problems and difficulties of both, and the beauty and reasonableness of both, he realizes the duties of both as well.[52] Lao She knows all too well that such a fixed scale of human characters could easily lead to simplified and formulaic caricature. Literary representations by no means proceed in the same way as number properties. For all his admiration of Charles Dickens, Lao She, in *Four Generations*, does not mean to ridicule his characters in order to disclose social ills. Ranbir Vohra rightly contends, "The streak of pessimism which comes out in practically every one of Lao She's writings contrasts strongly with the optimism which Dickens reveals in his."[53] What Lao She seeks to highlight, through a catalogue of human nature, is the unchanging essence of life in Beijing that seems able to survive any historical or political turmoil and remain an integral unity. However, the Japanese invasion ruthlessly smashes this enchanted image of an eternal hometown. After the latest dynastic change and the looting of Beijing, Old Man Qi's structure of feeling and his prediction of an undeviating Beijing have miserably lost their credibility. Old Man Qi's prophecy that the occupation would last no longer than three months did not come true. He never expected it would extend to eight years.

With the city overtaken by the Japanese, its daily life and cityscape have gone through dramatic changes. "The weather was hot and the hearts of all in the nation were cold. Peiping fell."[54] The fall of the city and the nation, and the poignant longing for a free and unconquerable city, prompt swirls of complex and even new emotions. Tracing the ups and downs of people living in the Little Sheepfold Lane, Lao She explores the structural transformations of family, society, city, and nation-state. To stay in the city means that the people have to revise their previous political, cultural, and emotional expectations and adapt to the military occupation. Some of them turn into traitors or collaborators, some docile conformists, some backlashers or revolutionaries, and others just try to survive. Whether choosing nonconformist or collaborative stances, these Beijing residents face serious emotional and moral dilemmas. Along with the formation of a new urban awareness and national consciousness, various structures of feeling start to develop in different social groups.

Collaboration becomes a passive, shameful, and guilty choice for urban survival in the cruel wartime conditions. A portion of Beijing inhabitants like Ruifeng, the second grandson of the Qis, seem ignorant of moral consequences of betrayal or loyalism, and indulge in sensual pleasure and escapist entertainment. For them, occupied Beijing offers a stimulating, sensual, and decadent city life: people "smelling of wine and belching loudly with satisfaction," crowded theaters where the

---

52 See Lau Shaw, *The Yellow Storm*, 37–38.

53 Vohra, *Lao She and the Chinese Revolution*, 160.

54 Ibid. 31.

fighting operas are performed with "lights so bright they made the heads of people ache," movie theaters with "the blare of love songs over the loud-speakers," lively and busy city streets swarming with "rickshaws, horse carriages, tram cars, motor-cars."[55] However, all these entertainment places with busy noises are soon engulfed by the vast darkness and silence of the night. "Peiping was silently weeping," and the "strange eyes of the invaders were searching the black night of Peiping."[56] And a strong feeling of shame and guilt emerges, untimely and unpleasantly, from deep in their hearts. The scenes of natural beauty stay the same, as if unaffected by war-time violence, affliction, and surveillance. However, the deep sense of shame that the inhabitants feel as members of a conquered nation changes the way they perceive the cityscape immensely. In a slightly melodramatic vein, the narrator laments,

> The spring water from the Jade Fountain Park was flowing leisurely as always. In the reservoir of the Ten Weirs and in the seas of the Three Palaces Parks the green lotus will give out its fragrance. To the north and the west the deep blue hills were still standing majestic beneath the bright blue sky. In the Temple of Heaven enclosure and in the imperial parks the old pines and green cedars still kept company with the red walls and the golden tiles. All the brave and splen-did scenes! But the people of Peiping had already lost the relationship they had had with Peiping. Peiping was no longer the Peiping of the Peiping people. The Japanese flag was flying above the green cedars and the yellow tiles. The eyes of the people, the hands of the artists, the minds of the poets, did not dare to see, did not dare to paint, did not dare to think of Peiping's majesty and great beauty. The eyes of the people all asked each other. "What shall we do?" The only answer was a shake of the head, and shame.[57]

Thomas Scheff examines wartime emotions, including shame, the construction and destruction of nationalist bonds, as well as family and small-group behavior, argu-ing, "Shame may be the most social of all emotions, since it functions as threat to the social bond."[58] Nevertheless, for traitors like Guan Xiaohe, they choose not to keep themselves in the loop of this social bond. The terms "state," "nation," and "society" are neologisms only existing on his lips, and he is unable or unwilling to understand their true meanings. The only thing he cares about is himself. He is the center of Beijing, or the whole universe. Even his wife and children are only his planets. The

---

[55] Lau Shaw, *The Yellow Storm*, 44–45.
[56] Ibid.
[57] Ibid., 47.
[58] Thomas J. Scheff, *Bloody Revenge: Emotions, Nationalism, and War* (Boulder, CO: Westview Press, 1994), 42.

four walls of his courtyard enclose his kingdom, where country, people, and race are only abstract concepts. The narrator comments with an ironic tone, "If by selling his country he could get better food to eat and more fashionable clothes, the god of this universe—Kuan the Morning Lotus—would go right out and sell his country."[59]

During the occupation, life in Beijing became so repressive and inhibiting that the daily communications among the inhabitants of the Little Sheepfold Lane are reduced to pure transactions and business. Within a single household, the familial relationships and structures considerably change and decompose. In this sense, *Four Generations* can be read as a family saga, but in a different vein than either Cao Xueqin's *Dream of the Red Chamber* or Ba Jin's 巴金 (1904–2005) *Jia* 家 (Family, 1933). While the former criticizes the ethical hypocrisy of the classical Chinese family, the latter tells how the patriarchal, oppressive traditional Chinese family system collapses in the maelstrom of the May Fourth enlightenment movement. Lao She's war epic probes the crisis in the domestic sphere not just from the perspective of the declining Confucian cultures and moralities or the conflicts between the traditional and the modern. It is also underpinned by a strong nationalist consciousness and pitches the family as the microcosm and the allegory of the nation.

After Poet Qian is arrested, a Japanese family moves into House Number One of Little Sheepfold Lane. As an imperial capital for many dynasties in Chinese history, Beijing did not treat foreigners as outsiders. Nor did its people. However, things were different this time—their neighbor was also their conqueror. The Japanese had first conquered their city and then moved in. "The people of the Little Sheepfold would never have looked out of the corners of their eyes at an English family, or a Turkish family, but they felt an unease in their hearts because of this family of Japanese."[60] The other families in the alley soon start to feel the reverse. They simply didn't feel that these Japanese were neighbors. "When they looked at Number One they felt that they were looking at a time bomb."[61] Guan Xiaohe, who wants to please every Japanese person he meets for his own interests, forces Sergeant Pai to take care of every daily need of this Japanese family. Intriguingly, what Guan Xiaohe stresses is not the fact that this Japanese family is from the hegemonic occupying country, but rather, that they are people of a modern nation, characterized by a sense of modern hygiene. Therefore, he tells Sergeant Pai, "[T]he Japanese must bathe every day. They use a lot of water. Other families can wait but Number One must never lack for water."[62]

---

[59] Lau Shaw, *The Yellow Storm*, 47–48.

[60] Ibid., 215. For the Chinese edition, see Lao She, *Sishi tongtang* [Four generations under one roof], in *Lao She wenji* 老舍文集 [Selected writings of Lao She] (Beijing: Renmin wenxue chubanshe, 1983), 4:289–290.

[61] Ibid., 215.

[62] Ibid., 205.

Da Chibao, Guan Xiaohe's wife, has a clandestine room where only special guests are allowed. In this secret place, Dao Chibao not only collects equipment for smoking opium but also reserves Western luxury goods such as red tea from the English Palace, authentic foreign brandy, and Chesterfield cigarettes.[63] In the list of her foreign commodities, no Japanese products can be found. The Guans always feel superior to their neighbors, which becomes even more evident in their communications with the Japanese after Beijing has fallen. Eager to subjugate themselves as the happy obedient slaves and servants of the conquerors, people like the Guans also see themselves as cultural mediators. Da Chibao honors herself as "the tutor of the Japanese in matters of eating, drinking and wearing,"[64] for not being a traitor nor a slave in a conquered country. She performs the role of the cultivator who sets out to assimilate the foreign barbarians into the refined and sophisticated Chinese culture. Such duality evidently marks the mentality of collaborators stuck in the power relationship of masters and slaves.

Ruixuan, a Hamlet-like hero in Lao She's works, struggles to choose between staying and leaving, between love and hatred. Regarded as the alter ego of Lao She himself, Ruixuan is proud of being born in the ancient cultural city of Beijing, where "he could speak a language honored as Mandarin Chinese, hang out in the parks that were previously imperial shrines for the emperors, read the rare books, and hear the most insightful comments. Even by listening and observing, people could gain much knowledge."[65] However, now he begins to hate the Beijingers, because in this occupied city, in the shadow of shame and humiliation, the remaining residents consider only their own lives. People like his grandfather are obsessed with celebrating their birthdays even though they are slaves without a country. They are just cocooned in their routine everyday life. As his friend, a Western priest living in Beijing, says, "[T]he people of Peiping really had less of the spirit of adventure than the Westerners and fewer heroic attitudes."[66]

The fallen city is permeated with the sentiments of emptiness and despair, and death looms large. If the city is like a human being, it has its own pain and pleasure, illness and health. The occupied city is like a dysfunctional organism whose metabolic system—the assimilation of the new and the excretion of the old—encounters severe problems such as local necrosis, partial degeneration, and mental stagnation. In his revisionist study of Hong Kong colony, John M. Carroll observes, "[C]olonial encounters were . . . fraught with overwhelming unfamiliarity, bewilderment, or

---

[63] Rey Chow, "Fateful Attachments: On Collecting, Fidelity, and Lao She," *Critical Inquiry* 28, no. 1 (2001): 286–304.

[64] Lau Shaw, *The Yellow Storm*, 199; *Sishi tongtang*, 281.

[65] See Lao She, *Sishi tongtang*, 67.

[66] Lau Shaw, *The Yellow Storm*, 53.

incompatibility—'the most complex and traumatic relationships in human history.' "[67] In Lao She's eyes, occupied Beijing is a coffin for slaves without a country, haunted by the overwhelming emotions of bewilderment, hatred, and shame. In this regard, the poet Qian remarks cynically, "Peiping is already dead. Inside the city there are ghosts only. You have to go outside the city to find men."[68]

For Beijing inhabitants, like Bannerman Little Wen and his wife, with no idea about nation or nationalism, the fall of the city seems remote from their daily lives. They have neither a strong emotional attachment to their past nor any worry about their future, provided they can survive the day. "They had passed through the greatest changes of history, yet they were living in as artless a way as babes."[69] Nevertheless, the national consciousness was forced upon them with the harsh reality of occupation and the Japanese militarist ideology. On the day when students were forced to a parade celebrating Japanese conquest and hegemony, "Peiping saw a sad and solemn parade, perhaps the first time . . . . No matter what they [students] studied, no matter how childish and young they were, no matter how obedient, these students knew the concept 'Nation'—a concept which their fathers had not known."[70]

The parade for the enemy proceeds past the Gate of Heavenly Peace, the symbol of Beijing. In this central locale of power of the ancient city, the occupational propaganda seems poignantly weak and futile. The Japanese celebration of their victory is engulfed by the massive, silent plaza, a spatial vacuum. The celebration turns into a funeral and mourning parade, carried out by Beijing citizens. The narrator says,

> In these majestic surroundings this effort at the dramatic was lost as the voice of an infant would be shouting to the ocean. The loudspeaker did not fill the space with sound. It was as though someone at a distance were chanting the sutras, or weeping. The soldiers between the Gate of Heavenly Peace and the great Front Gate of the city were so small they looked like small black pegs. In front of the great tower of the Front Gate all ugly things lost their power to frighten. On the platform those in long gowns and those in uniform all looked like puppets and not like anything alive.
>
> One of those in a long gown stood up and, facing the loudspeaker, began to talk. The voice coming from the instrument struck the red walls and was

[67] John M. Carroll, *Edge of Empires: Chinese Elites and British Colonials in Hong Kong* (Cambridge, MA: Harvard University Press, 2009), 13.

[68] Lau Shaw, *The Yellow Storm*, 210; *Sishi tongtang*, 297.

[69] Lau Shaw, *The Yellow Storm*, 127.

[70] Ibid., 135.

spread over the boundless space like a muffled cough. The students standing with heads hanging could hear nothing, nor did they want to hear. They called those standing in long gowns with the Japanese, traitors.

. . . On the towers and under the marble bridge were ambush soldiers and machine guns. But the great gate and the students seemed not to understand the meaning of these preparations. Silence and indifference seemed also to be military weapons.[71]

In addition to spaces of daily lives such as the residential lanes, places such as the Gate of Heavenly Peace, symbolic landmarks of Beijing, become significant wartime sites to channel and stimulate traumatic epiphany, to awaken new urban and national consciousness. Situated inside the gigantic space, a hollow center of power, the Japanese invaders feel terribly frustrated. At this majestic plaza and in the city at large, a dead silence dominates. It is impregnated with vibrations of revenge, detestation, and scorn. The resistance could be born anywhere, in any form, sporadic or organized. The Poet Qian's anti-Japanese confession releases his deep-seated and awakening wartime emotions of anger, antipathy, and resistance: "I had no plan and thought only of revenge . . . . I was like a madman urging everyone to 'kill' [the enemy]. I was angry. I hated . . . . I was a one-man army."[72]

The spatial trajectories of wartime emotions, including nostalgia, bewilderment, shame, agony, and hatred, mediate the interactions of family and city, self and society, individual and nation. The Little Sheepfold Lane, together with other real and fictional places and spaces ranging from a small clandestine room in the courtyard house to the gigantic Tiananmen Square in the heart of the city, constitute the lines of latitude and longitude that define the structures of feeling in occupied Beijing. Charged with nostalgic cultural memories, *Four Generations* creates an atlas of emotions, a performative psychogeography that accommodates and negotiates pain and catharsis, trauma and redemption, personal desire and collective guilt, loss and epiphany, and melancholy and hope.

---

[71] Ibid., 140–141.

[72] Ibid., 449. Poet Qian also mentioned the development of his awakening nationalist consciousness, his sense of the shared communities, stating, "Gradually I came to the second stage. My willingness to work and daring to work had brought me many friends. I saw clearly that I must have friends and work with them in one heart and one strength. Although I had not changed I saw that I was one end and my country the other of the same thing. That was my attitude. But I began to understand that one man daring to die was not as effective as many working together. Good—I cared not what the plans of others were, what political parties they belonged to, if only they came to me I was willing to help." He changes from a lonely individual "resist-the-enemy machine" to a member of patriotic team: "If my first stage was individual heroism, the second was co-operative patriotism" (449).

IDE©OLOGY AND THE SOCIALIST PRODUCTION OF SPACE

Ideology is a "representation" of the imaginary relationship of individuals to their real conditions of existence.

—LOUIS ALTHUSSER

The ecology of the city and the personalities of its inhabitants are mirror images of each other.

—DAVID HARVEY

As a unique work of experiment in Lao She's repertoire, *Longxu gou* (*Dragon Beard Ditch*, 1951),[73] a three-act drama composed right after the founding of the People's Republic of China, describes the renovation of a ditch to epitomize the great socialist transformation from pre-Mao "dystopia" to Maoist "paradise." The old Dragon Beard Ditch is a notorious hygienic dead corner, a typical shabby "courtyard tenements" (*daza yuan* 大雜院) east of the Bridge of Heaven (天橋) in southern Beijing, and more importantly, a symbolic miniature of the underprivileged ghetto of (Old) Beijing. The play shows how the new socialist government transforms an infamous stinking ditch and slum into a new tidy community, and bespeaks the pleasures and pitfalls of performing ide©ology and producing socialist space.

A well-known cultural rhetoric of early socialism in China is that "the old society turned human beings into ghosts; and the new society turns ghosts back into human beings" (舊社會把人變成鬼，新社會把鬼變成人). Reiterative and repetitive performances have pictured the melodramatic metamorphosis of social and political sufferers from haunting specters, living dead, poverty-stricken victims, sick or mad men and women in the old society all the way into healthy and robust citizens in the newly established socialist republic. With regard to the metamorphosis of "Dragon Beard Ditch," I take into consideration the space where the performance of "ide©ology" occurs, and the performance of/within this ide©ological space. Here I coin a term "ide©ology" to combine ideology and ecology, and to explore the simultaneously ideological and ecological performance of a particular space, "Dragon Beard Ditch."[74] Henry Sayer points out that "in ordinary usage, performance is a specific action or set of actions—dramatic, musical, athletic, and so on—which occurs on a given occasion, in a particular place. An artistic performance . . . is

---

[73] Yomi Braester translates "*Longxu gou*" as Dragon Whisker Creek; see his thorough and brilliant study in *Painting the City Red: Chinese Cinema and the Urban Contract* (Durham, NC: Duke University Press, 2010), esp. chap. 1 and chap. 3. Since the only available English translation of *Longxu gou* is entitled *Dragon Beard Ditch*, I will still use it in my analysis for practical purposes. The adaptations of *Dragon Beard Ditch* include Jiao Juyin's 焦菊隱 theatrical edition (1951), Xian Qun's 洗群 film production (1957), and most recently, a thirty-four-episode TV drama released in 2010.

[74] Ideology can be translated into Chinese as 意識形態, ecology as 生態(生態學，生態意識); then ide©ology can be rendered as 意識形(生)態.

further defined by its status as the single occurrence of a repeatable and preexistent text or score."[75] He furthermore brings to light that "performance is above all historical—that is, inevitably caught up in the social and political exigencies of the moment . . . . Finally, performance can be defined as an activity which generates transformation, as the reintegration of art with what is 'outside' it, an 'opening up' of the 'field.' "[76] Louis Althusser has argued, "[I]n ideology the real relation is inevitably invested in the imaginary relation, a relation that *express a will* (conservative, conformist, reformist or revolutionary), a hope or a nostalgia, rather than describing a reality."[77] I do not aim for an Althusserian reading of ideology as a whole, but for situating Louis Althusser's theory of "ideology and state apparatus" in the context of Lao She's representative plays and Chinese communist propaganda and socialist production of space. Therefore I argue, in Lao She's ide©ology, that a will, a hope, a nostalgia, a debate, and a reflection, to name a few possibilities, can be invested in ideological and ecological performance: the declaration of new citizenship and class consciousness, the baptism of socialist construction, and the inauguration of mass mobilization, among others.

In 1951, Lao She made a noteworthy confession in a short essay, "How I Wrote 'Dragon Beard Ditch' ": "the creation of this play was my biggest venture in more than twenty years as a writer."[78] The reason he offered is that he did not have enough time and experience to completely understand the Dragon Beard Ditch. Yet, Lao She does not describe, or intentionally represses, what is actually the biggest venture. As a matter of fact, Lao She is always fond of the topics he is familiar with, and the story settings of his major novels and dramas are mostly visualized in the past instead of the present or the future. However, *Dragon Beard Ditch* is an exception because the Beijing government had not yet finished the Dragon Beard Ditch project when

---

[75] Frank Lentricchia and Thomas McLaughlin, eds., *Critical Terms for Literary Studies* (Chicago: University of Chicago Press, 1995, second edition), 91. In the first edition of *Critical Terms for Literary Studies*, Frank Lentricchia and Thomas McLaughlin chose twenty-two keywords to map and chart the landscapes of literary theory and cultural criticism: representation, structure, writing, discourse, narrative, figurative language, performance, author, interpretation, intention, unconscious, determinacy/indeterminacy, value/evaluation, influence, rhetoric, culture, canon, literary history, gender, race, ethnicity, and ideology. The second edition added six terms: popular culture, diversity, imperialism/nationalism, desire, ethics, and class, so as to strengthen the liaisons among literary studies, cultural practices, and political (un)conscious.

[76] Lentricchia and McLaughlin, eds., *Critical Terms for Literary Studies*, 103.

[77] Louis Althusser, *For Marx*, trans. Ben Brewer (London: Verso, 1979), 234.

[78] Lao Sheh, "How I Wrote 'Dragon Beard Ditch,'" in *Dragon Beard Ditch: A Play in Three Acts*, trans. Liao Hung-ying (Peking: Foreign Languages Press, 1956), 7–8. The English version is a shorter edition of two Chinese essays regarding the process of writing *Dragon Beard Ditch*, one is "*Longxu gou xiezuo jingguo*" 《龍鬚溝》寫作經過 [The writing of *Dragon Beard Ditch*], in *Renmin ribao* 人民日報 [People's daily], February 4, 1951, and "*Longxu gou de renwu*" 《龍鬚溝》的人物 [Characters in *Dragon Beard Ditch*], in *Wenyi bao* 文藝報 [Literary gazette], February 25, 1951; these two essays are collected in *Lao She juzuo quanji* 老舍劇作全集 [Complete dramas of Lao She] (Beijing: Zhongguo xiju chubanshe, 1982), 2:174–181.

Lao She completed his play. Lao She envisions and performs a utopian future at the end of the play that the stinking ditch is cleaned up and has disappeared forever, and the inhabitants are released from the ecological and political morass and appreciate the timely help from the new government.[79] In other words, Lao She performs and promises an incomplete future for the present, or turns the urban future into a living presence or completed reality. To borrow Roland Barthes's words on the operation and mechanism of "myth," *Dragon Beard Ditch* has effectively become a "myth" because "myth hides nothing and flaunts nothing: it distorts; myth is neither a lie nor a confession: it is an inflection."[80] The strategy of presenting the past or the future, however, betrays a stunning "presentism,"[81] an ide©ological performance of a space, and a sort of revolutionary "special effects" in which the imagined is presented as the real in an otherwise realistic play. In this sense, *Dragon Beard Ditch* has set up a paradigm for socialist literature, especially for Seventeen-Year-Literature (1949–1966) in Maoist China.

In act 1 of *Dragon Beard Ditch*, Lao She sets the story in 1948, the year before Beijing became the capital of a new socialist China. Lao She's portrait of Dragon Beard Ditch, a notorious ditch in the east of the Bridge of Heaven, vividly illustrates the ecological portrait of the stinking and striking slum:

> The Ditch is full of muddy, slimy water, mixed with rubbish, rags, dead rats, dead cats, dead dogs and now and then dead children. The waste water from the nearby tannery and dyeworks flows into it and accumulations of nightsoil collect there to putrefy. The water in the Ditch is of various shades of red and green, and its stench makes people feel sick quite far away. Hence the district had earned the name of "Stinking Ditch Bank."[82]

Responding to Wen Yiduo's 聞一多 (1899–1946) powerful eco-critical image of "the dead water," the Dragon Beard Ditch is a hygienic dead zone and a filthy, crowded and cramped courtyard occupied by many poor households in the southern part of Beijing, and more importantly, a symbolic miniature of the underprivileged ghetto in Republican Beijing. Besides its physical location and the physiological

---

[79] See Chen Tushou 陳徒手, *Ren youbing, tian zhifou: 1949 nian hou zhongguo wentan jishi* 人有病，天知否？1949 年後中國文壇紀實 [People are sick, is heaven aware? Chronicles of the Chinese literary world after 1949] (Beijing: Renmin wenxue chubanshe, 2000), 44.

[80] Roland Barthes, "Myth Today," in *A Barthes Reader*, ed. Susan Sontag (New York: Hill and Wang, 1987), 116.

[81] See Mao Dun, *Rainbow*, trans. Madeline Zelin (Berkeley: University of California Press, 1992), 80, 89, 110; Daniel Fried, "A Bloody Absence: Communist Narratology and the Literature of May Thirtieth," *Chinese Literature: Essays, Articles, Reviews* 26 (2004): 23–53.

[82] Lao Sheh, *Dragon Beard Ditch*, 7–8.

action for the local residents, the ditch, a presocialist dystopia and an ecological living hell, was also a forgotten corner of the lower society, where the penniless city inhabitants settled down and made a hard living:

On the two banks, closely packed together, there live labourers, handicraft workers—the multifarious toiling poor. Day in and day out, all the year round and all their lives, they struggle in this filthy environment. Their houses may tumble down at any moment; most of their yards have no lavatories, let alone kitchens. There is no running water; they drink bitter and rank-tasting wellwater. Everywhere there are swarms of fleas, clouds of mosquitoes, countless bed-bugs and black sheets of flies, all spreading disease. [83]

In this slum, living conditions are incredibly tough: "Whenever it rains, not only do the streets become pools of mud, but water from the ditch overflows into the yards and houses, which are lower than the street level, and thus floods everything."[84] And who could imagine that, not very far from the splendid imperial palaces, a backwater emerged of itself and perished of itself?

The inhabitants of Dragon Beard Ditch live at the bottom of the society, and moreover, they are locked up in the prison house of the slum. Lao She deliberately designs a shabby and crowded courtyard, and defines it as "a small monument to illustrate the sin of the filthy Ditch."[85] In this courtyard of the ignored district, there are four tumbledown mud huts where four families painstakingly try to survive the hard times and spaces. In the Wang family, Mother Wang knows that the Ditch is foul, but she is conservative and inured to hardships. She earns her living and that of her second daughter, Erchun (Erh-Chun Ding), by soldering mirror frames and sewing. Erchun is semi-literate, and wants to find a new life outside of the ditch.

In the Ding family, Ding Si (Ting Sze) is a frustrated pedicab driver[86] who lives with a talkative and capable wife, Sisao (Sze-sao), a twelve-year-old son deprived of education, and a nine-year-old daughter, Little Niu, who became a victim of the filthy Ditch. As for the Zhao family, there is only one member, Lao Zhao (Old Chao), who is a sixty-year-old honest and righteous bricklayer. And the most significant figure is Mad Cheng, a folk artist, and his wife, Niangzi (Niang-tse), who supports her husband and herself by sewing and doing a little business in the market.

---

[83] Ibid.

[84] Ibid., 7–8.

[85] See Lao She, "*Longxu gou xiezuo jingguo*" [The writing of *Dragon Beard Ditch*], 175.

[86] The English version has a short note on the pedicab, which is "a tricycle rickshaw ridden by the driver in front, with the passenger seat behind." See Lao Sheh, *Dragon Beard Ditch*, 5.

Mad Cheng was formerly a popular performer, a good singer of ballads, especially "*shu-lai-pao*" 數來寶, in which he could recite, sing, and create stories in verse or prose to the accompaniment of a pair of bamboo castanets.

Suffering from physical and mental illness partly caused by the polluted environment, Mad Cheng is the only inhabitant with the ability to articulate things that ordinary people cannot speak about. From the very beginning, Mad Cheng prophetically sings out all the terrible past, the stinking presence, and the bright future of Dragon Beard Ditch. The madman is given an extraordinary capacity of traversing the paths from dystopia to utopia. Robert Stam addresses the relations between politics and language, power and utterance: "As Power is exercised in the right to speak, the right to interrupt, the right to remain silent. Politics and language intersect in the form of attitudes, of talking down to or looking up to, of patronizing, respecting, ignoring, supporting, misinterpreting."[87] Mad Cheng is always singing these two lines: "*The ditch won't stink, and the water will be sweet, / Our land will be great, the people happy, and the world at peace.*"[88] This sing-song man or "mad" storyteller takes a realistic and a metaphoric way to tackle his living conditions. For him, the prehistory of a formerly popular entertainer can be bittersweet—the happy days of singing ballads and earning a wage, and later on the miserable life in the ditch after he was cheated and deprived of pay. The material reality of being trapped in the ditch is absolutely terrible, and becomes the ultimate reason for all his physical problems and mental sufferings. However, the bright future exists in his ambivalent and ambiguous sensibility and songs.

Mad Cheng's metaphoric reading of the past, the present, and the future is at stake because once the metaphoric relations are created, they can be extended and even reversed. If the old society and old Beijing were like the filthy ditch, the ditch could be the incarnation of the previous urban life and old city. Terrible smells, fatal disease, and all negative things in general could be associated with the bitter past and needed to be scoured and cleaned. In the characters' combat and complaint in the first act, Old Chao lays the sins of the filthy ditch at the threshold of corrupt officials and the government. His ide©ological solution is that Beijing destitute must have clean officials before they can have clean water. This is the typical mentality in which the masses always long for an uncorrupted official, like the most distinguished archetype Bao Gong, who can play the role of Deus ex machina and solve the woes of the masses.

---

[87] Robert Stam, *Subversive Pleasures: Bakhtin, Cultural Criticism, and Film* (Baltimore: Johns Hopkins University Press, 1989), 9.

[88] Lao Sheh, *Dragon Beard Ditch*, 12.

Ding Si, a pedicab driver, like the rickshaw boy Xiangzi, is trapped in the trouble of encountering a soldier: "From Yungting Gate to Tehsheng Gate, ploughing through muddy roads, in pouring rain, and me sweating like a pig from head to foot. Of course he didn't pay, and on top of that he nearly beat me up."[89] Another common person in the streets, Ding Si is portrayed as a more complicated figure than Xiangzi in that he can complain with hatred, "trade or no trade, once in my cab, I'm away from this stinking Ditch."[90] Here, the pedicab is not only a tool for making a living but also a possible vehicle to go outside the ditch, the infrastructure of the family, and the dismal street corner. Erchun shares the imagined rebellious gesture of escaping the appalling misery, and is publicly against any physically and socially unreasonable rules upon her living situation. Occasionally, they enjoy constructing a hopeful linkage between their urban slum and the high buildings and broad avenues around the inner city. As a bricklayer, Old Chao has had a chance to know that wherever the big officials live there are tarred roads and large mansions.[91] Nevertheless, in act 1, in the presocialist nightmare and the urban dystopia, they are still confined in the muddy and stinking ghetto, with nowhere to hide or run away, and are hardly permitted to go outside the dead corner. Their encounters with Beijing lie in their physical perception of the unbearable smells, the precariousness in rain, the local gangsters, and the invisible corrupt officials mediated by the police sergeant Liu, a kind but powerless neighbor. Interestingly, old Beijing's official manipulation is quite loose in that the sergeant himself is a neighbor of the Ditch area, and does not play the role of surveillance. Amusingly, Sergeant Liu even becomes a face-to-face, kindhearted mediator between the corrupt government and the poor local inhabitants. The policeman himself is also a member and victim of the slum. In this sense, there is no Foucauldian Panopticon, but a personalized connection between the disciplined citizens and the man policing. So the Dragon Beard Ditch is more like a forgotten corner, a dead end in the city. The promiscuity, contagion, and contamination of the place are all geographical, rather than sexual or moral, in their register.

It is particularly worth noting that Old Chao catches malaria every year in the slum, and by any token, a typical poor Beijing proletariat complaint would be, "Huh, I have this every year, and always about this time; after the rain when houses tumble down; just the time when I should have plenty of work, I always go and get this malaria! After a few goes I feel like a wet rag."[92] Old Chao explains that his sickness is

---

[89] Ibid., 26.
[90] Ibid., 26.
[91] Ibid., 21–22.
[92] Ibid., 15.

due to mosquito bites, and to the bites from the environmental and social injustices evidenced in corrupt Nationalist Party officials, local gangsters, and even Japanese invaders after he is enlightened by the socialist propaganda. In his speech act performance, Old Chao deliberately constructs an ide©ological equivalence between his physical illness and the social cancers of old Beijing. This is the metaphor of sickness, in which socialist propaganda dominates the symbolic connections between natural diseases and antirevolutionary symptoms.

Following Maoist ideology and his own moral judgment, Lao She makes efforts to separate "moral wickedness" from "physical filthiness." Peter Stallybrass and Allon White illustrate that a writer can foreground "the connections between topography, physical appearance and morality."[93] In other words, Lao She's writing strategy is that he observes Beijing by tracing the ditch back to the old regime and the corrupt Nationalist government. Meanwhile, the new government can shed new light on the city's dark places and transform it into a bright and tidy community. The danger of contamination is eliminated by hygienic sweeping and ideological purification.

In act 2, after Beijing comes under the socialist reign, the social sickness is being cured, and the urban dead end is illuminated by an ide©ological utopia or a utopian ide©ology.[94] The real Dragon Beard Ditch project had not yet been completed, but the new government pushed the writer to praise the magnitude of the government and its new ide©ology and utopian imagination; Lao She envisioned the enlightened dwellers' enthusiastic and pleasant personalities in the newly established People's Republic. Erchun says loudly, "Just think, no more filthy water, no more stench, no more flies and mosquitoes. Oh, too, too wonderful."[95] The "imaginary relation" of the residents to the old stinking ditch is labeled as part of the bitter past in presocialist Beijing, and the imagined connections of the inhabitants with the forthcoming sanitary ditch can be named a socialist presence and future in the new Beijing. An overwhelming utopian longing for the future is produced and later on reproduced, and the future can be repeatedly designated as the present.

In the heat of the socialist urban planning, and in a state of bliss and even ecstasy, the four families dedicate their bodies and minds to the new ditch, the new Beijing and its government, and the new socialist China. Erchun develops a new urban consciousness, acquires a new socialist citizenship, regards the disappearance of the local

---

[93] See Stallybrass and White, *The Politics and Poetics of Transgression*, chaps. 3 and 4, esp. 129.

[94] For discussions of ideology and utopia, see Paul Ricoeur, "Ideology and Utopia," in *From Text to Action*, trans. Kathleen Blamey and John B. Thompson (Evanston, IL: Northwestern University Press, 1991), 308–324; and *Lectures on Ideology and Utopia*, ed. George H. Taylor (New York: Columbia University Press, 1986). See also Carles Prado-Fonts, "Beneath Two Red Banners: Lao She as a Manchu Writer in Modern China," in Shih, Tsai, and Bernards, eds., *Sinophone Studies*, 353–363.

[95] Lao Sheh, *Dragon Beard Ditch*, 57.

gangsters and the filthy ditch as signs of a new reality, and openly claims that "(i)n future, if anyone dares to say a word against the government, I'll split his skull open."[96] Old Chao consciously plays the role of propagandist and activist so as to pass on the new message, a possibility of socialist education and enlightenment, to his neighbors:

> The East Arch, the West Arch, the Drum Tower—everywhere needs repairing. Why does the government come to our stinking Ditch first? Instead of improving the appearance of the city first, they have come to look after *us*, because this Ditch gives me malaria every year and because it killed Little Niu. When it rains, Niang-tse can't put up her stall, you can't go out with your cab, stinking water floods our rooms with maggots. The government knows about these things, and they're doing something for you and me, and everyone in this district, so that we shan't have to be ill, and die, stink, and be filthy, and go hungry, any more. You and I are the people, and the government cares for the people; they're remaking the Ditch for *us*![97]

Individual memory of the concrete miseries, family trauma of the accidental death of Little Niu in the filthy ditch, and the ide©ological foul disease leading to illness, death, stink, and filth, among other problems, can all be swept away by ide©ological and utopian solutions in the "imagined community" of a socialist city. Mad Cheng's wife believes that again, in the near future, the Socialist Party can "really" get things done. She reports socialist propaganda, or more precisely, the socialist propaganda speaks out her will and enchants her to articulate, "They say, the Palace Lakes, Back Lake and Shih Cha Lake, as well as the whole city moat, are all to be dug out and new stone embankments built. Then all the roads will be repaired in turn."[98] Niangzi even goes further with another idea, that is, to persuade the dwellers to contribute a little money to put up a stone on which they inscribe the words, "There used to be a stinking Ditch here; the people's government made it into a fine road."[99] Besides the socialist propaganda from the high to the low, what this episode performs is the response from the reverse direction: a female pauper in the once forgotten corner of Republican Beijing figures out the strategy of constructing monuments and monumentality about socialist China. Niangzi's "urban planning" signifies a gesture of bidding farewell to the past in the name of a promised future and in the name of the people's government in the new Beijing.

---

[96] Ibid.
[97] Ibid., 64–65.
[98] Ibid., 83.
[99] Ibid., 89.

No doubt, as a professional performer, Mad Cheng can go further and conceive a more ambitious and ide©ological blueprint, a public space for all the citizens of Beijing: "we must have a park here . . . . We should change the Goldfish Pond into a park with trees all round it, and a swimming pool and some pavilions as well."[100] And the climax of the narrative lies in the crucial moment when Mad Cheng performs his new song, like a socialist and ide©ological utopian poem:

To all you people, I joyfully state,
The People's Government is truly great.
Is truly great, for it mended the Ditch,
And took great pains for us though we're not rich.
Think well of this, I beg you all,
East Arch, West Arch, Drum Tower tall,
Five Altars, Eight Temples, old Altar of Grain,
Summer Palace too needed mending again.
All needed repairing, I grant you this,
But why should they first mend Dragon Beard Ditch?
Simply because it was dirty, it stank,
When the Government saw it their very heart sank.
A first-rate Government, loving all poor men,
Help us to stand up proudly again.
They repaired the Ditch, made a road besides,
Help us to stand straight and march with great strides.
To march with great strides, and go laughing on,
All workers must strive with their hearts as one.
Must strive together, and work without cease,
Then our land will be great, the people happy,
And the world at peace![101]

This is a new ide©ological and utopian mapping of contemporary Beijing from the points of view of the poor people, such as a ballad singer, a bricklayer, and a pedicab driver, among others. The profound linkage among the new government and new citizens, among the marginal ditch, the central landmarks, the new Beijing city, and the socialist nation-state, can be established in physical and metaphoric spaces, no matter how petty or gigantic. Therefore, the image of the new Dragon Beard Ditch and new Beijing gains in strength and identity when set against the picture of the old

---

[100] Ibid., 85.
[101] Ibid., 91.

stinking ditch and old Beijing at large. In this sense, Dragon Beard Ditch has been granted rich meanings and developed into a super big "signifier" with overloaded "signified."[102]

When addressing the sewer, the gaze, and the contaminating touch, Peter Stallybrass and Allon White point out the difference between the bourgeois gaze and flâneur observation. The bourgeoisie stand on their balconies, from which they can gaze but not be touched; they can both participate in the banquet of the streets and remain separated. But the flâneur is afraid to be at home, mingles with the crowd but does not feel as one of them. The typical image of the flâneur is like what Baudelaire described: "even when he flees from town, he is still in search of the mob." And Baudelaire had been obsessed with writing "Hygiene Projects," "Hygiene Morality," and "Hygiene, Conduct, Morality."[103] In contrast, in his *Dragon Beard Ditch*, Lao She pays great attention to the alternative dimensions of Beijing's hygiene project, urban planning, and the socialist production of space. He explores the intersection of hygiene, morality, and ide©ology, which reveals a new modernist horizon that I would like to term a populist and ide©ological point of view. The division between cleanliness and filth, purity and impurity, is *not* that between the civilized and the savage, the high and the low in a moral sense. The representation of the filthy sewer can traverse social, moral, and political domains. The mapping of the city in sanitary terms tends to repeat the discourse of Maoist propaganda, that is, to live around the filthy ditch does not mean necessarily to be trapped in moral degradation. As the famous case of model worker Shi Chuanxiang 石傳祥 illustrates, in socialist China, not only could a professional worker removing excrement be named as a national labor model and hero, but it could also be claimed that the hands of such a worker are even cleaner than the minds of bourgeois intellectuals. The relation between body and mind is bestowed with a new ideological implication. From this perspective, moral depravity and crime are not rooted in physical disorder and depravity. If Chadwick "connects slums to sewage, sewage to disease, and disease to moral degradation,"[104] then the ide©ological myth of Dragon Beard Ditch upends that logic, and on the contrary, imbues the paupers with moral courage and spiritual victory.

The socialist sun shines over the Dragon Beard Ditch, where the inhabitants are endowed with new class consciousness and released from the hygienic and political morass, and warmly welcome ide©ological baptism and redemption performed by the fledgling socialist regime. The performance of/within "Dragon Beard Ditch"

---

[102] For a discussion of "eliminate the old in order to build the new," see Visser, *Cities Surround the Countryside*, 15–17.
[103] Stallybrass and White, *The Politics and Poetics of Transgression*, 136.
[104] See Stallybrass and White, *The Politics and Poetics of Transgression*, 131.

describes both an ecological and an ideological transformation of an infamous stinking ditch and slum into a new and sanitary socialist community, and exemplifies an imagined and theatrical ide©ological production of socialist space.[105]

TEAHOUSE, WARPED MINIATURE, AND SELF-MOURNING

For me it has always been a city of ruins and of end-of-empire melancholy.

—ORHAN PAMUK

This section explores the spatial form of the Yutai 裕泰 Teahouse in Lao She's 1957 three-act play, *Chaguan* (*Teahouse*), and its variant constructions in Jiao Juyin 焦菊隱 (1905–1975) and Xia Chun's 夏淳 (1918–2009) theatrical adaptation in 1958; Xie Tian's 謝添 (1914–2003) film in 1982; Lin Zhaohua's 林兆華 (1936–) theatrical version in 1999; He Qun 何群 (1956–), Ye Guangcen 葉廣岑 (1948–), and Yang Guoqiang's 楊國強 television drama released in 2010; and Yi Liming's 易立明 experimental and ephemeral reworking of Lao She's masterpiece in 2010. By depicting the lives of people who frequent the teahouse, a shrinking public space and a pessimistic miniature of old Beijing misery, the play reflects on the changing cityscape and social mores from the decline of the Manchu Empire, through the chaos of the warlord regimes, to the downfall of the Nationalist government. In the long sequence of sustained and shifting images of the teahouse produced from the seventeen-year socialist period to the post-Cold War era, the literary, theatrical, cinematic, and television drama illustrations recapitulate and attest to disparate political and cultural agendas. The teahouse series not only captures the political dimensions of entertainment, education, and edification but also stages a subtle and complex critique of the pre-Mao social morass and political violence.

When answering the question, "What led you to write a play about a teahouse?" Lao She said,

> People from all walks of life came to the teahouses; they were frequented by people of every possible character and persuasion. Thus the teahouses were a microcosm of society as a whole. In covering the [fifty years of historical change] it was

---

[105] Lao She's populist gaze is the viewpoint from underneath rather than above. His point of view is not an overlook from the top of Jing Mountain, or any privileged standpoint of imperial palaces or pavilions. Instead, Lao She himself is from the lower stratum of society in the northwestern part of Beijing, and he lives and walks with the ordinary people in the ancient capital and modern metropolis. Lao She's obsession with Beijing, or more precisely, his obsession with the "street corner society" and the underprivileged everyday life, provide a distinguished encyclopedia of modern Beijing, a kind of isomorphism of utopia and dystopia, of spiritual hometown and phantom "heart of darkness," which vividly highlights a vast yet repressed aspect of urban life in the modern times.

impossible to avoid political issues . . . . [In the teahouse] I would be revealing one face of the political change of the time.[106]

How do playwrights, multimedia directors, and stage designers imagine and envision the "one face of the political change of the time"? Using the teahouse images, from the original three-act play to its realist, expressionist, avant-garde, minimalist, and melodramatic adaptations, I aim to interpret the teahouse as a physical and psychological place and space, and a warped space-time continuum, that presents the interactions between material deformations and emotional vicissitudes over fifty years. My approach will focus on two aspects: the changing locations of material objects, such as tables, chairs, furniture, and ornaments within the shrinking and warped teahouse; and the intriguing relations between the teahouse and the street, between the interior and exterior spaces, and between nostalgic sympathy, sense of loss, and self-mourning that implode in the teahouse and urban horrors and darkness that extend and explode from within.

Lao She made a well-known confession that *Teahouse* buries the three former eras. Raymond Williams calls our attention to the relation among memoirs of the past, structure of feeling and social deformation.[107] My question is, does the Manchu playwright bury the three eras with a relatively homogeneous structure of feeling, or with related, yet distinct, feelings and emotions respectively in the three acts? Li Jianwu 李健吾 (1906–1982) points out that, in *Teahouse*, "there is no unified emotion or event, but repeated situations" (沒有一個統一的感情, 事件, 只有重複的情境).[108] The "repeated situations," as well as the diversified emotions and events, bring to limelight Lao She's affective mapping of the distorted teahouse and the warped hometown. Xiaomei Chen insightfully observes that *Teahouse* is "deeply rooted in the old culture of Beijing; however, one could also detect a resistance to change, no matter how frequently political regimes changed hands and claimed victory."[109]

[106] Lao She, "In Response to Some Questions about *Teahouse*," in *Teahouse: A Play in Three Acts*, trans. John Howard-Gibbon (Beijing: Foreign Languages Press, 1980), 82. See also Towery, *Lao She, China's Master Storyteller*.

[107] Williams, *The Country and the City*, 298.

[108] On December 19, 1957, the editorial board of *Renmin ribao* 人民日報 [People's daily] organized a symposium on Lao She's *Teahouse*, and invited Jiao Juyin, Zhao Shaohou 趙少侯, Chen Baichen 陳白塵, Xia Chun, Lin Mohan 林默涵, Wang Yao 王瑤, Zhang Henshui, Li Jianwu, and Zhang Guangnian 張光年, among others. Li Jianwu finished an article for *Renmin wenxue* 人民文學 [People's literature, the first issue in 1958], and talked about his discovery, which appeared as Jiao Juyin et al, "Zuotan Lao She de *Chaguan*" 座談老舍的《茶館》 [Symposium on Lao She's *Teahouse*] in the *Wenyi bao* 文藝報 [Literary Gazette] in 1958, and later is reprinted in Zeng Guangcan 曾廣燦 and Wu Huaibin 吳懷斌, eds., *Lao She yanjiu ziliao* 老舍研究資料 [Research materials on Lao She] (Beijing: Zhishi chanquan chubanshe, 2010), 793.

[109] Xiaomei Chen, ed., *Reading the Right Text: An Anthology of Contemporary Chinese Drama* (Honolulu: University of Hawai'i Press, 2003), 14.

How, then, can we locate the "resistance to change" in the physical and psychological, material and mental place and space inside and outside of the warped teahouse?

In the widely acclaimed act 1, Lao She sets the time of early fall of 1898 when the Reform Movement led by Kang Youwei, Liang Qichao and their followers has failed. The decline and fall of the Manchu Empire is approaching. The three male protagonists consist of Wang Lifa 王利發, a shrewd, sensitive, and somewhat self-centered proprietary of Yutai Teahouse, Chang Siye 常四爺 (Fourth Elder Chang), a well-built and morally upright Manchu bannerman, and Qin Zhongyi 秦仲義, Wang Lifa's landlord, a nationalist capitalist and follower of the Reformists. Minor characters range from an opium addict fortune teller (Soothsayer Tang) to a cruel and treacherous flesh merchant (Pockface Liu), from a western religion believer and bully (Fifth Elder Ma) to a former member of the Legislative Assembly but now an urban hermit (Cui Jiufeng), ... With a subtle yet detectable tone of nostalgia, Lao She gives an emotional description of Yutai Teahouse: "Large teahouses like this are no longer to be seen, but a few decades ago every district in Beijing had at least one."[110] While other large teahouses are disappearing, Yutai survives and becomes a relatively safe and sound shelter, open yet immune to the political change in the outside world. The teahouse provides an entertainment space for urban dwellers; a meeting place for discussions, negotiations, and transactions; a pseudopolitical newsroom for rumors, complaints, and opinions; and a center of cultural exchange for different classes of local people.

If we take a closer look at its interior space, then the dimensions of material culture, or the locations of objects and the order of things, can well present and illustrate life and the world, cultural and political change: "The building is extremely large and high-ceilinged, with rectangular tables, square tables, benches, and stools for customers. Through the window an inner courtyard can be seen, where there is a matted canopy for shade and seats for customers. There are hooks hanging up birdcages, both in the teahouse and in the courtyard."[111]

Amid the array of late imperial objects, Lao She does not indicate how many rectangular and square tables should appear in the scene, and later, on the stage. In Jiao Juyin and Xia Chun's classical adaptation premiered in 1958 by Beijing People's Art Theatre, a group of four stage designers, including Wang Wenchong

---

[110] Lao She, *Teahouse*, 5. Early in 1958, Scholar Zhang Geng 張庚 captured Lao She's tone of nostalgia, and a gesture of mourning for the late Qing past. See his "*Chaguan* mantan" 《茶館》漫談 [Random thoughts on Teahouse], *Renmin ribao* 人民日報 (People's Daily), May 27, 1958, reprinted in Zeng and Wu, eds., *Lao She yanjiu ziliao*, 800–804. See also Zeng Lingcun 曾令存, "Zai jiedu: *Chaguan* wenben de shenceng jiegou" 再解讀:《茶館》文本的深層結構 [Reinterpretation: The text structure of *Teahouse*], *Xiju xuekan* 戲劇學刊 [Taipei theatre journal] 11 (2010): 251–267; Guan Jixin 關紀新, *Lao She yu manzu wenhua* 老舍與滿族文化 [Lao She and Manchu culture], Shenyang: Liaoning minzu chubanshe, 2008.

[111] Lao She, *Teahouse*, 6.

王文衝, Guan Zhaisheng 關哉生, Song Yin 宋垠, and Qian Bin 錢斌, famously arranged and displayed eight tables total in act 1, and reduce the number to five in acts 2 and 3.[112] Xie Tian's film version in 1982 displayed a similar spatial structure centering on the tables as the skeleton framework of the teahouse. Yet Lin Zhaohua, an outstanding avant-garde theater director, and Yi Liming, Lin's longtime collaborator and a distinguished lighting/stage designer, intentionally challenged the classical design "eight tables surrounded by three-sided walls" (*bazhang zhuozi sanmian qiang* 八張桌子三面牆) in act 1 and changed the tables from eight to thirteen, which made Lin's theatrical space quite full of this significant teahouse furniture. Lin's 1999 theatrical version was controversial. Then he produced a 2005 version, extremely faithful to Jiao and Xia's 1958 edition, and changed the number of tables back to eight to celebrate the anniversary of the birth of director Jiao Juyin.

In addition to the leading material image of tea tables, changes of other objects and ornaments more or less indicate political changes. The spatial arrangements of the everyday objects in the teahouse, for instance, the counter and kitchen near the main entrance, traditional teahouse benches and stools, and the front hall and inner courtyard in the back, reveal vividly the kind of luxurious and large teahouses common in Beijing in the late imperial era. Interestingly, the political imperative DO NOT DISCUSS AFFAIRS OF STATE, on a paper notice in the play and a wooden board in Lin's drama, is pasted or hung up with hooks for hanging bird cages, which visualizes the coexistence of political self-censorship and leisurely enjoyment under the same high-ceilinged roof.

In act 2, this type of large teahouse is becoming extinct, and a material and mental loss becomes more observable and detectable. Even Wang Lifa's wife can mark out the trajectories of the disappearances of large teahouses: the few remaining "old and established names"—Detai 德泰 at Xizhimen 西直門, Guangtai 廣泰 at Beixinqiao 北新橋, and Tiantai 天泰 in front of the Drum Tower 鼓樓—have all had to close down. The Yutai Teahouse is the only survivor in the warlord era, and the reason is, as Wang Lifa realizes with perplexity, "that teahouses, like governments, have to reform."[113] Ironically, reform takes the form of deformation. The Yutai is forced to change its physical appearance by splitting the space: the front part remains a teahouse, while the rear section is renovated as a public lodging house. The chairs and tables have undergone a great "reform" as well: the tables are now smaller, with

---

[112] See Beijing renmin yishu juyuan *Yishu yanjiu ziliao* bianjizu 北京人民藝朮劇院《藝朮研究資料》編輯組 [Editorial board of *Art Research Archives* at Beijing People's Art Theatre], eds., Chaguan *de wutai yishu* 《茶館》的舞台藝朮 [Stage art of *Teahouse*] (Beijing: Zhongguo xiju chubanshe, 1980).

[113] Lao She, *Teahouse*, 24.

pale green tablecloths and wicker chairs. "The large painting of *The Eight Drunken Immortals* and even the shrine to the God of Wealth are gone, having been replaced by pictures of fashionable women in foreign cigarette advertisements. 'Don't discuss state affairs,' however, still stares down from every wall, written in even larger characters."[114] Politics and political change are revealed in the loss of material objects, the sense of anxiety and hurt, the dislocations of indoor ornaments and decoration, and the shrinking teahouse space.

In contrast to the material abundance, spatial fullness, and acoustic richness of the Teahouse in act 1 or the late Manchu Empire, the shabby interior scenes in act 2 and act 3 share a "family resemblance." Around the time of the downfall of the Nationalist government in 1948, the teahouse underwent greater changes and lost its dignity and substance. Even "the wicker chairs have disappeared, replaced by stools and benches. Everything, from the building to the furniture, looks gloomy." The only eye-catching things are the paper signs proclaiming, DO NOT DISCUSS AFFAIRS OF STATE—now in even bigger characters. The teahouse building itself and the interior furniture are "dull and shabby,"[115] reminiscent of Lao She's narrative strategy of envisioning urban darkness in horrible nights and mean streets in the stories of rickshaw puller Camel Xiangzi, a lonely individual who falls into unfathomable urban black holes. In the hostile political milieu, Wang Lifa has never forgotten about reform, change, and keeping up with the times in ways that he would not honor: a series of reluctant spatial rearrangements of the teahouse including opening a rooming house, bringing in a storyteller, and even hiring a come-on hostess. Yet a local gangster and opportunist, Little Pockface Liu, and behind him the KMT military officer Shen, conspire to occupy and possess the Yutai Teahouse, and re-envision it as a small dance hall, card room, cafeteria, or private club for their own purposes, indicating yet another material use and abuse of the place and space in a chaotic and reckless era.

Kwok-kan Tam 譚國根 rightly understands the teahouse as "the organizing principle," a stage, and an eyewitness to the political changes. He furthermore argues that *Teahouse* lacks "temporary unity," yet achieves "spatial unity," and the success of the play "lies precisely in its ambivalent ending and its Chekhovian sense of indirection."[116] I interpret the Yutai Teahouse as a warped space-time continuum illustrating historical and political violence. Anthony Vidler focuses on two types of spatial warping: psychological, "with its emphasis on the nature of space as a projection of

[114] Ibid., 23–24.
[115] Ibid., 46.
[116] Kwok-kan Tam, introduction to *Cha guan: Teahouse*, by Lao She, trans. Yan Liu (Hong Kong: Chinese University Press, 2004), xxxii–xxxvi.

the subject, and thus as a harbinger and repository of all neuroses and phobias of that subject"; and artistic, which is "produced by the forced intersection of different media—film, photography, art, architecture—in a way that breaks the boundaries of genre and the separate arts in response to the need to depict space in new and unparalleled ways."[117] The multimedia Yutai Teahouse is both concrete and conceptual, both physical and psychological, and depicts social and political transformation in the everyday scenes of a shrinking and malfunctioned public space. Significantly, the self-mourning performed by the three old men, Chang the Manchu Bannerman, Qin the industrialist, and Wang the property owner, evokes a spatial linkage between the half-open-half-closed Yutai and the turbulent street, a space stretch and exterior extension of the warped teahouse, by Master Chang's action of coming from the avenues and alleyways and stepping inside:

> MASTER CHANG: I love my country, but who loves me? See here (*taking paper money out of his basket*)—whenever I see a funeral, I try to pick up some of this paper money. I won't have any burial clothes. I won't even have a coffin. All I can do is save some paper money for myself. Ha, ha! (*Hearty laughter tinged with despair*)[118]

In act 1, Manchu Bannerman Master Chang realized "the Bannerman's subsidy was abolished," and signed, "The Great Qing Empire was done for after all!"[119] In act 3, as a lifelong inhabitant of Beijing from the late imperial to the Republican eras, Master Chang makes a complaint about his country that could also be rendered as "I love my city, but the city does not love me." The overlap between the city and the country (be it Manchu Empire or modern nation-state) highlights the perplexing political orientation, and the feeling of being abandoned conjures a melancholic resonance among the three aged urbanites. Qin Zhongyi responds, "Let's offer ritual funeral sacrifices for ourselves. Throw the paper money in the air. Something special for

---

[117] Anthony Vidler, preface to *Warped Space: Art, Architecture, and Anxiety in Modern Culture* (Cambridge, MA: MIT Press, 2002), vii. I describe this dimension of the literary mapping of Beijing, especially Lao She's Beijing narratives, as the warped hometown. The spatial warping, as Vidler suggests, indicates concrete and conceptual, physical and psychological changes and transformations in urban scenes and multimedia artistic practices.

[118] See also a new and forceful edition translated by Ying Ruocheng 英若誠 and revised by Claire Conceison, in Xiaomei Chen's *The Columbia Anthology of Modern Chinese Drama* (New York: Columbia University Press, 2010), 594. For John Howard-Gibbon's translation, see p. 75: "FOURTH ELDER CHANG: I love my country, but no one gives a damn about me. Look. (*Takes some paper money from his basket*). I gathered this bit of fake funeral money after a funeral procession had passed. I don't have burial clothes or a coffin; but why not at least gather together a little funeral money for myself? (*Hearty laughter tinged with despair*)."

[119] Lao She, *Teahouse*, trans. Ying Ruocheng (Taipei: Shulin chuban, 2004), 104, 110.

us three old fogies!"[120] Death comes in advance in the ceremony of self-mourning, which turns the physical place of the teahouse into a psychological space filled with frustration, pain, depression, and confusion.

Svetlana Boym states, "Nostalgia is a sentiment of loss and displacement, but it is also a romance with one's own phantasy."[121] Nostalgia contains a loss of the past and a longing for the past. Boym makes distinction of two types of nostalgias: "Restorative nostalgia stresses *nostos* (home) and attempts a transhistorical reconstruction of the lost home. Reflective nostalgia thrives on *algia*, the longing itself, and delays the homecoming—wistfully, ironically, desperately."[122] She also points out that "These distinctions are not absolute binaries, and one can surely make a more refined mapping of the grey areas on the outskirts of imaginary homelands."[123] In *Teahouse*, nostalgia, loss, melancholia, and mourning are intermingle and interconnected emotions. Loss leads to melancholia. The performance of mourning may overcome the sense of loss, and construct or reconstruct the lost objects or images in ongoing nostalgia, which embarks on a "restorative" and "reflective" journey back to an imagined home and idealized aura.

According to Sigmund Freud, mourning is the reaction to concrete loss, like a loved person, or abstract loss, like one's country, liberty, or an ideal. Rey Chow illustrates that the melancholic person "exhibits the symptoms of a delusional belittling of himself" and the sense of being unjustly abandoned.[124] Individual/private and collective loss can be concrete and abstract, and related to the absent body, damaged object, empty space, frustrated desire, loss of history, and the lack of social justice.[125] The three old fogies cannot come to terms with the strong sense of concrete and abstract loss, and this confirms their own worthlessness and feeling unjustly abandoned by their city, their country, and their eras. Now the falling paper money indicates the direction of gravity; the ashes of implosion; the trajectories of nostalgia, loss, mourning, and melancholia; the fragments of the melancholic urban subject suffering from historical and political violence; and the clashes of political black holes producing whirls, vortexes, and gusts of wind detectable in the warped teahouse. A social-political abyss appears in front of the three awakened urban subjects.

---

[120] Ibid.

[121] Svetlana Boym, *The Future of Nostalgia* (New York: Basic Books, 2001), xiii.

[122] Boym, *The Future of Nostalgia*, xviii, and chaps. 4 and 5. See also her webpage about nostalgic technology: http://www.svetlanaboym.com/main.htm.

[123] Boym, "Nostalgia and its discontents," *Hedgehog Review* 9.2 (2007): 7–18, esp. 13.

[124] Rey Chow, *Writing Diaspora: Tactics of Intervention in Contemporary Cultural Studies* (Bloomington: Indiana University Press, 1993), 3.

[125] See David L. Eng and David Kazanjian, "Introduction: Mourning Remains," in *Loss: The Politics of Mourning* (Berkeley, CA: University of California Press, 2003), 1–28; Judith Butler's psychoanalysis of loss, fragility, and political violence, in her *Precarious Life: The Powers of Mourning and Violence* (London: Verso, 2006);

The episode of self-mourning is a fabricated and displaced funeral for the living dead, and makes the Yutai a deserted place, a coffin, a grave, and a tomb. In the ceremony of burying the previous three eras, Lao She performs a "soul calling" for the dying subjects of pre-Mao Beijing right in the newly established socialist capital.[126]

As far as the theatrical structure of the three-act play *Teahouse*, Li Jianwu classifies the difference between "mu" 幕 (act) and "chang" 場 (scene): "Three acts would be better called three scenes, because they truly and vividly reflect three scenes. No matter acts or scenes, their nature would be close to scroll paintings, especially the scroll paintings or portraits of human life. We can sense this even in one single act." (叫做三幕其實不如叫做三場，因為它們只是真實地，生動地反映了三個場面。幕也好，場也好，它們的性質近似圖卷，特別是世態圖卷。甚至於一幕之中往往也有這種感覺。).[127] Jiao Juyin and Xia Chun's 1958 *Teahouse* presents a multifocused and horizontal urban scene, and provides the audience a panoramic point of view developed from looking at traditional Chinese scroll paintings (*tujuan xi* 圖卷戲), like Zhang Zeduan's 張擇端 (1085–1145) *Going on the River at the Qingming Festival* (*Qingming shanghe tu* 清明上河圖). Surrounded by three walls, with one transparent wall exposed to the spectators, the eight or five tables anchor the infrastructure of the interior space. The theatrical performance invites the audience to be on-site witnesses, or jury members during a live trial of pre-Mao political change.[128] Relying on cinematography, mise en scène, and soundtrack, Xie Tian's 1982 film version presents virtual scenes of streets, the city, and the country in documentary style, along with ballad singer Silly Yang's voice-over narration. In order to dispel "the

---

and E. Ann Kaplan's analysis of "quiet trauma," *Trauma Culture: The Politics of Terror and Loss in Media and Literature* (New Brunswick, NJ: Rutgers University Press, 2005).

[126] Lao She's *Teahouse* is, to borrow Edward W. Said's words on Kipling's *Kim*, an overwhelmingly male drama, and the masculine aspect the narrative is remarkably obvious because women in Lao She's works "are remarkably few by comparison, and all of them are somehow debased or unsuitable for male attention." Edward W. Said, *Culture and Imperialism* (New York: Vintage, 1993), 136–137. Tigress (*Rickshaw Boy*) is unpleasantly robust and wild, while Xiao Fuzi is tender and warm but hangs herself in the end of the novel. Yunmei is kindhearted but a minor character in *Four Generations Under One Roof*. In *Dragon Beard Ditch*, Er Chun is a "flat character," a rebelling and energetic girl. Moreover, the reason that there is no significant female character in *Teahouse* is that the waiters in old Beijing's teahouses were all male. In a word, Lao She's Beijing is a men's world, but his male characters are socially castrated and therefore have lost their masculinity because they are the oppressed class in Republican Beijing, where their life is replete with suffering, frustration, endurance, and distorted personality. The harmed and insulted male figures include not only Han people but also Manchu bannermen.

[127] Li Jianwu, "Du *Chaguan*" 讀《茶館》 [Reading *Teahouse*], *Renmin wenxue* 人民文學 [People's literature] 1 (1958): 45.

[128] Jiao Juyin, "Lun minzuhua" 論民族化 [On nationalization], *Xinwenhua shiliao* 新文化史料 [Historical materials of new culture] 2 (1996):11; Jiao's article was originaly written in 1963. Xia Chun, "Jiao Juyin he tade 'Zhongguo Xuepai'" 焦菊隱和他的"中國學派" [Jiao Juyin and his "Chinese School"], *Xinwenhua shiliao* 新文化史料 [Historical materials of new culture] 2 (1996):14–16.

anxiety of influence," Lin Zhaohua and his stage designer, Yi Liming, abandon the interior spatial form of the teahouse and instead remodel it into a tea canopy, which is a totally exterior space without walls, opens wide to the street, and becomes part of the street scenes. Although this unconventional adaptation weakens the theatrical tensions and symptomatic implosion condensed in the interior space, it effectively breaks the boundaries between the teahouse and the street and extends the spatial warping to street activities by the unnamable walking crowds. Lin wanted to rehearse an avant-garde production of *Teahouse*, which "departs from Lao She's play, centers on the three old men, with only nine tables and a huge reed curtain on the stage."[129] This 1999 theatrical performance introduced a debatable spatial discrepancy and a vertical exhibition of the Yutai as an asymmetric and gothic space of persistent urban darkness and horror. Yi Liming, the former designer of stage, lighting, and costumes for Lin, has become a director of experimental dramas, and released a bold and minimalist *Teahouse* with an expressionist understanding of the warped space in 2010.[130] However dim and vague the old Beijing flavor and aura have been, Yi's *Teahouse*, listed as a product from the Lin Zhaohua Studio, presents flamboyantly the crisis and climax of the self-mourning ceremony. Unsurprisingly, in the enormous television drama market, director He Qun, scriptwriters Ye Guangcen and Yang Guoqiang, and art designer Zhang Peng 張鵬 contributed a thirty-nine-episode melodramatic and problematic *Teahouse* in 2010, and daringly set fire to the teahouse to demonstrate dazzling visual effects and the suicidal impulse of resistance to political change.[131] In many ways, by condensing absurd politics and historical violence into a shrinking everyday space, Lao She conveys the warped teahouse as a volatile container that attests to an unsettled daily life distorted by political changes. The constant production and reproduction of the Yutai Teahouse present and perform a symbolic and chronotopic microcosm, as well as a warped and eventually implosive space, of modern urban horrors and darkness.

Lao She performs an affective mapping of his native city's streets, courtyard houses, ditch, and teahouse: everyday tyranny and despair in the phantasmal and entrapping avenues and streets; wartime atlas of emotions including nostalgia,

[129] Lin Zhaohua, "*Chaguan* buhui yuegai yueliang" 《茶館》不會越改越涼 [Adaptation of *Teahouse* cannot be getting worse. *Beijing Youth Daily* 北京青年報, September 30, 2005.

[130] Cheng Zhang 成長, "80hou yanyuan jiegou *Chaguan*" 80 後演員解構《茶館》 [The Post-80s generation actors deconstructed *Teahouse*], *Zhongguo wenhua bao* 中國文化報 [Chinese culture daily], January 29, 2010.

[131] See Lin Zhaohua, "Lin Zhaohua fangtanlu" 林兆華訪談錄 [An interview with Lin Zhaohua], *Xiju wenxue* 戲劇文學 [Drama and literature], 2003:8, 4–14, 38; He Qun, "He Qun fangtan" 何群訪談 [An interview with He Qun], *Dazhong dianying* 大眾電影 [Popular cinema], 16 (2010): 34–36; Zhang Peng 張鵬, "Jicheng yu fazhan" 繼承與發展 [Inheritance and development], *Zhongguo dianshi* 中國電視 [Chinese television], 10 (2008): 66–68.

mourning, shame, anger, and hatred; socialist sentiment and citizenship born in the ide©ological representation of Dragon Beard Ditch as a metamorphic space; and self-mourning in a warped and wounded teahouse as a distorted space-time continuum, a shrinking and pessimistic miniature of old Beijing misery and a sign of unfathomable urban darkness. Facing the arrival and (dis)advantage of modernity as well as the chaotic political and historical change, Lao She delineates modern Beijing as the locus of pain and pleasure, dystopia and dreamland, moral decline and physical performance, material deformations and emotional vicissitudes.

The capital teems with officials and dignitaries [冠蓋滿京華],
Yet you are haggard and lonely [斯人獨憔悴].
—DU FU 杜甫

2

Urban Snapshots and Manners

ZHANG HENSHUI AND THE BEIJING DREAM

THIS CHAPTER CONSIDERS a type of Beijing narrative that seizes instants in the floating, ephemeral, modern urban life while conveying a deep view of the city, its people, and social manners. Serialized in literary supplements of newspapers, these writings became enormously popular between the 1920s and the 1930s. Zhang Henshui's work represents the peak of the accomplishments in this subgenre.[1] Zhang's Beijing writings combine journalistic snapshots and observational portrayals of human behavior, social manners, and urban emotions. Through the curious eye of a city explorer, snapshot writings guide the readers in navigating the city, analyzing diverse and often conflicting pieces of information, and coping with stimuli and stresses from the fast-changing world around them. In contrast, his sophisticated and (un)sentimental depictions of social manners reveal the individual and collective mind, and also the ethos of modern experiences in the ancient capital of Beijing. These two disparate yet interrelated forms of observing, apprehending, and narrating Republican Beijing create an epistemological and psychological mechanism for modern citizens to come to grips with reality, with a version of life that is more real than reality.

Accordingly, Zhang's fiction is marked by two inherently conflicting modes of temporality: the condensation of time in news-style snapshot writings about palpably felt social changes and transformations, and the extension of time involved in

---

[1] For the dozens of Zhang Henshui's pen names, see Xiaowei Wang Rupprecht, *Departure and Return: Chang Hen-shui and the Chinese Narrative Tradition* (Hong Kong: Joint Publishing Co., 1987), 203.

the observation and representation of manners, customs, and social mores. Whereas the former compresses time and concerns events that are consequential because they demand attention within a short period of time, the latter deals with ways of life and being and registers a sense of time that is steady and continuous. This contradiction between instantaneity and duration is significantly visible in the narrative structure and constitutes the very form of Zhang's novels.

In the autumn of 1919, merely a few months after the May Fourth Movement was launched, Zhang Henshui, then an anonymous young man from Anhui province, exited the Beijing railway station and immediately caught sight of the grand majestic arrow tower 箭樓 of the Zhengyang Gate 正陽門, a vital symbol of the ancient imperial capital. Zhang was completely in awe, enchanted with profound emotional attachment to Beijing. His impression was shared by many visitors of the city during the Republican period. Jiang Deming (1929–), a distinguished Beijing expert who edited the influential two-volume anthology *Beijing hu* (Ah! Beijing), set his eyes firmly on the same arrow tower when he arrived in Beijing before its socialist reconstruction began. The sight of the massive tower and the dissipated yet still magnificent city instantly stirred up a deep historical and cultural consciousness in his mind.[2]

In the early years of the Republican period, most people came to Beijing by train, and Qianmen 前門 (the Front Gate, also called the Zhengyang Gate), where the city's main railway terminal was located, was often their first impression of the city. Zhengyang Gate was situated at the south end of the Inner City of the imperial capital, connecting the Inner City with the Outer City. A key point at the central south-north axis of the city, it was originally designed to protect the Inner City from access by the outside world. However, the Zhengyang Gate that Zhang Henshui saw when first arriving in Beijing no longer retained its original imperial architectural integrity. To meet the demand for access created by modern transportation, the protective walls of the Zhengyang Gate were dismantled, and the connections between the gate and its attached arrow tower were broken.[3] In 1915, the *wengcheng* 甕城 (the enceinte) at the Zhengyang Gate was demolished by the order of Zhu Qiqian 朱啓鈐 (1872–1964), Chief Director of the Department of Internal Affairs and the head of the Municipal Council under the Yuan Shikai 袁世凱 (1859–1916)

---

[2] Jiang Deming 姜德明, "Preface," in *Beijing hu: xiandai zuojia bixia de Beijing, 1919–1949* 北京平：現代作家筆下的北京 （一九一九ー一九四九） [*Ah, Beijing: Beijing in modern Chinese writings, 1919–1949*], ed. Jiang Deming (Beijing: Sanlian shudian, 1992).

[3] Wang Shiren 王世仁 and Zhang Fuhe 張復合, "Beijing jindai jianzhu gaishuo" 北京近代建築概說 [A survey of modern architecture in Beijing], in *Zhongguo jindai jianzhu zonglan: Beijing pian* 中國近代建築總覽：北京篇 [A review of modern architecture in China: The section of Beijing] (Beijing: Zhongguo jianzhu gongye chubanshe, 1993).

administration, to enlarge the passage into the city.[4] The reconstruction of the Zhengyang Gate area was a top priority in the Municipal Council's urban modernization project. Madeleine Yue Dong points out that the project "embodied an important principle in the reordering of the city: unifying the different parts of the city and connecting the city to the outside world."[5]

Deprived of its original political, military, or symbolic functions, the isolated Zhengyang arrow tower ushered Zhang Henshui and his fellow Beijing sojourners or residents into a city in its most dramatic moment of transition. The gigantic tower serves as an architectural mechanism dividing the inside and outside worlds. Like a painted screen in traditional Chinese art, it "always exhibits and conceals at the same time, and always invites the viewer to explore what is hidden and unseen."[6] For this outsider coming from a southern province, gazing at the arrow tower evoked a sense of awe, curiosity, and suspense, a desire to see what was unrolling behind it. Five years later, Zhang, who had already become one of the most prolific and popular writers in modern China, started to contribute new chapters to decode the myth and imagine the romance of the ancient capital.[7] In his major work, *Grand Old Family*, through the eyes of the protagonist Jin Yanxi 金燕西, Zhang paid another tribute to the Zhengyang arrow tower. After the collapse of his family, Yanxi decides to leave his native city and go abroad: "Yanxi walked over to the arrow tower of the Zhengyang Gate. He gazed at the tower and then sighed to the pair of stone lions at its entrance, 'Good-bye, my friend!'"[8] As the arrow tower and the city walls disappeared from his sight, his connection with Beijing was officially broken.

Beijing's grand yet irretrievably disintegrated spatial composition as represented by the Zhengyang Gate signifies not only the cosmological and political order of its imperial past but also a burgeoning modern city that the Republican state envisioned. The Zhengyang arrow tower defines two modes of temporality and spatiality, two

---

[4] For Zhu Qiqian's role in the urban reconstruction of Beijing in Republican China, see, for instance, Beijingshi zhengxie wenshi ziliao yanjiu weiyuanhui deng bian 北京市政協文史資料研究委員會等編, *Huogong jishi: Zhu Qiqian xiansheng shengping jishi* 蠖公紀事：朱啓鈐先生生平紀實 [The life of Zhu Qiqian] (Beijing: Zhongguo wenshi chubanshe, 1991); and Geremie R. Barmé, "Zhu Qiqian's Silver Shovel," *China Heritage Quarterly* 14 (June 2008), http://www.chinaheritagequarterly.org/.

[5] Dong, *Republican Beijing*, 22.

[6] Wu Hung, *The Double Screen: Medium and Representation in Chinese Painting* (Chicago: University of Chicago Press, 1996), 68.

[7] Zhang Wu 張伍, Zhang Henshui's son, once recalled his father's first sight of the significant monument, and some other daily objects, such as the passing cars with high speed and mechanical power, the mule carts decorated with sky-blue silk and window-glass, the cart driver's long whip and happy yell, which all summed up and compellingly situated Zhang Henshui in the cultural atmosphere of modern Beijing. See Zhang Wu, *Wo de fuqin Zhang Henshui* 我的父親張恨水 [My father Zhang Henshui] (Shenyang: Chunfeng wenyi chubanshe, 2002), 68.

[8] Zhang Henshui, *Jinfen shijia* [Grand old family] (Taiyuan: Beiyue wenyi chubanshe, 2000), 1039.

visions of culture and urbanity converging and competing at the advent of Chinese modernity. The conjunction of the old and the new, discontinuity and continuity, is also inscribed in Zhang Henshui's narrative forms and his literary position in modern China. In his *Memoirs of My Writing Career*, Zhang describes the duality in his intellectual and cultural formation as a result of unsystematic education, amateur readings, and the influence of modern culture and politics:

> I was a "revolutionary young man" [*geming qingnian*] and cut off my pig-tail queue when I was enlightened by modern education pedagogy and books of new culture. Nevertheless, I also worshiped the "traditional young talents" [*caizi*] because I read and accepted classical novels, poems, and song lyrics as well.[9]

A number of protagonists in his novels bear similar traits, be they a journalist-classical poet (*Unofficial History*), a flâneur-dandy-actor (*Grand Old Family*), a modern college student with classical learning and populist taste (*Fate in Tears and Laughter*), or a horse-carriage cart driver (*Deep Darkness of the Night*). Li Nanquan, the hero in *Bashan yeyu* 巴山夜雨 (Night rain over Ba mountain), for instance, can be read as the self-portrait of the author himself. Li is characterized by an intriguing mixture of *mingshi pai* 名士派 (self-indulgent literati style), *toujin qi* 頭巾氣 (a bookish cast of mind), and *geming xing* 革命性 (a revolutionary mentality) in turbulent modern times in China.[10] Zhang's Beijing narratives tiptoe among these polarities, contributing a series of characters possessing contradictory characteristics of both "enlightened new youth" and traditional literati-style "old souls."

Zhang Henshui established himself as a prolific writer of modern Chinese literature, and the majority of his work is set in Beijing, including *Unofficial History of Beijing, Grand Old Family, Fate in Tears and Laughter, Yinhan shuangxing* 銀漢雙星 (Pair of stars in the Milky Way, 1930), *Manjiang hong* 滿江紅 (All are red in the river, 1931–1932), *Meiren en* 美人恩 (Beauty's gratitude, 1931–1932), *Luoxia guwu* 落霞孤鶩 (Lonely duck under the colorful evening clouds, 1931–1932), *Yan guilai* 燕歸來 (Return of the swallow, 1932–1934), *Xiandai qingnian* 現代青年 (Modern youth, 1932–1934), *Deep Darkness of the Night, Dajiang dong qu* 大江東去 (The river flows east, 1938–1940), and *Sishui liunian* 似水流年 (Flowing years like a river,

---

[9] Zhang Henshui, *Xiezuo shengya huiyi*, in Zhang and Wei, eds., *Zhang Henshui yanjiu ziliao*, 13.
[10] See Yuan Jin 袁進, *Xiaoshuo qicai Zhang Henshui zhuan* 小說奇才張恨水傳 [Zhang Henshui: A talented fiction writer] (Taipei: Yeqiang chubanshe, 1992), 228.

1949), and so on.[11] Most of Zhang's novels were first serialized in newspapers and later published as monographic best-sellers. Taking Beijing as a locus of emotion, epiphany, and education, Zhang adopts the traditional form of *zhanghui xiaoshuo* 章回小說 ("chapter-titled" novels) to bring to the limelight encyclopedic registers of diversified urban stories, modern experiences, and the emotional vicissitudes of modern Beijing inhabitants from all walks of life and social status.[12]

Zhang Henshui's work was sensationally popular during the Republican era and today thanks to its continuous adaptations in films, local operas, and television dramas. In Republican China, "entertainment literature was still commercially successful in the hands of key writers such as Zhang Henshui."[13] After the publications of *Unofficial History of Beijing, Grand Old Family*, and *Fate in Tears and Laughter* in the 1930s, a huge group of Zhang Henshui fans formed, among which were both partisans of new literature and cultural conservatives.[14] However, in the standard literary histories of modern China, Zhang has been continuously categorized as a low-ranked popular writer (*tongsu zuojia* 通俗作家) belonging to the belittled "Mandarin Ducks and Butterflies" school (*yuanyang hudie pai* 鴛鴦蝴蝶派) of sentimental fiction. Given its focus on romantic love, Zhang's fiction was often interpreted as commercial, popular, and entertainment literature, or "fiction for comfort."[15] Such disparagement originated particularly from the leftist camp and intensified after the founding of the People's Republic of China in 1949 so much so that Zhang made a confession to mock himself as "Saturday school offspring."[16] In *Qingchun zhi ge* 青春之歌 (*The Song of Youth*, 1959), a post-1949 representative

---

[11] For a complete chronicle of Zhang Henshui's works, see Zhang and Wei, *Zhang Henshui yanjiu ziliao*, 318–556.

[12] Chapter-titled novel is the traditional Chinese literary form of full-length vernacular narrative, and remains an effective and popular literary genre that readers in the early modern times are still used to, and by which the readers can come to terms with the modern experiences written in premodern style.

[13] Bonnie S. McDougall and Kam Louie, *The Literature of China in the Twentieth Century* (New York: Columbia University Press, 1997), 28.

[14] The size of this fan group was only matched by that of Jin Yong, the most important and successful martial arts fiction writer in the Chinese language world since the late 1950s. Zhang's fervent readers include the female writer Zhang Ailing (Eileen Chang), the historian Chen Yinke 陳寅恪 (1890–1969), the politician Mao Zedong 毛澤東 (1893–1976), and mother of Lu Xun.

[15] Perry Link, *Mandarin Ducks and Butterflies: Popular Fiction in Early Twentieth-Century Chinese Cities* (Berkeley: University of California Press, 1981), 9. Actually, Zhang's fiction is not only for comfort, but also for discomfort because most of his works do not follow the popular model of a "happy ending." T. M. McClellan defines some of Zhang's novel as "oneiric romanticism," and correctly points out that the dreamlike quality contains beautiful daydreams but also haunting nightmares. See T. M. McClellan, "Change and Continuity in the Fiction of Zhang Henshui (1895–1967): From Oneiric Romanticism to Nightmare Realism," *Modern Chinese Literature* 10 (1998): 113–134.

[16] Zhang Henshui, *Xiezuo shengya huiyi*, in Zhang and Wei, *Zhang Henshui yanjiu ziliao*, 12; see also Chen Pingyuan, "Literature High and Low: 'Popular Fiction' in Twentieth-Century China," in *The Literary Field of Twentieth-Century China*, ed. Michel Hockx (Honolulu: University of Hawai'i Press, 1999), 113–133.

literary work of socialist realism, there is a subplot in which the progressive heroine, Lin Tao-ching (Lin Daojing) 林道靜, endeavors to politically enlighten Jen Yu-kuei (Ren Yugui), a furnace stoker on the Peiping-Hankow Railway, and imbue him with revolutionary ideas. The first step Lin takes is to eliminate the "negative influence" of urban romances by Zhang Henshui and other popular writers. With Lin's help,

> he improved both in health and in spirits. Whereas before he would lie in bed groaning or cursing to vent his frustration, or read old novels like *Seven Heroes and Five Gallants, Canonization of the Gods, Fate in Tears and Laughter*, and *Grand Old Family*, under Tao-ching's influence he now began to read *People's Life, World Culture* and other progressive literature which she smuggled in to him.[17]

For Yang Mo 楊沫 (1914–1995), a leftist woman writer, Zhang's *Fate in Tears and Laughter* and *Grand Old Family* not only are "old novels" but also hinder the cause of the Chinese revolution and revolutionary literature. The unyielding power of love and individual freedom unleashed from reading Zhang's romances could be dangerous if not controlled or rechanneled for the sake of the national salvation and socialist revolution. This episode in *The Song of Youth* bespeaks the sharp contrast between the new literature and the popular culture of the twentieth century. In the PRC's canonization of modern Chinese literature, popular literature including Zhang's is excluded from any literary or political taxonomy.

Reflecting on the tradition of Chinese vernacular literature and its variations in the twentieth century, T. A. Hsia 夏濟安 (1916–1965), C. T. Hsia's brother and a prominent literary critic, maintains that romance—including those of the *caizi jiaren xiaoshuo* 才子佳人小說 (talented scholar and beauty novel), martial arts fiction, military romance, and court-case fiction—has won the hearts and minds of generations of popular readers. Compared with the modern literary form of the novel, romance is mechanical, poorly organized, stereotypical, and conventional. Although the novel surpasses the romance in narrative structure and psychological depth, the romance is able to convey the Chinese mind. He regards Zhang Henshui's work as the best achievement of this genre. In a letter to C. T. Hsia in 1958, T. A. Hsia wrote, "Zhang Henshui is a genius. He can describe a scene in a vivid, lively manner. And of course, his limitations and deficiencies are quite obvious; but he has ears, eyes, and imagination. It is really a shame that you did not discuss Zhang

---

[17] Yang Mo, *The Song of Youth*, trans. Nan Ying (Beijing: Foreign Languages Press, 1964), 455–457. The English translation is modified by the author according to the original Chinese text.

Henshui in your study of modern Chinese fiction. At least he is a greater and better artist than Wu Jingzi."[18] For T. A. Hsia, Zhang's work is characterized not only by its exploration of the Chinese mentality but also by its artistic merits. Therefore, it deserves a serious position in the literary history of modern China.

C.T. Hsia comments on the popular "Chapter-titled" fiction of the Republican period in his pioneering and field-redefining work, *A History of Modern Chinese Fiction*:

> Contemporary novels in the old styles were avidly read by a large audience seeking primarily escapist entertainment. Ranging from sentimental romance to incredible adventure, these novels stemmed from the earlier vernacular tradition and have little in common with the new fiction except for their use of the pai-hua. Though contemptuously dismissed by the partisans of the new literature for its unconcern with social issues and its unawareness of the Western tradition, this fiction actually boasts several practitioners who are in narrative skill much superior to their more ideologically enlightened fellow craftsmen. It should be instructive to attempt a serious study of this fiction, if not to discover literary merits, at least to analyze the kinds of daydream and fantasy to which a large section of the reading public yielded during the Republican period.[19]

For the Hsia brothers, good vernacular fiction is able to transcend mere "escapist entertainment" or fabrications of "daydream and fantasy." Although it might not be "ideologically enlightened" and lack a deep social concern, it adeptly describes popular psychology and the complexity of human nature, thereby speaking for and speaking to a large population of its time. Since the last few decades, with a reconsideration of the resilient divide between high and low, serious literature and popular culture, Zhang's sophisticated portrayal of social life and urban experiences in Republican Beijing has eventually won a belated re-evaluation and recognition by literary critics and historians.[20]

This chapter scrutinizes Zhang Henshui's Beijing narratives in terms of two modes of representation: urban snapshots and social manners. I examine four representative novels, *Unofficial History of Beijing, Grand Old Family, Fate in Tears and*

---

[18] T. A. Hsia, "On Chinese Popular Literature," in C. T. Hsia, *Jichuang ji* 雞窗集 [A collection of the study] (Shanghai: Sanlian shudian, 2000), 206.

[19] Hsia, *A History of Modern Chinese Fiction*, 25.

[20] In 2006, *Asia Weekly* (Hong Kong) named the 100 Best Chinese Fictional Works in the twentieth century. Zhang Henshui's *Fate in Tears and Laughter* ranked twenty-seventh.

Laughter, and *Deep Darkness of the Night*, which were written at different stages of his career. Zhang explained,

> Generally speaking, my writing career could be divided into three periods. The first was the period during which I published *Unofficial History of Beijing*, *Grand Old Family*, and some other novels. The second period fell at a time when China was at war [with Japan], and our country was in extreme difficulties. It was during this period that I wrote *Madness* and *Worlds of Demons* [*Wangliang shijie*] (its original title was *Niu ma zou* [Oxen and horses prevail]). The third period is the present.[21]

Hsiao-wei Wang Rupprecht identifies the three phases respectively as 1919 though 1931 (Zhang as a journalist-*littérateur*); 1931 though 1949 (Zhang as an editor-writer during the Second Sino-Japanese War and its aftermath); and 1949 though 1963 (Zhang as an aging writer under communism).[22] Accordingly, *Unofficial History of Beijing*, *Grand Old Family*, and *Fate in Tears and Laughter* were composed in the first period, in which the "double personality" of both "the revolutionary young man" and the old-style "talented youth" set the personal, romantic, sentimental, and melancholic tones with sophisticated interpersonal and social observations. *Deep Darkness of the Night* can be categorized as an early stage of the second phase and bears more evident social criticism.

Peter Brooks interprets Balzac's Paris and literary reality as "both the scene of drama and mask of the true drama lies behind" within "the realm of emotional and spiritual reality."[23] Beijing to Zhang Henshui, like Paris to Balzac, exhibits an (un)masked and emotional reality. Zhang captures the conflicting and competing moments of fleeting urban scenes and social mores and manners that accumulated in the turbulent transitional time in Beijing. I argue that the inherent duality of temporality informs the very narrative form of Zhang's writings. I begin with the notion of curiosity as a way of reading and surviving the city in *Unofficial History of Beijing*. I then consider *Grand Old Family* through the prism of family romance. In the third section, I depart from the implications of tears (*ti* 啼) and laughter (*xiao* 笑) in *Fate in Tears and Laughter* to trace the genealogy of novels of social manners.

---

[21] See Zhang's self-critical essay "Guanyu du xiaoshuo" 關於讀小說 [On reading novels], quote in Hsiao-wei Wang Rupprecht, *Departure and Return: Chang Hen-shui and the Chinese Narrative Tradition* (Hong Kong: Joint Publishing Co., 1987), xxi.

[22] Wang Rupprecht, *Departure and Return*, 2–31.

[23] Peter Brooks, *The Melodramatic Imagination: Balzac, Henry James, Melodrama, and the Mode of Excess* (New Haven, CT: Yale University Press, 1976), 2.

CURIOSITY, NOVELTY, AND THE GHOST HOUSE

Curiosity becomes more than an idle pleasure in spectacle;
it becomes the mode of urban survival.

—BARBARA M. BENEDICT

In early 1924, after reluctantly giving up his original study plan at Peking University, Zhang Henshui was invited by Cheng Shewo 成舍我 (1898–1991), an established newspaperman and Zhang's countryman, whom he met at the Anhui provincial association (*huiguan* 會館), to be the editor of *Yeguang* 夜光 (Moonlight), the literary supplement of *Shijie wanbao* 世界晚報 (World evening news), published by Cheng himself. While working as a journalist and editing articles, Zhang started to write his first fictional work, *Unofficial History of Beijing*, which was serialized from April 12, 1924, to January 24, 1929, in the same literary supplement.[24] An instant success, Zhang's first novel acquired a large audience and provided a main draw for the *World Evening News*.

Consisting of eighty-six chapters, *Unofficial History of Beijing* depicts life in Beijing in the 1920s through the story of Yang Xingyuan 楊杏園, a journalist and classical poet, recently arrived from Anhui province. A navigator of the maze of city streets and alleys and a sensitive poet, Xingyuan falls in love with a delicate courtesan named Liyun 梨雲 (pear-blossom cloud) and subsequently the talented woman poet Li Dongqing 李冬青. Both romantic relationships end tragically: Liyun dies of an intestinal disease, and Dongqing, suffering from an incurable illness since birth, has to reject Xingyuan's marriage proposal and leave Beijing forever. At the end of the novel, exhausted by these two failed romantic liaisons, Xingyuan dies of tuberculosis, spitting blood. *Chunming* 春明 (spring brightness) is the original name of the main gate in the eastern wall of Chang'an 長安, the capital city of the Tang dynasty, and was later adopted to refer to an ancient imperial capital. For the misfortunate sojourner, the ancient capital turns out to be a "soul-slaying" place.[25]

Unofficial History has every pronounced element of the genre of Butterfly sentimental romance. Its main characters are young, talented, virtuous, and delicate; they have sensitive personalities and frail physiques, and are extremely susceptible

---

[24] Hsiao-wei Wang Rupprecht points out that Zhang Henshui was still a writer of traditional sensibility and technique when he wrote *Chunming waishi*. He formulated five guidelines for the composition of chapter headings in this chapter-titled novel: 1) the couplet chapter heading should indicate the climax of the chapter; 2) the language of the couplet should be elegant; 3) the couplet should be antithetically worded; 4) the couplet should end in a syllable with a level tone; 5) there should be the same number of syllables in the couplet chapter headings throughout the novel. See Wang Rupprecht, *Departure and Return*, 14.

[25] For an amazing representation of the meaning of "soul-slaying" and the spirit of the folklore world in old Beijing, see Lao She's short story "*Duanhun qiang*" 斷魂槍 [Soul-slaying spear], in Lao She, *Crescent Moon and Other Stories* (Beijing: Chinese Literature, 1985), 149–164.

to illness and melancholy. And both love stories unfold following the formulaic six stages of the "Romantic Route through Life" that Perry Link charts as a conventional pattern in popular romance of early twentieth-century China: 1) extraordinary inborn gifts; 2) supersensitivity; 3) falling in love; 4) cruel fate; 5) worry and disease; and 6) destruction.[26] When Yang Xingyuan first arrives in Beijing, he chooses to rent a small courtyard house with three rooms as his first residence. Located inside the Anhui provincial association, it is a deserted house everyone shuns. Rumor has it that this is a "ghost house," haunted by the soul and mishaps of the previous tenant. The deceased resident of this "ghost house," also an urban sojourner from Anhui province, attempted to pass the imperial civil service examination but failed three times and finally died of madness.[27] Xingyuan, however, does not mind the ghost story and enjoys the beautiful pear blossoms in the quiet and graceful courtyard.

I understand Zhang Henshui's "ghost house" as a distinctive trope, competing with yet supplementing his contemporary writer Lu Xun's "iron house." In his reflections on Chinese tradition and national rejuvenation, Lu Xun uses the metaphor of an "iron house," which itself is a familial, private, and residential space, to criticize the stifling ethical and cultural status of Chinese society. Frederic Jameson's notion of national allegory might be debatable; however, it rightly notes that Lu Xun's criticism—anchored in the private, familial system—targets society writ large.[28] When examining Lu Xun's early work as representative May Fourth new literature, Leo Ou-fan Lee defines the New Culture Movement as "voices from the iron house."[29] If China can be metaphorically depicted as an "iron house," in which the unenlightened people fall asleep and need to be awakened, the ancient capital Beijing in Zhang Henshui's work turns into a "ghost house" that accommodates fragments of the old and the new and specters of history and memories.

Furthermore, this ghost house constitutes "the realm of emotional and spiritual reality,"[30] a private space for the solitary subjectivity to find tranquility and vitality and cope with unruly, modern, urban life. Eileen Chow observes,

> There is also a temporal disjunction here that is marked by a physical border: Yang has been self-enclosed in this older temporality of the haunted courtyard for the past five years (though we know that he works for a

---

[26] Link, *Mandarin Ducks and Butterflies*, 65–77.

[27] Zhang Henshui, *Chunming waishi* (Taiyuan: Beiyue wenyi chubanshe, 2000, reprint), 1.

[28] Frederic Jameson, "Third-World Literature in the Era of Multinational Capitalism," *Social Text* 15 (Autumn 1986): 65–88.

[29] See Lu Xun, *Diary of a Madman and Other Stories*, trans. William Lyell (Honolulu: University of Hawai'i Press, 1990); and Leo Ou-fan Lee, *Voices from the Iron House: A Study of Lu Xun* (Bloomington: Indiana University Press, 1987).

[30] Brooks, *The Melodramatic Imagination*, 4.

newspaper); at the onset of the novel, we see him traversing these boundaries, into the different temporality of the city that surrounds him. However, within the "older" temporal space, Yang composes classical poetry, dreams (an activity that plays a central narrative and expository role in this novel), and writes to friends.[31]

Indeed, the circular moon gate that leads to Xingyuan's "ghost house" not only separates it spatially from the chaotic outside world but also ensures a disparate cultural form and temporality, a classical world vanishing at the threshold of the modern.

Xingyuan's "ghost house" represents an alternative type of private, familial space that accommodates a new mode of enlightenment subjectivity and sociality in modern Chinese cities. It is the main location where the romance unfolds. It is not merely a daily living compartment inside the Anhui association but also a lyrical, highly stylized space of self-identity. In this enclosed private space, the lyric aspect of Xingyuan's life is foregrounded with sophisticated depictions of his psychology.[32] In the courtyard covered by pear blossoms, which epitomize purity and frailty, Xingyuan treats close friends to tea, composes classical poems, or, occasionally, writes martial arts fiction for entertainment, seeks spiritual serenity, or indulges himself in melancholy. The lyrical subjectivity fostered through the trajectory of classical Chinese heritage unfolds in this interior space. Xingyuan and his fellow urban citizens act as autonomous moral agents, without interventions or injunctions from parental authority in a traditional patriarchal household. "In the great city," Franco Moretti observes, "the heroes of the *bildungsroman* change overnight from 'sons' into 'young men': their affective ties are no longer vertical ones (between successive generations), but horizontal, with the same generation."[33] This change of interpersonal connections from "vertical" to "horizontal" in early twentieth-century Chinese cities signifies the emergence of what Haiyan Lee calls "the enlightenment structure of feeling," which "breaks with the Confucian structure of feeling in staking uncompromising and nonnegotiable claims for individual freedom and autonomy."[34] Xingyuan's mother and relatives live in southern China, and his family ties recede into the background of his life in Beijing. Instead, horizontal "affective ties" dominate in his connections with his friends, lovers, and

---

[31] Eileen Cheng-yin Chow, "Spectacular Novelties 'News' Culture, Zhang Henshui, and Practices of Spectatorship in Republican China" (PhD diss., Stanford University, 2000), 110.

[32] For a study of the narrative speeds, see Zhao Xiaoxuan 趙孝萱, *Zhang Henshui xiaoshuo xinlun* 張恨水小說新論 [New thesis on Zhang Henshui's novels] (Taipei: Xuesheng shuju, 2002), 69.

[33] Franco Moretti, *Atlas of the European Novel, 1800–1900* (London: Verso, 1998), 65.

[34] Haiyan Lee, *Revolution of the Heart: A Genealogy of Love in China, 1900–1950* (Stanford, CA: Stanford University Press, 2007), 95–96.

colleagues of the same generation, for whom romantic sentiment, literature, theater, painting, journalism, finance, law, and politics constitute the essential contents of their daily lives.

Unofficial History is marked by a dual temporality: a tranquil romantic mode of time associated with a lyrical subjectivity, and a journalistic mode that rapidly presents disinterested, timely snapshots of social life. Zhang Henshui regards the Chinese lyrical tradition as a formation accumulated over a long period of time, a *longue durée*, in Fernand Braudel's terms.[35] The lyrical subjectivity fostered through the classical cultural duration is preserved and unfolds in private, intimate spaces such as Yang Xingyuan's courtyard house and Li Dongqing's rented room. Meanwhile, the multifaceted social occurrences take up the fast-paced external temporal spaces. Xingyuan's romantic liaisons are interspersed with volatile outside news that he captures and reports. In passages dealing with social circumstances, the narrative pace and plot development are exceedingly fast, the descriptions of culture and life in Beijing are sketchy, and the characters are portrayed in a relatively caricatured manner.

The sentimental romance is only one narrative thread of the kaleidoscopic and panoramic world of *Unofficial History*. Indeed, neither Yang Xingyuan nor his romance is the main subject of this novel; rather, it is a story of the city, Beijing. In news-style urban snapshots, information, and anecdotes, Beijing narratives constitute the antiromantic counterpart of the romantic thread in the novel. The rich, vast tapestry of urban life is observed and presented through the curious eye of a journalist, the other identity of Yang Xingyuan. A professional newspaper reporter, Xingyuan visits brothels, teahouses, theaters, clubs, schools, province hostels, bathhouses, parties, and exhibitions—any place in Beijing that is conducive to his reporting of news. One time, when he feels reluctant to visit a sleazy, low-class brothel, his friend teases him: "Haven't you said that you should do field work to investigate various kinds of societies in Beijing, including the small teahouse for the rickshaw pullers?"[36] Along with his routine empirical investigations of the ancient capital, he encounters prostitutes, opera singers, housewives, shopkeepers, vendors, teachers, students, poets, bureaucrats, politicians—people of all walks of life, native Beijingers and sojourners. The novel is composed of digressive accounts of Beijing customs, tourist attractions, political scandals, social commentaries, opera reviews, restaurant guides, and so on. Zhang Henshui once talked about his own identity as a journalist and a fiction writer: "I am not a prophet, nor am I a Doctor of Philosophy, so

---

[35] See Fernand Braudel, "History and the Social Sciences: The *Longue Durée*," in *On History*, trans. Sarah Matthews (London: Weidenfeld and Nicolson, 1980); and his preface to *The Mediterranean and the Mediterranean World in the Age of Phillip II*, trans. Sian Reynolds (New York: Harper and Row, 1972–1974).

[36] Zhang, *Chunming waishi*, 4.

I can use the realities of the past to assess the realities of the present, and to extrapolate from here on, to talk about the future."[37] His literary hero in *Unofficial History* observes Beijing's social reality with an objective eye and responds to social injustice in a timely manner.

Driven by journalistic instincts, Xingyuan becomes an avid chaser of news, knowledge, and novelty in town. He shows a great appetite for information, a capacity to analyze the world around him, and an insatiable curiosity. That is how he navigates the city: he gets into trouble from time to time, but he also gets to know the city inside and out, and he survives. In this sense, Xingyuan becomes a modern Robinson Crusoe in the urban jungle, the "ghost house" of Beijing. In her study of curiosity in the early modern period in England, Barbara M. Benedict argues that Robinson Crusoe exemplifies "a cultural ideal of transcendent curiosity,"[38] which conceives the passion of curiosity not as vulgar, transgressive, or monstrous, but as a heroic ambition. She regards Robinson as a curious hero in early modern times: "Robinson's head is always filled 'with rambling Thoughts,' thoughts of rambling that themselves are disorganized . . . . Survival gives them shape."[39] In modern times, curiosity remains a state of mind other than insignificant, random, or idle pleasure that people share in their leisure time—or, sometimes, working time. It serves as the key to modern sensibility. Benedict maintains that curiosity becomes the "mode of urban survival" more than "an idle pleasure in spectacle."[40]

Zhang Henshui's Beijing narratives construct a kind of aesthetics of "curiosity." In the liminal transitional time in Beijing, the term "curiosity" carries controversial implications, including a passionate chase after new things—consumer commodities, new fashion shows, and funky markets, and/or after the opposite, old, and outdated things such as those in curiosity shops, where antiques, historical artifacts, and archaic objects are collected and priced to sell. The mentality of curiosity propels Zhang's protagonists to capture the city with professional journalists' eyes, and to illustrate it with the passion and patience of a painter. Such urban snapshots are defined by their instantaneous and punctual quality. The instantaneity refers to the brief exposure time for the event to be captured by the writer and transcribed into a segment of literary text, as well as the short turnaround time for this text to be published and distributed. The rapidity of snapshot writings also indicates the timeliness and liveness of the represented event. Therefore, the event is measured by its

---

[37] Zhang Henshui, "Weilai de Beijing" 未來的北京 [Beijing in the future], appeared as seven-part series in the Beijing *Shijie ribao* 世界日報 [World daily news] from September 27, 1926 to October 7, 1926.

[38] Barbara M. Benedict, *Curiosity: A Cultural History of Early Modern Inquiry* (Chicago: University of Chicago Press, 2001), 109.

[39] Ibid., 108.

[40] Ibid., 94.

consequences and social impact. The flip side of urgency is forgettability. The serialized chapters in the literary supplement *Moonlight* by Zhang Henshui, who was
himself a journalist, can be viewed as quick and timely responses to Beijing's daily
news and events. Behind the veneer of daily sketches of the city lie a city outsider's
curiosity and a lonely poet's sentimentality. The sketches of these social occurrences,
ranging from political events and social scandals to daily goings-on, are timely,
immediate, and novel, hence perishable. Urban snapshots satisfy curious readers yet
are easily recyclable.

In the transitional formative age when the traditional and the modern meet and
compete, curiosity becomes the way people obtain information, comprehend the
drastically changing world, attain access to illicit political intrigues or celebrity gossip, and handle anxiety and confusion generated by modern existence. Zhang Ailing
famously notes that reality is more dramatic, or even more melodramatic, than any
fictional writings in the urban turbulence of modern China, and that "people feel
curious about what really happened around them."[41] In transitional times, reality
itself increasingly attracts people's attention, which could be more dramatic than
any fictional imaginations. To be curious about the reality in the city where one
lives by reading newspapers, live reports, and pamphlets rather than pure imaginary
works becomes a strategy for surviving calamities and miseries in the transforming
ancient capital in modern times.

Indeed, sharing the discovery of the city through newspapers—especially through
reading Zhang Henshui's phenomenally popular work—was a method of firmly
attaching oneself to the urban milieu. Anecdotes, tabloids—especially those stories
and news about social celebrities—become a focus of the novel. Hence, the serialization of *Unofficial History* resembles a literary version of the daily news and stories
because it reports what actually occurs in real life in 1920s Beijing. It is a literary
index to the historical context, and its fictional characters have counterparts in
reality. For example, Shi Wenyan is the modern romantic poet Xu Zhimo 徐志摩;
Hu Xiaomei is Xu Zhimo's second wife, Lu Xiaoman 陸小曼; Wei Jifeng is the
warlord Cao Kun 曹錕; Zeng Zuwu is the famous genius, literatus, and politician
Yang Du 楊度; Shu Jiucheng is actually Zhang's friend and colleague Cheng Shewo;
Han Youlou is the legendary general Zhang Xueliang 張學良; He Da is the spiritual
leader in the intelligentsia Hu Shi 胡適; Jin Shizhan is the distinguished literatus
and politician Zhang Shizhao 章士釗.[42] In this light, the book becomes one major
composite myth for curious readers, who indulge in activities of uncovering hidden

[41] Zhang, "Tan kanshu," in *Zhang Kan*, 188.
[42] For a more detailed study regarding this issue, see Zhang Wu, *Wo de fuqin Zhang Henshui*; and Zhao, *Zhang Henshui xiaoshuo xinlun*.

secrets and hunting curiosities (*jiemi lieqi* 揭秘獵奇).[43] These readers were local inhabitants who were fond of reading newspaper columns as a way of accessing the concealed corners of the city. At the same time, thanks to the mass dissemination of newspapers, readers in Shanghai, Nanjing, and other cities were able to glimpse the ancient remote city by reading Zhang's stories in installments. Following Zhang's narrative lines, they were now able to see the unseen, know the unknown, and participate in previously esoteric or forbidden topics as a way of virtually living in the city.

Unofficial History feeds the reader's hunger for information and plays "a key role in regulating the way in which questions are asked and the forms curiosity can take in the public arena."[44] The readers of Zhang Henshui's novels are dealers in second-hand information. Like the rising curious man in early modern England defined by Barbara M. Benedict, the audience in early Republican Beijing developed a voracious appetite for urban encyclopedic items. Sometimes their curiosity is not manipulated very well, and these men and women in the city might "spread malice, invent secrets, breed divisiveness by turning public facts into private gossip; they colonize information and reverse the public categories of meaning and insignificance. Parodies or rivals of the moral mediator of information, they embody unregulated curiosity."[45] The unregulated curiosity and uncategorized news, stories, and rumors weave into a social and literary panorama in which true dramas and fabricated stories could happen simultaneously in 1920s Beijing.

In incorporating social news and tabloids, Zhang's urban romance is therefore marked by a prevailing antiromantic color. However, the serialization of *Unofficial History* in newspaper supplements, framed by other newspaper columns, also nourishes a new mode of reading: rather than a contemplative, absorptive repose often associated with the rise of the modern novel, it is characterized by a short attention span, which urban novelty stirs curiosity and encourages distractions. This new reading experience defines an audience by its thirst for information and knowledge. It is shaped by and in turn shapes a new mode of writing, the timely, instantaneous urban snapshot, fertilized by the booming periodicals in Republican Beijing. Eileen Chow stresses the crucial connection between newspaper supplementary pages (*fukan* 副刊) and Zhang Henshui's installment writings. She observes,

> *Chunming waishi* is often filled with . . . digressive discussions about the merits of this or that custom or habit, and at times corresponding with news items and other issues covered in the various editorials and articles in the "Moonlight"

[43] Zhao, *Zhang Henshui xiaoshuo xinlun*, 76–77.

[44] Benedict, *Curiosity*, 98.

[45] Ibid., 103.

page. Could one argue that these digressions, in fact, constitute the very form of the novel, and that the pastiche quality of the novel is part and parcel of the experience of reading the *fukan*? You read a little fiction, you read a little classical poetry; then there is the main commentary of the day, usually on contemporary affairs or national politics; then a section on Beijing's theatres, restaurants, popular haunts; usually a comical, anecdotal piece, or letters from readers debating a fashion trend, etc. Finally, there are the occasionally pieces of regional dialects or customs—also very present in the novel. So essentially all the various sub-genres that are present in *Chunming* are also present in the *fukan*, and so the reading of the novel becomes pedagogically oriented readings of the newspaper, and vice versa.[46]

Indeed, *Unofficial History* absorbs such diverse journalistic writings into its novelistic narrative that it is often hard to distinguish between the fictional and the factual. It produces a series of fragmented, patched urban snapshots, forming a panorama that spins like a kaleidoscope. Thus Zhang catalogues the private life and the public affairs of the city. However, this endeavor does not aim at creating a closed, complete system of knowledge. Rather, it is random, digressive, and eclectic. This unsystematic, sometimes contradictory mapping of the chaotic urban life of 1920s Beijing speaks to the very nature of modern urbanism and the precise way of experiencing and surviving the city. Reflecting on modern urban experiences in 1930s Europe, Walter Benjamin argues, "The greater the shock factor in particular impressions, the more vigilant consciousness has to be in screening stimuli; the more efficiently it does so, the less these impressions enter long experience [*Erfahrung*] and the more they correspond to the concept of isolated experience [*Erlebnis*]."[47] In Zhang Henshui's narrative snapshots, the city is presented with pieces of *Erlebnis* that will never be integrated into a coherent totality organized according to any single taxonomy. In this sense, the more the novel offers an encyclopedic knowledge of Beijing, the greater the satisfaction for readers yearning to comprehend the city. Or paradoxically, the more intricate and specific the details offered, the harder it is for readers to acquire a total view, to access the heart of darkness of the city.

Zhang portrays Beijing in a way that brings together a scattered but panoramic view, reminiscent of the famous Song dynasty painting *Qingming shanghe tu* (Going on the river at the Qingming Festival), one of the most well-known hand-scrolls in Chinese art history. Jerome Silbergeld interprets it as a representation

---

[46] Chow, "Serial Sightings," 70.

[47] Marcus Bullock and Michael W. Jennings, eds., *Walter Benjamin: Selected Writings*, vol. 1, *1913–1926* (Cambridge, MA: Harvard University Press, 1996), 319.

of the capital city of the northern Song dynasty, Kaifeng, on the verge of the onslaught by the Jurched Tartars.[48] Valerie Hansen proposes that the handscroll portrays "an idealized city" with buildings and urban features present in any twelfth-century city; and the painter Zhang Zeduan aimed at creating an ideal cityscape, not necessarily that of Kaifeng. For that purpose, Hansen argues, Zhang Zeduan "deliberately left out all identifying marks."[49] In this way, the *Qingming* scroll foresees the Italian writer Italo Calvino's fictional construction of an ideal city. In *Invisible Cities*, the character Marco Polo conceives of any city not on its own terms but in terms of its relationship to his native Venice. He breaks Venice's landmarks and defining qualities into pieces and uses them to imagine all cities: "Each time I describe a city I am saying something about Venice."[50] The ideal city is only visible in the re-collection of all invisible cities.

Zhang Henshui's Beijing narrative is imbricated with journalistic observations and sentimental stories, constructing a kind of "unofficial history" (*waishi* 外史) of modern Beijing. In the tradition of vernacular Chinese literature, Wu Jingzi's 吳敬梓 (1701–1754) *Rulin waishi* 儒林外史 (*The Scholars*), written in the Qing dynasty, is a key work creating an unofficial history of the scholarly world. In T. A. Hsia's discussion of Zhang Henshui, quoted above, he argues that Zhang surpasses Wu Jingzi in terms of narrative strategies and artistic merit. Addressing the tradition of "unofficial history," Wei Shang, in his study of Wu Jingzi's *The Scholars*, maintains that "*waishi* signals its generic category as a vernacular novel,"[51] and raises the following questions: "Is *waishi* meant to encompass what is excluded from the *zhengshi* or to revise what they include? Does it suggest a narrative undertaken from a peripheral perspective and thus refusing to confirm the central narrative of the *zhengshi*?"[52] Interestingly, whereas *waishi* claims to be a fictional, imaginative work, it actually defines its narrative legitimacy in relation to *zhengshi* 正史, an official history that is marked by authority, authenticity, and factuality. *Waishi* might supplement, question, or even repudiate *zhengshi*; however, no matter what, it must not be official history; otherwise it would lose its raison d'être as fiction. *Waishi* is thus a literary category that walks the fine line between fiction and history.

In a broad sense, works of *waishi* include historical fictions and social novels in late imperial and early modern times. Zhang Ailing, a passionate reader of Zhang

---

[48] See Jerome Silbergeld, *China into Film: Frames of Reference in Contemporary Chinese Cinema* (London: Reaktion Books, 1999), 129–130.

[49] Valerie Hansen, "The Mystery of the Qingming Scroll and Its Subject: The Case Against Kaifeng," *The Journal of Sung-Yuan Studies* 26 (1996): 184.

[50] Calvino, *Invisible Cities*, 86.

[51] Shang Wei, *Rulin waishi and Cultural Transformation in Late Imperial China* (Cambridge, MA: Harvard University Press, 2003), 122.

[52] Shang, *Rulin waishi and Cultural Transformation in Late Imperial China*, 124.

Henshui, uses the English term "novels of manners" to refer to 1920s social novels. In justifying her propensity for such works, Zhang writes, "Occasionally one can find some details of life that cannot be found in formal histories and biographies. They capture and trigger the reader's imagination, enabling the reader to come into touch with the texture of another age."[53] What she appreciates is this genre's capacity to offer not what formal history forbids or excludes but what it would not care to include, that is, the trivial details that enable the reader to imagine what life might have been like in a past age. In this regard, fictional accounts might be more reliable than historical records in rendering an original, genuine flavor of life.

In addition to such a capability to preserve life's true flavor, Zhang Henshui's *Unofficial History* reveals further significant implications of the notion of "unofficial history." "Unofficial," or "periphery," indicates a space outside of the mainstream, official narratives, historical or fictional. Zhang's novels are precisely located beyond the prevalent orthodox May Fourth new literary discourse. "Unofficial history" never makes a grand narrative. It takes on a supplementary or contradictory position vis-à-vis the linear, teleological form of history as revolution, modernization, and national salvation. Replete with minor details, incongruous information, and even contradictions, the novel adds "popular" or "vernacular" features to the fundamental constitution of modern Beijing. In this way, *Unofficial History* creates an unofficial history in a time without official history.

Moreover, *waishi* also signifies the narrative position taken by Zhang Henshui, who observes and illustrates the city both as an urban sojourner from the provinces and as an objective, impartial journalist. However, the work from the outside, on the margin, of the city, is in effect accepted and consumed as being from the inside (*nei* 內). Achieving massive popularity, Zhang's work is regarded as providing authentic, indigenous information regarding Beijing. Indeed, Zhang Henshui, like his fictional character Yang Xingyuan in *Unofficial History*, was invited by leading official presses and tourist enterprises to offer insider accounts of the city. He even worked with other renowned, authoritative Beijing experts, the so-called *lao Beijing* (Old Beijing inhabitants) and *Beijing tong* (Beijing experts), such as Ma Zhixiang 馬芷庠 and Qi Rushan, to account for and classify local social and cultural customs and manners of Beijing. In this way, the outsider turns into the insider with authority and resources. Like his protagonist, Zhang Henshui is both a Beijing sojourner and a Beijing expert, both a tourist and a city guide, who presents an ethnographical introduction of the city and its cultural spaces and a personal and

---

[53] Quoted from Tze-lan Sang, "Romancing Rhetoricity and Historicity: The Representational Politics and Poetics of *Little Reunion*," in *Eileen Chang: Romancing Languages, Cultures, and Genres*, ed. Kam Louie (Hong Kong: Hong Kong University Press, 2012), 208.

an affective account of a changing Beijing. Some readers would indeed take Zhang's "unofficial history" as "official history" to guide their visits or even their lives in the capital, to find ways to survive daily stresses and strains in an unsettling time of transition.

Unofficial History constitutes a literary mapping of 1920s Beijing, creating a literary panorama that is explicit and random, romantic and antiromantic. Yang Xingyuan, an early modern man of sentiments and of curiosity, observes the city from both a subjective and a professional journalist's perspective. As both a classical Chinese lyricist and a modern flâneur, Xingyuan best represents the transitional, formative age of modern Beijing. His sentimental romances and urban experiences are marked by the immense weight of history, in the sense of official, unofficial, and personal histories in his "ghost house" and the transformation of Beijing on the threshold between traditional and modern. The historical spectrality embodies not only the vanishing lyric tradition of talented youth and beauty but also the emergent modern city life. Whereas the protagonist Jiusi yisheng 九死一生 (A man with nine lives) in Wu Jianren's 吳趼人 (1866–1910) *Ershinian mudu zhi guai xianzhuang* 二十年 目睹之怪現狀 (Strange things observed over the past twenty years, 1903–1910) suffers from but eventually survives specters and spectacles in late Qing Shanghai, Yang Xingyuan is by no means a survivor in a modern urban milieu. In the chaotic Beijing of the 1920s, he is not the type of May Fourth enlightenment hero who is able to hold open the "gate of darkness" for the nation and its people, as Lu Xun anticipates at the advent of modernity.[54] At best, he is a petty soldier wandering in the old yet new capital. Exhausted mentally and physically, this romantic and curious hero is haunted by shattered romances and existential anxieties, and ultimately collapsing and dying in a transitional urban milieu.

THE CITY AND ITS FAMILY ROMANCE

Romance is a journey toward a supreme trial, after which home is possible, or else homelessness will suffice.
—HAROLD BLOOM

Bertolt Brecht once noted that Honoré de Balzac "writes gigantic genealogies," in which "families are organisms, individuals grow within them."[55] In the second half of the nineteenth century, when the organic type of bourgeois family started to

---

[54] See T. A. Hsia's pioneering analysis, *The Gate of Darkness: Studies on the Leftist Literary Movement in China* (Seattle: University of Washington Press, 1968).

[55] Quoted in Patrizia Lombardo, *Cities, Words and Images: From Poe to Scorsese* (New York: Palgrave Macmillan, 2003), 64.

collapse, Brecht believes, montage rather than Balzacian realism was a more adequate technique to assemble fragmented social, ethical, or human imageries and
respond to the familial and cultural crisis in late capitalism. In 1920s China, when
Zhang Henshui presented his gigantic genealogy of families, it was the moment
when the Confucian family as an organism went through a crisis and was gradually
replaced by the antagonist bourgeois nuclear form of family. In *Grand Old Family*,
Zhang portrays the decline of the distinguished Jin family in Beijing, a city changing from an imperial capital into a Republican city. Headed by Jin Quan 金銓, the
prime minister of Republican China, this grand old Chinese family is not an affirm-
ative organism where free, modern individuals are shaped. The final disintegration
of the Jin family into multiple nuclear families, however, does not provide the ideal
solution for colliding ethical and affective values in a transitional age. Confronted
with the Jins' ethical decay and the equally hypocritical and petty bourgeois way of
life emerging in modern cities, the author has to resort to Buddhist sutras for a temporary spiritual refuge.

A magnum opus in Zhang Henshui's literary career, *Grand Old Family* was originally serialized from 1926 to 1932 in *Mingzhu* 明珠 (Bright pearl), the literary supplement of the *World Daily News*. After a major revision by the author, it was later
published as a monograph. With its publication, *Grand Old Family* immediately
became a commercial hit and even surpassed the popularity of *Unofficial History of
Beijing*. Zhang explained that "the stories are so relaxed, so bustling, and so sentimental as to make the classes of urbanites feel intimate and tasteful."[56] Zhang Youhe
張友鶴 (1907–1971), Zhang Henshui's colleague and bosom friend, also stressed
the novel's sentimentality and entertainment value. Depicting dozens of women
characters and exploring their aspirations and frustrations in a society newly blessed
with modernity, the novel appealed especially to Republican women readers. From
Unofficial History to *Grand Old Family*, Zhang Henshui's literary journey not only
zooms in from a tale of the city to that of a family but also shifts from an unofficial
history (*waishi*) to a form of official history, namely, the history of a grand family (*shijia* 世家). Accordingly, the urban hero who navigates modern Beijing turns
from the modern journalist/classical poet (Yang Xingyuan) into the dandy/flâneur
(Jin Yanxi). Yang Xingyuan's ghost house in the Anhui province association turns
into the majestic Jin family mansion and its filmic projection by means of "shadow
magic," the arising modern medium of motion pictures.

In *Grand Old Family*, Zhang made Beijing a site of tragic comedy and considered to what extent and under what conditions a city legend can be structured as

---

56 Zhang, *Xiezuo shengya huiyi*, 41.

a "family romance," even though not a perfect one. For Sigmund Freud, "family romance" is a conscious fantasy in which the child dreams of "getting free from the parents of whom he now has such a low opinion and of replacing them by others, occupying, as a rule, a higher social station."[57] The family romance may thus be considered a crucial stage in development when someone attempts to doubt and escape the supreme authority of the parents and seeks his or her own position in the generational transition. In her seminal work, *The Family Romance of the French Revolution*, Lynn Hunt uses the notion of family romance broadly and considers how the narratives of the family order structured the collective political unconscious during the French Revolution. Following Hunt, Aihwa Ong applies the construct of family romances to her investigation of how familial images become an integral component of state policies and political imaginaries in Asian societies.[58] In my discussion of Zhang Henshui's family romance, I use the notion in a broad sense to examine the prevalent type of "family novels" in modern Chinese literature that deals with tensions, desires, loves, conflicts, illusions, and disillusionments between father and son. Given the essential position of the Confucian family system in traditional Chinese culture, a break with the family and its underlying ethics was the central goal of the May Fourth New Culture Movement. From Lu Xun's "Kuangren riji" 狂人日記 (A madman's diary) to Ba Jin's *Family*, from Bai Wei's 白薇 (1894–1987) *Dachu youlingta* 打出幽靈塔 (Fight out of the Ghost Tower, 1928) to Cao Yu's 曹禺 (1910–1996) *Beijing ren* 北京人 (Peking Man, 1940), the cannibalistic, patriarchal traditional family has been the main site onto which various literary and national imaginations have been projected. The modern nation was to be established on a clean ground deprived of "the Confucian family shop" (*kong jia dian* 孔家店).[59] As the oppressive patriarch was to be replaced by an enlightened father, the absolute power of a monarch replaced by the government of a republic, the literary imaginations of modern China were organized around a family romance quest.

Zhang Henshui's family romance responds to the crisis of a Confucian family caught in the maelstrom of modernization and conceives the changing imperial city as a grand old family at large. When composing *Grand Old Family*, Zhang places his literary imagination under the historiographical category of "hereditary houses" (*shijia* 世家), which bespeaks the essential relation among the individual, the family, and the state in Confucian ethics. In portraying the city through the

[57] Sigmund Freud, "Family Romance," in *The Freud Reader*, ed. Peter Guy (New York: Norton, 1989), 297–300.

[58] See Lynn Hunt, *The Family Romance of the French Revolution* (Berkeley: University of California Press, 1993); and Aihwa Ong, *Flexible Citizenship: The Cultural Logics of Transnationality* (Durham, NC: Duke University Press, 1999), esp. chap. 5.

[59] Hu Shi's phrase, see Tse-Tsung Chow, *The May Fourth Movement: Intellectual Revolution in Modern China* (Cambridge, MA: Harvard University Press, 1960), 307.

lens of family history, the novel foregrounds the intricate connection between family romance and political morality, or, using Lynn Hunt's words, between "private sentiments and public politics."[60] "Hereditary houses" denote an old and distinguished family that has held high official positions for generations. It is one of the essential categories in the paradigm of historiography created by the great historian Sima Qian 司馬遷 (145–186 B.C.). As is well known, Sima Qian established a historiography based on annals-biographical accounts of human lives (*jizhuan ti* 紀傳體), instead of the annals-chronicle style (*biannian ti* 編年體) that dominated the composition of official imperial histories. When clarifying different categories in his historiographical construction, Sima Qian made the following distinctions: *benji* 本紀 (basic annals) referred to the imperial biographies of the kings from the Three Dynasties through the Han, and *liezhuan* 列傳 (arrayed biographies) was conceived for ordinary people who achieved extraordinary merit. Under the category of *shijia*, he classified biographies of notable feudal lords, aristocracy, and ministers, mostly from the Spring and Autumn and the Warring States periods, including the eminent scholar Confucius.[61] Sima Qian started his work *Shiji* 史記 (Records of the grand historian) as a private narrative of historiography, which, according to Andrew Plaks, later stimulated the emergence of fiction in Chinese tradition.[62] Tracing records of hereditary houses in Beijing, *Grand Old Family* provides an account of the city from within *zhengshi* (the official history), and differs from *Unofficial History of Beijing*, which adopts the unofficial, external viewpoint to challenge a grand narrative of the city and the nation and straddles the border between fictional and historical accounts of the city.

Depicting the decline of the prestigious Jin family in a changing Beijing, *Grand Old Family* is often viewed as a modern version of the Qing classic, Cao Xueqin's *The Story of the Stone* (also known by the title of *The Dream of the Red Chamber*). Zhang Henshui's family romance unfolds around the romance between Leng Qingqiu 冷清秋, "a modernized Lin Daiyu" from a traditional middle-class family, and Jin Yanxi, who is a "Jia Baoyu in Western suit" and the youngest son of Prime Minister Jin.[63] In the 1920s, the demise of the Confucian family and the ascendancy of the nuclear bourgeois family had profound implications in literature. Both May Fourth new literature and Butterfly school popular culture use family as a social and cultural

---

[60] Hunt, *The Family Romance of the French Revolution*, 4.

[61] For a study of traditional Chinese historiography, see On Cho Ng and Q. Edward Wang, *Mirroring the Past: The Writing and Use of History in Imperial China* (Honolulu: University of Hawai'i Press, 2005).

[62] Andrew Plaks, "Toward a Critical Theory of Chinese Narrative," in *Chinese Narrative: Critical and Theoretical Essays*, ed. Andrew Plaks (Princeton, NJ: Princeton University Press, 1977), 309–352.

[63] Zhang and Wei, *Zhang Henshui yanjiu ziliao*, 308.

institution to reflect on the changing social and cultural values in modern China. Whereas May Fourth literature revolts vehemently against the traditional family system, *Grand Old Family* explores the desires, strictures, and aspirations in a family of the transitional age that seeks to reconcile the old and the new values and customs.

Jin Quan, the liberal prime minister in Republican Beijing and the sole authority of the family, is presented as an ideal patriarch. Having studied in Europe, he is an enlightened head of a grand family, an ideal father, and a supporter and practitioner of both Confucian ethics and selected modern Western ideas. He creates a meaningful alliance between traditional values and modern Western knowledge, which manifests in the family's eclectic attitude toward tradition and modernity, an attitude characterized as half-new and half-old. When she spent her first lunar New Year in the Jin house, Leng Qingqiu was struck by the peculiar way of celebration:

> Talking about being new, their family's very new; talking about being old, it's very old. They celebrate the lunar New Year by paying respects to ancestors, but at the same time they've taken on the Europeanized superstition in regarding black as an inauspicious color; should there be a grand gathering, black clothes mustn't be worn.[64]

When meeting his youngest daughter-in-law, Qingqiu, for the first time, Jin Quan is very satisfied with the girl because "he is mostly fond of people who can mix the new and the old in harmony," and Qingqiu is exactly the type.[65] The Jin family precisely embodies the characteristic of Beijing, which harbors the new and the old, and accepts the traditional rituals and ethics while being open to Westernized manners.

As an eclectic who appreciates a harmonious balance of the traditional and the modern, Jin Quan differs sharply from Jia Zheng 賈政, head of the Jia family in *The Story of the Stone* and a tyrant apologist of orthodox Confucian ethics. Master Gao 高老太爺 in Ba Jin's *Family*, another contemporary popular family novel, stands for a modern version of Jia Zheng. Critiquing the oppressive nature of the traditional hierarchical family, Ba Jin's novel dramatizes the irreconcilable confrontation between the generations of the conservative father and the rebellious son, and it embodies the radical May Fourth iconoclastic mentality. Enlightened by modern values, the rebel sons in the Gao family have to fight against the restrictions of traditional ethics, practiced by the father, to pursue free love and individual independence. Zhang Henshui's *Grand Old Family*, however, writes the May Fourth family romance against the grain. The relationships among family members are portrayed in

---

[64] Zhang, *Jinfen shijia*, 506. I am using Xiaowei Wang Rupprecht's translation; see her *Departure and Return*, 61.
[65] Zhang, *Jinfen shijia*, 464.

a harmonious manner. Jin Quan maintains the basic Confucian ethical relationships in the family, but meanwhile embraces notions of individual freedom and the right for equality. Whereas Master Gao in Ba Jin's novel treats family servants as slaves, Jin Quan announces that servants are equal human beings and even invites the maids to sit together at the dinner table at his son's birthday gathering. Whereas his fellow May Fourth writers organize family conflicts around the quest for free love and individual choice, Zhang Henshui portrays a father who supports monogamy and a loving marriage for all his children. When Yanxi falls in love with Qingqiu, a girl from a social class lower than the Jins, Jin Quan approves this relationship willingly, for he appreciates Qingqiu's artistic talent and placid disposition. Whereas the son's rebellion against the patriarchal feudal family is often epitomized by the final destruction of a multigenerational family clan into numerous modern nuclear families, Madame Jin initiates the division of the family and distributes the family inheritance equally among all the children—both male and female descendants.

Despite its relatively liberal and enlightened attitude toward the new and the foreign, the Jin household is by no means depicted as the ideal family. The efforts to comply with both the old and the new are not always successful. When the Jins strive to embrace Western values and manners to show that they are modern and civilized, they also adhere to the traditional Chinese order underlying the family's distinguished history over eight generations. The narrator often mocks the hypocrisy of the family philosophy of patching old and new so as to present the flimsy façade of a harmonic unity. A salient example is the argument among the sons and daughters about the format of the funeral ceremony for Jin Quan. Between a traditional Chinese extravagant funeral procession and a modern, simplified style, the Jin family members, especially Jin Fengchu, Jin Quan's eldest son, are on the horns of a dilemma:

> If the rites of the civilized Occident had been adopted, a limousine would have been used to tow the coffin and, at most, the officer in command of the infantry would have been asked to assign two platoons of soldiers to march. But regrettably, there was no precedent for the burial of a premier in Beijing. Further, friends and relatives all reckoned that the Jin family would definitely make a pompous show out of the procession. If it had been carried out in a simpler manner, a few civilized individuals would have understood it as civilized conduct, but eight or nine out of ten would surely have said that the Jins could not have spent money: as soon as the head of the family had passed away, it had turned so poor that it could not have financed a grand funeral procession—this would have greatly affected the honor. After such considerations, he talked it over with Mrs. Jin: except for superstitious paper-made sacrificial articles and those feudal insignia form the former Qing dynasty, many

lama and monk groups, Chinese and Western bands, units of the armed forces would be accepted, so as to avoid others' gossip that money was a problem. Although Mrs. Jin was very civilized, she agreed fully that honor had to be preserved. Accepting Fengchu's words, she let him go ahead with the plan.[66]

The sudden death of Jin Quan, the ideal father, triggers the final disintegration of the grand old family. The veil of the family romance is stripped away. With no son competent enough to continue the family legacy and secure wealth, power, and prosperity, the Jin family is soon on the verge of collapse.

In the novel's interlude, the narrator, in a journalistic and storytelling tone, informs the reader that he will tell a tragic story about Leng Qingqiu, a poet, calligrapher, and now single mother. The romance between Qingqiu and Yanxi, the pampered youngest son of Jin Quan, unfolds alongside the prosperity and demise of the Jin family. Together, the individual love story and the family history are woven into the tapestry of a transformative modern Beijing. By describing the desires and agonies of the younger generation as represented by Yanxi and Qingqiu, the author reflects on the texture of life in a city lingering between its glorious imperial history and the dawn of the modern age. Yanxi is a subtle mixture of an aimless flâneur, a supercilious dandy, and finally a modest actor after surviving a dreadful family tragedy when his wife and son disappear after a mythical fire that causes the final collapse of the Jin family. In his analysis of Charles Baudelaire's work in mid-nineteenth century Paris, Walter Benjamin defines "flâneur" as a heroic pedestrian in the crowds. Addressing *flânerie* in European novels, particularly in early Weimar texts, Anke Gleber argues that "the flâneur appears in various forms, often in relation to other figures of modernity, such as the collector, the historian, or the spectator. As a city stroller, the flâneur is at once a dreamer, a historian, and a modern artist, someone who transforms his observations into texts and images."[67] Yanxi in Zhang Henshui's *Grand Old Family* is by no means a modernist hero or artist. He is also different from those cosmopolitan urban characters in works by the Shanghai "Neo-sensationalists," such as Shi Zhecun 施蟄存 (1905–2003), Mu Shiying 穆時英 (1912–1940), Liu Naou 劉吶鷗 (1905–1940), and Shao Xunmei 邵洵美 (1906–1968). Yanxi is, at best, a refined but amorous ambler in the city, a man of fashion. "With his drifting and shifting, deliberately nonjudgmental and noncalculatory existence,"[68] he becomes superfluous.

---

[66] Zhang, *Jinfen shijia*, 761; see Wang Rupprecht, *Departure and Return*, 61–62. I slightly changed her English translation.

[67] Anke Gleber, *The Art of Taking a Walk: Flanerie, Literature, and Film in Weimar Culture* (Princeton, NJ: Princeton University Press, 1999), viii.

[68] Gleber, *The Art of Taking a Walk*, 26.

This superfluous man, in the chapter-titled best-seller and in the vein of the popular narrative, is diametrically opposed to the type of "superfluous man" in May Fourth new literature, epitomized by the melancholic and schizophrenic protagonist in Yu Dafu's 郁達夫 (1896–1945) short story "Chenlun" 沈淪 (Sinking). An overseas young Chinese student in Japan, Yu's protagonist is tortured by psychological and sexual frustrations that are intricately related to a nationalist sentiment.

Yanxi's aimless wandering and his life of leisure point to a lack of particular purpose—whether national, patriotic, or political. Although born into a prestigious patrilineal family, he has no particular propensity for or training in classical literature and learning. Although enjoying the comforts and conveniences of modern city life, he has no interest in modern science, culture, or politics. Safely backed by his family's fortune, he does not have any profession or useful social connections. A superficial carefree dandy, Yanxi is never short of money, time, or the freedom to pursue his adventures in the city. Wandering aimlessly in dance halls, cafeterias, theaters, teahouses, and labyrinthine alleyways, he always projects his gaze onto beautiful ladies. However, deep in his mind, Yanxi is searching for peace that could help him at least partly escape the anxiety and confusion of the modern urban milieu, which are greatly aggravated after the grand old family falls apart. Qingqiu, a modern schoolgirl with fine classical training, provides him with a temporary spiritual anchor in the hustle and bustle of modern city life.

Leng Qingqiu is reminiscent of Li Dongqing or Yang Xingyuan in Zhang's first Beijing narrative, *Unofficial History*. A classical lyricist, Qingqiu is also an "old soul" walking in the modern world, seeking happiness and spiritual consolation in poetry and Buddhist sutras. The enclosed enclaves or historical sites in the city and within the Jin mansion constitute nurturing spaces for her to rejuvenate her mind and attain a sense of independence: the small house in the hidden historical alley where she grows up, the attic in the garden of the Jin mansion where she retreats, the secluded street at the margin of the city where she sells her calligraphy to make a living after fleeing from the grand old family in the fire, and even the movie theater, where she bursts into tears when she watches her ex-husband performing their family tragedy on the silver screen.

After she falls in love with Yanxi, Qingqiu believes that she might find happiness in his distinguished grand family. In response to their different social backgrounds and family upbringings, Yanxi claims that "with regard to love, there is no gap of poverty and wealth.... As long as I love you and you love me, our marriage is legitimate."[69] Shortly after their marriage, Qingqiu realizes that Yanxi is just a spoiled

---

[69] Zhang, *Jinfen shijia*, 72.

playboy spending his family fortune chasing girls. She lacks the inclination for social occasions in the Jin house, including numerous mahjong parties. Disappointed, she locks herself in the attic and immerses herself in poetry and Buddhist classics. This is arguably a Chinese version of the "madwoman in the attic." However, in Zhang Henshui's treatment, Qingqiu does not go crazy or lose her sense and sensibility. Fully aware of her position in the prison of the hierarchical family, she chooses to shut the door and stay in her enclosed, inner boudoir. In Zhang Ailing's novel *Shiba chun* 十八春 (Eighteen springs, 1950) and its revised edition *Bansheng yuan* 半生緣 (Half a lifelong romance, 1969), the female protagonist Gu Manzhen 顧曼楨 was locked in the attic after being raped by her brother-in-law; yet unlike Zhang Ailing's tragic heroine, Qingqiu creates a female space of serenity to suit her poetic self within the labyrinth-like grand old family. Such a withdrawal inside the patriarchal family also differs from the radical, romantic gesture of breaking away to achieve spiritual freedom, which was upheld by most of Zhang's contemporary May Fourth intellectuals. This does not suggest that Zhang Henshui is a cultural conservative in the new age. A strong advocate of women's rights, he adheres to the premise of the women's emancipation project. However, he never envisions in extreme rebellions or revolution the ideal solution and individual fulfillment for Chinese women. He deals with the social conditions and problems that Chinese young women confronted in big cities in a more realistic manner. In his well-known speech at Beijing Women's Normal College, "Nala zouhou zenyang" 娜拉走後怎樣 (What happens after Nora leaves home, 1923), Lu Xun raises the question about Nora's future after she leaves home at the end of Henrick Ibsen's play, *A Doll's House*. Lu Xun cautions that there are two possible options for China's would-be-Noras, prostitution or returning home, in order to survive. Based on his own journalist experiences, he sees more possibilities for modern women at the transitional age to achieve financial independence. Disillusioned with her marriage life, Qingqiu manages to escape from the doll's house with her son during the unexpected fire, and lives on her own as a calligrapher and teacher.

The mysterious fire becomes the final straw that breaks up the prestigious grand family. It is a moment of both disenchantment and hope. It can be read as a form of punishment for Yanxi's infidelity but also as a form of illumination for Qingqiu that liberates her from the marriage and wins her the opportunity to stay independent. Yanxi leaves Beijing for Germany with one of his elder sisters. Years later, he returns to Beijing as a modest actor in the emerging film industry. Ironically, it is through film, the best medium for melodrama, that Yanxi obtains a narrative voice for his cinematic fabrication of his life story. With regard to the true nature of melodrama, Peter Brooks states, "Melodrama at heart represents the theatrical impulse itself: the impulse toward dramatization, heightening, expression, acting out."[70] No wonder Yanxi grasps the "theatrical impulse," and thus figures out an unsurpassable way to dramatize, heighten, express, and act out his family tragedy. His performance of the fire scene is worth particular attention. In his film *Huodun* 火遁 (The fire escape), the wife is portrayed as an unpleasant and jealous woman who sets fire to the house. Holding her one-year-old baby, she jumps into the fire and is burned to death. The husband is so shocked that he eventually goes mad, suffering from pyrophobia. Whenever he catches sight of flames, he will jump to put out the fire. When he is dying in the film, he keeps shouting, "Help, help, there are a woman and a boy in the fire!" (臨死的時候，口裡還喊著，火里有個女人，有個孩子，救哇救哇！)[71]

In this story within a story, Zhang Henshui subtly combines the modern experience of watching a film and the traditional storytelling of love and desire. This is a melodramatic rewriting of Lu Xun's famous slogan "*jiujiu haizi*" 救救孩子 (save the children). However, in Zhang's text, the public plea is transformed into a personal call to "save my child" and "save my woman." By creating his own fire scene on the big screen, Yanxi conveys his explanation of the marriage between a modern dandy and a traditional female lyricist. By means of the modern medium of motion pictures, a private story becomes a public image. The city and the family, the swirling vortex of modern urban experiences and the traumatic memories of the destruction of a family, are entangled and imbricated in the melodramatic cinematic exhibition for contemporary consumers, including Qingqiu.[72]

Yanxi's phantasmagoric cityscape is juxtaposed with the transcendental view of the city and human life held by his mother, Madame Jin. For this Buddhist advocate, the glorious family history and the splendid past of the imperial city are nothing but empty shadows that reflect a negative enchantment. On top the Western Hills of the city, Madame Jin contemplates the disintegration of the Jin family after Jin Quan's death:

Let's take a look at Beijing; it is besieged in the sunset smoke, foggy and misty; around the city dark shadows accumulate level by level. The tower of *Beihai* and the arrow tower of Zhengyang Gate stretch out into two black tips above the level of

---

[70] Peter Brooks, *The Melodramatic Imagination: Balzac, Henry James, Melodrama, and the Mode of Excess* (New Haven, CT: Yale University Press, 1976), xi.

[71] Zhang, *Jinfen shijia*, 1049.

[72] The scream from the role that Yanxi played in his film can be reminiscent of Henshui's novel *Pinghu tongche* 平滬通車 (Shanghai express), which was serialized for a complete year in the Shanghai magazine *Lüxing zazhi* 旅行雜誌 (Travel magazine) in 1935. A wealthy banker, Hu Zi'an encountered a beautiful young woman and lost his money and fame in the Express from Beijing to Shanghai because, according to Hu's yell, "she is a con artist and a thief." Zhang Henshui, *Shanghai Express: A Thirties Novel*, trans. William A. Lyell (Honolulu: University of Hawai'i Press, 1997), 237. But Hu would regard every attractive lady as a thief, and

the dark circle. Madame Jin turns back her head and says to the second wife: "See, the murky dark shadow *is* the city. We hang out there for dozens of years. But now we glance at it from the top of the hill, the capital is just like the small ant kingdom where they invoke a future husband for the ant princess. Alas, life is a dream."

看看北京城，在夕陽煙裡籠罩著，霧沈沈的，一圈圈黑影子。北海的塔，正陽門的城樓，在一圈黑影中，透出兩個黑尖。金太太回頭對二姨太道："你看，那烏煙瘴氣的一圈黑影子，就是北京城，我們在那裡混了幾十年了。現時在山上看起來，那裡和書上說的在螞蟻國招駙馬，有甚麼分別？哎！人生真是一場夢。"[73]

Prosperity and decline—familial, dynastic, or national—are merely dark shadows in the tiny ant kingdom. Madame Jin takes an aerial viewpoint from the top of Western Hills, and "up there one is a voyeur, a nonparticipant."[74] Having survived the collapse of the imperial capital and her disintegrated family, she is able to view the city and its past "in a thoroughly objectifying" way, which creates a visual metaphor for a Buddha-like, omniscient yet human position. Such a stance is utterly different from the aesthetic observations of the city by writers such as Lin Yutang and Lin Huiyin. At this disenchanted moment, Beijing is transformed into an abstract object, an allegory in the Buddhist scriptures and an opaque image that mirrors the emptiness of secular human life. The city eventually evaporates in the dust of history and memory.

In his accounts of the city and the family, Zhang reveals the inevitable degeneration of the Confucian grand family, an institution that the May Fourth intellectuals accused of being cannibalistic and that they declared should be smashed mercilessly. However, unlike his radical antitraditionalist fellow writers, Zhang expresses a profound lament about the organic, harmonious moments of traditional households. Whereas he spells out the advantages of the modern nuclear family, which facilitates the ultimate independence of the young generation, he also is well aware of the deceits and hypocrisy of the emerging bourgeois family ethics. In his recasting of family romance in the early modern era in China, Zhang carves out an independent space for his protagonists pursuing individual autonomy, no matter how modest it could be, in the emerging modern metropolis.

---

he himself was laughed at by the tourists and driven out of the train on a heavy snow day, whereafter he continued shouting his warning in the direction of the departing train. Rey Chow uses the railway journey from Beijing to Shanghai as the trip from tradition to modernity, and Hu, a framed banker from Beijing, was horribly trapped and abandoned by the modernizing progress itself. Rey Chow, *Woman and Chinese Modernity*, 75–76.

[73] Zhang, *Jinfen shijia*, 1026.

[74] Joan Ramon Resina, "The Concept of After-Image and the Scopic Apprehension of the City," in *After-Images of the City*, ed. Joan Ramon Resina and Dieter Ingenschay (Ithaca, NY: Cornell University Press, 2003), 7.

AN UNOFFICIAL HISTORY OF EMOTIONS

Exhibitions represent identity, either directly, through assertion, or indirectly, by implication . . . . Exhibitions are privileged arenas for presenting images of self and "other."
—IVAN KARP

In his reflection on the decline of storytelling and the emergence of the novel as a genre of modern times, Walter Benjamin observes that "memory is the epic faculty par excellence" and that it plays an essential role in literature.[75] Both story and novel reside in memory, although in different ways. Zhang Henshui's Beijing narratives are characterized by both "perpetuating the remembrance of the novelist" and the "short-lived reminiscences of the storyteller."[76] Their accounts of the urban adventures of modern Beijing heroes are interpolated by penetrating observations of social manners and mores. With its anthropological bearings and ethnographical concerns, Zhang's work indicates a close affinity with late imperial *shiqing xiaoshuo*, which, according to Lu Xun, was born out of the writer's "profound understanding of human life" and holds "a variety of human interest."[77] Later, in her brief comments on Zhang Henshui, Zhang Ailing renders the notion *shiqing xiaoshuo* into English as "novel of manners" and places Zhang's work in the lineage of *The Plum in the Golden Vase* and *Sing-song Girls of Shanghai*.[78]

Zhang Henshui's Beijing story *Fate in Tears and Laughter* (hereafter *Fate*) represents a salient example of the transformation from late imperial vernacular literature to the modern genre of novel. *Ti* (tears) and *xiao* (laughter) in the title merit special attention. As "tears" suggest literary tradition of love, romance, and emotional matter (*yanqing* 言情), "laughter" indicates the social (*shehui* 社會) dimension of Chinese literature. "Laughter" signifies the author's intention to reveal and criticize the unjust conditions of social reality, an effort that can be traced back to the satirical realist tradition, as particularly embodied by the late Qing exposé novels, which, according to David Der-Wei Wang's study of the genre, are "characterized by topical urgency, vigorous cynicism, and a compulsive need to laugh at everything high and low."[79] Zhang's *Fate* continues the significant tradition of social satire and

---

[75] Walter Benjamin, "The Storyteller: Reflections on Nikolai Leskóv," in *Illuminations*, trans. Harry Zohn (New York: Harcourt, Brace & World, 1968), 97.

[76] Ibid., 98.

[77] Lu Xun, *Zhongguo xiaoshuo shi lue* 中國小說史略 [A Brief History of Chinese Fiction] in *Lu Xun Quanji*, 9:325.

[78] Zhang, "Yi Hu Shizhi," in *Zhang Kan*, 147.

[79] David Der-wei Wang, *Fin-de-siècle Splendor: Repressed Modernities of Late Qing Fiction, 1849–1911* (Stanford, CA: Stanford University Press, 1997), chap. 4, esp. 183.

establishes a close intertextual connection with late Qing fictions such as Liu E's 劉鶚 (1857–1909) *Lao Can youji* 老殘遊記 (*The Travels of Lao Can*, 1907), Wu Jianren's *Strange Things Observed over the Past Twenty Years*, and Li Boyuan's *Guanchang xianxing ji* 官場現形記 (*Officialdom Unmasked*), among others.[80] Like his fellow late Qing writers, Zhang seeks to condemn the dark side of social reality with a compulsive pose of parody and laughter to mock social perversities and human absurdity.

On the other hand, the word "tears" underscores the affective concerns of Chinese literature of sentiments. Tears as a form of human expression denote both personal, romantic feeling and an emotive response to social and political conditions. Human sentiments refer not only to the type of romantic love unto death conceived in the late Ming *qing* cult but also to the emotional economy of political engagement and social concern. In the preface to *The Travels of Lao Can*, Liu E regards weeping as an expression of the spiritual nature of human beings. He asserts, "We of this age have our feelings stirred about ourselves and the world, about family and nation, about society, about the various races and religions."[81] By weaving a discourse of tears into one of laughter, Zhang Henshui carries on both the romantic tradition as exemplified by Cao Xueqin's *The Story of the Stone* and Wei Zi'an's 魏子安 (1818–1873) *Huayue hen* 花月痕 (Traces of the flower and the moon) as well as late Qing social satire. Zhang's notion of weeping insinuates the sentimental and the social dimension in his literary response into a historical moment when both social morality and human relations were reshaped at the advent of modernity.

In 1929, after accepting an invitation by Yan Duhe 嚴獨鶴 (1889–1968), a prominent newspaperman, editor, and writer based in Shanghai, Zhang Henshui started to write *Fate* for *Xinwen Bao* 新聞報 (News Daily), one of the two most popular newspapers in modern Shanghai. During its 1929 through 1930 serialization in *News Daily*'s literary supplement *Kuaihuo lin* 快活林 (Forest of lightheartedness), *Fate* was read with enormous enthusiasm and became the greatest literary hit of the time. Although Zhang himself suggested that *Unofficial History* and *Grand Old Family* are equally important Beijing stories, *Fate* has been regarded as the most popular fiction about Republican Beijing and was widely adapted into film, drama, local opera, TV series, and other media.[82]

---

[80] For more intertextual relations between Zhang's novels and other Qing narratives, see Zhao, *Zhang Henshui xiaoshuo xinlun.*

[81] Liu T'ieh-yün, *The Travels of Lao Ts'an*, trans. Harold Shadick (New York: Columbia University Press, 1990), 2.

[82] C. T. Hsia observes that "the phenomenal best-seller of the early Republican period . . . sold several hundred thousand copies during its years of fame, and reached even larger audiences when it was made into a silent movie." *C. T. Hsia on Chinese Literature* (New York: Columbia University Press, 2004), 270. See also Zhang

The novel tells of a complicated romance among several young people of different social backgrounds, interposed by minute depictions of human life in early Republican Beijing, in particular, a wide array of folklore and social customs around topographical imaginations of Tianqiao 天橋 (Heaven's Bridge) as a cultural site. Because the novel was mainly written for readers in Shanghai, Zhang Henshui, a self-proclaimed resident of Beijing, illustrated the city from an indigenous and ethnographical perspective, mapping and elucidating the city like the Weimar writers investigated Berlin: "street by street, scene by scene, sign by sign, shop by shop, window by window, and doing so with the freshness of a foreigner's first gaze."[83] Such a refreshing dual gaze at Beijing by a city stranger and a local informant inspires and defines the literary imagination and readers' perception of Republican Beijing.

Fate is a romantic urban adventure that consists of stories of romantic love and fraternity, moral conflicts and social abuses, historical cultural heritage and modern urban spectacles, heroic knights-errant and political assassins. Like Yang Xingyuan in *Unofficial History*, *Fate*'s protagonist, Fan Jiashu 樊家樹, is also a Beijing sojourner from a southern province. However, unlike Xingyuan, who inhabits a transitional zone between a classical poet and a modern journalist, Jiashu is an idealistic modern college student who embarks on a romantic journey in the ancient capital. The main plot centers on the quadrilateral romance between Fan Jiashu and three women, Shen Fengxi 沈鳳喜, He Lina 何麗娜, and Guan Xiugu 關秀姑, with starkly different upbringings, social backgrounds, and personalities. Fengxi is a drum singer from a humble family in the poor district of Heaven's Bridge. Lina, who looks like Fengxi's identical twin, is a modern girl from a wealthy, distinguished family. The third woman, Xiugu, is portrayed as a knight-errant from a traditional martial arts world. Jiashu seems to confront three different types of women, who represent three different routes of development in this modern city: a queen of the ghetto of the Heaven's Bridge district, Fengxi turns from an innocent and gullible girl into the mistress of a powerful warlord; He Lina endeavors to change from a shallow modern girl into someone accommodating both traditional and modern femininity; and Xiugu is preoccupied with a premodern chivalric spirit and a desire to redress social injustice.

Behind the sentimental romance is Zhang's notion of the ideal social order, one that is underlined by both traditional and modern values and envisions a new type of citizen and his/her relation to family, society, and the state. The novel's concept of

---

Wu, *Wo de fuqin Zhang Henshui*. According to incomplete statistics, *Fate in Tears and Laughter* has been reproduced in various versions since its publication in the late 1920s, and Zhao Xiaoxuan provides a detailed investigation of the border-crossing and multimedia adaptations in the Chinese-language world, see Zhao, *Zhang Henshui xiaoshuo xinlun*, 90–94.

[83] Gleber, *The Art of Taking a Walk*, 9.

"fate" (*yinyuan* 因緣) signifies its focus on transformations that the main characters undergo. By exploring the cause and effect of their transformative journeys, it can be regarded as a complex of several Bildungsromans. The educative process that each character experiences is closely related to the modern transitions the city and the nation go through.

Fengxi grows up in a poor section in Beijing. She sings drum songs in the low-class Heaven's Bridge area to make a living. She falls in love with Jiashu, and with his help, becomes a modern school student. Zhang Henshui explicitly emphasizes that what strongly attracts Fengxi are the modern features of Jiashu—his fashionable personal belongings and ornaments, as well as the material temptation of the new-type schooling environment.[84] At school, Fengxi is not really interested in new thoughts and knowledge offered by the modern institution of education. She feels exhilarated by novel and exotic fashions and objects, such as Western glasses, pens, high-heeled shoes, and stylish jewelry. Her enlightenment aspirations are, after all, only about chasing the superficial images of Western civilization and modern material life, which anticipates her subsequent degeneration. When Fengxi later visits the warlord's majestic mansion, she becomes deeply engrossed by its palatial grand hall, extravagant furniture and decorations, lavish carpets and drapery, huge brass bed, a radio broadcasting foreign tunes, electric fans, and so on.[85] After careful calculation, Fengxi agrees to become the aged warlord's concubine, dreaming of "the foreign mansion, car, jewelry, luxuriously furnished rooms, servants gathering in crowds and groups" (洋樓 , 汽車 , 珠寶 , 如花似錦的陳設 , 成群結隊的傭人 , 都一幕一幕在眼面前過去).[86] She is finally driven mad by the warlord's torture and abuse.

While relentlessly condemning the cruelty and perversity of warlords, the author cautions contemporary readers about Fengxi's moral deterioration in being seduced by modern material life, which derives also from the weakness of her personality. In attributing Fengxi's downfall to her vanity and shallow character rather than merely to social oppression and corruption, Zhang Henshui drew leftist criticism for his lack of correct class consciousness. However, these politically engaged critics often overlooked that Zhang's notion of moral integrity is defined by one's attitude to the lure of material life, not by one's social identity. In *Fate*, all the characters, whether rich or poor, are described as morally weak if they are obsessed with modern,

---

[84] An interesting episode is that when Fengxi played the episode of "Farwell, My Concubine" in front of Jiashu, all of sudden, the string broke, which was taken as an omen indicating the unhappy ending of the love between Jiashu and Fengxi.

[85] Zhang Henshui, *Tixiao yinyuan* (Taiyuan: Beiyue wenyi chubanshe, 2000), 108–109.

[86] Zhang, *Tixiao yinyuan*, 123.

luxurious things. On the contrary, those characters—no matter what social class they belong to—who are illustrated as morally superior and sincere often have a propensity toward classical Chinese culture.[87] Although open to modern ideas, Zhang nevertheless places more emphasis on traditional values and moral cultivation. In so doing, Zhang reveals an oscillating position—both rebelling against and depending on tradition; both longing for the modern and keeping a distance from radical Westernization.

He Lina, an upper-class, modern, educated woman, lives a privileged life and enjoys the vibrant and dynamic urban lifestyle. From Jiashu's perspective, she is arrogant and pretentious, excessively fashionable, lacking in the beauty of innocence, and amounting to nothing but a fake foreign lady.[88] After Lina falls in love with the "old" youth Fan Jiashu, she decides to downgrade her modern Westernized characteristics to become a modest Chinese woman for him. She starts to read Buddhist scriptures, becomes a vegetarian, and lives a reclusive life in the Western Hills on the margins of the city. By reversing her modern education, her determination to return to tradition finally wins the heart of the male protagonist.

Guan Xiugu, a female knight-errant in the modern society, embarks on a different type of transformative journey, which bespeaks Zhang Henshui's distinctive idea of heroism. She is the daughter of Guan Shoufeng 關壽峰, who was a bandit for twenty years before becoming a martial artist and doctor in Beijing and a close friend of Jiashu because of their shared notion of social justice. Zhang stated that the martial-arts storyline in *Fate* was intentionally written for the Shanghai literary market, where this genre entertained a loyal and large readership.[89] However, there is more at stake in Zhang's modern, urban, martial-arts fantasy. In a 1945 article entitled "On Martial Arts Novels," Zhang addressed the popularity of martial arts fiction among Chinese readers: "There always exists an ambiguous heroism in the minds of low-class Chinese people. Having nowhere to ask for redress of an injustice or to assuage indignation, they turn to these fabricated knights-errant novels for comfort" (中國下層社會里的人物,他們的思想,始終有著模糊的英雄主義的色彩,那完全是武俠故事所教訓的。他們無冤可伸,無憤可平,就托諸這幻想的武俠人物,來解除腦中的苦悶).[90] In *Fate*, Xiugu represents the modern heroic spirit: she kills the malicious warlord who abducted Fengxi and helps her

---

[87] Zhao, *Zhang Henshui xiaoshuo xinlun*, 183.

[88] Zhang, *Tixiao yinyuan*, 153–160.

[89] Early in the 1930s, enlightened writers and critics including Zheng Zhenduo 鄭振鐸 (1898–1958) and Shen Yanbing 沈雁冰 (1896–1981) denounced martial arts fictions as daydream literature.

[90] Zhang Henshui, "Lun Wuxia xiaoshuo" 論武俠小說 [On martial arts novels], in Zhang and Wei, eds., *Zhang Henshui yanjiu ziliao*, 268.

escape from the warlord's mansion; together with her father, Xiugu rescues Jiashu from local gangs who kidnapped him to the Western Hills.

Whereas Xiugu saves Jiashu's life by means of her martial-arts skills, Jiashu serves as her teacher and spiritual guide. The education of a woman knight-errant is conducted through book reading. The author goes to great lengths to describe the reading matter of these Republican Beijing inhabitants. What gave rise to modern serious readers? What composed their reading lists? In what sorts of spaces did they commit themselves to absorbing the reading material? When Guan Shoufeng is seriously ill, Fan Jiashu brings him a pile of books, including martial-arts novels, to entertain him and boost his morale. When Jiashu comes home from a dance club, exhausted by the noise and daunting colors,[91] he picks up a book beside his pillow. It is *The Story of the Stone*, and he accidentally turns to the page that depicts Lin Daiyu playing the *qin*, a classical Chinese musical instrument. Fengxi happens to have performed the same musical interlude on that very day. Jiashu's bedroom reading of *The Story of the Stone* not only provides peace and tranquility to heal his painful experiences in the dance hall but also evokes his romantic sentiments toward Fengxi.

Xiugu's feelings (from love to friendship) towards Jiashu develop and change along with her reading of two Qing vernacular romances and later Buddhist sutra prepared by Jiashu. While recovering in the hospital, Xiugu first reads Cao Xueqin's *The Story of the Stone*, a classical Qing novel of melancholic triangle love among the male protagonist Jia Baoyu and his two beautiful and talented cousins, Lin Daiyu and Xue Baochai. Keith McMahon regards Jia Baoyu as the incarnation of "the exquisitely ephemeral nature of *qing*, especially as captured in the perfect moment of love that is fleeting or just missed."[92] Artistic sensitivity and romantic sentimentality are projected onto the utopian Grand View Garden, initiates the sentimental education of the modern-day female knight-errant. The nurse mistakes Jiashu for Xiugu's Jia Baoyu, a moment when Xiugu realizes her feelings (*qing* or love) for Jiashu. The next book Jiashu brings Xiugu is the late Qing chivalric novel *Ernü yingxiong zhuan* 兒女英雄傳 (A tale of heroes and lovers), which tells a story of how the talented Confucian young scholar An Ji 安驥 wins the hearts of a Confucian fair lady, Zhang Jinfeng 張金鳳, and a woman knight-errant, He Yufeng 何玉鳳. Using her martial-arts skills, Yufeng saves An Ji and Jinfeng time and time again from the oppression of corrupt bureaucrats. After An Ji and Jinfeng get married, they together persuade Yufeng to marry An Ji as well. In his discussion of *A Tale of Heroes and Lovers*, David Der-wei Wang points out the Confucian edifice that structures this late Qing

---

[91] Zhang, *Tixiao yinyuan*, 20.

[92] Keith McMahon, *Polygamy and Sublime Passion: Sexuality in China on the Verge of Modernity* (Honolulu: University of Hawai'i Press, 2010), 31.

martial arts romance and reads Yufeng's story as "the taming of women warriors."[93] After reading the novel, Xiugu inevitably guesses that Jiashu means to tell her that he already has a lover and insinuates a possible happy ending of their triangular relationship. Xiugu, however, refuses to become a modern Yufeng, who tolerates An Ji's ideal polygamy and subordinates herself to the Confucian order. After she finds out that Jiashu loves Fengxi, Xiugu hides her feelings and starts to read the *Lotus Sutra*. By reading Buddhist classics, she learns to treat her love and frustrations as fetters on her mind. Only by transcending these secular desires can a modern woman warrior reach pure moral integrity. In the sequel to *Fate* that Zhang finished a few years later, Xiugu's personal feelings are further elevated and sublimed to nationalist passion as she becomes a modern Hua Mulan, a national heroine, who sacrifices her life for the nation in a battle against the Japanese invaders. Xiugu's reading list, which mixes works from vernacular romances, Confucian thoughts, and Buddhist teachings, bespeaks the evolution of her emotional experiences and a modern notion of heroism.

The sentimental education Zhang's Beijing new youth undergoes is supplemented by an ethnographical and spatial edification. Zhang's Beijing romance charts a literary and emotional topography, both of which are essential to his agenda of modern enlightenment. In *Fate* and other Beijing stories, Zhang Henshui sought materials and information from a variety of sources and created a rich exhibition of public spaces in Republican Beijing, including Heaven's Bridge, the Altar to Agriculture (Xiannong tan 先農壇), Lake of the Ten Temples (Shichahai 什刹海), North Lake Park (Beihai 北海), and Western Hills (Xishan 西山). If public spaces in Shanghai, as portrayed in Neo-sensationalist or Zhang Ailing's writings, are minute and crowded, dark and humid, then Zhang's Beijing public spaces are always stately, rich in historical flavor. Heaven's Bridge is an entertainment center for the masses and also attracts elite intellectuals. The Altar to Agriculture is where Fan Jiashu had his first date with Fengxi and dreamed of turning this illiterate drum singer into a modern coed. There are various levels and styles of teahouses. As Guan Shoufeng reminds Jiashu, the snobbish teahouses in the Central Park (Zhongshan gongyuan 中山公園) are far less enjoyable than the down-to-earth teahouses around the Lake of the Ten Temples. Moreover, Zhang Henshui offers detailed accounts of a wide array of private spaces, where the romances unfold and the characters' personalities develop, such as Jiashu's spacious courtyard house, the small but organized residence of Guan Shoufeng and his daughter Xiugu, the shabby adobe of Fengxi, and the colossal mansion of He Lina. Through traveling between various social and cultural spaces, the social and affective relations are constructed.

---

[93] Wang, *Fin-de-siècle Splendor*, 156–174.

No doubt, a key site in *Fate*'s emotional geography is "the sound and the fury" in Heaven's Bridge. As the story begins, a servant of Jiashu's Beijing relatives tells Jiashu he should definitely pay a visit to the Water Heart Pavilion in Heaven's Bridge because many beautiful girls sing Peking opera there. At first, Jiashu feels reluctant to go because, according to stereotypes, Heaven's Bridge is a dreadful location where low-class people congregate. Coming from Westernized Shanghai, Jiashu always imagines Beijing as an elegant and refined place. However, bored with being home alone, Jianshu decides to take a risk. He is immediately intrigued by the sights and sounds of Heaven's Bridge, where various forms of popular entertainment compete for audiences. It is also the point of departure for the romances between Jiashu, Fengxi, and Xiugu. The charm of Heaven's Bridge prompts Jiashu to become an active explorer of the historical city. From the Water Heart Pavilion to the daily humble teahouses, from the martial arts club where Guan Shoufeng and other martial artists gather to the intimidating mansions of ministers and warlords, from modern-style schools to dance halls, his trajectory of urban adventures crosses the boundaries of social classes and of the traditional and the modern.

Shortly after its serialization in *News Daily*, *Fate* became phenomenally popular among Shanghai readers. Zhang Youluan 張友鸞 (1904–1990) attributed its success to its ability to present an exotic Beijing to southern readers, especially Shanghai citizens who were tired of stories set locally:

> *Fate* was written about Beijing, introducing Beijing's scenery, customs, and peoples with great liveliness. In particular, the descriptions of the Heaven's Bridge area were so vivid that even today readers from the south who travel up north to Beijing make the pilgrimage to Tianqiao.[94]

Heaven's Bridge is a fascinating stage on which stories of native Beijingers are shown. For a lot of Zhang Henshui fans, it became the epitome of original Beijing, full of historical relics and folklore stories. Paradoxically, the exoticism of Heaven's Bridge lies precisely in its being part of the native and authentic Beijing. It is the ethnographic knowledge of Beijing as embodied in the folk society and culture in Heaven's Bridge that represents the outlandish, the other city for generations of *Fate* readers.

Zhang Henshui's spatial and poetic topography of Beijing is completed by an acoustic mapping of the city and its culture. A novel of social manners would not be complete without rendering the cacophony of sounds in everyday life. Zhang Henshui's Beijing narratives capture the acoustic traces of the city. What defines the

---

[94] Zhang Youluan, "Zhanghui xiaoshuo dajia Zhang Henshui" 章回小說大家張恨水 [Zhang Henshui: the master of the chapter-titled novel], in Zhang and Wei, eds., *Zhang Henshui yanjiu ziliao*, 134. I adopted Eileen Chow's English translation and made a slight modification.

sound of Beijing is not the piercing whistle of the train arriving at the Zhengyang Gate, the relentless beat in modern dance halls or on radios, the voices of the vendors down the winding alleys, or the gunfire that looms large in the political chaos. For Zhang, the sound that haunts every corner of this ancient city is the antiquated tunes filtered and transmitted through dynasties and generations. Including arias from Peking opera and drum songs, such as "Daiyu beiqiu" 黛玉悲秋 (Daiyu moans about autumn), "Bawang bieji" 霸王別姫 (Farewell, my concubine), and "Ye shenchen" 夜深沈 (Deep darkness of the night), these ancient tales about sad romances, tragic kings and heroes, familial separations, everlasting sorrows, or dynastic decline constitute the acoustic memories of the city. In *A Thousand Plateaus*, Deleuze and Guattari reflects on the vocal component that structures the prehuman origins of art. They observe,

> A child in the dark, gripped with fear, comforts himself by singing under his breath. He walks and halts to his song. Lost, he takes shelter, or orients himself with his little song as best he can. The song is like a rough sketch of a calming and stabilizing, calm and stable, center in the heart of chaos. Perhaps the child skips as he sings, hastens or slows his pace. But the song itself is already a skip: it jumps from chaos to the beginnings of order in chaos and is in danger of breaking apart at any moment.[95]

The song provides a shelter against the intrusion of the outside world. It also establishes a point of departure from which the human being can venture out and create positive relations with the outside world. In Zhang Henshui's much ignored 1937–1938 Beijing story, *Deep Darkness of the Night*, which takes its title from a Peking opera tune of the same name, the operatic melody not only catalyzes the romantic relationship between the Peking opera singer Yuehong and the horse carriage driver Ding Erhe but also functions as a key narrative line in their urban disillusion. This well-known Peking opera excerpt draws its material from the tragic legend about King Xiang Yu 項羽 (232–202 B.C.) and his concubine Consort Yu 虞姬 who committed suicide before Xiang Yu started and fatally failed the final battle against Liu Bang 劉邦 (256–159 B.C.), the future emperor of the Han dynasty. In Zhang's account, the melancholic melody articulates personal and collective memories for the downtrodden and for the privileged, and also conveys the weight of history in the ancient city of Beijing, which has witnessed endless dynastic changes and the maelstrom of modernization. Mapping Beijing from the affective, poetic, sonic, spatial, and

---

[95] Deleuze and Guattari, *A Thousand Plateaus*, 311.

ethnographic perspectives, Zhang Henshui's urban imagination provides a sophisticated cityscape in a time when tradition and modernity meet and compete, and personal, familial, social, and national relations are redefined. The characters in Zhang's Beijing dreams create and materialize their spatial fantasies, but suffer from their misapprehension of daytime and nighttime, false lures and cruel traps, safety exits and prison houses, and the enchanting and disenchanting city chronotopes.

If we take only a distant, bird's eye view of the history of China in the twentieth century, it is often hard not to see it mainly as a century of colossal *waste*: *wasted* opportunities, *wasted* resources, *wasted* lives.

—JONATHAN SPENCE

3

The Aesthetic versus the Political

LIN HUIYIN AND THE CITY

IN 1936, AT the Hall of Prayers for Good Harvest (祈年殿) of the Temple of Heaven (天壇) in Beijing, Lin Huiyin (Phyllis Lin or Lin Whei-yin) and Liang Sicheng, "partners in exploring China's architectural past,"[1] stood on the roof of this sacred imperial site, and on the figurative heads of all previous emperors and ministers. The Hall of Prayers for Good Harvest was where the rites of state religion were performed and offerings were made to heaven. Emperors invoked heaven and the gods to bestow their dynasties with auspicious years and good harvests.[2] Thanks to photography, a new Western technology imported to China around the mid-nineteenth century, a black-and-white snapshot captured the evocative moment and preserved the couple's image for later generations. On that day, Lin remarked with deep pride her belief that she was the *first woman* ever to stand on top of the Temple of Heaven.

In this poignant moment, Lin Huiyin publicly inhabited a unique place in Beijing, not only defying the traditional restriction of woman's space to the domestic sphere, but also bespeaking an intriguing relationship between modern Chinese female subjectivity and the city. Michelle Yeh observes, "[W]omen have been traditionally marginalized in Chinese society, barred from participating in the sociocultural

---

[1] See Wilma Fairbank's subtitle and major theme of her book, *Liang and Lin*.
[2] Naquin, *Peking*, 324.

sphere on equal terms with men and deprived of physical, intellectual, and social autonomy."[3] At this particular temporal and spatial site, Lin physically transgressed the ideological and gender boundaries drawn between man and woman, masculinity and femininity, society and family, as well as between modernity and tradition. Lin and Liang were among the earliest modern architects in China. Lin was the first female architect and an important architectural historian with distinguished literary talent and sensibility. Standing atop the Hall of Prayers for Good Harvest, a historically privileged place, and facing the horizon of this old yet modern city of Beijing, what intellectual and sensual pleasure and passion would emerge from her literary mind? What new modes of observation and perception had the modern discipline of architecture provided her?

By the early 1930s, Lin Huiyin was already a well-established literary figure, a poet, essayist, and short story writer, and a vital member of significant literary groups including the Beijing School and the Crescent Moon Society (新月社).[4] Her writings contributed considerably to the literary topography of modern Beijing. Furthermore, she was a charismatic hostess and the guiding spirit of "Madam's Salon," a regular literary gathering and famous cultural salon in Republican Beijing. Located in her residence, Number 3 North Zongbu Lane (北總佈胡同三號), Lin's Salon was an influential literary public space.

From the rooftop of an imperial hall to the interior salon of a modern Beijing household and beyond, Lin spent most of her life in Beijing and left traces at all sorts of historical and cultural sites.[5] Saul Bellow points out that a city is "the expression of the human experience it embodies, and this includes all personal history."[6] For Lin Huiyin, a "renaissance woman,"[7] Beijing was like a huge vessel, filled with hopes,

---

[3] Michelle Yeh, ed. and trans., *Anthology of Modern Chinese Poetry* (New Haven, CT: Yale University Press, 1992), xlv.

[4] For recent studies of modern Chinese literary societies, see Michel Hockx, *Questions of Style: Literary Societies and Literary Journals in Modern China, 1911–1937* (Leiden: Brill, 2003); Kirk A. Denton and Michel Hockx, eds., *Literary Societies of Republican China* (Lanham, MD: Lexington Books, 2008).

[5] Born in Fujian and raised in Beijing, Lin Huiyin lived out her childhood (1914, 1916–1920), her youth (1921–1924, 1928, 1929), and most of her adulthood (1930–1937, 1946–1955) in Beijing. See Chen Xueyong 陳學勇, *Cainü de shijie* 才女的世界 [World of a talented lady] (Beijing: Kunlun chubanshe, 2001), 199–236.

[6] Saul Bellow, *More Die of Heartbreak* (London: Secker & Warburg, 1987), 124.

[7] The Italian Renaissance was a source of inspiration for modernity in the twentieth century. Giants like Dante Alighieri, Leonardo da Vinci, and others were the ideal models for modern Chinese literati and intellectuals to follow. See Liang Congjie 梁從誡, "Shuhu renjian siyue tian" 倏忽人間四月天 [Suddenly the Beautiful April on the Earth], in *Lin Huiyin wenji—Wenxue juan* 林徽因文集·文學卷 [Selected writings of Lin Huiyin: Volume of literature], ed. Liang Congjie (Tianjin: Baihua wenyi chubanshe, 1999), 447. On May 3, 1953, Lin Huiyin and Liang Sicheng published an essay entitled "Da Fenqi: Juyou weida yuanjian de jianzhu gongchengshi" 達·芬奇——具有偉大遠見的建築工程師 [Leonardo da Vinci: An Architectural Engineer with Great Foresight], in *Lin Huiyin wenji: Jianzhu juan* 林徽因文集·建築卷 [Selected writings of Lin

aspirations, disappointments, pain, frustrations, and bliss. Her eyes looked back into the city's past, and her ears could even hear the secret voices of long ago, reverberating around Beijing. As she and Liang Sicheng described in their famous piece on architectural and aesthetic investigations, "No matter whether you come across a towering ancient city gate or an abandoned palace foundation, all silently tell you or even sing out to you the unbelievable changes wrought by time" (無論哪一個 巍峨的古城樓，或一角傾頹的殿基的靈魂里，無形中都在訴說乃至歌唱時 間上漫不可信的變遷).[8]

Hou Renzhi 侯仁之 (1911–2013), an eminent geologist and historian of Beijing, who returned from England three days before Chairman Mao Zedong declared the founding of the People's Republic of China on October 1, 1949, recalled that this passage offered inspiration for understanding Beijing's history and architecture.[9] The aesthetic illumination of the city and its historical relics creates an indelible image of Beijing imbued with historical and lyrical allusions for professional scholars and amateur readers. Gaston Bachelard has argued that "great images have both a history and a prehistory; they are always a blend of memory and legend . . . . Every great image has an unfathomable oneiric depth to which the personal past adds special color."[10] Personal stories are visibly or invisibly inscribed in the processes of naming, representing, historicizing, and recollecting the city. From Lin and Liang's point of view, Beijing was "a gigantic exhibition hall,"[11] a "living" city (活"的城市) and an organic museum (活著的博物館)[12] that needed to be understood, charted, and protected. When facing the museum/city, Lin Huiyin would be a purposeful rambler, a serious investigator, an earnest curator, a sophisticated interpreter, and a secret storyteller who could tell or retell the stories buried beneath the silent, gigantic places and the desolate ruins.

Huiyin: Volume of architecture], ed. Liang Congjie (Tianjin: Baihua wenyi chubanshe, 1999), 356–362. See also Hu Shih, *Chinese Renaissance* (New York: Paragon Book Reprint Corp., 1963).

[8] Liang Sicheng and Lin Huiyin, "Miscellaneous Records of Peiping Suburban Architecture," in Wilma Fairbank, *Liang and Lin*, 181. For the Chinese version, see Liang, ed., *Lin Huiyin wenji: Jianzhu juan*, 16.

[9] "It is Beijing's marvelous beauty of architecture and history that always stimulates my research," Hou said while recalling parts of his life. The remark by professors Liang Sicheng and Lin Huiyin, two famous architectural specialists—"Every grand ancient castle or even a corner of collapsed palace eulogizes the endless and incredible changes of time"—has never left Hou's memory. The octogenarian expert still keeps a close watch on Beijing's city construction today. A map of Beijing printed during the reign of Emperor Qianlong 乾隆 (1711–1799) in the Qing dynasty (1644–1911) hangs on a wall in his house, and maps of different scales are spread on his desk. Hou always travels around the city calling for more concern about and understanding of Beijing from the public. See *People's Daily*, December 15, 2000.

[10] Gaston Bachelard, *The Poetics of Space: The Classic Look at How We Experience Intimate Places*, trans. Maria Jolas (Boston: Beacon Press, 1994), 33.

[11] Wilma Fairbank, *Liang and Lin*, 182.

[12] Liang, *Lin Huiyin wenji: Jianzhu juan*, 440, 453.

This chapter considers the aesthetic versus the political aspects of Beijing representations as conveyed by Lin Huiyin's literary and architectural productions. I first examine how Lin's literary works configure the city as an aesthetic object and how urban spaces shape her literary imagery and vocabulary. Then I map the literary circles and public spaces in Beijing that made the city a cultural capital par excellence of Republican China, particularly Lin's well-known "Madam's Salon." I conclude by examining the distinctions between Lin's aesthetic ideals of urban planning versus the Maoist and Socialist urban imagination, as well as highlighting the return of the once-missing "Renaissance woman" and her significance in the aesthetic understanding of Beijing as ancient capital, modern metropolis, and socialist city.

THE POETICS AND POLITICS OF URBAN OBJECTS

Levels and dimensions . . . serve as lexical items (readings) in urban texts and writing, or maps, and as "urban things," which can be felt, seen, and read in the environment.
—HENRI LEFEBVRE

Lin Huiyin's literary topography of Beijing in the 1930s conveys a distinctive blend of aesthetic sensibility and critical urban consciousness. By reading her lyrical poems "Chenglou shang" 城樓上 (On the gate tower, 1935) and "Gucheng chunjing" 古城春景 (Spring scene of the ancient city, 1937), her stream-of-consciousness short story "Jiushijiu du zhong" 九十九度中 (In ninety-nine-degree heat, 1934), and her self-reflexive essay "Chuangzi yiwai" 窗子以外 (Outside of the window, 1934), I aim to explore Lin's unique lexicons and positions, creative imagery and mapping, and intriguing exhibition of "urban things" in her less prolific yet more innovative and multigenred literary texts.

In 1931, Lin Huiyin was diagnosed with severe pneumonia and went to stay in Beijing's suburban sanatorium, Shuangqing Villa (雙清別墅), in Fragrant Hills Park (香山公園). In this western suburb of the city, Lin's literary career was given its point of departure. While convalescing, Lin composed her first poems, characterized by distinctive melodic and rhythmic patterns evoking spatial images spreading in horizontal and vertical directions. These poems include "Shui ai zhe buxi de bianhuan" 誰愛這不息的變幻 (Who loves the restless change, 1931), "Ji'ang" 激昂 (Excitement, 1931), "Yishou taohua" 一首桃花 (A peach blossom, 1931), and "Liandeng" 蓮燈 (A lotus light, 1932). Fragrant Hills Park provided a remote, pastoral environment where Lin could retreat from the city, recuperate from pneumonia, connect with nature, and enjoy bucolic pleasure and tranquility.[13] Her brother

---

[13] Liang, *Lin Huiyin wenji: Wenxue juan*, 156–157. See also Liang Congjie's comments on the poem "Shuhu renjian siyue tian," in *Lin Huiyin wenji: Wenxue juan*, 419.

Lin Xuan 林宣 recalled that in the evening, Lin Huiyin would burn incense, arrange flowers, wear white silk pajamas, face the lotus leaves of a pond, and recite and "brew" a fine poem in a fleeting cool breeze.[14] The sound and fury of the city could be converted into quietness during the night.[15] As portrayed in her poem "Excitement," the young poet even knelt down in this pure stillness with gratitude, bliss, and conviction.[16] In the poem "A Lotus Light," the poet's heart and mind are transformed into a lotus lit with a candle, and they sail along the river of destiny and comprehend the myth and beauty of life and death. The delicate lyric imagery and elegant wording in Lin's poems are further enriched with a touch of Buddhist meditation. Life is a dreamy journey, and time unfolds as a series of spatial images: "The roving journey is also— / Is also a beautiful dream" (這飄忽的途程也就是個— / 也就是個美麗美麗的夢).[17]

Michelle Yeh argues that early modern Chinese women poets made painstaking efforts to revise conventional poetic language, images, and motifs, so that they could "free themselves from *wanyue*, or 'feminine,' tradition in Chinese poetry, in which typically a woman sits alone in her boudoir, perhaps leaning on the windowsill overlooking a beautiful yet confining garden, and pines for her absent lover or husband or wallows in melancholy over lost love."[18] With regard to Lin Huiyin's 1930s poetic creation, Yeh maintains,

> We also see the woman as at once freer, more complex, and in more control of her physical and emotional life than before. One of her last poems, entitled "Life," written in 1947, . . . goes on to compare the narrator to a traveler and life to "fields, forests, and mountain peaks." The implication that she decides where she goes in life and takes responsibility for her self-fulfillment generally reflects the burgeoning individualism of the 1920s, the May Fourth era, and specifically relates to the new definition of womanhood in the whole modern period.[19]

---

[14] Chen Yu 陳宇, "Yilu jiedu Xu Zhimo: Xu Zhimo qinpeng caifang shouji" 一路解讀徐志摩：徐志摩親朋採訪手記 [Reading Xu Zhimo all along: Notes on Interviews with Xu Zhimo's Relatives and Friends], in *Zhuanji wenxue* 傳記文學 [Biographical literature] 12 (1999), http://www.shuku.net/novels/zhuanji/sahqz-wrpbj/zlsj14.html.

[15] Lin Huiyin, "Shui ai zhe buxi de bianhuan" 誰愛這不息的變幻 [Who loves the restless change], in Liang, *Lin Huiyin wenji: Wenxue juan*, 145.

[16] Lin Huiyin, "Ji'ang" 激昂 [Excitement], in Liang, *Lin Huiyin wenji: Wenxue juan*, 154–155.

[17] Lin Huiyin, "Liandeng" 蓮燈 [A lotus light], in Liang, *Lin Huiyin wenji: Wenxue juan*, 158.

[18] Yeh, *Anthology of Modern Chinese Poetry*, xlv–xlvi. Julia C. Lin also points out Lin's "pioneering efforts in employing the vernacular, experimenting with new themes and forms, and carving out a niche for women poets in a field long dominated by men," in her edited volume *Twentieth-Century Chinese Women's Poetry: An Anthology* (Armonk, NY: M. E. Sharpe, 2009), xxx, 5–8.

[19] Yeh, *Anthology of Modern Chinese Poetry*, xlv–xlvi.

Indeed, Lin's poetic imagination was by no means confined to the female or feminine "physical and emotional" spaces of interiority. Widely regarded as a poet of the Crescent Moon School and a novelist of the Beijing School, Lin displays similar imagery and aesthetic tastes. Nevertheless, she was not a typical Crescent poet. When she began to write poetry in the early 1930s, the Crescent Moon School had already come to an end. During her time in Fragrant Hills Park, Xu Zhimo (1897–1931), the leading figure of the Crescent Moon School, was a regular houseguest. They read and discussed poetry and held similar opinions about poetry criticism, which might be the reason she was often regarded as a follower and practitioner of this school. But Lin was not merely an imitator of Xu's poetic style. Her poems are laden with architectural imagery and spatial consciousness. For example, her poem "Shenxiao" 深笑 (Deep smile, 1936) reads,

Who smiles like a hundred-story tower,	是誰笑成這百層塔高聳，
letting nameless birds circle around? And who	讓不知名鳥雀來盤旋？是誰
smiles like the spins of thousands of Aeolian bells,	笑成這萬千個風鈴的轉動，
from the eaves of every level of the glazed pagoda	從每一層琉璃的簷邊
waving above	搖上
cloudy sky?	雲天[20]

A smile, a facial and acoustic expression of human feeling, is captured and represented as a series of moving images of the erection of "a hundred-story tower" and the "spins of thousands of Aeolian bells" waving all the way up to the cloudy sky. This spatialized smile demonstrates a state of happiness that Lin described elsewhere as "an aesthetic pleasure." In a letter to her friend Shen Congwen dated February 27, 1936, Lin wrote,

> This is the supreme pleasure I talked about, a spiritual, transparent, and beautiful happiness . . . . I believe that this type of happiness strikes you in a momentary manner, like a flash of light, like magic . . . at that moment, what you see, what you hear, what you feel, everything is beautiful. Emotions flow naturally like lyric verses, like fragrances of which you can't trace the origin.
>
> 我方才所說到極端的愉快 靈質的 透明的 美麗的快樂. . . . 我認為最愉快的事都是一閃亮的 在一段較短的時間內迸出神奇的. . . . 在那時那刻眼所見，耳所聽，心所觸無所不是美麗，情感如詩歌自然的流動 如花香那樣不知其所以。[21]

---

[20] Lin Huiyin, "Shenxiao" 深笑 [Deep smile], in Liang, *Lin Huiyin wenji: Wenxue juan*, 181–182. See also her poetry commentary, "Jiujing zenmo yihuishi" 究竟怎麼一回事 [What's the matter?], in Liang, *Lin Huiyin wenji: Wenxue juan*, 42–46.

[21] Liang, *Lin Huiyin wenji: Wenxue juan*, 333.

From the 1930s, particularly after Xu Zhimo's accidental death in 1931, Lin Huiyin did not maintain communication with the members of the Crescent Moon Society, and was not even fond of the term "crescent moon" itself.[22] The modern poet Bian Zhilin 卞之琳 (1910–2000) observes, "her poetry is not like Crescent Poets' poems with rhyme scheme, but rather it creates unique images and artistic conceptions by weaving vernacular words into classical and foreign vocabulary. It is scintillating with superb talent" (她的詩不像新月詩人那樣的方塊格律詩，而是將口語融入古典的和外國的詞語，創造出獨特的形象和意境，才氣過人).[23] Lin Huiyin continued to write poetry throughout the 1940s, with crucial poems such as "Linggan" 靈感 (Inspiration, 1935), "Zhoumeng" 畫夢 (Daydream, 1936), and one of her last poems, "Women de xiongji" 我們的雄雞 (Our rooster, 1948).

The poem "On the Gate Tower" merits particular attention. Published in 1935, it depicts a pastoral autumn scene viewed from the top of the gate tower of the ancient city walls, and conveys the aesthetic pleasure spreading to various spatial sites in the city.

What did you say?	你說甚麼？
About ducks, the sun,	鴨子，太陽，
The moat below the gate tower?	城牆下那護城河？
Me?	——我？
I was just thinking,	我在想，
It wasn't that I didn't hear you.	——不是不在聽
I was thinking about . . .	——想怎樣
the past . . .	從前 . . .
That's right,	對了，
it was autumn then too!	也是秋天！
You have been there as well,	你也曾去過，
no? That little forest?	你？那小樹林？
Don't you remember?	還記得麼；
The mountain cave, the leaves as red as flames?	山窩，紅葉像火？
The reflection,	映影
Floating upside down upon the lake?	湖心裡倒浸，
The quiet?	那靜？
And the sky! . . .	天！ . . . .
(It's just as blue today, look!)	（今天的多藍，你看！）

[22] Liang Congjie, "Jianzhujia de yanjing, shiren de xinling" 建築家的眼睛，詩人的心靈 [Architect's eyes, poet's mind], in *Lin Huiyin wenji: Wenxue juan*, 421.

[23] Liu Xiaoqin 劉小沁, ed., *Chuangzi neiwai yi Huiyin* 窗子內外憶徽因 [In memory of Huiyin inside and outside of the window] (Beijing: Renmin wenxue chubanshe, 2001), 342.

The white clouds,	白雲，
billowing like smoke.	像一縷煙。
Who's talking too much again?	誰又羅嗦？
You prefer this gate tower,	你愛這裡城牆，
the ancient tombs, the solemn dirges,	古墓，長歌，
wildflowers blooming on vines.	蔓草里開野花朵。
Fine, I won't speak more	好，我不再講
of the past. I'll think only of us here on the gate tower,	從前的，單想我們在古城樓上
today	今天，——
White doves,	白鴿，
(did you know that they were white doves?)	（你准知道是白鴿？）
flying before us.	飛過面前。[24]

The lyric portrayal composed of visual fragments in a free-verse style represents the transformation from "a moment of perception into a crisp colloquial poem."[25] The poetic subject presents a little forest decorated with red leaves, floating reflections upon the lake, and idyllic quietness on a beautiful autumn day. The poem also recalls Lin and Liang's essay "Miscellaneous Records of Peiping Suburban Architecture," which conceptualizes the aesthetic notion of "an architectural flavor." Ban Wang writes, "[A]esthetic experience is about our perceptual, sensory, sensuous, emotional, and bodily experience."[26] Enlightened by the aesthetic experience, one is capable of hearing the "solemn dirges" around the "ancient tombs" and seeing the blooming wildflowers as never before. Two years later, in 1937, Lin wrote another poem about Beijing, "Spring Scene of the Ancient City," a subtle meditation on Beijing and its environmental conditions at a time when modern science and technology had begun to emerge and change the city profile and landscape.

Lin demonstrates her aesthetic sensibility with a distinctive interpretation of the modern age from the perspective of space. Modernity and its discontents are reconfigured in perceptions and representations of different kinds of places and spaces, such as temples, fortresses, bridges, city walls, gate towers, and everyday scenes with urban objects, which form an aesthetic and lyrical constellation interspersed with minimal and gigantic spatial images. In "Spring Scene of the Ancient City," Lin

---

[24] Lin Huiyin, "On the Gate Tower," in *Writing Women in Modern China: An Anthology of Women's Literature from the Early Twentieth Century*, ed. Amy D. Dooling and Kristina M. Torgeson (New York: Columbia University Press, 1998), 304. For the Chinese version, see Liang, *Lin Huiyin wenji: Wenxue juan*, 179–180.

[25] Dooling and Torgeson, eds., *Writing Women in Modern China*, 301.

[26] Ban Wang, *The Sublime Figure of History: Aesthetics and Politics in Twentieth-Century China* (Stanford, CA: Stanford University Press, 1997), 6–7.

Huiyin not only expresses deep admiration for the sublime ancient gate tower and the colorful daily objects but also glimpses the advent of urban modernization and industrialization, which is embodied by the incongruous, unsettling image of towering smokestacks intruding into the harmonious city view.

The era can't rein in its own worries,
   pouting simply can't be called the grumblings of a new era—
but it will congeal back into resentment, piling up into a black heap of thick smoke,
   pour forth from smokestacks, a looming new concept facing the ancient gate tower!

No wonder this flat expanse of tender grey sky, this skeptic spring
   wants the mud-yellow sandstorm, trailing along the white plaster alleys,
to once more bow its head and search for that lost romance
   among the indigo curtains, swastika-pattern balusters, and thresholds of old shops.

Go search—no need for newfangled finds, the timeworn are reliable
   though a bit antique, in need of an emerald sugarcane crutch
to prop up the little fruit stands beneath the city walls; their crimson candied hawthorns
   still ablaze, stick upon stick, like aged coral—still unafraid of the new era's dust.

時代把握不住時代自己的煩惱，—
輕率的不滿，就不叫它這時代牢騷—
偏又流成憤怨，聚一堆黑色的濃煙
噴出煙囪，那矗立的新觀念，在古城樓對面！

怪得這嫩灰色一片，帶疑問的春天
要泥黃色風沙，順著白洋灰街沿，
再低著頭去尋覓那已失落的浪漫
到藍布棉簾子，萬字欄桿，仍上老店鋪門檻？

尋去，不必有新奇的新發現，舊有保障
即使古老些，需要翡翠色甘蔗做拐杖
來支撐城牆下小果攤，那紅鮮的冰糖葫蘆
仍然光耀，串串如同舊珊瑚，還不怕新時代的塵土。[27]

---

[27] Liang, *Lin Huiyin wenji: Wenxue juan*, 212. The English translation is by the author and Nick Kaldis and Linda Rui Feng. I also appreciate and adopt an anonymous reader's wonderful correction and translation of a few lines.

The smokestack, a prevalent symbol of modern times, confronts the ancient capital like an ominous dark ghost. Through these spatialized outdoor images, the abstract "new era" is rendered visible and tangible. In contrast, the poet depicts a set of smaller-scale, warm, cozy, and colorful images of the old city: "indigo curtains," "swastika-pattern balusters," and "crimson candied hawthorns." For Lin Huiyin, these daily objects symbolize the old, romantic urban experience. In spite of the "sandstorms" or the "gust and dust" of the spring, a sweet old Beijing was like "candied hawthorns," a small but radiantly utopian image, still ablaze, bunch after bunch, like aged coral—uncontaminated by and fearless of the New Time's dust. In Marshall Berman's terms, this can be seen as the juxtaposition of the pastoral and the counterpastoral.[28] Lin's vision of Beijing is composed of ambivalent scenes: the colorful and romantic everyday life and the intrusion of the newly built smokestacks, the incarnation of modern industry. As early as 1937, in her nostalgic depiction of Beijing, Lin's aesthetic and lyrical poem already expressed her anxious awareness of an increasingly polluted and disappearing ancient capital.

Amid these contrasting images, what and where is the "authentic" Beijing? Perhaps there is no pure Beijing untainted by modernity, only the vestiges of bygone scenes. In this poem, the relatively "authentic" vision of Beijing lies not in its architectural grandeur and magnificence, but in those ephemeral, trivial images of snacks displayed under vendor's tarps at the foot of the city wall. To be sure, imperial palaces and other grand buildings dominate the landscape. However, in Lin's eyes, the cultural textures and basis of this city are constituted by apparently sensuous and superfluous everyday objects, which have outlived the traditional time and the turbulent history. Confronting the invasion of modern industry, these urban cultural objects remain preserved from the dust of modern times. In juxtaposing ancient grand buildings, factory smokestacks, and those quotidian things, Lin not only tells a different story about Beijing's everyday life but also provides an intriguing reconfiguration of the city's spatial-temporal topography. Rey Chow argues that the representation of irrelevant details may be as heavily politically and ideologically charged as that of nation and revolution.[29] Such a politics of details also helps us understand Lin's poetic and cultural agenda in the transitional time of Beijing. It is in this poetics and politics of urban objects that her modern urban sensibilities and perceptions are most fully manifested.

Considering the enthusiastic praise of modern science and technology by her contemporaries, Lin's conception of modernity was unique. Here it is necessary to outline their starkly different vision of the modern in early twentieth-century China.

---

[28] Marshall Berman, *All That Is Solid Melts into Air: The Experience of Modernity* (New York: Penguin, 1982), 135.

[29] Chow, *Women and Chinese Modernity*, 85–86.

Almost ten years earlier, some radical modern Chinese writers enthusiastically embraced the introduction of modern technology to China. Early in 1923, writers of the Creation Society, who were teased by Lu Xun as "caizi jia liumang" 才子＋流氓 (talents plus rascals), published a book series about new science and technology, fantasizing about its benefits in China and urging the dissemination and popularization of scientific knowledge among common people. It includes Cheng Fangwu's 成仿吾 (1897–1984) *Xuanzhan qiji* 漩轉汽機 (Revolving steam machine) and *Gongye shuxue* 工業數學 (Industry mathematics) and Zhang Ziping's 張資平 (1893–1959) *Haiyang xue* 海洋學 (Oceanography) and *Diqiu shi* 地球史 (A history of the earth). The column "Chuangzao ri" 創造日 (Creation day) published several scientific essays, such as Zhou Quanping's 周全平 (1902–1983) "Du *Kexue dagang* diyice hou" 讀《科學大綱》第一冊後 (After reading the first volume of *The Outline of Science*) and Zhang Ziping's "Xinzhi kuangwuxue jiaokeshu" 新制礦物學教科書 (Textbook of new mineralogy) and "Gaodeng kuangwu jiangyi de piping" 高等礦物講義的批評 (Critique of advanced mineralogy). Highlighting the importance of science and technology in changing Chinese society, members of the Creation Society also yearned for modern material civilization. Guo Moruo 郭沫若 (1892–1978), the leading figure of the Society, wrote a poem eulogizing the spectacles of a prosperous industrial metropolis, in which he created a vital metaphor of a "wanglai gongming de jiaoxiangyue, ziran yu rensheng di hunli" 萬籟共鳴的交響樂，自然與人生底婚禮 (harmonious symphony and happy wedding between nature and human life). In his poetic imagination, the smokes of steamboats are "heise de mudan" 黑色的牡丹 (black peonies), "ershi shiji de minghua" 二十世紀的名花 (the noble flowers of the twentieth century), and "jindai wenming de yanmu" 近代文明的嚴母 (the strict mother of modern civilization).[30]

Such images, and especially the "black peonies," exerted a powerful influence on popular perceptions of the "modern" and "modernity" in this period. The sharp contrast between Guo Moruo's eulogy and Lin Huiyin's allergy to smokestacks and modern industrialization foreshadows the later conflicts between Lin Huiyin's aesthetic perspective and urban planning of Beijing and the Maoist political blueprint of a socialist capital after 1949.

---

[30] Run Hua 潤華, "Chuangzao she de lixiang shehui" 創造社的理想社會 [Creation Society's Ideal Society], *Ershiyi shiji* 二十一世紀 [The 21st century] 8 (1999): 85–91; Jiayan Mi, *Self-Fashioning and Reflexive Modernity in Modern Chinese Poetry* (Lewiston, NY: Edwin Mellen, 2004). Modern writers' perception of modern machines is an intriguing topic. For example, Xu Zhimo was fond of riding a bike to pursue the gradually setting sun along a countryside dirt road when he was at the University of Cambridge, and romantically observed the holy interaction between the heaven and the earth. See Zhang Qingping 張清平, *Lin Huiyin* (Tianjin: Baihua wenyi chubanshe, 2002), 138. Every modern reader could be deeply shocked by the stunning sentences of Mao Dun's *Midnight*: "To the west, one saw with a shock of wonder on the roof of

Like her 1930s poems, Lin Huiyin's prose and short stories, including the essay "Zhusi he meihua" 蛛絲和梅花 (Spider's web and plum blossoms, 1936), the short story "Jiong" 窘 (Embarrassing, 1931), and the four-part short story "Moying ling-pian" 模影零篇 (Fragments of vague impressions, 1935–1937), express great interest in nature and the environment, from the city to the country. Nevertheless, Lin was distinct from her fellow Beijing School writers such as Fei Ming 廢名 (1901–1967) and Shen Congwen. Fei and Shen are known for their negative depictions of modern urbanism and their emphasis on a pastoral lifestyle and rural aesthetics. Lin, however, deals with modern Western technologies that inevitably changed daily culture and urban mores in a much more complicated way. A good example is the short story "Jigong" 吉公 (Mr. Ji), which constitutes one section of Lin's series of "Fragments of Vague Impressions." It portrays the life of Mr. Ji, who was adopted by his great-grandmother and was never really accepted by the patriarchal family. A half-professional, half-amateur photographer and craftsman, he is capable of tackling various kinds of new technology. To be sure, his shabby room is like a forgotten, derelict, and exotic corner, but it is also a "romantic location"[31] and a "private laboratory."[32] Mr. Ji is enchanted by different kinds of foreign inventions, such as clocks, telescopes, and cameras, as well as various sizes of maps and oil paintings of topics ranging from trains, steamboats, and foreign royalty to Prussian-French war scenes.[33] These objects stir his imagination, and he sets off for Shanghai to see a true steamboat with his own eyes. Sometimes, in front of an elder who is fond of traditional Chinese martial arts, Mr. Ji talks about Western firearms and spouts eloquent speeches on guns, cannons, steamboats, trains, and even on naval navigation, foreign countries, and the reasons for learning foreign languages.[34] Finally Mr. Ji embarks on his journey to Shanghai, where he finds a job on a steamship, becomes a

a building a gigantic NEON sign in flaming red and phosphorescent green: LIGHT, HEAT, POWER!" See Lee, *Shanghai Modern*, 3. For a heuristic interpretation of "light, heat, power" in Western modernity, see Wolfgang Schivelbusch, *The Railway Journey: The Industrialization of Time and Space in the Nineteenth Century* (Berkeley: University of California Press, 1986); and *Disenchanted Night: The Industrialization of Light in the Nineteenth Century* (Berkeley: University of California Press, 1991).

[31] Lin Huiyin, "Jigong" 吉公 [Mr. Ji], in Liang, *Lin Huiyin wenji: Wenxue juan*, 112.

[32] Ibid. 113.

[33] Ibid. 114–116.

[34] For instance, "They discussed the Suez Canal, and then Mr. Ji went upstairs to bring down his map with pleasure and sympathy. They talked about geography and history, such as the Opium War and the foreign army's looting of Beijing in 1900, which I heard about for the first time. What impressed me more was that Mr. Ji, who had previously always been silent, fluently expressed his indignation. I'm very proud of him, although I cannot understand why his conclusions always return to machines" (他們講到蘇彝士運河，吉公便高興地，同情地，把樓上地圖拿下來，由地理講到歷史，甲午呀，庚子呀，我都是在那時第一次聽到。我更記得平常不說話的吉公當日憤慨的議論，我為他不止一點的驕傲，雖然我不明白為甚麼他的結論總回到機器上). Ibid. 117.

wharfinger, and later establishes his own small textile mill. Lin Huiyin's impressionistic sketches of this man who indulges in modern technologies and novel objects are
quite uncommon among the Beijing School writings.

Published in the first issue of *Xuewen yuekan* 學文月刊 (Xuewen monthly), Lin's
representative short story "In Ninety-Nine-Degree Heat" is another piece of the
"Fragments of Vague Impressions," and it shows a shift from an aesthetic perception
of the city to a more realist, in certain aspects modernist, account of everyday life
in the cruel heat of the Beijing summer.[35] This is a view "from above to street level
to below,"[36] which diverges further from the literary practice and aesthetic expectations of the Beijing School. In the short story, the omniscient narrator tears off the
curtain of the disorderly everyday life of modern Beijing, so as to feel the city's pulse
and diagnose its symptoms in a literary form. Here, tradition and modernity are
not exhibited in a sharp contrast or distinctive rupture, but rather are presented in a
tangible and random manner: a luxurious old-fashioned wedding ceremony versus
modern romantic love in college, a country girl versus a modern lady, traditional
Chinese cuisine versus Western-style desserts, food porters versus rickshaw men,
sweet-sour plums versus ice cream, old ideas versus new terminology, Peking opera
versus foreign cinema, feudal ethics and rites versus new fashion and knowledge, traditional Chinese medicine stored in porcelain pots versus Western medicine practiced in missionary hospitals, and so forth. In this way, Lin offers an impressionist
and panoramic picture of daily life in 1930s Beijing.

In her short preface to the anthology of Beijing School works published in
Dagongbao 大公報 (*Ta Kung Pao*, formerly *L'Impartial*) in 1936, Lin Huiyin pointed
out one distinct deficiency of the school's early writings:

> In terms of depiction, we feel that most of the short stories choose an episode
> of a story, or center on one or two characters, or set its main plot from the sim-
> ple beginning and ending of an event happened in some location. This is also
> a weak method. We are wondering whether many authors misunderstand the
> limits of the short story, looking down upon its possibilities. *Few attempt to*

---

[35] As far as the heat of Beijing is concerned, Lao Chin 老金 (Chin Yueh-lin, or Jin Yuelin 金岳霖, 1895–1984),
a leading logician, one of Lin and Liang's best friends, wrote in a short letter in 1934, "[T]he weather has
been rather negligent of our feelings, it teases us, irritates us, and put us into that terrible state in which we
are way below our sense of humor and just slightly above our level of consciousness. I, for one, am far from
civilized. I was going to say that I am far more like the animals than they are like me, but upon reflection
there seems to be something wrong with the statement." John K. Fairbank, *Chinabound: A Fifty-Year Memoir*
(New York: Harper & Row, 1982), 108. The last sentence is evidence that the logician had not yet lost his sense
of humor, which seems to partly relieve the exhausting and frustrating heat of summer in the city.

[36] Burton Pike, *The Image of the City in Modern Literature* (Princeton, NJ: Princeton University Press, 1981), 52.

touch upon the naked fragments of life, or the contradictions of everyday life around
the writers. This is also a regret among us.

在描寫上，我們感到大多數所取的方式是寫一段故事，或以一兩人物為
中心，或以某地方一椿事發生的始末為主幹，單純的發展與結束。這也是
比較薄弱的手法。這個我們疑惑或是許多作者誤會了短篇的限制，把它
的可能性看得過窄的緣故。生活大膽的斷面，這裡少有人嘗試，剖示貼
己生活的矛盾也無多少人認真的來做。這也是我們中間的一種遺憾。[37]

With "In Ninety-Nine-Degree Heat," Lin attempted to capture the "naked fragments" and "contradictions of everyday life" so that she could remedy the regret
mentioned in her preface, and demonstrate and develop the potential of the
short-story form.

The story also uses some key modernist narrative tactics. It lacks a conventional,
main plot or leading protagonists. In its minute descriptions of indoor activities and
street scenes, everyday life unfolds in speedy and arbitrary montages. City life is presented as a sequence of random snapshots, tracing diverse locales and "the state of
mind" of urban residents. The "fragmentation of people through the dynamism of
the street"[38] is a familiar theme that many Beijing writers try to explore. In modern
Chinese literature, Lu Xun added a moral dimension to a story about an anonymous rickshaw man to criticize the urban middle class. Through rickshaw puller
Xiangzi, Lao She tested the ambitious yet unfulfilled dream of lonely individual-
ism and approached the modern antihero's disillusionment and despair in terms of
morality, economy, and body. Hu Shi (1891–1962) and Chen Duxiu 陳獨秀 (1879–
1942) used the figure of the rickshaw boy to mirror modernity's negative effects on
the masses in the city. Yet in Lin Huiyin's story, the striking and absurd street fight
between two rickshaw pullers and the bitter destiny of a food porter, whose miserable life ends suddenly in the summer, expeditiously posit the fragments of daily
existence against the background of the transforming Beijing.

What intrigued Lin Huiyin were not merely the streets where great historical
events took place. She offered modern sketches to depict the small maelstroms of
the rich and the poor. There are neither monumental nor spectacular moments, neither sentimental nor melodramatic narratives. "In Ninety-Nine-Degree Heat" is
replete with random impressions of modern Beijing on a hot summer day. Richard
Lehan examines "the distinction between descriptive detail (the detail controlling

---

[37] Lin Huiyin, ed., *Dagongbao wenyi congkan xiaoshuo xuan* 大公報文藝叢刊小說選 [Anthology of short stories published in the Literary Supplement of *Dagongbao*] (Shanghai: Dagongbao guan, 1936; repr., Shanghai
shudian, 1990), 2–3; italics added.
[38] Berman, *All That Is Solid Melts into Air*, 276.

the mind) and impressionistic detail (the mind controlling the detail)."[39] In Lin's description of the cruel summer day, the "descriptive detail," is tensely interwoven with the "impressionistic detail." Ah Shu, the old-style girl in this story, finds out that "her real marriage is not less problematic because she pays more attention to the various kinds of problems with marriage, family, love discussed in newspapers and new literatures" (並沒有因為她多留心報紙上，新文學上，所討論的婚姻問題，家庭問題，戀愛問題，而減少了問題).[40] Her lover, Yijiu, a modern young man majoring in politics and law and striving for new perspectives, still oscillates between Ah Shu, a traditional girl, and Qiong, a modern female student. Yijiu is fond of modern style. He always spoke English when he was in middle school, and collected lots of pictures and posters of exotic female movie stars and displayed them on his bedroom walls. He even went to Shanghai for two years to learn modern dance. On that hot summer day, Yijiu and two friends go to a Western-style restaurant in Beijing, where "ice cream, coffee, milk, and various desserts" are served. The young lovers sitting at the next table catch his attention. The beautiful girl reminds him of his beloved Qiong, and a vague memory of an episode emerges in his mind: one time, Qiong played around with Yijiu at her father's house, pretending to grope for fish in the garden pond; when her authoritarian uncle came out to scold her, she giggled. However, all of a sudden, Yijiu recalls Ah Shu, a totally different type of woman. Ah Shu is never dressed in up-to-date fashion, but she represents an alternative beauty, intelligence, and femininity. Yijiu cannot think further in such hot and humid weather—he only feels an unnamable sorrow gnawing at his heart.[41]

This was Beijing in Lin Huiyin's literary imagination, with the old and the new, the traditional and the modern arbitrarily juxtaposed in both temporal and spatial terms. In this story, the consciousness and inner voices of the city's inhabitants emerge and flow like brimming streams. Lin Huiyin's narrative perspective moves like a camera lens in a smooth and fluid manner. In the ancient city, new ideas and values ferment and brew while the old customs persist. Lin's writing of Beijing is a complex aggregation or accumulation, not just in demographic, economic, or social terms but also, and more importantly, in affective and cultural terms. Thus Beijing becomes "more than their built environment, more than a set of class or economic relationships;" it is "also an experience to be lived, suffered, undergone."[42]

---

[39] Lehan, *The City in Literature*, 77–78.

[40] Lin, "In Ninety-Nine-Degree Heat," in Liang, *Lin Huiyin wenji: Wenxue juan*, 84.

[41] Ibid. 87–88.

[42] Peter Preston and Paul Simpson-Housley, *Writing the City: Eden, Babylon and the New Jerusalem* (London: Routledge, 2002), 2.

Although this story by Lin Huiyin differs from other Beijing School works in its experimental, modernist depiction of urban experiences, it was surprisingly well received by her fellow writers and contemporary critics. They applauded Lin's experimental short story without complaining about its obvious nonfiction elements, such as the fundamental lack of a real plot or climax, themed environment, and unity of narrative voice.[43] Li Jianwu observed in 1936,

> In such sweltering summer weather, the author reveals all the hues of a day. The short story has organization without organization, has consecutiveness without consecutiveness, has story without story and even tells so many stories, and is replete with crafts without craft.
>
> 在這樣一個溽暑的北平,作者把一天的形形色色披露在我們的眼前,沒有組織,卻有組織;沒有條理,卻有條理;沒有故事,卻有故事,而且那樣多的故事;沒有技巧,卻處處透露匠心。[44]

Other critics claimed they had no ability to write a modern piece like this. They highly evaluated Lin Huiyin's perception of modern Beijing in her spatialization of time, her appropriation of camera-like perspectives, and her construction of montages of the fragments of everyday life. In his comparison of Liu Na'ou's and Mu Shiying's Shanghai narratives, Leo Ou-fan Lee argues, "Mu Shiying's mis-en-scène is more ambitious than Liu's, as the street scene leads to a series of panoramic shots of the city crowd."[45] Lin Huiyin also illustrates a panorama of everyday life in Beijing, but in a more impressionist and rapid manner that is characterized by a brisk stream-of-consciousness narrative and explorations of deep urban psychologies. Burton Pike asserts that "during the nineteenth century the word-city was increasingly represented in literature as an unstable refraction of an individual consciousness rather than as an object fixed in space."[46] In Lin's case, the spatial objects and images are configured along the stream of consciousness originating from the flat characters, thus forming a "modernist montage and episodic narrative."[47] Shu-mei Shih points out, "like a camera capturing diverse scenes of life and presenting them in montages, Lin's narrative

---

[43] Berman, *All That Is Solid Melts into Air*, 216.

[44] Li Jianwu, "Jiushijiu du zhong—Lin Huiyin nüshi zuo" 《九十九度中》—林徽因女士作 [In Ninety-Nine-Degree Heat—Written by Madam Lin Huiyin], in Liu, ed., *Chuangzi neiwai yi Huiyin*, 21.

[45] Lee, *Shanghai Modern*, 225.

[46] Pike, *The Image of the City in Modern Literature*, 71.

[47] Shu-mei Shih contextualizes the method of "episodic narrative" in Chinese literature, and Wu Jingzi's *The Scholars* is a representative work: "The fragmentary nature of the narrative harkens back to the traditional episodic narrative, where events are frequently merely juxtaposed or connected as if by coincidence and form a vast 'interweaving' and 'reticular' relationship rather than a linear, causal one." *The Lure of Modern*, 213.

perspective moves in a fluid manner without explanatory subtitles or voice-overs."[48] Carles Prado-Fonts suggests that "thanks to this episodic, disrupted narrative—in terms of structure and also as a combination of dialogue, monologue, indirect speech, stream-of-consciousness style and so on—Lin Huiyin is able to suitably depict a set of social contrasts and juxtapositions."[49] Lin's urban "scrolls" unfold and fold at three transitory moments within the same day: high noon, afternoon, and evening. They can be categorized into three different spatial types: first, interior and enclosed spaces, including the grand Zhang Mansion and the food porter's shabby home; second, exterior and open spaces, such as the streets and winding alleyways; and third, a semiopen space embodied by the wedding hall. The stream of consciousness flows along the short temporal framework and runs across different types of spaces, which are then captured and woven into episodic descriptions and observations, scroll by scroll.

Shortly after the publication of "In Ninety-Nine-Degree Heat," Li Jianwu hailed it as a work "of utmost modernity."[50] Both Zhu Ziqing 朱自清 (1898–1948) and Bian Zhilin pointed out the relationship between Lin's short story and Virginia Woolf's experimental "stream-of-consciousness novels."[51] The omniscient narrator rapidly recounts the daily activities of the upper class enjoying life in leisure and of the lower class struggling to make a living in the hot Beijing summer.[52] However, what the "omniscient point of view" put in practice was not the "aesthetics of exclusion" adopted by both Beijing and Shanghai School writers, who deliberately focused on selective aspects of life and bracketed or ignored others. In "In Ninety-Nine-Degree Heat," Lin Huiyin seeks to achieve a full-scale observation of life in Beijing in terms of social class, politics, economics, gender, and psychology, and to open up a larger aesthetic and social view than her contemporary Beijing or Shanghai School writers.

Li Jianwu notes, "The modernity of a work lies in not only in the materials themselves (we should avoid using the terms 'form' and 'content'), but also, more importantly, in the observation, choice, and technique" (一件作品的現代性,不僅僅在材料(我們最好避免形式、內容的字樣),而大半在觀察,選擇和技巧).[53] Lin Huiyin's experimental literary techniques can be considered through a reading of her

---

[48] Ibid., 212.

[49] Carles Prado-Fonts, "Fragmented Encounters, Social Slippages: Lin Huiyin's 'In Ninety-Nine Degree Heat,'" *Lectora: Revista de Dones i Textualitat* 16 (2010): 128.

[50] Li, "Jiushijiu du zhong—Lin Huiyin nüshi zuo," 21.

[51] See Yu Xiaoxia 俞曉霞, "Lin Huiyin xiaoshuo changzuo zhong de wuerfu yinsu" 林徽因小說創作中的伍爾夫因素 [Virginia Woolf Elements in Lin Huiyin's Short Stories], *Zhongguo xiandai wenxue yanjiu congkan* 中國現代文學研究叢刊 [Modern Chinese literature studies] 6 (2012): 59–67.

[52] If we compare Lin's narrative and Lao She's description in *Rickshaw Boy*, we can figure out the different writing strategies and narrative paces of two Beijing writers.

[53] Li, "Jiushijiu du zhong—Lin Huiyin nüshi zuo," 20.

essay entitled "Outside of the Window." This can be viewed as a self-reflexive work by an urban ethnographer, in which Lin contemplates her aesthetic and lyrical position vis-à-vis the city and its history. I consider the window image as building a framework, a boundary between inside and outside. In his well-known poem "Duanzhang" 斷章 (Fragment, 1935), Bian Zhilin creates a set of images of bridges, balconies, and windows:

You are standing on a bridge enjoying the view;
Someone's watching you from a balcony.
The moon adorns your window;
You adorn someone else's dream.

你站在橋上看風景，
看風景人在樓上看你。
明月裝飾了你的窗子，
你裝飾了別人的夢。[54]

Like Lin, Bian portrays a subtle scenario of seeing/being seen, subject/object, inside/ outside (of a window). Lin's "Outside of the Window" ponders the intricate connections between observation and reflection: "when stopping by the lively avenues, you are still watching operas from a specific balcony, with no need to participate in the performance; leaning against the rail, you are appreciating them with an aesthetic distance, and with a bit of leisure" (到了熱鬧的大街了，你仍然像在特別包廂裡看戲一樣，本身不會，也不必參加那齣戲；倚在欄杆上，你在審美的領略，你有的是一片閒暇)。[55] Lin's prose features an observer, the "you," who walks in the crowd on the street while simultaneously maintaining a constant distance, both aesthetic and spatial, from the surrounding people and the hustle and bustle of everyday life.[56] The observer is a bystander described by another bystander, who witnesses the pleasure and pain of the masses, unrelated to his or her own interests. In this sense, the second-person narrative "you" resembles an urban ethnographer observing and classifying city life in a detached, scientific manner. Yingjin Zhang maintains, "[F]rom the ethnographic perspective, the configurations of space, time, and gender may provide a route that reaches down to the level of mentalities."[57] In a reflexive and confessional tone, Lin writes, "[Y]ou're still seated inside of a window, whether a train's, a car's,

[54] Bi Zhilin, "Fragment," in Yeh, *Anthology of Modern Chinese Poetry*, 51.

[55] Liang, *Lin Huiyin wenji: Wenxue juan*, 20.

[56] With regard to literary walking, Leo Ou-fan Lee remarks, "To be sure, there is no shortage of literary references to walking (*sanbu*) itself in Chinese poetry and fiction, both traditional and modern. But such literary walks often take place against or amidst a pastoral landscape." See his *Shanghai Modern*, 39.

[57] Zhang, *The City in Modern Chinese Literature and Film*, 52.

or an inn's, as well as the window constructed by invisible habit, and where you're entrenched" (你是仍然坐在窗子以內的, 不是火車的窗子, 汽車的窗子, 就是客棧逆旅的窗子, 再不然就是你自己無形中習慣的窗子, 把你攔在裡面).[58] Her conscious contemplation of a physical and metaphorical window between herself, the observing subject, and the places and people, the observed objects, is also different from two other significant perspectives of urban observation: the balcony in E. T. A. Hoffman's last story, "The Cousin's Corner Window," which houses a bourgeois male observer's gaze; and Edgar Allen Poe's "man of the crowd," the flâneur figure discussed by both Charles Baudelaire and Walter Benjamin, which epitomizes an observer who mingles with the crowd but does not feel like one of them.[59] In Lin's essay, the "you" is an abstract position taken by some disinterested observer. She put it well, saying, "[Y]ou do not expect that no matter where you go, you always take a seat within a window. Yes, many 'modern' scholars often proudly put on airs, wear 'scientific' glasses, and occasionally stop by a strange place to observe. Nevertheless, the invisible window is still there" (想到不管你走到哪裡, 你永遠免不了坐在窗子以內的。不錯, 許多時髦的學者常常驕傲地帶上"考察"的神氣, 架上科學的眼鏡, 偶然走到哪裡一個陌生的地方瞭望, 但那無形中的窗子是仍然存在的).[60] Lin, also a self-reflective observer, notices the transparent barrier of her own window: the predicament she had to confront in a transitional, formative age of the modern, in order to go in and out of her well-known "Madam's Salon," develop her literary and architectural aesthetics, and decipher and map out people, places, and things in Beijing and beyond.

PASSION AND PAIN IN PLACE

In space, one can be another person. Time does not give one much leeway: it thrusts us forward from behind, blows us through the narrow funnel of the present into the future. But space is broad, teeming with possibilities, positions, intersections, passages, detours.
—SUSAN SONTAG

"There are times when our little courtyard is inundated with joy."[61] Thus wrote Xu Zhimo in the spring of 1923, when he recalled those happy moments in a notable

[58] Liang, *Lin Huiyin wenji: Jianzhu juan*, 23. Wang Ping 王平 addressed the connection of Lin's window image and "architectural flavor" (jianzhu yi 建築意) in "Chuangzi neiwai 窗子內外 [Inside and outside of the window], *Wenyi zhengming* 文藝爭鳴 [Literary debates] 5 (2011): 108–112.

[59] For a further discussion of these two bourgeois observational perspectives, see Peter Stallybrass and Allon White, *The Politics and Poetics of Transgression* (London: Methuen, 1986), esp. chaps. 3 and 4.

[60] Liang, *Lin Huiyin wenji: Wenxue juan*, 22.

[61] Xu Zhimo, "Number 7, Stone Tiger Lane," in Jonathan D. Spence, *The Gate of Heavenly Peace: The Chinese and Their Revolution, 1895–1980* (New York: Viking, 1981), 16.

literary salon in Beijing. A few years later, in 1927, Lin Huiyin and Liang Sicheng's house at Number 3 North Zongbu Lane, another "little yard . . . inundated with joy," had become one of the most influential cultural salons among Beijing literati and intellectuals.[62] Lin Huiyin was the longtime hostess and the guiding spirit of her salon,[63] called by friends "Madam's Salon."[64] The key figures and regular guests included the philosopher and logician Jin Yuelin, the writer and professor of literature at Peking University Shen Congwen, the journalist Xiao Qian 蕭乾 (1910–1999), poet Xu Zhimo, professor of political science Zhang Xiruo 張奚若 (1889–1973), the physicist Zhou Peiyuan 周培源 (1902–1993), the economist Chen Daisun 陳岱孫 (1900–1997), professor of aesthetics and art theory Deng Yizhe 鄧 以蟄 (1892–1973), the expert on international politics Qian Duansheng 錢端升 (1900–1990), the sociologist Tao Menghe 陶孟和 (1887–1960), the archaeologist Li Ji 李濟 (1896–1979), and the historian John K. Fairbank (1907–1991) and his wife, the art historian Wilma Fairbank (1909–2002), among others.

In his discussion of Zeng Pu's guest room and publishing house at the beginning of the twentieth century, Leo Ou-fan Lee compares it to "a genuine French salon" and emphasizes the resemblances between these two cultural spaces.[65] Inspired and influenced by the Bloomsbury Group, Lin Huiyin created her famous "Madam's Salon" by combining cultural features of the turn-of-the-twentieth-century English and also the mid-nineteenth-century French-style salon. In his study of French salon culture from the seventeenth to the nineteenth century, Steven Kale regards the salon as a significant cultural and political space of "sociability of leisure, a form of communication and an arena for social encounters, providing opportunities for conviviality, intellectual exchange, and unconventional social relationships."[66] Craig Calhoun states that, in nineteenth-century France, salons were "public institutions located in a private home," and "were also distinctive in including, even being organized by women."[67] Lin's "Madam's Salon" was situated in her home, and she was the

---

[62] Jin Yuelin lived in the other half of the courtyard house, and his salon was named "Hunan Hotel," a complementary salon to Lin Huiyin's.

[63] Here, "salon" means a place primarily for communications among intellectuals, which is different from the classical and Western sense of "salon," where intellectuals meet with the aristocracy.

[64] In 1930s, Bing Xin 冰心 (1900–1999) wrote a short story entitled "Women taitai de keting" 我們太太的客 廳 [Our madam's salon], which is said to refer to Lin Huiyin's salon with a satirical tone. See *Bing Xin quanji* 冰心全集 [Complete writings of Bing Xin] (Fuzhou: Haixia wenyi chubanshe, 1994), 3:21–39.

[65] Lee, *Shanghai Modern*, 20.

[66] Steven Kale, *French Salons: High Society and Political Sociability from the Old Regime to the Revolution of 1848* (Baltimore: John Hopkins University Press, 2006), 4.

[67] Patricia Laurence, *Lily Briscoe's Chinese Eyes: Bloomsbury, Modernism, and China* (Columbia: University of South Carolina Press, 2003); Craig Calhoun, ed., *Habermas and the Public Sphere* (Cambridge, MA: MIT Press, 1992), 12, 43n18.

charming hostess and organizer. It treaded the blurred boundaries between the private and the public, between a female inner boudoir and the patriarchal domain of a traditional Chinese family. From 1931 to 1937, "Madam's Salon" hosted guests on Saturday afternoons in Beijing. After 1946, when the couple returned to the city following their exile during the Sino-Japanese War, it became the daily afternoon tea party, relocated to their new home in Number 12 Shengyin Court. Liang Sicheng greatly valued the significance of leisurely chatting, and traced it back to Cambridge University's seven-hundred-year tradition of formal and informal conversations among intellectuals from different disciplines to exchange ideas.[68] As the smart salonnière and the "magisterial" leader, Lin Huiyin moderated conversations on topics ranging from poetry style (her debate with Liang Zongdai 梁宗岱 [1903–1983] is an outstanding example), literary trends, and the historical study of Beijing architecture to Wang Guowei's 王國維 (1877–1927) suicide and its cultural implications.[69]

Many times, Lin dominated the conversations in her salon while other members, including her husband, sat there and listened to her. John K. Fairbank once recalled, "She was creatively gifted as a writer, a poet, a woman of great aesthetic sensitivity and broad intellectual interests, and socially charming. The household, or any scene she was in, tended to revolve around her."[70] Xiao Qian, a native Beijinger, affectionately called Lin "the soul of the Beijing School." He recalled that in the autumn of 1933, shortly after Xiao's debut, "Chan" 蠶 (Silkworm), appeared in the "Literary Supplement" of *Dagongbao*, Lin invited him to her "Madam's Salon" and highly praised his literary skill and sincere feeling. These remarks encouraged Xiao Qian to choose literature as his career; he later became an established reporter and literary translator.[71]

Lin Huiyin's salon, situated within a familial space, functioned as a literary and cultural public space. In his study of the bourgeois public sphere, Jürgen Habermas proposes an interactive relationship between literature and politics, or more

---

[68] Li Daozeng, "The Significance of Chatting," in Liu Xiaoqin, *Chuangzi neiwai yi Huiyin*, 43.

[69] Lin pointed out that Zhu Yixin's 朱一新 study, *Jingshi fangxiangzhi* 京師坊巷志 (Records of streets and alleys in Beijing), only went back to the Yuan dynasty. Actually, earlier, during the Sui and Song dynasties, the markets had already begun to take shape, though not in Beijing. She also talked about the names of Beijing's alleyways, which highlight the changes in the city's life. For example, some names are related to the size and shape of the alleys, like "ladder alley," "pocket alley," "frosty gourd alley," or to various kinds of wells, such as "sweet water well," "bitter water well," "three-hole well," "four-hole well," "high well," "Prince's Court well"; some other names are connected with the districts of Beijing, such as "sheep market," "pig market," "mule and horse market," "arrow yard," "fine brick yard," "glaze yard," "Military and Horse Department," etc. See Zhang, *Lin Huiyin*, 123–125, 128–130.

[70] John K. Fairbank, *Chinabound*, 105. For a Chinese version, see Liu, *Chuangzi neiwai yi Huiyin*, 31.

[71] Xiao Qian, "Yidai cainü Lin Huiyin" 一代才女林徽因 [The talented lady of a generation, Lin Huiyin], *Dushu* 讀書 [Reading] 10 (October 1984): 114–115.

precisely, between the literary public sphere and the formation of public opinion, which could change the making of state policy.[72] Although the social, cultural, and political contexts of modern Beijing differed substantially from late eighteenth- and early nineteenth-century Europe, Habermas's theoretical framework may help open up new perspectives into the cultural implications of Lin's "Madam's Salon." As a cultural public space, the salon did not intend to create any direct connections between literature and real politics.[73] In fact, writers of the Beijing School were known for their resolution to separate literature from politics to maintain intellectual autonomy. For Habermas, "the public sphere in the political realm evolved from the public sphere in the world of letters."[74] The intellectuals in Lin Huiyin's literary public space, however, emphasized the quality of language, the purity of aesthetic experiences, and pastoral simplicity in literary representations, separate from political involvements. Literature thus became an autonomous aesthetic realm that could contest and compete with that of politics. This did not mean that Lin and her friends were not interested in political topics. However, they did not regard literature as a supplementary instrument to intervene in the political situation. As a public space inside the world of letters, Lin's "Madam's Salon" was also marked by a collegial intimacy. It formed a cultural institution that not only introduced new ideas and branches of knowledge but also edited and produced literary anthologies of Beijing School writers, thus creating a "symbolic capital" that circulated in the "market of culture products."[75]

In addition to these distinguished communities, literary and cultural public spaces were not uncommon among general Beijing residents.[76] The diversity and popularity of such clubs and gatherings in Beijing is reminiscent of the cultural scene in

---

[72] Jürgen Habermas, *The Structural Transformation of the Public Sphere*, trans. Thomas Burger (Cambridge, MA: MIT Press, 1991), 30.

[73] For a volume shedding new light on the public sphere (public space) in the context of transnational communications, see Mayfair Mei-hui Yang, ed., *Spaces of Their Own: Women's Public Sphere in Transnational China* (Minneapolis: University of Minnesota Press, 1999).

[74] Habermas, *The Structural Transformation of the Public Sphere*, 32. For a discussion of the salons as female "public sphere," see Seyla Benhabib, *The Reluctant Modernism of Hannah Arendt* (Lanham, MD: Rowman & Littlefield, 2003).

[75] Another famous salon was Zhu Guanqian 朱光潛 (1897–1986) and Liang Zongdai's monthly "poetry reading party" that gathered key figures of modern Chinese poetry: Feng Zhi 馮至 (1905–1993), Zhu Ziqing, Bing Xin, Ling Shuhua 凌叔華 (1900–1990), Bian Zhilin, and He Qifang 何其芳 (1912–1977). See, for instance, Li Lei 李蕾, "Jingpai zuojia de juhe xingtai kaojiu: Yi shalong wei lunshu zhongxin 京派作家的聚合形態考究：以沙龍為論述中心 [Beijing school writers' group gathering: Salon as a distinctive form], *Jilin daxue shehui kexue xuebao* 吉林大學社會科學學報) [Jilin University journal of social sciences] 4 (2009): 106–110.

[76] Mingzheng Shi, "Beijing Transforms: Urban Infrastructure, Public Works, and Social Change in the Chinese Capital, 1900–1928" (PhD diss., Columbia University, 1993).

mid-nineteenth-century London, where "every profession, trade, class, party, had its favourite coffee-house."[77] In Beijing's Zhongyang gongyuan 中央公園 (Central Park, later renamed 中山公園 Zhongshan Park), three teahouses in modern or traditional styles attracted various groups of patrons. The Chunmingguan chazuo (Spring brightness teahouse 春明館茶座, with chunming referring to Beijing) was a space favored by old-fashioned celebrities, who wore Qing-style gowns, robes, and watermelon-shaped hats (長袍馬褂, 瓜皮小帽). The food offered there consisted mainly of Beijing local specialties, including haw (山楂紅), yellow split pea cake (豌豆黃), glutinous rice cake with a sweet filling (艾窩窩), Poria cake (茯苓餅), steamed chestnut bread (栗子面窩頭), and Beijing-style buns and noodles, such as steamed buns stuffed with sweetened bean paste (豆包), noodles served with fried bean sauce (炸醬麵), vegetarian sauce noodles (素鹵面), and cake with ground meat (肉末兒燒餅). The teahouse provided a special area for Chinese chess (象棋) and the Go game (围棋). The customers enjoyed the leisure of playing games, reciting classical Chinese verses, improvising Peking opera, or just sitting back and relaxing.

Another teahouse, the Bosixing chazuo (柏斯馨茶座), was a favorite hangout for *modeng* (modern 摩登) young people and foreign patrons. It was entirely decorated in Western style, and offered a Western beverage menu including lemonade, orange juice, soda, coffee, beer, and wine. Its customers read English-language newspapers, and their conversations were often interspersed with phrases from different foreign languages. The third teahouse, the Changmeixuan chazuo 長美軒茶座 (Always beautiful teahouse), was a more eclectic place. In between the fashionable edge of Bosixin and the archaic tone of Chunmingguan, Changmeixua was regarded as a proper venue frequented by modern Beijing intellectuals and academics. This teahouse offered daily snacks such as sunflower seeds (葵花子), peanuts (花生米), walnuts (核桃仁), and dried apricots (杏乾). The main menu consisted of steamed dumplings with seasonal fillings (燒賣), meat-filled buns fresh from the food steamer (小籠包), rice fried with eggs (蛋炒飯), and *huntun* with light soup (清湯餛飩). It was common to see writers or professors in their regular seats, reading books or writing over a cup of tea.[78]

The three teahouses varied in size, composition of customers, and topics of debate. However, they all demonstrated an important aspect of city life in modern Beijing, which featured a juxtaposition of diverse, competing cultural spaces and values. In addition to literary salons located in private homes, teahouses were indispensible

[77] "The Clubs of London," *National Review* 4, no. 8 (April 1857): 301, quoted in Habermas, *The Structural Transformation of the Public Sphere*, 257.

[78] Zhang, *Lin Huiyin*, 177–178; Tang Xiaobing 唐小兵, "Sanshi niandai Beiping de liangdao fengjingxian" 三十年代北平的兩道風景線 [Two landscapes in 1930s Beijing], *Shuwu* 書屋 [House of books] 9 (2007): 61–64.

places where new ideas were brewed, debated, and contested. In the spring of 1936, to promote the Beijing School as a more coherent literary entity and win over a larger audience, Shen Congwen invited Lin Huiyin, Zhu Ziqing, Yang Zhensheng 楊振聲 (1890–1956), Zhu Guangqian 朱光潛 (1897–1986), Li Jianwu, and other fellow writers to meet in Laijinyu xuan 來今雨軒 (The hall of the coming of today's rain) inside the Changmeixuan Teahouse.[79] At this gathering, they decided to compile an anthology of their recent writings and selected Lin, "the soul" of the Beijing School, as the editor. This anthology was later published as *Selections of Beijing School Literature* (京派文學作品選集), and it collected works by Shen Congwen, Lao She, Xiao Qian, Li Jianwu, Zhang Tianyi 張天翼 (1906–1985), Yang Zhensheng, Lu Fen 蘆焚 (Shi Tuo 師陀, 1910–1986), Jian Xian'ai 蹇先艾 (1906–1994), Sha Ting 沙汀 (1904–1992), Yang Jiang 楊絳 (1911–2016), and Ling Shuhua, among others, as well as two short pieces by Lin Huiyin herself.[80]

Interestingly, Lin Huiyin's "Madam's Salon" not only constructed a community of elite intellectuals but also was open to the general public. Its open type of public space was similar to its nineteenth-century counterparts in European cities. This space, as Habermas describes, "not merely made access to the relevant circles less formal and easier; it embraced the wider strata of the middle class, including craftsmen and shopkeepers."[81] According to Chen Daisun's recollections, Lin's guests included professors; students of Peking University, Tsinghua University, and Yenching University; traditional-style literati; actors and actresses; craftsmen; and even aged cricket players.[82] After the department of architecture was founded at Tsinghua University, Lin's salon became the regular department party site and the preparatory place for the Association of Architecture in China.[83]

The 1936 photography of Liang and Lin on the top of the Temple of Heaven depicted a key moment when Lin's literary and artistic activities extended from the interior literary salon to exterior, historical sites during field trips where she and her colleagues conducted architectural and art historical investigations. During her journey to Shanxi province to examine ancient buildings, she wrote,

> Everything I see is a wonderful picture, and all the days are ancient records that could be sung and recited . . . . In order to investigate the ancient traces,

---

79 Zhang, *The City in Modern Chinese Literature and Film*, 25; Zhang, *Lin Huiyin*, 178.

80 See Lin, *Anthology of Short Stories Published in the Literary Supplement of Dagongbao*.

81 Habermas, *The Structural Transformation of the Public Sphere*, 33.

82 Chen Daisun, "Renwu de guangfanxing shi zhe chahui de tedian" 人物的廣泛性是這茶會的特點 [The tea party is characterized by its wide-ranging participants], in Liu, *Chuangzi neiwai yi Huiyin*, 36–37.

83 Liu, *Chuangzi neiwai yi Huiyin*, 29–48.

we marched a lot, and noted the rise and decline of the past and the present. Reading inscriptions on tablets buried in wild grass, or casually encountering Buddha's hands or smile in the disordered pile of bricks—all of these could stimulate some uncommon feelings.

旬日來眼看去的都是圖畫,日子都是可以歌唱的古事。. . . . 我們因為探訪古跡走了許多路,在種種情形之下感慨到古今興廢。在草叢裡讀碑碣,在磚堆中間偶然碰到菩薩的一雙手一個微笑,都是可以激動起一些不平常的感覺來的。[84]

Lin's aesthetic sensibility and architectural training enabled her to appreciate the lost "romance, beauty, and innocence" of the forlorn historical relics and buildings that she sought to record, measure, and study.[85] Stepping out of the modern city, or a privileged imperial capital represented by the Temple of Heaven, Lin took the opportunity to investigate ancient temples, fortresses, ruins, and relics, constantly searching for abandoned and neglected sites and cultural artifacts. In 1937, with John K. Fairbank and Wilma Fairbank, Lin Huiyin took measurements for scale drawings. John K. Fairbank vividly recalled,

> They finally found a true Tang building, the oldest then known, in the Wu-t'ai Mountains northeast of Taiyuan, they knew its general age from the size of the brackets (called *tou-kung*) which carry the roof's weight down onto the columns. . . . But they found no date until Phyllis caught sight of an inscription high up on a beam, left by a donor. Ironically this discovery was made on July 7, 1937, the day the eight-year Sino-Japanese war began, putting them out of the business of North China field trips.[86]

Eight days later, Lin Huiyin learned belatedly from a local newspaper that the Second Sino-Japanese War had already broken out. A critical date of a significant finding in Chinese architectural history was the very day when the Japanese army invaded China. Aesthetic discovery was forced to give way to political catastrophe. That year, Lin Huiyin and Liang Sicheng finally decided to leave the city under the Japanese occupation and began their strenuous exile—an experience shared by hundreds of thousands of Chinese intellectuals. Number 3 North Zongbu Lane, the literary and cultural public space, was abandoned during the war. During the prolonged wartime

---

[84] Lin Huiyin, "Shanxi tongxin" 山西通信 [Letter from Shangxi], originally appeared in *Dagongbao*, August 25, 1934, reprinted in Lin Huiyin, *Heping liwu* 和平禮物 [Presents of peace] (Beijing: Beijing daxue chubanshe, 2009), 121.

[85] Zhang, *Lin Huiyin*, 239.

[86] John K. Fairbank, *Chinabound*, 109.

exile, Lin's health suffered severely.[87] Drawing on Lin Huiyin's diaries, letters, memoirs, and several biographies, Jonathan Spence writes,

> We hear Whei-yin's voice through the illness, the work, and the renewed misery and relocation caused by the full invasion of China by Japan in 1937, and the flight of the Liangs, first to Changsha and then to Kunming and Chungking in China's southwest. For Whei-yin this was not only a world of loss and horror but one of "delicate bare branches that scatter silver, small quiet temples, and the occasional bridge one can cross with romantic pride." . . . Rasping with tuberculosis and shivering with cold in dank lodgings, Whei-yin could still note how "the sun steals in curious angles into one's aching sense of awareness of quietness and beauty."[88]

This long journey of exile not only mapped "a world of loss and horror" with an "aching sense of awareness of quietness and beauty" but also traced the passion and pain, intellectual and sentimental, in places where Lin's aesthetic observations shed light.

AN ALTERNATIVE URBAN BLUEPRINT

> Literature had its own politics. And that politics was part of the wider politics—or metapolitics—of aesthetics: a metapolitics of the sensory community, aimed at achieving what had been missed by the "merely political" revolution—freedom and equality incorporated in living attitudes, in a new harmony between the distribution of bodies and the distribution of words, between the places, the occupations and the modes of being and speaking.
> —JACQUES RANCIÈRE

> How can he understand that the balance is precisely the dignity of symmetry? 他哪裡懂得那均衡即對稱的莊嚴？
> —LIN HUIYIN

As a literary author, architectural historian, and one of the founders of the discipline of architecture in China, Lin Huiyin had an aesthetic ideal and produced work

---

[87] Zhang, *Lin Huiyin*, 263. During the nine-year exile, Lin Huiyin could not help missing Beijing, like Lao She in London, even though the living conditions were distinctively different. Familiar sounds and tints emerged from their memories (294). And Lin Huiyin's numerous and mixed reading list was as follows: *War and Peace, Passage to India, Disraeli, Queen Victoria, Indecent Tales of Anatole France, Memoirs of Casanova*, Shakespeare, Andre Gide, Samuel Butler's *The Way of All Flesh, Alice in Wonderland* for her kids, Liang Sicheng's manuscripts, *Palaces in Yuan Dynasty* (Chinese), *Palaces in Qing Beijing*, her son's writing, and so on (Liu, *Chuangzi neiwai yi Huiyin*, 320).

[88] Jonathan Spence, foreword to *Liang and Lin*, by Wilma Fairbank, ix.

deeply embedded in the historical and cultural texture of Beijing.[89] Her Beijing narratives and images take a wide range of viewpoints, spatial and semiotic, literary and scientific. Lin mapped the city in terms of cultural tradition, architectural beauty, historical complications, and the living conditions of the populace.[90] After the Communists reunified the Chinese mainland in 1949, Lin's professional visions of urban planning and reconstructions differed substantially from the official socialist mission of building a modern capital.

In 1948, the Chinese People's Liberation Army sought to take Beijing over from the Nationalist Party Army commanded by General Fu Zuoyi 傅作義 (1895–1974), marking the turning point in the history of Beijing and the whole nation. One day, two Chinese Communist Party cadres paid a visit to Lin Huiyin and Liang Sicheng and asked them to mark on a map of the city the most important historical buildings and sites. They told Lin and Liang that the CCP Army would try to protect those ancient places if they had to occupy Beijing by military means. Lin and Liang were profoundly moved. After the founding of the PRC, Lin and Liang enthusiastically participated in the reconstruction of the city, which became the capital of the new socialist state. In 1951, they published an influential essay, "Beijing: dushi jihua de wubi jiezuo" 北京——都市計劃的無比傑作 (Beijing—Unparalleled masterpiece of urban planning) in *Xin guancha* 新觀察 (New observation). In this essay, they remarked,

> Beijing, the capital of People's China, is an extremely old city, but also an extremely young city. Beijing, once the center of feudal kings' authority, the fortress of warlords and antirevolutionary forces, is today newly rebuilt, a towering beacon of Democracy illuminating the whole world. Once an ancient capital

---

[89] For a discussion of the different names of Beijing, see Naquin, *Peking*, xxxiii–xxxiv, 701–702. Previous generations' experiences and expectations cannot be ignored. Liang Qichao's *Ouyou xinying lu* 歐游心影錄 [Record of impressions of travels in Europe], without doubt, opened Liang Sicheng and Lin Huiyin's perspectives on both the Occidental and Oriental worlds. In April 1929, *American Historical Review* published an essay in memory of Liang Qichao's death, in which the author Liang Sizhuang 梁思莊 (Liang's daughter) stated, "In a little autobiographical sketch entitled, 'On Reaching the Age of Thirty' ['Sanshi zishu'], Mr. Liang remarked, 'Prior to my visit to Shanghai at the age of eighteen, when a world atlas for the first time fell into my hands, I did not know of the existence of the five continents. (When I visited Shanghai on the way home after having failed in the civil service examination, I purchased in the market and read the *Yinghuan zhilüe* 瀛環志略 [A brief survey of the maritime circuit], and for the first time I came to understand that there various countries in the five continents)," quoted in Joshua Fogel, *Between China and Japan: The Writings of Joshua Fogel* (Leiden: Brill, 2015), 239. See also Xiaobing Tang, *Global Space and the Nationalist Discourse of Modernity: The Historical Thinking of Liang Qichao* (Stanford, CA: Stanford University Press, 1996).

[90] Most ancient cities, like Troy, were gradually toppled by wars, plagues, natural disasters, or geological changes. However, the city of Beijing, which has survived over three thousand years, may be considered an exceptional case. Built in 1054 BC, this capital city of the People's Republic of China is now one of the oldest cities in the world, and many people have tried to explain why it has such strong vitality.

so decrepit it could only stir up a boundless nostalgia, enduring wanton tram-
pling invaders, today Beijing is a new capital, basking in the welcome radiance
of Socialism.

人民中國的首都北京,是一個極年老的舊城,卻又是一個極年輕的新
城。北京曾經是封建帝王威風的中心,軍閥和反動勢力的堡壘,今天它
卻是初落成的,照耀全世界的民主燈塔。它曾經是沒落到只能引起無
限"思古幽情"的舊京,也曾經是忍受侵略者鐵蹄踐踏的淪陷城,現在它
卻是生氣蓬勃地在迎接社會主義曙光中的新首都。[91]

The new capital, Beijing, had a new physical appearance: its tidiness and freshness
were unprecedented. Tons of garbage, which had accumulated along the city walls
and the banks of the moat for centuries, were removed and cleaned up. The filthy
and stinking "Dragon Beard Ditch" was filled in and smoothed over. The alleys and
streets were made level and tidy. According to official statistics, from 1949 to 1950,
Beijing Municipality cleared away 330,000 tons of garbage accumulated since the
Ming dynasty; closed down 809 manure pits, manure boxes, and manure facto-
ries; cleaned away 10,000 tons of accumulated excrement; restored 160,000 square
meters of drainage; and repaired 252,000 square meters of streets and alleys.[92]

Lin Huiyin and Liang Sicheng were thrilled with Beijing's new sanitary condition
and devoted fully to the project of city building and nation building. One of their
contributions was the design of the National Emblem and the Monument to the
People's Heroes, two significant projects symbolically legitimizing the new republic.
It was a great challenge for Lin and Liang to create modern monumental patterns to
memorialize Chinese revolutions and fit them into the ancient cityscape dominated
by imperial palaces and ceremonial buildings. They had to find a solution to maintain a visual, aesthetic, and ideological balance in the fledgling Socialist city.

After a fierce competition with the Central Academy of Fine Arts, the design
created by Tsinghua University's group, led by Liang and Lin, was officially chosen by Chairman Mao Zedong and Premier Zhou Enlai 周恩來 (1898–1976) for
the National Emblem 國徽. Their version of the emblem incorporates four key
components—the red background and yellow stars of China's national flag, a wheel,
a wheat head, and a relief of the Tiananmen Gate. The elements of the flag, the wheel,
and the wheat head symbolize the New China, with the Communist leadership supported by an alliance of workers and peasants. The Tiananmen Gate symbolizes the

[91] Liang, *Lin Huiyin wenji: Jianzhu juan*, 317. The English Translation is by the author and Nick Kaldis.

[92] Cao Zixi 曹子西 and Yu Guangdu于光度, *Beijing tongshi*北京通史 [General history of Beijing]
(Beijing: Zhongguo shudian, 1994); Zhang, *Lin Huiyin*, 370.

May Fourth Movement, a patriotic demonstration against imperialism that laid the foundation for the Chinese Communist Party.

Liang and Lin were also involved in the design of the Monument to the People's Heroes. Chang-tai Hung observes, "[F]or the Chinese communists, the building of a giant memorial in the capital's most sacred space was more than an act of commemoration; it was a cultural production that addressed present political needs: affirming the legitimacy of the Chinese Communist Party (CCP), rewriting China's turbulent history according to a carefully scripted Marxist text, and establishing the regime's control over the nation's collective memory."[93] Through their art and architectural undertaking, Liang and Lin were engaged in the legitimization of a new sovereignty. In 1951, the newly designed National Emblem was hung high at the center of the rostrum of Tiananmen, facing the "central axis" of Beijing. In 1958, three years after Lin Huiyin passed away, a gigantic construction, the Monument to the People's Heroes, was erected at the center of the Tiananmen Square, honoring the martyrs during Chinese revolutions that ultimately led to the Communist victory.[94]

In the first years of the PRC, Lin Huiyin's architectural career reached its climax. She was appointed First Class Professor at Tsinghua University, offering courses such as "History of Chinese Architecture" and "Introduction to Housing." She was a member of the Committee of Beijing Urban Planning, the Team for the National Emblem Design, and the Committee for the Design of the Monument to the People's Heroes. She was also a representative in Beijing's First People's Congress and a member of the National Literature Assembly. While Lin was explicitly engaged in political participation in the early Chinese Socialist stage, during the same time period, her beloved friend Shen Congwen fell into a profound depression, attempted suicide but failed, and later became a victim of Maoist constraints and controls.[95] Moreover, many Chinese intellectuals had to suspense their incomplete project of a Chinese modernity, and sooner or later they began to incorporate Maoist principles in their new imaginations, if intellectual agency was at all possible.

In addition to their new design projects, Lin and Liang worked tirelessly to preserve the architectural beauty of old Beijing, which was on the verge of demolition and destruction to make room for the Maoist plan of building up a modern socialist

---

[93] Chang-tai Hung, "Revolutionary History in Stone: The Making of a Chinese National Monument," *The China Quarterly* 166 (June 2001): 457.

[94] Wilma Fairbank, *Liang and Lin*, 170. Are Lin's aesthetic sophistication and sensibility still traceable in this national emblem or in the colossal revolutionary monument located in what is now the largest plaza on earth, Mao's center of world revolution?

[95] For a recent study of Shen Congwen's crisis and redemption, see Wang, *Modernity with a Cold War*, 54–107.

capital. In spite of their enthusiasm for a new China, they insisted on preserving their architectural and aesthetic vision of an ideal city.[96] An initial moment of disillusionment occurred in the early 1950s when Liang met the mayor of Beijing, Peng Zhen 彭真 (1902–1997). At this casual meeting, Peng described to Liang how the Maoist blueprint of modernization and urban planning would look. Jianying Zha wrote,

> The mayor of Beijing, Peng Zhen, had taken Liang up to the rostrum of Tiananmen to see the big picture. Mayor Peng, a robust man from the military, belonged to the trusted clique of leaders around Mao until he was purged during the Cultural Revolution. Looking out over the city from the rostrum, Peng told Liang that Chairman Mao had stood there with him recently and said the view would be quite different in the future: "We'll see a forest of chimneys from here!" the chairman had grandly pronounced. So Mayor Peng patted Liang on the shoulders: "Imagine that, Mr. Liang! You must have a broad mind and see the big picture." Liang almost fainted at these words.[97]

For Liang and Lin, the episode must have been the recurrence of a continuous modern nightmare in which Guo Moruo's "black peonies" and the dark "noble flowers" would be blooming in the very heart of Beijing. Some twenty years earlier, in her poem "Spring Scene in the Ancient City," Lin had expressed her anxiety about the threat of the modern, how industrialization might break down the tranquil, harmonious cityscape in Beijing. Now, in the Maoist project of modernization, this nightmare was a sanctioned state policy. These conflicting visions of a modern city marked the beginning of socialist modernity's maelstrom, which gradually erased much of the historical landscape of old Beijing. The massive urban renovation and construction decades later, for the 2008 Olympics, carried the socialist modernization further into the age of globalization.

One key conflict between Liang and Lin's urban planning and the socialist state's agenda concerned the preservation of Beijing's city walls. The party authorities were

---

[96] Wang Jun provides a nuanced study of Beijing's modern urban planning, and the controversy about and "natural death" of the 25,000-word "Liang-Chen proposal," suggested by Liang Sicheng and Chen Zhanxiang 陳占祥 (1916–2001) and jointly supported by Lin Huiyin, which aimed at protecting Beijing intact as ancient capital, historical city, and history museum; see his *Chengji*. Regarding the urban planning of Beijing in a longer historical period, see Jianfei Zhu, *Chinese Spatial Strategies: Imperial Beijing, 1420–1911* (London: Routledge, 2003); and Lillian M. Li, Alison Dray-Novey, and Haili Kong, *Beijing: From Imperial Capital to Olympic City* (New York: Palgrave Macmillan, 2007). For the relationship between utopia and city planning, see, for instance, Roland Schaer et al., eds., *Utopia: The Search for Ideal Society in the Western World* (New York: Oxford University Press and Smithsonian, 2000).

[97] Jianying Zha, *China Pop: How Soap Operas, Tabloids and Bestsellers Are Transforming a Culture* (New York: The New Press, 1996), 63.

eager to demolish all of the city walls. According to the political propaganda, these walls were officially designated as physical chains around the socialist capital's neck, an obsolete but imperious sign of feudal and imperial power, and a barrier to the modernization process of the socialist city. But for Liang and Lin, rather than fetters or chains, the city walls constituted a precious necklace, an unparalleled masterpiece in the architectural history of Beijing and of the whole world.[98]

In Liang and Lin's vision, industry should be barred from Beijing, as it would definitely generate environmental, traffic, and population problems. A new administrative center for the government should be constructed in the west suburbs, in parallel with a cultural center remaining at the location of the Forbidden City. The city walls and gate towers could be transformed into city gardens, a public space where Beijing people could enjoy their leisure time. Here, let me return to Lin Huiyin's 1935 poem, "On the Gate Tower," in which she describes a fantastic view on one fine autumn day in Beijing.

> You prefer this gate tower,
> the ancient tombs, the solemn dirges,
> wildflowers blooming on vines.[99]

The colorful forest in the poem was now under the threat of a socialist forest of smokestacks. The aesthetic subjectivity established from atop the tower was now banished or obliterated. In Lin and Liang's project and in her poem, this aesthetic perspective belonged to *all* citizens of Beijing; it was not a privileged position for political authorities. Her transformation from a poet to an architect, from individual pleasure to collective amusement, is incarnated in the change from a small poem into a grand project of urban planning some fifteen years later.

However, the new government resolutely rejected Lin and Liang's proposal to turn portions of Beijing's ancient city walls into public parks. It ordered the city walls torn down to make way for new construction and urban expansion. Jacques Rancière rightly points out that "the essential work of politics is the configuration of its own space."[100] This political decision led to the demolition not only of the

---

[98] Zhang, *Lin Huiyin*, 404. Andrew F. Jones explores Liang's efforts to (re)construct a Chinese architectural "Order"; see his "Portable Monuments: Architectural Photography and the 'Forms' of Empire in Modern China," *positions* 18, no. 3 (2010): 599–631. I appreciate an anonymous reviewer's constructive and insightful comments and calling my attention the late development of socialist urban planning: ironically, in 2007, the Beijing municipal government, adhering to the new CCP dictate of "harmonious society," again adopted the rhetoric of a precious necklace, yet now the *metaphorical* ring around the city center was intended to rationalize the development of eleven satellite towns (and the relocation of urban poor to these satellite towns prior to the Olympics).

[99] Lin Huiyin, "On the Gate Tower," in Dooling and Torgeson, *Writing Women in Modern China*, 304.

[100] Jacques Rancière, *Dissensus: On Politics and Aesthetics*, ed. Steven Corcoran (London: Continuum, 2010); and Kristin Ross and Alain Badiou, *Jacques Rancière: History, Politics, Aesthetics*, ed. Gabriel Rockhill and Philip Watts (Durham, NC: Duke University Press, 2009).

physical walls but also, I would argue, of the idea of a modern public space and with it, a modern, cosmopolitan, democratic subjectivity. During later political purges and campaigns, Liang Sicheng and Lin Huiyin were condemned as reactionary for their preservation proposals. While her poems reached readers, Lin's vision of a great city was never to be realized or experienced by her fellow citizens. In the 1950s, when the Maoist modernization blueprint became the exclusive authority, what was left for a poet to hear—the sorrowful silent sighs emanating from deep recesses of old Beijing?[101]

In the 1990s, the government started to re-evaluate Liang and Lin's urban preservation and renovation plans, decades after the state had carried out its projects to "dismantle the magnificent city walls, an architectural wonder of history, and use the bricks to build useless anti-air raid tunnels."[102] In the early 1950s, Lin lamented with profound sorrow that one day in the future, people would have to produce "fake antiques" when they eventually recognized the value of the original relics that had been lost. At a university meeting, she publicly confronted Wu Han 吳晗 (1909–1969), Vice Mayor of Beijing and a distinguished historian at Tsinghua University, because she believed Wu was incapable of defending Beijing's old city walls, for which he was then responsible. Lin Huiyin's warnings and laments have haunted later generations. Today, people can find original or, mostly likely, reproduced bricks of old city walls for sale in Beijing's antique stores. Beijing, Lin's dream city, has been modernized and transformed into a metropolis that seriously suffers from ecological crisis, climate challenges, human destruction, and the abuse of natural resources, in social, cultural, political, physical, and psychological terms. Lin Huiyin's aesthetic

---

[101] However, we cannot reduce the negative attitudes toward city walls and other similar cultural relics to pure products of Maoist ideology. Early in 1925, when pondering the meanings of the Great Wall, Lu Xun concluded,

> Our wonderful Great Wall!
>
>   This engineering feat has left its mark on the map, and is probably known to everyone with any education the whole world over.
>
>   Actually, all it has ever done is work many conscripts to death—it never kept out the Huns. Now it is merely an ancient relic, but its final ruin will not take place for a while, and it may even be preserved.
>
>   I am always conscious of being surrounded by a Great Wall. The stonework consists of old bricks reinforced at a later date by new bricks. These have combined to make a wall that hems us in.
>
>   When shall we stop reinforcing the Great Wall with new bricks?
>
>   A curse on this wonderful Great Wall! (Lu Xun, *Selected Works of Lu Hsun*, trans. Yang Hsien-yi and Gladys Yang [Peking: Foreign Languages Press, 1957], 151)

Besides its aesthetic significance, the Great Wall is also a gigantic construction that imparts to the inhabitants a closed mindset, a tendency to be isolated from and indifferent to the outer world and changes. From Lu Xun's perspective, the Great Wall is wonderful, but it also must be cursed.

[102] Zha, *China Pop*, 59.

and lyrical representations of Beijing are still illuminating for a city that never ceases to transform itself.[103]

OBLIVION AND RECOLLECTION

Remembrance restores possibility to the past, making what happened incomplete and completing what never was. Remembrance is neither what happened nor what did not happen but, rather, their potentialization, their becoming possible once again.

—GIORGIO AGAMBEN

From the Anti-Rightist Campaign in the late 1950s to the early stage of the post-Mao or early Deng Reform Era, the name of Lin Huiyin has been scarcely visible in the standard histories of modern Chinese literature. On the one hand, she lived in the shadow of two giants, Xu Zhimo and Liang Sicheng: Xu was a renowned romantic poet, and the affair between Xu and Lin became one of the most popular romances in modern China, which eclipses considerably Lin's literary merit; Liang was Lin's husband and the founding father of modern Chinese architecture, and his fame overshadows Lin's contributions and achievements as a female architect.[104] On the other hand, although her literary and artistic activities involved a wide range of genres, she was by no means prolific. Nevertheless, Lin Huiyin can be seen as a modern "Renaissance woman," with her versatile talents displayed in poetry, prose, drama, design, and architecture, among many other areas. As a poet, she penned a small collection of distinctive poems. As a fiction writer, she left behind merely six short stories, each a minor masterpiece. As a dramatist, her "Meizhen tong tamen" 梅真同他們 (Meizhen and them), an incomplete draft, has been hailed by the aesthetic philosopher Zhu Guangqian as "a cool drink in stuffy weather" (悶熱天氣中的一劑清涼散).[105] In 1923, Lin translated Oscar Wilde's essay "Nightingale and Rose" into Chinese; it was published in "Supplement of the Fifth-Anniversary Issue of Morning Newspaper."[106] In 1924, she played the leading role, Princess

---

[103] In 2010, a critically acclaimed eight-episode documentary, *Liang Sicheng Lin Huiyin,* directed by Hu Jingcao, was released and shown on CCTV's high-definition channel (http://jishi.cntv.cn/program/lianglin/lianglinft/index.shtml). In 2010, Liang Sicheng and Lin Huiyin's former residence, No. 24 Beizongbu Hutong (formerly No. 3) was about to be demolished by some Beijing developers, but later luckily confirmed as "immovable cultural heritage" under the protection of cultural heritage protection laws by China's State Administration of Cultural Heritage. http://www.gg-art.com/news/newsread/artnews47092.html.

[104] For a succinct re-evaluation of Lin Huiyin's contribution to Chinese architecture, see Zhao Chen 趙辰, "Zuowei zhongguo jianzhu xueshu xianxingzhe de Lin Huiyin" 作為中國建築學術先行者的林徽因 [Lin Huiyin as a pioneer of Chinese architecture], *Jianzhu shi* 建築史 [History of architecture] 21 (2005): 1–12.

[105] Chen Xueyong, "Meizhen kangzhan qule" 梅真抗戰去了 [Meizhen goes for anti-Japanese war], in his *Cainü de shijie,* 150–151.

[106] Liang, *Lin Huiyin wenji: Wenxue juan,* 307–313.

Chitra, in Nobel laureate Rabindranath Tagore's (1861–1941) poetic drama *Chitra*, and served as Tagore's interpreter during his China visit, along with Xu Zhimo. In 1927, Lin Huiyin enrolled in the distinguished stage-design program directed by the renowned scholar George P. Baker (1866–1935) at Yale University; she had just graduated from the School of Fine Arts at the University of Pennsylvania, where she worked briefly with Paul P. Cret (1876–1945), leader of the Beaux-Arts tradition of architecture in the United States.[107] As a designer, she worked as the set designer for Cao Yu's drama *Caikuang* 財狂 (Moneygrubber), an adaptation of Molière's *L'Avare* (The miser).[108] She designed the cover of "Supplement of the Fifth-Anniversary Issue of *Morning Newspaper*" in 1924, the Northeastern University emblem in 1928, the cover for Chen Menjia's 陳夢家 (1911–1966) anthology of poetry, and a cover for the journal *Xuewen Monthly* (Learning literature). She also created the poster for the International Exhibition of Chinese Art in London in 1938, as well as an illustration entitled "Qifu" 祈福 (Praying for happiness) for Shen Congwen's short story "Shenwu zhiai" 神巫之愛 (Love of a necromancer).[109]

As an architect, Lin designed a dorm for female undergraduates and the Geology Hall at Peking University, and a traditional/national-style storefront for Renli Carpet Company in Beijing's Wangfujing (王府井) in the 1930s.[110] The peak moment in her architectural career was her involvement in the design of the National Emblem and the Monument to the People's Heroes of the People's Republic of China in the early 1950s. She was a distinguished professor of architecture at Tsinghua University, and she assisted Liang Sicheng in composing his invaluable monograph *A Pictorial History of Chinese Architecture: A Study of the Development of Its Structural System and the Evolution of Its Types*. Since the Anti-Rightist Campaign, which broke out in 1957, all Lin's literary, artistic, and architectural productions, which were deeply connected with Beijing, have been erased from official narratives and cast into oblivion. One wretched yet illuminating incident in Lin's afterlife was that, during the unprecedented Cultural Revolution in the 1960s and 1970s, Red Guards wiped out the inscription on her tombstone, "Tomb of Architect Lin Huiyin" (建築師林徽因墓) and left a blank stele without any words, only the flower ornament on the

---

[107] At the University of Pennsylvania, Lin and Liang were employed by Paul P. Cret as assistants. For a recent study of the important of the Beaux-Arts school and its influence on Chinese architecture, see Jeffrey W. Cody et al., eds., *Chinese Architecture and the Beaux-Arts* (Honolulu: University of Hawai'i Press, 2011). See also Shih, *The Lure of Modern*, 208.

[108] Xiao Qian wrote an essay remembering his experience in the audience of Cao Yu's drama with Lin Huiyin's stage design; see Chen, *Cainü de shijie*, 158.

[109] Chen, *A Talented Lady's World*, 156–159.

[110] Liang, "Shuhu renjian siyue tian," in *Lin Huiyin wenji: Wenxue juan*, 424–425.

bedding base of the tablet, the same pattern that Lin designed for the Monument to the People's Heroes.[111]

During the Japanese invasion and occupation, Lin Huiyin led a nine-year vagrant life in vast inner China, suffering from pneumonia and other diseases. She almost collapsed when she learned that the invaluable research materials she and Liang Sicheng had stored in the safe of a bank in Tianjin were destroyed by an unexpected flood. In his touching preface for Wilma Fairbank's biography of Liang and Lin, Jonathan Spence reflects upon the "colossal waste," which remains a haunting weight of a past era, an enduring historical specter even with the belated recognition or resurrection of some writers and scholars who were repressed at various times of political turbulence in twentieth-century China.[112] In the late 1990s, Lin Huiyin was rediscovered and returned to the limelight of the Chinese cultural arena. Her son Liang Congjie (1932–2000), an eminent ecologist, compiled the authoritative two-volume anthology *Selected Writings of Lin Huiyin: Volumes of Literature and Architecture* (1999), which brought Lin back to public attention. As the nostalgic trend of "Republican fever" (民國熱) swept China at the turn of the twenty-first century, Lin was transformed into an icon of Republican China overnight by the partly inaccurate but tremendously popular TV melodrama *Renjian siyue tian* 人間四月天 (April rhapsody, 2000), based on the love affairs among Xu Zhimo, Lin Huiyin, Lu Xiaoman 陸小曼 (1903–1965), and Zhang Youyi 張幼儀 (1900–1988). Lin was reconfigured as one of the most beautiful, talented, and legendary female intellectuals in modern China, and was greatly admired for her beauty, intellectual versatility, refined rhetorical style in the cultural salon, and elegant taste in humanities and arts. After years of waste and oblivion, Lin's aesthetic perspective and visions of modern urbanity, once culturally conditioned toward the early Socialist political ends, re-emerged from the horizon of post-Cold War history, and illustrate and illuminate the future urban planning of the old yet new city.

---

[111] Wang Jun writes (translated into English by Li Zhurun), "[G]rief-stricken, Liang Sicheng designed her tomb with a wreath in white marble relief placed in its front. The relief was designed by Lin Huiyin for the Monument to the People's Heroes in the Tiananmen Square." In Wang Jun, *Beijing Record: A Physical and Political History of Planning Modern Beijing* (Singapore: World Scientific, 2011), 222.

[112] The sad silhouettes of a few important modern writers come to mind: Shen Congwen, who planned to write dozens of novels after 1949, gave up his career as a novelist after a failed suicide attempt, and eventually took refuge in a dark corner of the Chinese Historical Museum; Qian Zhongshu 錢鐘書 (1910–1998), a resourceful and cynical genius, discontinued and destroyed his manuscript *Mon Coeur* (*Baihehua* 百合花), the sequel to his masterpiece, (*Weicheng* 圍城 [*Fortress Besieged*], 1947); Hu Feng 胡風 (1902–1985), who prophetically announced, "Time has begun" 時間開始了, was accused of antirevolutionary activity and jailed for several decades; and Lu Ling 路翎 (1923–1994), the ultimate and dissident Marxist/modernist writer, was also involved in the so-called "Hu Feng Antirevolutionary Circle" (胡風反革命集團) and stayed in jail and even a madhouse for over twenty years. The list can be extended.

Only those who will risk going too far can possibly find out how far one can go.
—T. S. ELIOT

4

A Comparative Imperial Capital

LIN YUTANG, PRINCESS DER LING, VICTOR SEGALEN,
AND THE VIEWS FROM NEAR AND AFAR

FROM A COMPARATIVE and cross-cultural perspective on the Occidental and the Oriental city, Max Weber (1864–1920) conceptualizes the ideal-type Occidental city as follows:

> To constitute a full urban community a settlement must display a relative predominance of trade-commercial relations with the settlement as a whole displaying the following features: 1. a fortification; 2. a market; 3. a court of its own and at least partially autonomous law; 4. a related form of association; and 5. at least partial autonomy and autocephaly, thus also an administration by authorities in the election of whom the burghers participated.[1]

Based on this definition, Weber further argues, "in contrast to the Occident, the cities in China and throughout the Orient lacked political autonomy."[2] Therefore, "an urban 'community,' in the full meaning of the word, appears as a general phenomenon only in the Occident."[3] How to define a Chinese city, if it apparently

---

[1] Max Weber, *The City*, trans. and ed. Don Martindale and Gertrud Neuwirth (Glencoe, IL: The Free Press, 1958), 80–81.

[2] Max Weber, *The Religion of China: Confucianism and Taoism*, trans. and ed. Hans H. Gerth (Glencoe, IL: The Free Press, 1951), 13.

[3] Weber, *The City*, 80.

defies the conceptual taxonomy of an urban community in Weber's East and West dichotomy? In the field of historical studies of Chinese cities, there have been significant scholarly contributions: Rhoads Murphey examines late imperial Chinese treaty ports opened to foreign trade by the unequal treaties; G. William Skinner focuses on rural markets and the dynamic "trade-commercial" activities in a newly defined city-countryside relationship; and William T. Rowe proposes in his study of Hankow that the locality "reflected the highest stage of the indigenous development of Chinese urbanism before wholesale imitation of Western models."[4] These historical, comparative studies of Chinese cities bear on our understanding of the unique trajectories and development of Chinese urbanity.

While historians and social scientists compare Occidental and Oriental cities in terms of legal systems, political institutions, economic structures, public health, and so forth, literary authors deal with the cities as decipherable texts, and rely on imaginative forms to conceive and map the cross-cultural and translingual differences and similarities. Walter Benjamin asserts that "perception is reading."[5] Kevin Lynch calls to mind that "legibility is crucial" in the city setting.[6] Mikhail Bakhtin remarks that "the chronotope in literature has an intrinsic generic significance. It can even be said that it is precisely the chronotope that defines genre and genric distinctions."[7] The chronotope in city-texts indeed invokes generic varieties and diversities. How to imagine and decipher cities in comparative and cross-cultural contexts is a challenge for all storytellers and scholars in the sphere of world literature.

Zeami (or Seami) Motokiyo (1363–1443) once said that a good actor must be able to see himself in the way that his spectators see him, that is, to take the view from afar. Claude Levi-Strauss borrowed Zeami's insight, entitling his third volume of structural anthropology *The View from Afar* to illustrate a significant viewpoint from which anthropologists should observe their own cultures and societies.[8] Yue Daiyun 樂黛雲 calls attention to intersubjectivity, mutual recognition, and cross-cultural dialogue in comparative and world literature, to explore the literary contacts and transcultural communications among transnational authors.[9] In this chapter,

---

[4] Rhoads Murphey, "The City as a Center of Change: Western Europe and China," *Annals of the Association of American Geographers* 44 (1954): 349–362; and "The Treaty Ports and China's Modernization," in *The Chinese City Between Two Worlds*, ed. Mark Elvin and G. William Skinner (Stanford, CA: Stanford University Press, 1974), 17–72; Rowe, *Hankow: Commerce and Society in a Chinese City, 1796–1889*, 8–9, 13–14.

[5] Bullock and Jennings, *Walter Benjamin: Selected Writings*, vol. 1, *1913–1926*, 92.

[6] Kevin Lynch, *The Image of the City* (Cambridge, MA: MIT Press, 1960), 3.

[7] Mikhail Bakhtin, "Forms of Time and of the Chronotope in the Novel," in *The Dialogic Imagination*, 84–85.

[8] Claude Levi-Strauss, *The View from Afar*, trans. Joachim Neugroschel and Phoebe Hoss (New York: Basic Books, 1985); Du Xiaozhen, *Yaoyuan de muguang* 遙遠的目光 [The view from afar] (Beijing: Sanlian shudian, 2003).

[9] Yue Daiyun, "Dangdai zhongguo bijiao wenxue fazhan zhong de jige wenti" 當代中國比較文學發展中的幾個問題 [Issues in the development of contemporary Chinese comparative literature], *Beijing daxue xuebao* 北

I examine "the view from afar" and the close-up view to consider Lin Yutang, Princess Der Ling, and Victor Segalen's Beijing narratives centering on imagery of the city as the imperial capital. All three writers were cosmopolitan subjects who were educated in both Chinese and Western cultures and traveled across several continents. They endeavored to represent imperial Beijing from a cross-cultural, comparative perspective. Written in English or French, their works have been translated into Chinese and enjoyed wide circulation in both the source and the target languages. They dip broadly into both Oriental and Occidental traditions and consciously deploy a comparative and double vision: their Beijing narratives are both insiders' elucidations of a native city that they inhabit and outsiders' observations and investigations of a foreign land. Their combined cultural, linguistic, and, in the case of Der Ling, gender position makes them fully aware of the traps of fetishizing Beijing as an Orientalist spectacle or an antiquated imperial museumification.

Lin Yutang's Beijing imagery is deeply embedded in historical and cultural specificities. Incorporating Confucian and Taoist notions of harmony, leisure, and modesty into the Chinese cosmological notion of the city, he creates a Beijing that gracefully survives the late Qing and Republican political turbulence and offers a spiritual anchor to transmit the cultural heritage and embrace changes. Der Ling diagnoses the symptoms of decline in the Forbidden City at the end of the Qing Empire; unveils inaccessible places, characters, and things; and provides a synoptic vision of imperial history and individual perceptions and memories. Unraveling the "Great Within," the dark heart of the imperial city, Der Ling's narratives are permeated with an awareness of her split identity and the predicament of how to resolve the tensions between her Chinese and Western educations, Chinese and Manchu ethnicities on the verge of the demise of the Manchu Empire, official historiography and private memoirs, a feminine sensitive self, and the narrative authority predominantly associated with men. Victor Segalen is obsessed with pure difference and disparity, and the Forbidden City and the fictional city beneath it are the incarnation of his creative exoticism in space. In pursuit of knowledge about the imperial city and the ancient civilization, he approaches the edge of spatial, cognitive vertigo displaced in imagery of an underground city and the "horizontal wells." Propelled by an insatiable yearning for difference and comparison, his urban expeditions are devoured in the abyss of the unfathomable center.

京大學學報 [*Journal of Peking University*] 4 (2009): 15–20; and "Hudong renzhi: Bijiao wenxue de renshilun he fangfalun" 互動認知：比較文學的認識論和方法論 [Reciprocal cognition: Epistemology and methodology in comparative literature], *Zhongguo bijiao wenxue* 中國比較文學 [Chinese comparative literature] 1 (2001): 1–7.

AN IDEAL-TYPE CITY AND THE PERFORMANCE OF PLEASURE

Confucianism stood for a rationalized social order through the ethical approach, based on personal cultivation. It aimed at political order by laying the basis for it in a moral order, and it sought political harmony by trying to achieve the moral harmony in man himself.

—LIN YUTANG

Appeals to the past are among the commonest of strategies in interpretation of the present. What animates such appeals is not only disagreement about what happened in the past and what the past was, but uncertainty about whether the past really is past, over and concluded, or whether it continues, albeit in different forms, perhaps.

—EDWARD SAID

Lin Yutang regarded himself as "a bundle of contradictions" (*yikun maodun* 一綑矛盾): he was a Christian believer, a Taoist advocate, and a Confucian supporter; he liked the revolution but was tired of the revolutionaries; he cherished his childhood memories of villages and mountains but also enjoyed urban life and cosmopolitan culture, and wanted to be a world citizen; he was trained at Western-oriented institutions, and later on became a spokesman of Chinese Confucianism, Taoism, Buddhism, and Chinese culture at large.[10] These contradictions are disseminated in Lin's urban narratives, ranging from literary works (*Moment in Peking, Leaf in the Storm*, and *The Vermillion Gate*) to nonfiction writings (*Imperial Peking, The Importance of Living*, and *My Country and My People*), and interweave into a euphoric illustration of the quintessence of the ideal-type Chinese city from the diversified material and mental life of urban inhabitants in Beijing, Xi'an, Nanjing, Shanghai, among others. He does not close his eyes to personal pain, cultural crisis, social crimes, moral decline, and political decay. Like the pleasant genius Su Dongpo 蘇東坡 (1037–1101) about whom he wrote, Lin attempts to perform and promote leisure and enjoyment of an idealized urban life and transcend the paradoxes, contradictions, and dilemmas in the secular world.[11]

One of the central concerns for modern Chinese writers is how to deal with the relationship between the countryside and the city. Zhang Ailing, Lao She, and Zhang

---

[10] The role that Lin Yutang played in modern Chinese literature and thought is similar to that of Rabindranath Tagore (1861–1941) for Indian spirit, and D. T. Suzuki (1870–1966) for Japanese culture. For a discussion of the "middling liberal cosmopolitan road," see Suoqiao Qian, *Liberal Cosmopolitanism: Lin Yutang and Middling Chinese Modernity* (Leiden: Brill, 2011). Shuang Shen puts Lin into a larger group of cosmopolitan writers and scholars in her *Cosmopolitan Publics: Anglophone Print Culture in Semi-Colonial Shanghai* (Piscataway, NJ: Rutgers University Press, 2009).

[11] See Lin Yutang, *The Gay Genius: The Life and Times of Su Tungpo* (New York: The John Day Company, 1947). Lin's notion of leisure and everyday pleasure is deeply influenced by his reading of late Ming Dynasty scholars such as Yuan Zhonglang and the other two Yuan brothers, later regarded as the leaders of the Gong'an School. For a discussion of this intellectual impact, see Suoqiao Qian, *Liberal Cosmopolitanism*, 127–160.

Henshui focus on urban lives in Shanghai and Beijing, although using disparate literary strategies. For Shen Congwen and Fei Ming, the city often represents social crimes, moral decline, and political decay, an antithesis of the innocent, pastoral rural life. Some other writers, such as Lu Xun, Mao Dun, and Ba Jin, set out to expose the dark sides of both the Chinese countryside and the newly emergent bourgeois cities. Lin Yutang's urban imaginations are often concerned with the great transformation of ancient, historical cities in modern times. Through his protagonist's eyes, he reflects on the changes occurring in Xi'an (Si-an):

> He had seen the sedate ancient city, the famed capital of the Tang emperors, change hesitantly, unwillingly, but perceptibly. Si-an was far inland, in the heart of China's northwest. He called it "The Anchor of China's Conservatism." It was his home town and he loved everything connected with it. Si-an would not change gracefully. The changes in men and morals, government and costumes, meant chaos and confusion. He loved this big, buzzing confusion.[12]

Through filters of confusion and chaos brought by the maelstrom of modernization, Lin seeks to create an ideal archetypal Chinese city as a world city to enrich human civilizations. His understanding of Confucius, Confucianism, and Confucian wisdom plays a significant role in his urban narratives (Beijing is the major motif), in which he configures the ideal Chinese city as an earthly paradise, a harmonious moral and political unity, a rationalist humane environment, and a place with open attitudes to the modern and the new.

In 1932, Lin Yutang founded a bimonthly magazine, *Lunyu* 論語 (Analects), to promote witty writings. His contributions to the magazine seek to reconfigure Confucius as a humanist and humorous philosopher. From 1929 to 1935 in Shanghai, Lin was also the editor of a few other literary magazines, such as *Renjianshi* 人間世 (This human world) and *Yuzhoufeng* 宇宙風 (Cosmic wind), which were devoted to humor, leisure, pleasure, and self-cultivation.[13] When Pearl S. Buck (1892–1973), the female Chinese-born writer who would become a Nobel Prize laureate in literature (1938), visiting China on a world tour, made Lin's acquaintance in 1933, they admired each other's works and soon became friends. Dissatisfied with the shallow and stereotypical writings of China provided by American missionaries and tourists, Pearl Buck persuaded Lin to introduce Chinese culture from his distinctive cross-cultural perspective. The resulting book, *My Country and My People* (1935), containing a

---

[12] Lin Yutang, *The Vermillion Gate* (New York: The John Day Company, 1953), 4.

[13] For a detailed study, see Charles A. Laughlin, "The *Analects* Group and the Genre of *Xiaopin*," in Denton and Hockx, *Literary Societies of Republican China*, 207–240.

preface by Buck, became first on the best-seller list in the United States.[14] When Japan and China were on the brink of war in 1936, Lin moved with his family to New York City. The next year he published his second best-seller, *The Importance of Living*, a blend of philosophy and humor justifying a moderate hedonism. Invited by Random House, Lin edited *The Wisdom of Confucius* (1938). After finishing this anthology, he wanted to translate *Dream of the Red Chamber* into English. However, considering the reality of the Sino-Japanese War in China, Lin determined to create a novel reflecting on modern China, employing Cao Xueqin's artistic strategies and techniques. The result was *Moment in Peking*, completed in 1939 in Paris. Shortly after it was published, *Moment in Peking* was chosen for special recommendation by the American Book-of-the-Month Club. Later he published a few other literary and nonliterary works relevant to Confucian imaginations and Chinese cities, including *Leaf in the Storm* (1940), *The Wisdom of China and India* (1942), *The Vermilion Gate* (1953), and *Imperial Peking: Seven Centuries of China* (1961). All these works were translated into Chinese, and have been widely anthologized, reprinted, and well circulated in Taiwan, Hong Kong, and post-Maoist China.[15]

Lin's bilingual literary, historical, and philosophical works composed from the 1930s to the 1970s have constituted a sustained, diversified, and multifaceted Lin Craze traveling from the 1930s and the 1940s English- and Chinese-language worlds to post-1949 Taiwan and Hong Kong and to the post-Mao mainland Chinese communities. Hundreds of editions of Lin's works, including a large number of pirated copies in mainland China, have been published and distributed. In the campaign to

---

[14] At midnight on August 10, 1936, Lin Yutang left China and went to America to start his new career. He lived at Pearl S. Buck's house for a while, and then left for New York City and settled down there. In New York, he got to know Eugene O'Neill, Thomas Mann, Lillian Gish (the actress in Griffith's masterpiece *Broken Blossom*), Chinese American movie star Anna May Wong, and others. The mainland Chinese-language editions of *My Country and My People* have been best-sellers and drawn critical attention since the 1980s.

[15] For a comprehensive study of Lin Yutang's works and life, see Wang Zhaosheng 王兆勝, *Lin Yutang de wenhua qinghuai* 林語堂的文化情懷 [Lin Yutang's cultural complex] (Beijing: Zhongguo shehui kexue chubanshe, 1998); Wan Pingjin 萬平近, *Lin Yutanglun* 林語堂論 [On Lin Yutang] (Xi'an: Shanxi renmin chubanshe, 1987); Shi Jianwei 施建偉, *Lin Yutang zai dalu* 林語堂在大陸 [Lin Yutang in mainland China] (Beijing: Beijing shiyue wenyi chubanshe, 1991); and *Lin Yutang zai haiwai* 林語堂在海外 [Lin Yutang overseas] (Tianjin: Baihua wenyi chubanshe, 1992); Lin Taiyi 林太乙, *Lin Yutang zhuan* 林語堂傳 [Biography of Lin Yutang] (Taipei: Lianjing, 1990); Liu Yansheng 劉炎生, *Lin Yutang pingzhuan* 林語堂評傳 [Annotated biography of Lin Yutang] (Nanchang: Baihuazhou wenyi chubanshe, 1994); Chen Pingyuan, *Zai dongxi wenhua pengzhuang zhong* 在東西文化碰撞中 [Between the conflict of Eastern and Western culture] (Hangzhou: Zhejiang wenyi chubanshe, 1987); A. Owen Aldridge, "Lin Yutang," in *American National Biography Online*, American Council of Learned Societies (New York: Oxford University Press, 2000); Elaine Kim, *Asian American Literature: An Introduction to the Writings and Their Social Context* (Philadelphia: Temple University Press, 1982), 91–121; Diran Sohigian, "The Life and Times of Lin Yutang" (PhD diss., Columbia University, 1991); and Suoqiao Qian, *Liberal Cosmopolitan*.

promote the 2008 Beijing Olympic Games as a megaevent, the city was represented as a cultural token to embody a modern China in the globalizing world. In the mass-market media industry or "the institutional matrix,"[16] Lin Yutang's imagery of Beijing, in particular that in his *Moment in Peking* and *Imperial Peking*, has become a beloved source of inspiration. His portraits of ancient and modern Beijing prompt multimedia productions and reproductions of Beijing stories, engaging in the circulation of the ideal city.[17]

In *My Country and My People*, Lin portrayed Confucius as "our great humanist" and proposed Confucianism as a true humanism. At its heart is Chinese realism with a positive attitude toward life and even turbulent times.

> This realism and this attached-to-earth quality of the Chinese ideal of life has a basis in Confucianism, which, unlike, Christianity, is of the earth, earth-born. For Jesus was a romanticist, Confucius a realist; Jesus was a mystic, Confucius a positivist; Jesus was a humanitarian, Confucius a humanist.[18]

For the Chinese humanists, people live under the same roof of heaven, and the "greatest achievement is to attain a measure of harmony and happiness in this earthly life."[19] When addressing the nature of Confucianism, Max Weber emphasizes the harmonious relationship among "innerworldly morality of laymen," the cosmic orders of the world, the order of society, and "the happiness of the world and especially the happiness of man."[20] Lin's distinctive interpretations of Confucius, Confucianism, and humanism are substantiated in his Confucian imaginations of the ideal-type Chinese city, especially in the "harmony and happiness" of the earthly and secular urban life. In 1937, two years prior to completing the manuscript of his masterpiece, *Moment in Peking*, he published a short essay, "Captive Peiping Holds Soul," in the *New York Times*. In it he proclaimed that Beijing was still amazing, fundamentally pleasant and attractive, although it had just fallen under the control of the Japanese army. Under Japanese rule, Beijing is a king's dream and a gourmet's paradise, shoppers' heaven, a place both for the rich and the poor, and more notably, "the ideal city, where there is space for everyone to breathe in, where rural quiet is

---

[16] See Janice A. Radway, *Reading the Romance: Women, Patriarchy, and Popular Literature* (Chapel Hill: University of North Carolina Press, 1991), especially the first chapter, "The Institutional Matrix."

[17] The popular and melodramatic adaptations of Lin's *Moment in Peking* include two sensational television drama serials: a forty-episode rendition coproduced by Taiwan and Hong Kong in 1987, and a forty-four-episode mainland Chinese version produced by CCTV in 2005.

[18] Lin Yutang, *My Country and My People* (New York: Halcyon House, 1938), 104.

[19] Lin, *My Country and My People*, 108.

[20] Weber, *The Religion of China*, 152–153.

matched with city comforts."[21] In his *Moment in Peking*, Beijing is represented as a wonderful amalgamation of civilization and nature, sublime monuments and pleasant everyday life, as well as pastoral beauty and metropolitan stimulus:

> In that city, man lives in civilization and yet in nature, where the maximum comforts of the city and the beauties of rural life are perfectly blended and preserved, where, as in the ideal city, man finds both stimulation for his mind and repose for his soul . . . . The city was planned by a master architect as no other city was even planned on this earth, with a breadth of human spirit, an understanding of sublimity and grandeur and the amenities of domestic living, paralleled nowhere else.[22]

No doubt, this pastoral and ideal city contains natural beauty, humanist spirits, and harmonious people, things, and places. Personal lifestyles, political glory, and moral order can live harmoniously under the same roof of the ancient capital, which is, according to Lin's understanding, the incarnation of Confucian ideals. His emphasis on the cultural and historical heritage Beijing represents does not make him a conservative who rejects modern civilizations. He embraces the advantages of modern science, technology, and industrial civilization, and champions dynamic communications between Beijing and other cities and nation-states. *Moment in Peking* is a poetic and panoramic exhibition of tradition and modernity, ranging from the striking scenes viewed from Coal Hill 煤山 (just to the north of the Forbidden City) to the modern conveniences and comforts. Lin's embrace of modern civilization is not without reservations. He holds a strongly negative attitude toward the type of urban modernization epitomized in Shanghai. From his standpoint, Shanghai is a city of disease derived from the bizarre mixture of Eastern and Western culture. He opens his satirical essay entitled "A Hymn to Shanghai" with the following remarks:

> [Shanghai] is terrible in her denaturalized women, dehumanized coolies, devitalized newspapers, decapitalized banks, and denationalized creatures. She is

---

21. "Captive Peiping Holds the Soul" has at least two Chinese versions: "Miren de Beiping" 迷人的北平 [Amazing Peiping], in *Beijing ren, Shanghai ren* 北京人，上海人 [Beijingers, Shanghaines], ed. Lu Xun, Zhou Zuoren, Lin Yutang, et al., (Hong Kong: Sanlian shudian, 2001), 73–76; and "Shuo Beiping" 說北平 [On Peiping], in *Lin Yutang sanwen jingdian quanbian* 林語堂散文經典全編 [Complete prose of Lin Yutang] (Beijing: Jiuzhoutushu chubanshe, 1997), 4:409–413.

22. Lin Yutang, *Moment in Peking: A Novel of Contemporary Chinese Life* (New York: The John Day Company, 1939), 171.

terrible in her greatness as well as in her weakness, terrible in her monstrosities, perversities, and inanities, terrible in her joys and follies, and in her tears, bitterness, and degradation, terrible in her vast immutable stone edifices that rear their heads high on the Bund and in the abject huts of creatures subsisting on their discoveries from refuse cans.[23]

In a deliberately stereotypical, negative, and exaggerating tone, Lin ridicules and attacks the dehumanized urban milieu in modern Shanghai. He teases the shining neon lights as the vulgar brightness of modernity, the fashionable skyscrapers as "vast immutable stone edifices" on the Bund. However, this does not mean that he opposes the advancement of science and technology and modern urbanization. He envisions his ideal city not in an alienated modern metropolis like Shanghai, but in cities like Beijing, Paris, or Vienna, which are able to encompass the glory of the arts, a profound history of culture, and a harmonious secular individual and political life.

To be sure, the height of Beijing's traditional gate towers and imperial buildings was considerably lower than that of the skyscrapers in Shanghai in the first half of the twentieth century. Whereas the horizontal vastness of the former invokes a strong sense of history, tradition, and solemnity, the vertical spectacle of the latter suggests the advent of modernity in a Westernized metropolis with modern building materials and technology. Literary representations of modern urban experiences in Shanghai are permeated with sensuous imageries of neon lights, ominous pressing highrises, stylish automobiles, decadent music, and so on. In a literary map of Beijing, especially in prose writings of modern times, the depiction of these modern objects and material culture is not predominant. Often the force of the modern is moderated and balanced by the sophisticated presentation of ancient architectures

---

[23] Lin Yutang, "A Hymn to Shanghai," in *With Love and Irony*, 63–64. See also Lin's positive imagination of Xi'an city in *The Vermillion Gate*, 4. It is worth noting that Shanghai, a new and a semicolonial metropolis tremendously influenced by Western capitalism and having no burden of (pre)history, has become an extremely "hot" subject and virtually the sole focus in the field of Chinese urban studies in American universities. In recent years, in addition to the literary remapping of Shanghai in terms of writers, literary schools, literary journals, and the publishing and printing industries, there have also emerged many a study on "Shanghai capitalists, workers, students, native-place associations, rural immigrants, gangs, prostitutes, municipal government, and police" (Joseph W. Esherick, *Remaking the Chinese City*, ix). To be sure, it is illuminating to consider modern traces in Shanghai inscribed in literary circles, the printing industry, international commerce, Westernized lifestyles and tastes, dance halls, coffeehouses, movie theaters, department stores, public parks and race clubs, various types of casinos and night clubs, foreign-style architecture, façades, and streets. Scholars argue that the birth and development of a "Shanghai Modern" primarily follows the models of Western cities. Therefore, the city could be interpreted by adapting some Western conceptual frameworks and key notions such as those of "public sphere," "civil society," "print culture," "imagined communities," "flâneur" and "cosmopolitanism"—all of which, to a certain extent, can heuristically fit in with the experiences and interpretations of indigenous Shanghai.

or peaceful daily objects, such as the city walls, gate towers, stately imperial palaces, historical relics, idyllic pastoral scenes and natural landscape, solemn camels, mule carts, humble vendors and peaceful pedestrians along the historical alleys, and so forth.

From Lin Yutang's perspective, the hills, lakes, trees, palaces, and amiable and harmonious pace of life in the old yet new Beijing constitute the essential texture of an ideal-type city. Tranquil scenery testifies to the concept of nature, and imperial grandeur bespeaks political order. These two dimensions correspond to each other delightfully in this urban harmony. One of his favorite places in the city is Back Lakes area (Shichahai),

> for it is particularly in this northwestern quarter of the city that the scene is rustic and one has the impression of living in the country. Trees and lotus-covered lakes and willow-bordered embankments abound. This is the great area for relaxation in summer. In the late afternoons young college students and girls saunter under the generous shade and sip *suanmeitang*, a delicious cold drink made of wild plums. The rhythmic clanging of the copper saucers of the men who sell this fruit juice can be heard along its embankments.[24]

Besides these geographical and climatic advantages, Beijing offers abundant places and facilities for recreation and relaxation. The enclosed courtyard of a residential compound, connected with the main street by the winding *hutungs*, or alleyways, is reminiscent of a rural cottage, and a secluded niche deep in the urban center. For Lin, alleyways in Beijing are

> hidden away from the broad avenues, but still within walking distance of the main streets, they provide much of Peking's charm. The broad open spaces of the city create the illusion of living in the country, especially where big trees cast their shadows on the yards and twittering of birds and the tap-tap of woodpeckers are heard in the morning. Unlike the main thoroughfares, the hutungs twist and turn upon each other, or lead unexpectedly to a square before some old temple.[25]

If avenues are the cardinal locations for political events and grand narratives, then alleyways mark the spatial and figurative line of personal stories and *petit récit*. In contrast to Lao She's alleyways full of ill-fated urbanites afflicted by poverty and

---

[24] Lin, *Imperial Peking*, 39.
[25] Ibid., 114.

disease or Zhang Ailing's Shanghai alleyways crowded by pragmatic, shrewd petit bourgeois, Lin Yutang's alleyways are the urban site where a pastoral aesthetics is born and a Confucian happiness and harmony (or a "central harmony," his translation of *zhongyong* 中庸) is substantiated.

Lin further illustrates the cultural implications of Chinese humanism and Confucianism and highlights the significant meaning of home: "The Chinese roof suggests, therefore, that happiness is first to be found in the home. Indeed, the home stands for me as a symbol of Chinese humanism."[26] The homes and courtyard houses in his works can be regarded as small cities within the great city of Beijing; meanwhile, the ideal-type city, be it Beijing, Nanjing, or Xi'an, is epitomized in minute yet detailed spaces of enclosure such as houses, courtyards, and gardens. Homes, or the courtyard houses, in *Moment in Peking* offer a key clue to illuminate Lin's Confucian imaginations of the ideal-type city. Spatially, *Moment in Peking* begins in the courtyard house of the Yao family, the doorway to which "was not an imposing entrance—a small black door with a red disc in the center." But the Yao house itself "was solid, well-proportioned, and exquisitely furnished and had none of the features of shabby gentility," and from this family atmosphere, Mulan, the ideal Chinese woman in Lin Yutang's magnum opus, "derived her style and self-confidence."[27] Whereas the Yao residence makes a visual statement of the Taoist spirit, which follows the cosmic order and appreciates a casual and adaptive lifestyle, the Tseng family occupies a stately mansion that bespeaks their position in imperial officialdom underpinned by orthodox Confucian teachings. The narrator describes the Tseng mansion:

> The white walls stretched over a hundred feet in length, and at the entrance was raised pavement over twenty-five feet wide, with the walls on both sides slanting inward toward the gate, which was shining red with golden knobs. On the top of the gate was a black-varnished signboard, bearing in golden characters a foot high the inscription, "The Air of Luck Brings Blessed Peace." Beside the gate hung a vertical signboard in white and sprinkled gold, bearing cabbage green characters which read, "Residence of the Vice-Director Tseng of the Government Telegraph Bureau." In front of the raised pavement were a pair of maliciously grinning stone lions, and the road at that point widened with "screen walls" facing the gate and receding in the opposite direction, giving a large space for parking carriages.[28]

---

[26] Lin, *My Country and My People*, 108.

[27] Lin, *Moment in Peking*, 3, 133. For historical and architectural features of the traditional courtyard house and how it represents old Beijing architecture, city planning and culture, see Lin, *Imperial Peking*, and Dong, *Republican Beijing*.

[28] Lin, *Moment in Peking*, 100–101.

Like the Yao house, the Tseng mansion is an independent and autonomous complex of buildings. Besides the exterior grandeur, the interior structure is massive and imposing: "The Tseng mansion was a spacious house, four courts deep, with a narrow but long patch of vacant space lined with tall elm trees on the east of the main courts, and a number of rambling, zigzag promenade corridors leading to well-concealed courtyards on the west."[29] While Chinese courtyard houses in the works of Lao She, who is primarily concerned with the lives of commoners or the lower class, are shabby, cramped places where several households of the underprivileged live together, Lin Yutang's courtyard houses are spacious, comfortable, elegant, and highly cultivated. For him, the style and decoration of the Yao house demonstrate the values and tastes of Yao Si'an, who is a Taoist believer, runs traditional Chinese businesses such as tea and Chinese medicine commerce, and at the same time is open to modern Western knowledge. Yao Si'an is representative of Beijing's elite intellectuals, although he is a businessman. Tseng Wenpu, an imperial minister, a Confucian believer and practitioner, represents another important social stratum in Beijing, mandarins. Since Beijing was the capital for the Ming and Qing dynasties, government officials constituted a significant social class in the city's population. The design and construction of the Tseng mansion differentiate it from the Yaos' and reflect the moral and cultural mentality of the mandarin class. The Tseng house is close to the east city gate and next to the city wall, in a luxurious, independent, and self-sustaining community, while the Yaos' is located in a district for businessmen. While Beijing's spatial layout provides for all its inhabitants multiple possibilities in culture and everyday life, Lin Yutang's urban image is a combination of the lifestyles of Tseng and Yao, namely, the perfect blend of Confucian and Taoist ideals. Not until after Mulan, the perfect daughter of Taoism, marries the youngest son of the Tseng/Confucian family does the ideal lifestyle emerge, exemplifying Lin's idea of "Great Harmony."

From Lin's point of view, the courtyard houses present the orders of the world and the society, the "innerworldly morality," and the harmony of human and nature. These ideal-type homes and houses can be taken as the starting point, the fundamental basis, on which the ideal-type city is to be created. Residents can go to *Shichahai* to enjoy the beauty of the lakes and the fragrance of lotus flowers, stop by the bank of the city moat to collect dewdrops to cook tea, sit idly under the shade of pine trees in the Central Park, or visit the Forbidden City. When illustrating the aesthetic dimension of space, or more specifically, the emotional and even rational sense of a house, Edward W. Said borrowed Gaston Bachelard's poetics of space and further argued:

The inside of a house . . . acquires a sense of intimacy, secrecy, security, real or imagined, because of the experiences that come to seem appropriate for it.

---

[29] Ibid., 102.

The objective space of a house—its corners, corridors, cellar, room—is far less important than what poetically it is endowed with, which is usually a quality with an imaginative or figurative value we can name and feel: thus a house may be haunted, or homelike, or prisonlike, or magical. So space acquires emotional and even rational sense by a kind of poetic process, whereby the vacant or anonymous reaches of distance are converted into meaning for us here.[30]

In the literary and cultural topography of Beijing, the Chinese courtyard house can also be regarded as a small poetic "city" within the city—from Lin's perspective, a wonderfully designed space for everyday life and an idealized domestic place. The outer city culture of Beijing is perceived from within this walled and closed space of courtyard houses: the sound, the smell, the taste, changing seasons, social customs. . . . The observer experiences a combination of the poetics of daily life and the poetics of space.

To English readers, Lin's works are fantastic reference books about alternative daily experiences, a far-reaching encyclopedia of a foreign civilization, and an idealized and intellectualized portrayal of the ideal Chinese city culture.[31] *The Importance of Living* (1937) is a salient example. Lin's letter to Tao Kangde 陶亢德 (1908–1983) accurately elucidates his understanding of the art of daily life, and why he chooses this as his major subject matter. *The Importance of Living* was specially recommended by the American Book-of-the-Month Club for December 1937 and became popular throughout the whole country, staying at the top of the American best-seller list for fifty-two weeks in 1938. Orville Prescott, columnist of "Books of the Times" for the *New York Times*, commented that after reading this book, he wanted to run into

---

[30] Gaston Bachelard, *The Poetics of Space*, trans. Maria Jolas (Boston: Beacon Press, 1994); the first English translation was published by New York: Orion Press in 1964. Edward W. Said, *Orientalism* (New York: Vintage, 1978), 55.

[31] It is also worth noting that Zhou Zuoren offers a significant understanding of ancient and modern Beijing. As Susan Framji Daruvala points out, Zhou Zuoren's alternative responses to modernity occur in three interrelated ways: 1) traditional aesthetics, 2) locality in a writer's identity and self-representation, and 3) construction of a literary history in opposition to the dominant one; see *Zhou Zuoren and an Alternative Chinese Response to Modernity* (Cambridge, MA: Harvard University Asia Center, 2000), 12. When coming back to China from Japan, Zhou Zuoren began to construct a whole set of local knowledge (the locality is historicized) and alternative utterances about Beijing. His close relationship with the writers of the Beijing School and his cooperation with the Japanese invaders betray the continuing question of the relationships between intellectual life and politics, which was earlier crystallized in the event of Wang Guowei's death; and Zhou's understanding of modern Beijing as a particular city in the general pan-Asian context of Chinese and Japanese cultures, and his contradictory image of himself—a collector of antiquities, a protector of a living museum, and a traitor in a political turmoil.

Chinatown and deeply bow to every Chinese he met.[32] Such was the effect of Lin's introduction of Chinese culture. In the Cold War and post-Maoist sociocultural contexts in mainland China, readers have discovered a bygone era, a lost legend, and a profound nostalgia, all projected into an idealized city image polished by Lin's constructed and imagined happiness and pleasure. What Lin seeks to establish is a universalist discourse of humanism and humanity that goes beyond the East-West dichotomy. In response to the chaos and calamities the world went through in modern times, Lin proposes an Oriental philosophy, including Confucian wisdom characterized by idleness and "the doctrine of the mean," as a way of cultivating one's inner world. Only when one learns how to appreciate leisure and pleasure in practices of everyday life is one able to confront and redress political turbulence and morass.

By advocating beauty and performing pleasure in urban settings, Lin Yutang puts into effect a poetics of urban objects against the backdrop of imperial buildings, connecting pastoral representations with individual and lyrical evocations. In the opening paragraph of his preface to *The Importance of Living*, Lin confesses that his writing is a "personal testimony," not an objective record but a "lyrical philosophy" expressed in terms of a "highly personal and individual outlook." And thanks to such a "convenient form for personal, inadvertent disclosures," he brings in "the significant trivialities of our daily life," above all, "idle rambling about the pastures of sweet, silent thought."[33] This narrative strategy, therefore, bestows a unique personality on his ideal-type city.

Lin once said that he himself was positioned in both Eastern and Western cultures. He commented with his whole heart on universal works and indulged in self-contradictions. In fact, this person of contradictions never lacked the capacity to locate or build ways toward happiness and harmony. Rather than rejecting illusions, he observes that daydreams and fantasies are essential to life, and the purpose of surviving would be lost if the secular world is stripped of illusions.[34] He endeavors to create a universalized Beijing, although he always claims that nobody can understand Beijing as a whole. Lin's essays for the *New York Times*, his verbal and visual constructions of Beijing in *Imperial Beijing*, and his novel *Moment in Peking* are not indigenous works providing colonists with information on primitive knowledge and customs, as defined by the anthropologists. Instead, these writings function as a self-indulgent performance of the Oriental character and Chinese principle of pleasure

---

[32] Quoted in Lin Taiyi, *Lin Yutang zhuan* [Biography of Lin Yutang] (Taipei: Lianjing, 1989), 176. Lin Taiyi mistakenly wrote "Orville Prescott" as "Peter Prescott."

[33] Lin Yutang, *The Importance of Living* (New York: The John Day Company, Inc., 1937), vii.

[34] See Lin Yutang, *Looking Beyond* (New York: Prentice-Hall, 1955), also called *Unexpected Island* (1955), and the Chinese version entitled *Qidao* 奇島, trans. Zhang Zhenyu 張振玉 (Taipei: Jinlan chubanshe, 1986).

for an ideal readership based in the West. Lin's ideal-type city is cosmopolitan and universal:

> A man—let him be Chinese, Japanese, or European—who has lived in Peking for a year wouldn't want to live in any other city in China. For Peking is one of the jewel cities in the world. Except Paris and (by hearsay) Vienna as they once were, there is no city in the world that is quite so nearly ideal, in regard to nature, culture, charm, and mode of living, as Peking.[35]

Here, the image of Beijing evolves from a pastoral city to a cultural and symbolic capital and ultimately a cosmopolitan metropolis. In a subtle manner, Lao She's Beijing captures the contradiction between tradition and modernity, between the old ways of life and the challenging modern values amid the melodious Beijing accents and the citizens' slow rhythms of life.[36] But for Lin Yutang, all the distinctions between the old and the new, the vulgar and the refined—subaltern versus aristocracy, Manchu madams versus modern women, rickshaws versus foreign-style carriages—are juxtaposed harmoniously, and, more importantly, are assimilated and merged into the cultivated Beijing culture:

> It has variety—variety of men. It has laws and breakers of laws, police and accomplices of police, thieves and protectors of thieves, beggars and kings of beggars. It has saints, sinners, Mohammedans, Tibetan "devil-expellers," fortune tellers, boxers, monks, prostitutes, Russian and Chinese taxi dancers, Japanese and Korean smugglers, painters, philosophers, poets, collectors of curios, young college students, and movie fans. It has political scoundrels, retired old magistrates, New Life followers, theosophists, wives of former Manchu officials, now serving as maids.[37]

---

[35] Lin, "Captive Peking," 55. Lin's *Juniper Loa*, an autobiographical and nostalgic novel, reveals another perspective from which to see Beijing, that is, to catch sight of the historical changes from the point of view of a "kid on the top of a mountain." He revealed his own philosophy of life like this: "If you are born in the high mountain, you meditate on everything by the help of the high mountain. If seeing a skyscraper, you compare it with the mountain peak that you saw before, and then the skyscraper seems to be absurd and negligible." See Lin Yutang, *Juniper Loa* (New York: Dell, 1963). Lin Yutang's view of Beijing from afar is not only from New York or Paris but also from the height of a mountain and the perspective of a naïve child. Even in noisy Shanghai, Lin Yutang still searches for and listens attentively to the rhythmic sounds of the city, like he heard and enjoyed in modern Beijing.

[36] It is best manifested in works such as "Kaishi daji" 開市大吉 [The grand opening], "Lao zihao" 老字號 [An old and established name], "Heibai Li" 黑白李 [Black Li and White Li], "Linju men" 鄰居們 [Neighbors], "Waimaoer" 歪毛兒 [Crooktails], and even "Duanhunqiang" 斷魂槍 [Soul-slaying spear]. See *Blades of Grass: The Stories of Lao She*, trans. William A. Lyell and Sarah Wei-ming Chen (Honolulu: University of Hawai'i Press, 1999).

[37] Lin, "Captive Peking," 58.

Beijing "harbors the old and the modern," but significantly, the city is "unmoved herself."[38] Or, as Lin well put it in another set of urban images, "Modern young misses in high-heeled shoes brush shoulders with Manchu ladies on wooden soles, and Peking doesn't care. Old painters with white, magnificent long beards live across the yard from young college students in their 'public hostelries' (*kungyü*), Peking doesn't care. Packards and Buicks compete with rickshas and mule carts and caravans, and Peking doesn't care."[39] In this way, Lin Yutang, a self-appointed representative of Beijing culture, creates an eternal city image that is not and can never be corroded by historical changes and human behaviors. *Moment in Peking* is a wonderful example illustrating the transcendental, cosmopolitan, and universal aspects of modern Beijing. In delineating a family history, the novel describes significant historical transformations that Beijing and the Chinese nation have undergone in the modern age. As the title of the novel suggests, all the complicated and turbulent historical incidents in modern Chinese history are nothing but transient moments, passing like floating dreams. The true and only constant is the city itself. Lin Taiyi notes that the subject matter of *Moment in Peking* is the fleeting vicissitudes of life. I argue that this novel also tries to illuminate the "super-stable structure" of Beijing. In the first chapter of *Imperial Peking*, Lin Yutang reflects on the mentality of old Beijing: "dynasties come and go, and tyrants rise and fall, but in Peking the life of the common people continues unperturbed . . . . With eternal cities, . . . short moments pass and are forgotten. The happy life of the people goes on. Every city is greater than the personalities which momentarily dominate it."[40]

Lin pictures Beijing as a universal code or sign surviving from and going beyond historical transformations and cultural differences. The rise and fall of dynasties, nation-states, or political ideologies cannot change its essence. He bridges the city and his notion of Confucianism with his principle of performing pleasure. Lin maintains, "[T]here is a centrality or, shall I say, universality, about the Confucian attitude and point of view, reflected in a joy in Confucian belief that I see even among maturing modern Chinese who have received a Western education."[41] The "joy in Confucian belief," and the "centrality" or "universality" of the Confucian point of view, can be decoded from Lin's Confucian configuration of the ideal-type Chinese city. This is a city that encompasses the pleasant and the painful, creates harmony out of contradictions, promotes leisure and pleasure in the practice of everyday life, and substantiates Confucian aesthetics and poetics of human life.

---

[38] Ibid., 58.

[39] Ibid., 56.

[40] Lin, *Imperial Peking*, 11–12.

[41] Lin Yutang, *The Wisdom of Confucius* (New York: The Modern Library, 1938), 3.

THE TWILIGHT OF EMPIRE AND THE DISCLOSURE
OF THE FORBIDDEN CITY

The possibility of the production of the native informant by way of the colonial/postcolonial route . . . is lodged in the fact that, for the real needs of imperialism, the in-choate in-fans aboriginal para-subject cannot be theorized as functionally completely frozen in a world where teleology is schematized into geo-graphy (writing the world). This limited access to being human is the itinerary of the native informant into the post-colonial, which remains unrecognized through the various transformations of the discussions of both ethics and ethnicity.

—GAYATRI SPIVAK

In the sunset years of the Manchu Empire, the inner city and the outer city of imperial Beijing were defined and confined by walls, gates, and enclosed circles. As the center of centers and circles, the Forbidden City, or the "Great Within," constitutes the most sealed, concealed, and enchanting place for Chinese and foreigners, who want to see behind the massive and ancient palace walls, the visual and symbolic barriers, and access the heart of Beijing and the Chinese Empire.[42] Among the privileged group who inhabited or lived temporarily inside the Forbidden City in turn-of-the-century Beijing, Princess Der Ling, pseudonym of Yu Der Ling 裕德齡, not only enjoyed access to but also strove to unfold the "Great Within" in written words. Of paternal Manchu and maternal American-Chinese ancestries, Der Ling was brought up with no shortage of Western references, and spent her late childhood and adolescent years in Tokyo (1895–1898) and Paris (1898–1903) with her father, Lord Yu Keng 裕庚 (?–1905). Lord Yu was a member of the Manchu White Banner Corps and one of the most liberal Manchu aristocrats in his generation.[43] At the turn of the century, he was appointed by the Qing government as Minister to Japan and later Minister to the French Third Republic. Together with her sister, Rung Ling 容齡 (Rong Ling, 1882–1973), and her brother, Hsun Ling 勳齡 (Xun Ling, ca. 1880–1943),

---

[42] For recent books about the chronicle and history of *Zijincheng* in English, see Geremie Barmé, *The Forbidden City* (Cambridge, MA: Harvard University Press, 2008); May Holdsworth and Caroline Courtauld, *The Forbidden City: The Great Within*, rev. ed. (London: Frances Lincoln Ltd, 2008).

[43] Grant Hayter-Menzies published the first English-language comprehensive biography of Der Ling with a foreword by Pamela Kyle Crossley, *Imperial Masquerade: The Legend of Princess Der Ling* (Hong Kong: Hong Kong University Press, 2008). Crossley points out the dubious identity of Yu Keng: "Der Ling's father, Yu Keng, was not a Manchu. Neither was he Chinese. He belonged to the old and misunderstood Chinese-martial caste of mixed origins who conquered China alongside the Manchus in the seventeenth century. To Chinese civilians the entire conquest elite was 'Manchu,' despite a range of cultures and family histories." Foreword to *Imperial Masquerade*, by Grant Hayter-Menzies, xvi; see also Thomas F. Millard's preface to Princess Der Ling, *Two Years in the Forbidden City* (New York: Moffat, Yard and Company, 1911), vii. One of the Chinese versions is entitled *Qinggong ernian ji* 清宮二年記, trans. Gu Qiuxin 顧秋心 (Kunming: Yunnan renmin chubanshe, 1981), 85.

Der Ling was educated in missionary schools. She also learned modern dance under the tutelage of Isadora Duncan (1877–1927). She was fluent in English and conversant in French, Japanese, German, Spanish, and Russian. At the age of seventeen, she returned to Beijing and became First Lady-in-Waiting and multilingual translator to the Empress Dowager Cixi from 1903 to 1905. After two years of service in the Forbidden City, Der Ling was allowed to leave the Qing court when her father passed away in 1905. She was married to Thaddeus C. White, the American vice-consul in Shanghai, in 1907, and went to the United States with her husband. In 1927–1928, she returned to Shanghai and played the role of Empress Dowager Cixi (her sister Rung Ling starred as Der Ling) in a stage performance at Shanghai's Lanxin Theatre. During the Sino-Japanese War, she participated in fundraising programs, including "Voyage of China," in America to aid wartime China. She died in a car accident outside the University of California, Berkeley in 1944. From 1911 to 1935, Der Ling published eight popular books in English, mostly memoirs, about the Forbidden City, the imperial capital, and her personal journeys between the Oriental and Occidental worlds. Grant Hayter-Menzies, biographer of Der Ling, draws her portrait: "A memoirist, raconteur, and a European-educated, multi-lingual Asian woman who gleefully crossed all the lines of cultural expectations both oriental and occidental, Princess Der Ling was a unique character on the stage of late Qing and early Republican China."[44]

A modernized and Westernized young Manchu lady, Der Ling served Empress Dowager Cixi during the waning years of the Qing Empire, experienced the inertia and changes of the imperial capital, and witnessed the enigmas surrounding the mythical and inaccessible Forbidden City from a cross-cultural view both near and far. She is a rare combination of multiple identities of female translator, cross-cultural observer, and enlightened "native informant." Der Ling's works in English and their constant Chinese renditions and multimedia adaptations enjoy wide translingual and transnational circulation.[45] Her Beijing narrative straddles the boundaries between fiction and history, individual memories and dynastic politics, reliable record and consumable story. Imbricating gender and empire, female consciousness

---

[44] See http://solongletty.tripod.com/princessderling/id1.html.

[45] Regarding the characteristics of unofficial history in Princess Der Ling's works, see Rung Ling's preface to the 1936 Chinese version *Yuxiang piaomiao lu* 御香縹緲錄 of Der Ling's *Imperial Incense* published in English in 1933, and another preface by Qin Shouou 秦瘦鷗 (1908–1993), the Chinese translator. One recent Chinese version is *Cixi hou sishenghuo shilu* 慈禧後私生活實錄 (Nanjing: Jiangsu guangling guji keyinshe, 1998). See also Chen Lirong 陳禮榮's two essays, "Shenmi de Princess Der Ling" 神秘的 "德齡公主" [Mythical Princess Der Ling], in *Guangming ribao* 光明日報 [Guangming daily], July 13, 2000; and "Yong yingwen xie gongwei" 用英文寫宮闈 [Writing Qing court stories in English], in *Hubei ribao* 湖北日報 [Hubei daily], May 15, 2003; and Lydia H. Liu, *The Clash of Empires: The Invention of China in Modern World Making* (Cambridge, MA: Harvard University Press, 2004), chap. 5.

and urban sensitivity, these imperial Beijing stories feed the desires of both Anglo-American and Chinese-language readers to uncover "the secret of her greatness" and the myth of the "Great Within" at the twilight of the "Celestial Empire."

Two Years in the Forbidden City, Der Ling's first and most popular English work, was published in October 1911, a time when Qing rule was being over-thrown and Republican China was about to be born. Up until the early twentieth century, in the English-language world, there had been few faithful and detailed accounts about Qing imperial court life. In 1905, Miss Katharine A. Carl (1865–1938), an American artist who painted a portrait of the Empress Dowager Cixi for the 1904 St. Louis World Exposition, published a memoir entitled *With the Empress Dowager*.[46] Sarah Pike Conger (1843–1932), the wife of Edwin Hurd Conger (1843–1907), the US minister to China during the Boxer Rebellion, composed *Letters from China with Particular Reference to the Empress Dowager and the Women of China* (1907). 1910 saw the publication of the seminal book, *China Under the Empress Dowager: Being the History of the Life and Times of Tzu Hsi, Compiled from State Papers and the Private Diary of the Comptroller of Her Household* (1910), by J. O. P. Bland (1863–1945) and Sir Edmund Backhouse (1873–1944). While evoking broad interest among Western readers in the figure of the Empress Dowager Cixi, these writings also created a stereotypical image of Cixi as the malicious and moody female ruler of an ancient empire, a mysterious and formidable "Dragon Lady" in the Oriental kingdom.[47] However, as foreigners, these authors had limited views of and restricted contacts with the Qing court; therefore their sketches of Qing imperial life were far from accurate or comprehensive. In contrast, Der Ling's special position endowed her with privileged and intimate access to the "Great Within" and to the enigmatic core of the absolute form of sovereignty in the Manchu Empire. Her perspective from within and beyond allowed

---

[46] The first edition is entitled *With the Empress Dowager*, by Katharine A. Carl; illustrated by the author and with photographs (New York: The Century Co., 1905). Later editions are issued as *With the Empress Dowager of China*. See also David Logge, "The Empress Dowager and the Camera: Photographing Cixi, 1903–1904," http://ocw.mit.edu/ans7870/21f/21f.027/empress_dowager/.

[47] See, for instance, Sterling Seagrave, *Dragon Lady: The Life and Legend of the Last Empress of China* (New York: Knopf, 1992). Geremie Barmé mentioned Sir Edmund Backhouse's unpublished manuscript, "Décadence Mandchoue" (1943), in his *The Forbidden City* (Cambridge, MA: Harvard University Press, 2008), 216. Backhouse's bold accounts were published as *Decadence Mandchoue: The China Memoirs of Sir Edmund Trelawny Backhouse* (Hong Kong: Earnshaw Books, 2011), and its Chinese translation, entitled *Taihou yu wo* 太后與我 (The Empress Dowager and I, translated by Wang Xiaoge), appeared simultaneously in Hong Kong and Taiwan in 2011, and mainland China in 2012. The English publisher describes Backhouse's self-promotion in eye-catching terms: "In 1898 a young Englishman walked into a homosexual brothel in Peking and began a journey that, as he claims, took him all the way to the bedchamber of imperial China's last great ruler, the Empress Dowager. Published now for the first time, the controversial memoir of sinologist Sir Edmund Backhouse provides a unique and shocking glimpse into the hidden world of China's imperial palace with its rampant corruption, grand conspiracies and uninhibited sexuality."

her to provide firsthand accounts and insider information interspersed with literary imagination and East-West comparative observations. Many of her works were instant best-sellers in the English-language world and were followed by Chinese translations and multimedia adaptations.[48]

Two Years in the Forbidden City combines the author's "near views" of the Empress Dowager Cixi with her own story of growth and development in a cross-cultural environment, and extends her personal experiences to social and political domains in the final years of the Manchu Empire. From a comparative perspective, Der Ling, an interpreter and observer, describes Cixi's political and private life, and Her Majesty's remaining power and changing psyche after the suppression of the disastrous Boxer Uprising and the foreign looting of Beijing in 1900. She also reveals the Emperor Guangxu's (Kwang Hsu) political frustrations and tragic personal life after the failure of the Hundred Days' Reform in 1898. In her first visit to the Empress Dowager Cixi and the Emperor Guangxu in the Summer Palace, Der Ling was requested to dress in her Parisian costumes. Cixi showed great interest in her foreign education and wanted her to stay in the inner court. Later on, after Der Ling changed from her Western clothes to a Manchu dress, everybody commented that she now looked more beautiful and "natural," except for the Emperor Guangxu, who sighed and said, "I think that your Parisian gowns are far prettier than this."[49] The Empress Dowager Cixi laughed loudly and said, "I can't believe you are the same girl. Just look at yourself in this looking-glass . . . . See how you have changed. I feel that you belong to me now."[50] This seemingly trivial differentiation in fashion senses reveals the disparate attitudes of the Emperor and the Empress Dowager toward the West and its cultures. The large Western-style mirror in Her Majesty's room not only reflects the sartorial homecoming of Der Ling but also points to the close connection between fashion preferences and political-cultural positions.

Der Ling's ongoing Beijing narrative focuses on the Empress Dowager Cixi and depicts her extravagant lifestyle and multiple personalities. In her novel *Lotos Petals*, she sketches the image of Her Majesty as follows:

> Inside the Forbidden City, in the heart of Peking, Her Majesty was the sun about which all China revolved. Even the humiliating experience of the

---

[48] The Chinese translation of Der Ling's *Two Years in the Forbidden City* first appeared in 1911 in the form of classical Chinese (*wenyan* 文言), and later in vernacular Chinese, including Chen Yixian 陳貽先 and Chen Lengtai's 陳冷汰 1914 translation and Gu Qiuxin's 1948 edition. Recent adaptations of Der Ling's debut work include Han Gangji's 韓剛繼 popular twenty-two-episode TV series *Der Ling gongzhu* 德齡公主 (2006), based on famous female writer Xu Xiaobin's 徐小斌 novel; He Jiping's 何冀平 spoken drama *Der Ling yu Cixi* 德齡與慈禧 [Princess Der Ling and Empress Dowager Cixi] was staged in Hong Kong and Beijing in 2008.

[49] Der Ling, *Two Years in the Forbidden City*, 155.

[50] Ibid., 156. For a discussion of her changing clothes, see Wang Shuo, "Der Ling: Manchu Princess, Cultural Advisor, and Author," in *The Human Tradition in Modern China*, ed. Kenneth James Hammond and Kristin Eileen Stapleton (Lanham, MD: Rowman & Littlefield, 2008), 73–92.

Boxer Uprising could not rob Tzu Hsi of the reverence of her subjects. Her court was magnificent. Her gowns and those of her court ladies were studded with precious stones. She was surrounded by thirty-six hundred eunuchs whose duty it was to be as servant maids for the court. They held their jobs by flattery, each eunuch humbling himself before the eunuchs next in rank above him, and all of them paying abject homage to Old Buddha, the nickname by which Her Majesty was known. Certain hours of the day were set aside by Her Majesty for audience with her ministers, and war would scarcely have changed her habits in this regard, while securing a special audience for any reason was almost as difficult as for a rich man to enter the kingdom of heaven.[51]

Coming from a young female translator returning home (Beijing) from afar (Paris), Der Ling's demarcations of Cixi highly complicate the stereotypical caricature of a devious despot or femme fatale. Der Ling's exploration of Her Majesty's personality and psychology is characterized by her gender standpoint, which focuses on, from time to time, feminine details such as hairstyles, flowers, jewels, costumes, and interior decorations. Der Ling once recalled, "Her Majesty told us the way we must have our hair dressed, and what kind of flowers we should wear, in fact she was very happy arranging to make us into Manchus."[52] Shifting from the feminine gaze to political observations, Der Ling discovers the cruel and cunning character of Cixi as a capricious ruler in imperial politics as well as in everyday life. If a eunuch let any strand fall while combing her hair, he would be killed. If she was in a bad mood, she would punish the cook willfully.[53] Nevertheless, Der Ling also captures the pleasant and amiable side of the temperament of the "Old Buddha." One winter, Cixi was thrown out of the sedan chair after one carrier fell down on the icy, slippery road, yet surprisingly, forgave the bearer. Every year on the death anniversary of her late husband, the Emperor Xianfeng 咸豐 (1831–1861), she would feel sad and morose and "hardly had a word to say to any of us and cried almost incessantly."[54]

For Der Ling, a Manchu lady with modern Western values who spent her formative years in Japan and Europe, a suffocating darkness emerges as the defining feature of the Forbidden City: "The Palace in the Forbidden City was so old, and built in such a queer way. The courtyards were small, and the verandas very broad. All the rooms

---

[51] Der Ling, *Lotos Petals* (New York: Dodd, Mead, 1930), 3–4.

[52] Der Ling, *Two Years in the Forbidden City*, 138–139.

[53] See the Chinese version translated by Gu Qiuxin, *Qinggong ernian ji*, 272–273.

[54] Der Ling, *Two Years in the Forbidden City*, 249.

were dark. No electric light. We had to use candle light. One could not see the sky except by going into the courtyard and looking up."[55] Enclosed by towering walls, rectangular courtyards, and gigantic pressing roofs, the "Great Within" is described as a dim and inconvenient environment for daily activities. She writes that "Her Majesty never liked to stay in the Forbidden City, and I was not a bit surprised, as I hated the place. We had to use candles to dress by, in the morning, as the rooms were in absolute darkness even in the middle of the afternoon."[56] As an alternative, the Summer Palace becomes their favorite place to stay and enjoy. The shadow world of the Forbidden City is haunted by imperial conspiracies, intrigues, and cover-ups: "One of the principal reasons for Her Majesty's dislike to the Forbidden City was the mysteries which it contained, many of which she did not know of herself."[57]

While dark and hidden secrets in the "Great Within" were sealed, the great outside world and foreign powers were irresistibly approaching the walled enclosure of the Forbidden City. Cixi was conservative and suspicious toward new, especially Western, ideas and practices, which were introduced to China rapidly after the 1900 looting of Beijing. However, she could occasionally put away her "pride and prejudice" to try the new things with the "alien influence." [58] One intriguing example is Cixi's changing responses to Western painting and photography.[59] When Mrs. Conger first brought the American artist, Miss Katherine Carl, to draw the Empress Dowager's portrait, Cixi was quite provoked by this idea. According to Chinese custom, a portrait was only to be drawn after the person died. However, Cixi was soon fascinated with the artist's work and appreciated and criticized the Western principle of perspective in painting shadows on the face: half of the face is white and half black. She also agreed to have her picture taken by Hsun Ling, Der Ling's brother, who had studied photography for a considerable time in Europe and became Cixi's only photographer in the Forbidden City. At first Cixi was utterly shocked when seeing people upside down through the camera lens. But Her Majesty soon learned the optical principle and was mesmerized by the novel technology. In minute observations, Der Ling portrays Cixi as both "the highest authority and an ordinary woman."[60] A. Owen Aldridge observes, "Western fiction has transfigured

---

[55] Ibid., 134.

[56] Ibid., 139.

[57] Ibid., 320.

[58] Princess Der Ling, *Imperial Incense* (New York: Dodd, Mead, 1933), 9.

[59] Der Ling, *Two Years in the Forbidden City*, chap.13, "The Empress's Portrait." For a critical reading of Cixi's pictures, see Cheng-hua Wang, "Going Public: Portraits of the Empress Dowager Cixi, Circa 1904," *Nannü* 14, no. 1 (2012): 119–176; *Empress Dowager Cixi: Her Art of Living* (Hong Kong: The Regional Council and the Palace Museum, 1996); and Liu, *The Clash of Empires*, esp. chap. 5.

[60] Liu Zhongjie's 劉中傑 words; see the Chinese version translated by Gu Qiuxin, *Qinggong ernian ji*, 3.

the Empress Dowager Ci-Xi into a cultural icon for the Far East embodying the contradictory characteristics of the femme fatale and the eternal mother. The mystery surrounding her personality has been attributed to aesthetic sensitivity, lust for power, and obsession with sex. Some novels about her border on pornography, but the one most widely circulated portrays her as an ordinary woman rather than a stereotype."[61] Aldridge refers to Der Ling's writings, including *Two Years in the Forbidden City*, as contributing a more humanized image of Cixi.

Moreover, Der Ling exhibits in flamboyant detail imperial rituals and courtesies of the Qing court, her own social life with other Manchu royal family members, and her communications with foreign ladies. Der Ling was astonished by the low level of education of the Manchu royal ladies, by their narrow vision, stunning ignorance about the Western world, and xenophobia. For instance, the Qing court ladies believed that a person who had drunk Western water would forget everything in his or her native land. Der Ling was by no means an obedient court servant. Xiaoyu Wang points out her self-promotion:

[S]he cultivated a modern cosmopolitan vantage point that stood her as equal to Western commentators on China. Father's support and daughter's giftedness also explain how Der Ling negotiated the other major episodes upon which she built her life story. These included an incredibly daring refusal of a proposed marriage to the Guangxu Emperor's uncle by none less than the Empress Dowager Cixi, her ability to earn extraordinary favours with both the Dowager and the emperor, her refusal of marriage proposals from other prominent Manchus, and her decision to choose an American husband with whom to launch a publishing career in California.[62]

In spite of her admiration and worship of Cixi, Der Ling was not blind to the fact that Cixi governed the empire in an extremely tyrannical and conservative way. During her two-year service in the court, Der Ling, sometimes with the help of her father, explained Western etiquette to Cixi, translated selected articles from foreign newspapers for Her Highness, and endeavored to open the empress's eyes and convince her to implement political reforms. Moreover, the father and daughter introduced the trends of Western modernization to Emperor Guangxu and occasionally taught him foreign languages and Western musical instruments. In concluding her

---

[61] A. Owen Aldridge posits a rhetorical yet important question in his article, "The Empress Dowager CI-XI in Western Fiction: A Stereotype for the Far East?," *Revue de littérature comparée* 1 (2001): 113–122.

[62] Xiaoyu Wang, review of *Imperial Masquerade: The Legend of Princess Der Ling*, by Grant Hayter-Menzies, *Journal of Historical Biography* 4 (Autumn 2008): 125.

debut work, Der Ling expressed her deepest wish: "Although I was not able to do much towards influencing Her Majesty in the matter of reforms, I still hope to live to see the day when China shall wake up and take her proper place among the nations of the world."[63]

Gu Hongming (Ku Hung-ming) 辜鴻銘 (1857–1928) highly complimented Der Ling's first book, *Two Years in the Forbidden City*. Trained in Europe, Gu won a controversial reputation for his erudite knowledge of Western literature and his bitter criticism of Western imperialism. He was a good friend of Yu Keng, as they had been colleagues in Wuchang for more than five years. Gu wrote a book review for the Shanghai English newspaper *International Reviews*, which acclaimed Der Ling as a modern Manchu woman and regarded *Two Years in the Forbidden City* as without artistic exaggeration, a simple and unembellished book surpassing any other works on similar subjects because it offered the most accurate information on authentic Manchu life.[64] Chen Yixian, who cotranslated *Two Years in the Forbidden City* and authored its preface, also highly evaluated Der Ling's personal testimony and vivid depictions of imperial life and politics:

> Everyday details are minutely and subtly recorded, and scenes of the inner court are vividly illustrated. It is not only highly interesting to read, one can also vaguely envisage the raison d'être of the rise and fall of a dynasty. In the former imperial time, there was a strict boundary between the court and the outside world. For the ordinary people, the Forbidden City is utterly unattainable, like the legendary Jade Island or Jasper Lake. Hearsay makes it appear more mysterious than betraying its true face. Now, this book reveals the enigmatic court life to us.
>
> 日常瑣碎，纖悉必錄，宮闈情景，歷歷如繪。不獨閱之極饒趣味，而隱微之中，亦可以覘廢興之故焉。至於一支一節，足備掌故之資者，更復不鮮。間嘗竊嘆昔在帝制之世，宮府隔絕。吾民之視皇宮，若瑤池瓊島之可望而不可即。雖或傳聞一二，亦惝恍而莫得其真。今得是書，一旦盡披露於前，不亦快歟。[65]

Grant Hayter-Menzies discusses Der Ling's intriguing alternations between the roles of "principal translator" on diplomatic occasions and "Her Majesty's First Lady-in-Waiting" in the Forbidden City: the former as a cross-cultural agent, and

---

[63] Der Ling, *Two Years in the Forbidden City*, 382–383. See also the Chinese version translated by Gu Qiuxin, 364.

[64] See Chen Lirong's two essays.

[65] Chen Yixian, preface to his Chinese translation of *Two Years in the Forbidden City*, *Qinggong ernian ji* 清宮二年記 (Shanghai: Shangwu yinshuguan, 1937), 1. The original remarks are in classical Chinese, and the English translation is mine.

the latter as a privileged position to access invaluable secrets in proximity, which was envied by Miss Katherine Carl.[66] Furthermore, Der Ling herself noted and publicly admitted her dual identity as a Westerner at heart. In *Two Years in the Forbidden City*, she wrote,

> While in Shanghai I made many new friends and acquaintances and gradually began to realize that after all, the attractions of Court life had not been able to eradicate the influences which had been brought to bear upon me while in Europe. *At heart I was a foreigner, educated in a foreign country*, and, having already met my husband the matter was soon settled and I became an American citizen.[67]

Despite all the appeal of imperial court life, this Manchu woman showed a strong affinity for the cosmopolitan lifestyle in Shanghai. Der Ling's Forbidden City narrative is characterized by cross-cultural comparison and deeply embedded in the encounter of the Occidental and Oriental worlds.

With *Two Years in the Forbidden City*, Der Ling made a sensational debut in the Anglo-American world. Years later, when her second book, *Old Buddha*, was published, Arthur J. Burks wrote confidently in his preface, "For most of the readers, it is not necessary for me to introduce Princess Der Ling. The popularity of her *Two Years in the Forbidden City* published in 1911 makes me believe so."[68] With encouragement and endorsement from writers, scholars, and the publishing industry, Der Ling continued to provide otherwise inaccessible information about Qing court life, and attempted to revise the stereotypes about the words and deeds, heart and mind of the Empress Dowager Cixi, in her popular series including *Old Buddha* (1928), *Kowtow* (1929), *Jades and Dragons* (1932), *Golden Phoenix* (1932), *Imperial Incense* (1933), and *Son of Heaven* (1935). All these English works were translated into Chinese immediately and drew much attention from a wide spectrum of Chinese readers across the world.

Imperial Incense continues to describe court life inside the Forbidden City and Her Majesty's mental world from the unique perspective of an ethnic Manchu cosmopolitan subject. Der Ling functions like a double agent negotiating between Chinese and non-Chinese cultures, and develops "reciprocal recognition" in her individual and feminine views of the Empress Dowager from within and without.

---

[66] Hayter-Menzies, *Imperial Masquerade*, 262–263.

[67] Der Ling, *Two Years in the Forbidden City*, 382; italics added.

[68] See Arthur J. Burks, "Princess Der Ling," preface to *Old Buddha*, by Princess Der Ling (New York: Dodd, Mead, 1928), xi. One of the Chinese versions of *Old Budhha*, see Li Baozhen 李葆真 trans., *Yuyuan lanxin ji* 御苑蘭馨記 (Hong Kong: Baixin shudian, 1954), which is reprinted as *Cixi lianai jishi* 慈禧戀愛紀實 [Empress Dowager Cixi's romance] (Beijing: Zuojia chubanshe, 1989).

One narrative line is centered around the introduction of trains into China. The invention of the locomotive marks one of the most significant moments in the process of Western industrialization and modernization. Wolfgang Schivelbusch argues in his seminal work, *The Railway Journey*, "[N]othing else in the nineteenth century seemed as vivid and dramatic a sign of modernity as the railroad."[69] The "mechanical horse" not only had a great impact on transportation but also profoundly changed the temporal and spatial perceptions of modern men and women. When the locomotive train was introduced into the Manchu Empire, it aroused vehement controversy in the inner court, and, to borrow Schivelbusch's words, "introduced a new system of behavior: not only of travel and communication but of *thought, of feeling, of expectation*."[70] Cixi wanted to take a railroad journey from Beijing to Mukden to try this new Western technology. When she asked her ministers for advice on this matter, not surprisingly, she ran into strong opposition. The train was in their eyes something like "wind and flash, thus very dangerous." Der Ling portrays the communication between Her Majesty and her ministers:

As soon as the word went forth the ministers got very busy indeed, sending memorials of protest to the throne. They ran somewhat as follows:

"Never before in Chinese history has a sovereign made a journey by railroad. It is very dangerous. Particularly it is dangerous to Her Majesty, who is becoming old. Nor can Her Majesty be spared so long from the Forbidden City where she has so many duties to perform. Her Majesty's humble servants beg that she will give over her plan; that she will not be swayed by alien influence."[71]

In these memorials, which came in daily and hourly during the twenty days of trip preparation, Der Ling and her sister Rung Ling were labeled as the "alien influence." However, Cixi showed a more liberal and positive attitude toward the gigantic token of Western industrial civilization. She tore the papers into pieces and embarked on the "foreign-devil train." "Her Majesty was like a child with Christmas toys."[72] In addition to the episode of the railway journey, Der Ling touches upon a wide range of objects and events taking place within the Forbidden City, from the splendid and exotic costumes of Manchu officials and Her Majesty to the lavish court meals and

---

[69] Schivelbusch, *The Railway Journey*, esp. xiii.

[70] Ibid. Italics added.

[71] Der Ling, *Imperial Incense*, 9. See also the Chinese version translated by Qin Shouou, *Yuxiang piaomiao lu* 御香縹緲錄 (Shanghai: Shenbao guan, 1936). Some scholars question the truth of this episode and regard it as Der Ling's fabrication. Even so, the train scene captures a fascinating moment of the reception of a new technology in the central kingdom.

[72] Der Ling, *Imperial Incense*, 11.

musical instruments, from the exile life of the Emperor Guangxu to Yuan Shikai's political strategies at the turn of the century, from the imperial palaces and the Qing emperors' holy relics to Cixi's hobbies of collecting jades and pets, and even her peculiar diet of drinking human breast milk. These mysterious and sometimes outlandish anecdotes deliberately catered to the taste of both Chinese and Western readers of the time; they also satisfied the curiosity of Der Ling the cosmopolitan observer.

Another of Der Ling's notable works is *Kowtow*, the Chinese translation of which was titled *Memoir of My Childhood*. *Kowtow* extends Der Ling's scope of observation from the "Great Within" at the center of the imperial capital to the vast exterior world beyond the imperial borders. This memoir seeks to construct a more ambitious geopolitical landscape. It touches upon Der Ling's childhood memories, diplomatic adventures, and identity crisis after the 1900 looting of Beijing by the military forces of the Eight-Nation Alliance. By describing two incidents revolving around kowtow, part of traditional Chinese etiquette, from her personal experiences, she demonstrated the disparity and conflicts between Eastern and Western cultures and social customs. The first kowtow incident is narrated against the backdrop of the relationship between the Qing Empire and Germany. During the Boxer Rebellion, many Western nations looked with scorn at the late Manchu Empire. And in Paris, Der Ling's family and staff were blamed as "the representatives of the hateful barbarians who had fired upon the foreign legations" in Beijing.[73] The Kaiser of the German Reich demanded that a Manchu prince of royal blood, as closely allied to the throne as possible, should come to Berlin to apologize in person to the Kaiser for the death of Clemens Von Kettler (1853–1900), a German diplomat murdered during the Boxer Rebellion. Prince Chun, father of Puyi, the last emperor of the Qing dynasty, was sent to Berlin on this mission. He confronted the Kaiser's imperial will that "I will receive you only on condition that you kowtow before me."[74] Frightened half out of their wits, Prince Chun's staff wished the prince to go through with it and abase himself at the feet of the foreign emperor. However, when asked whether or not the prince should kowtow to the Kaiser, Yu Keng's reply was brief and decidedly to the point:

"No! It is not a German custom! It is our own custom, and the kowtow is for your own emperor and none other!" . . .

"Did I kowtow to Loubet when I presented my credentials? Does our minister to England kowtow to the king? Prince Chun will return to China without tendering the apology before he will kowtow to the German Kaiser!"[75]

---

73 Princess Der Ling, *Kowtow* (New York: Dodd, Mead, 1929), 295.
74 Der Ling, *Kowtow*, 304.
75 Ibid., 305.

Confronting death threats, Yu Keng insisted on equal respect between the Qing Empire and Germany, and what the French reporters "lacked in knowledge they made up for in the picturesqueness of their imaginations."[76]

In his *Cherishing Men from Afar*, James Hevia probes the international trade failure of the British Empire as a result of clashes of Eastern and Western customs. The malfunction of the McCartney Embassy of 1793 to the Qing court was attributed to disagreement on observing the Chinese tradition of kowtowing. Hevia also points out that hidden underneath this apparent cultural disparity is a whole series of problematics regarding the tributary system that had been practiced by the Qing Empire with its subject countries over decades.[77] In the kowtow incident that Der Ling describes, what matters is maintaining the mutual respect in international diplomatic communications. She acts as both a storyteller recollecting tales from her childhood and a witness of a political and diplomatic episode between the Qing Empire and Western powers. In this way, her memoir constitutes a highly stimulating concoction of imperial history and unofficial stories, individual experiences and eyewitness accounts of diplomatic affairs.

While the first kowtow story is of a political nature, the second one comes from the author's childhood. Indeed, cultural divergences between East and West are a significant subject in Der Ling's works. Such conflicts take place not only between Chinese and Western nations but also between conservative and liberal groups within the Manchu ethnic community. Der Ling participated in the rehearsal of the play *Sweet Lavender* in Paris when she was fifteen years old. In one scene, Der Ling's character wept bitterly and a boy was supposed to pat her on the back, stroke her hair, and kiss her, in order to stop her from crying.[78] The wife of Yu Keng's secretary thought such a shameless performance offended traditional "Chinese" conceptions of courtesy and public morality. She stood up in the middle of this scene and took her ten-year-old son out of the theater, because she felt that this scene was too indecent for him to watch. As a gesture of protest, the old-fashioned secretary himself vehemently criticized such an improper performance: "A Manchu gentleman of your rank, whose ancestor came to China with the first Manchu Emperor, to even allow your daughter to associate with a man! It is not according to custom, and your daughter's reputation will be ruined."[79] However, Yu Keng thought that Der

---

[76] Ibid., 306.

[77] James L. Hevia, *Cherishing Men from Afar: Qing Guest Ritual and the McCartney Embassy of 1793* (Durham, NC: Duke University Press, 1995); his chapter "Looting Beijing: 1860, 1900," in Liu, *Tokens of Exchange*, 192–213; and his essay "Cong chaogong tizhi dao zhimin yanjiu" 從朝貢體制到殖民研究 [From tributive system to colonial study], trans. Weijie Song, *Dushu* 讀書 [Reading] 8 (1998): 61–69.

[78] Der Ling, *Kowtow*, 297.

[79] Ibid., 298.

Ling participated in a perfectly innocent play, and could not tolerate his secretary's narrow-minded accusation: "You should be thoroughly ashamed of your attempt to blacken the character of a mere child!"[80] He even rejected the secretary's apology, saying coldly, "You must make your apologies to Der Ling in my presence, and must kowtow to her to show your sincerity!"[81] The secretary refused to kowtow to a mere child. Yu Keng countered, "Did you think of her as a mere child when you tried to ruin her reputation?"[82] In the end, the secretary, who was the same age as Der Ling's father, kowtowed in front of Der Ling for his rude and disrespectful behavior. The girl "stood rather stiffly, wondering not a little, to receive the kowtow of our secretary, who dropped to his knees before me, and touched his head most humbly to the floor."[83] With the elder kneeling on the ground, Der Ling was completely startled. Although the secretary's attack provoked her, she felt unease at the expression of apologies in the traditional gesture of kowtow. What upset her was that the solution her liberal and affectionate father offered to his subordinate was the conservative traditional custom. Just as the caress on stage was deemed improper by the secretary, who came from a culture that sets strict rules on contact with the opposite sex, having an elder man kowtowing before her was equally shocking for Der Ling, who embraced Western rites and manners. Perched between the East and the West, Der Ling questioned the boundaries between courtesy and cruelty, discipline and penalty.

Der Ling's family was also a victim of the Boxer Uprising. As described in a letter from Rong Lu (Yung Lu), Der Ling's father learned that their house in Beijing had been destroyed; their curio room was "utterly looted and such things as could not be carried away have been rendered valueless." Conservative Manchu officials regarded Yu Keng as a traitor: "He is no longer a Manchu. He has turned Chinese." Meanwhile, foreign people took him as the representative of the hateful Chinese barbarian. Der Ling's interpretation of her father's identity is akin to a self-portrait: "You must understand that the Chinese regarded the Manchus as invading barbarians, and that, to the Manchus, to be called a Chinese was considered an insult. Father did have many friends among the Chinese, just as he had friends among all other nations, for he firmly believed that the future of China rested in her ability to strengthen her relations with foreign powers. At this time Father was already looking forward to the time when there would be no 'Manchus' and 'Chinese,' but all would be 'Chinese.'"[84]

---

[80] Ibid., 299.

[81] Ibid., 299.

[82] Ibid., 299.

[83] Der Ling, *Kowtow*, 299–300. The secretary was eventually aware how bad-mannered his wife had been to leave in the middle of the rehearsal.

[84] Der Ling, *Kowtow*, 289–290.

In Der Ling's writings, the binary oppositions between the Manchu and Chinese, between the civilized and the barbarian, are investigated through an intriguing view from near and afar, across the ambiguous boundaries of ethnicity, race, gender, language, and culture.

Der Ling's Beijing narratives can be read within, and against, the genealogy of Orientalist fantasies about the mysterious and tyrannical Empress Dowager Cixi, the Forbidden City, and the Qing imperial court, as well as Beijing, the imperial capital, at large, composed in English and other Western languages.[85] In the opening of "Nietzsche, Genealogy, History," Michel Foucault points out,

> Genealogy is gray, meticulous, and patiently documentary. It operates on a field of entangled and confused parchments, on documents that have been scratched over and recopied many times .... Genealogy, consequently, requires patience and a knowledge of details and it depends on a vast accumulation of source materials ... [and is] constructed from "discreet and apparently insignificant truths and according to a rigorous method."[86]

Foucault follows the direction taken by Nietzsche and questions the traditional historiography that narrow-mindedly focuses on the noblest times, the most graceful forms, the most abstract ideas, and the purest individuals. The "affective history" proposed by Foucault and Nietzsche pays attention to decline, ignorance, and chaos. Der Ling's Beijing narratives originate from and respond to an era of decline, when the Manchu Empire was on the verge of collapse with Western military intrusion, domestic political oppression and peasant rebellions, and the incompetent and corrupt Qing administration and bureaucracy.

On the other hand, thanks to the Chinese translations of Der Ling's writings, which enjoyed wide circulation, her Beijing narratives can also be placed in the genealogy of Chinese historical fictions recounting the imperial trauma, dynastic crisis, and national catastrophe in the late Qing and early Republican periods. Some crucial works of this literary category include Wu Jianren's *Henhai* 恨海 (*The Sea of Regret*, 1906), Li Boyuan's *Gengzi guobian tanci* (Tanci, on the Boxer Rebellion of 1900, 1902), and Lin Shu's *Jinghua bixue lu*

---

[85] For a recent study of the image of Beijing as an Oriental capital, see Lü Chao 呂超, *Dongfang didu: Xifang wenhua shiye zhong de Beijing xingxiang* 東方帝都：西方文化視野中的北京形象 [Oriental imperial capital: The image of Beijing in Western cultures] (Jinan: Shandong huabao chubanshe, 2008). With regard to the study of the images of China in Western literature and culture, see, for instance, Meng Hua 孟華, *Bijiao wenxue xingxiangxue* 比較文學形象學 [Imagology in comparative literature] (Beijing: Beijing daxue chubanshe, 2001); and Zhou Ning 周寧, ed., *Zhongguo xingxiang: xifang de xueshuo yu chuanshuo* 中國形象：西方的學說與傳說 [Images of China: Western theories and stories] (Beijing: Xueyuan chubanshe, 2004).

[86] Michel Foucault, *Language, Counter-Memory, Practice* (Ithaca, NY: Cornell University Press, 1977), 139–140.

(Record of blood shed in righteous death in Beijing, 1913), all addressing the 1900 Genzi Indemnity, or the looting of Beijing.[87] By depicting lives of regret, pain, and dislocation resulting from this infamous incident, Wu Jianren's *The Sea of Regret* conceptualizes a unique notion of *qing* (passion). The protagonists, Dihua and Zhongai, struggle with and suffer from the tension between "passion" and "reason" in a tumultuous time. The crisis of social mores and family ethics in the late Qing era is illustrated through the lens of personal pain and agony. Li Boyuan's *Tanci, on the Boxer Rebellion of 1900* romanticizes the Empress Dowager Cixi's escape from Beijing to Xi'an and fantasizes about an amiable communication between the Empress Dowager and the ordinary people at the time the Qing Empire was under serious foreign attack. Lin Shu's *Record of Blood Shed in Righteous Death in Beijing* describes the national calamity by tracing a couple's romantic yet tragic story. Meanwhile, Der Ling, as a witness and a member of the Manchu aristocracy, tells about the secret court life of the Empress Dowager Cixi from an intimate angle, as she came back from war exile to the Forbidden City and lived through happiness, anger, and grief.

Furthermore, Der Ling's work is to be considered in Chinese/Asian American literature and the diaspora writings at large. Der Ling can be examined in the same cultural contexts as other pioneer Chinese American female writers, such as Edith Maude Eaton (Sui Sin Far, 1865–1914), Virginia Lee (1923–), Jade Snow Wong (1922–), and Mai-mai Sze (1910–1992), to name a few. Whereas Der Ling's works are mainly focused on the Forbidden City and the last splendor of the Manchu Empire, they are autobiographical writings dealing with female experiences and feelings born in the cultural contact between the Oriental and Occidental worlds.

As an inside outsider and an outside insider, Der Ling had a cross-cultural hybrid identity formed and transformed within and without indigenous and foreign cities—the Forbidden City, the Imperial Capital, Tokyo, Paris, and Los Angeles, among others—which cultivated her multiple and flexible personas, including imperial messenger, native informant, Qing court translator, First-Lady-in-Waiting, westerner at heart, Manchu princess, unique observer/witness, and patriotic "Chinese" lady. Der Ling's Beijing narratives appealingly incorporate both reflective elucidations of cultural contrasts between East and West and nuanced descriptions of trivialities and novelties of Qing court life, which, in views from near and afar, unfold the "Great Within" and release messages from the heart of the Empire. In his succinct work "An Imperial Message," Franz Kafka (1883–1924) depicts the impossible mission of a messenger who is about to deliver an imperial message regarding the death of the emperor. In order to reach the vast world outside of the "Great Within"

---

[87] For the English translation of *Henhai*, see Patrick Hanan, *The Sea of Regret: Two Turn-of-the-Century Chinese Romantic Novels* (Honolulu: University of Hawai'i Press, 1995).

to spread the imperial message to *tianxia*, the geographical empire and political sovereignty under heaven, the messenger attempts arduously to transverse countless chambers, thresholds, courtyards, and palaces within the Forbidden City.

> The messenger . . . would have to stride through the courtyards, and after the courtyards through the second palace encircling the first, and, then again, through stairs and courtyards, and then, once again, a palace, and so on for thousands of years. And if he finally burst through the outermost door—but that can never, never happen—the royal capital city, the centre of the world, is still there in front of him, piled high and full of sediment.[88]

If a Kafkaesque imperial messenger makes painstaking, sometimes futile efforts to deliver a secret message that is invisible, unheard, and inaccessible to ordinary people, then Der Ling serves as an innocent yet articulate imperial messenger. With limited views of the secrets of the Manchu Empire, the Empress Dowager Cixi, and the Forbidden City, her narrative is not contained by the inaccessible heart and the spatial enclosure of the Forbidden City. In emplotting the imperial family and the imperial capital with her personal experiences and imagination, she writes with a distinctive ease, navigating the forbidden within and the vast without, spreading the imperial messages to the native land and the foreign world. However, this messenger with hybrid identity is not unaware of the constraints of her capacity of knowing. Her journey to chart the imperial heart is often permeated with a sense of frustration and anxiety at the impenetrable imperial secrets and dynastic intrigues, labyrinthine political traps and ethnic disparity.

Der Ling's Oriental tales dissolve the boundary between fiction and history, facts and fabrications. She adeptly took advantage of the problematic translation, or intentional misinterpretation, of her title "Princess" in English and Chinese. In effect, it is questionable to call Der Ling "Der Ling Gongzhu (Princess Der Ling)."

---

[88] Franz Kafka, "An Imperial Message" (Ian Johnson's translation, http://www.kafka-online.info/an-imperial-message.html). Another translation quoted reads, "But the multitudes are so vast; their numbers have no end. If he could reach the open fields how fast he would fly, and soon doubtless you would hear the welcome hammering of his fists on your door. But instead how vainly does he wear out his strength; still he is only making his way through the chambers of the innermost palace; never will he get to the end of them; and if he succeeded in that nothing would be gained; he must fight his way next down the stair; and if he succeeded in that nothing would be gained; the courts would still have to be crossed; and after the courts the second outer palace; and once more stairs and courts; and once more another palace; and so on for thousands of years" (Franz Kafka, "The Great Wall of China," trans. Edwin Muir and Willa Muir, in *The Metamorphosis and Other Writings*, ed. Helmuth Kiesel [New York: Continuum, 2002], 171); see also Kafka's "Building the Great Wall of China," in *Kafka's Selected Stories: New Translations, Backgrounds and Contexts, Criticism*, trans. and ed. Stanley Corngold (New York: W. W. Norton, 2007), 113–123. For Jonathan Spence's discussion of Kafka and other major western writers' imagination of China, see his *The Chan's Great Continent: China in Western Minds*.

The original English word "princess" can be used to designate both daughters and other female relatives of the emperor, and ladies with high morality. In Chinese, however, "Gongzhu" 公主 is restricted to denoting daughters or sisters of the emperor. The accurate title of Der Ling is "Junzhu" 郡主, a rank of noblewoman lower than "Gongzhu," often conferred on nieces of the emperor. Rung Ling, for instance, always signed her name as "Rung Ling Junzhu" in her prefaces to her sister's works or on other occasions. The first time the title "Princess Der Ling" was employed was in Arthur J. Burks' preface, "Princess Der Ling and Me," to Der Ling's novel *Old Buddha*.[89] In order to attract more Western readers, Burks raised Der Ling's rank. And the Chinese publishing houses seemed eager to welcome such a commercial strategy and promotion. They used the title "Gongzhu" instead of "Junzhu" to refer to Der Ling in the Chinese translations of her works.

In his 1946 essay *"Jieshao yuanzhuzhe"* 介紹原著者 (Introducing the author), Qin Shouou, the Chinese translator of *Son of Heaven* (*Yingtai qixue ji* 瀛台泣血記) and a distinguished writer himself, questioned the noble title of Der Ling. He remarked, "Actually, according to Chinese customs, all sorts of titles issued in the previous dynasty must become invalid the day the dynasty falls. Even if we preserve her title from the previous Qing dynasty, she should only be called Junzhu" (其實不但照中國的習慣,已經覆亡的一朝所頒給的種種頭銜都得一律作廢;便是真要保留她在遜清一朝所得的封號的話,也只應稱為郡主).[90] Der Ling indeed served as the First Lady-in-Waiting to the Empress Dowager Cixi, and in fact, was one of her favorites. Thomas F. Millard, who wrote a preface for Der Ling's debut, states, "Her opportunity to observe and estimate the characteristics of the remarkable woman who ruled China for so long was unique, and her narrative throws a new light on one of the most extraordinary personalities of modern times."[91]

In Der Ling's accounts of the imperial life, there is an unmistakable strategy of self-orientalization, which fashions the Forbidden City as an Oriental space that cannot be decoded and also resists being deciphered. An old civilization and its dark yet magnificent imperial heart, the unfathomable "Great Within," are reified as an exotic, mummified collection composed of treasures, antiques, and peculiar customs. The articulation of the inarticulate center of the city is transformed into a deliberate construction of Orientalist exoticism catering to implied readers, especially those from the Western world. The Forbidden City, the imperial capital, the Manchu Empire, and the image of China are created as the "other" in Der Ling's works written in English. Her Beijing narratives help to substantiate the notion of

---

[89] See Arthur J. Burks, "Princess Der Ling," preface to *Old Buddha*, xi–xiv.

[90] See Chen Lirong, "Shenmi de Princess Der Ling."

[91] Millard, preface to *Two Years in the Forbidden City*, viii.

difference from the Western world in the cultural, economic, and political dimensions. In this sense, Der Ling becomes one of what Rey Chow calls "their culture's anthropologists and ethnographers, capturing the remnants of a history that has undergone major disasters while at the same time imparting information about 'China' to the rest of the world."[92]

As Der Ling's narrative position stands close to that of an anthropologist or ethnographer, she is also a native informant, in that the exoticism in these Forbidden City tales is a blend of the Oriental's Orientalism and the Occidental's Orientalism. Gayatri Spivak calls attention to the role of the "native informant" as the other and its cultural implications in the colonial and postcolonial worlds. She reminds us of the problematic use of autobiographies as "objective evidence" in scientific investigations conducted in anthropology and ethnolinguistics and cautions against "the curious 'objectified' subject-positioning of this other in 'oral history' politicized by exceptionalized 'testimony.'"[93] Der Ling's "autobiographies" and "oral histories" revolving around the Forbidden City considerably blur the boundaries between the foreign, "enlightened," and authoritative observer, or the fieldworker, on the one hand, and the primitive, not-yet-enlightened "native informant" on the other. Given her Western training and living experiences in Europe, Der Ling is a double agent who consciously plays the dual role of a foreign observer and a native informant. Equipped with an "enlightened" state of mind, she gazes at her native culture during the last years of the Manchu Empire through the lens of Westernized values and concepts. Her portrayal of the Forbidden City becomes an Orient, the exoticist Great Within colored by a cross-cultural female representation. Constructed by a self-Orientalist for the Occidental audience first, these stories subsequently gained an even more extensive circulation among the Oriental (Chinese) audience.

In her fictional self-performance and self-representation, Der Ling appears as what Grant Hayter-Menzies calls in his *Imperial Masquerade* a "chameleon figure," self-Orientalized in cross-cultural masquerades. In his review of Hayter-Menzies's biography, Xiaoyu Wang writes, Der Ling "chose to invent attachments to a vanished Manchu world, to a Chinese republic with which she had little contact, and to the broader Chinese nation in which she always felt like an alien."[94] In gliding between the East and the West, the Manchu and the Han Chinese, the language of English and of Chinese, this female observer/native informant is more capable and functional than a Kafakesque imperial messenger or an anthropological and

---

[92] Rey Chow, *Primitive Passions: Visuality, Sexuality, Ethnography, and Contemporary Chinese Cinema* (New York: Columbia University Press, 1995), 38.

[93] Gayatri Chakravorty Spivak, *A Critique of Postcolonial Reason: Toward a History of the Vanishing Present* (Cambridge, MA: Harvard University Press, 1999), 153.

[94] Wang, review of *Imperial Masquerade: The Legend of Princess Der Ling*, 127.

ethnolinguistic "native informant." After relocating to Los Angeles, Der Ling show-cased herself as a Manchu princess, and as a patriotic Chinese woman during World War II. The hybrid, flexible, and shifting identities reveal the intriguing heterogene-ous positions that Der Ling occupied, displaying an "authentic" and "authoritative" view of the "Great Within" in her cross-cultural and comparative Beijing narratives.

BENEATH THE "GREAT WITHIN," HORIZONTAL WELLS, AND SPATIAL EXOTICISM

In the end, I came here looking for neither Europe nor China but for a vision of China.
—VICTOR SEGALEN

The imposing Gate of Spiritual Valour through which I made my first entrance into the Forbidden City on March 3rd, 1919, led me into a new world of space and time. It was through that portal that I passed not only from a republic to a monarchy but also from the New China of the twentieth century into a China that was old before the foundation of Rome.
—REGINALD F. JOHNSON

Victor Segalen occupies a distinctive position in the field of *Imagologie* (Imagology, or the study of exotic images and stereotypes in national literature).[95] Just before he died, Jorge Luis Borges (1899–1986) remarked to a French poet friend who had never heard of Segalen,

> The French talk about Valery and even the preposterous Peguy with adoration—don't they know that in Victor Segalen they have one of the most intelligent writers of our age, perhaps the only one to have made a fresh synthesis of Western and Eastern aesthetics and philosophy?...You can read Segalen in less than a month, but it might take you the rest of your life to understand him.[96]

Tzvetan Todorov observes that Segalen is arguably the most profound French writer describing exotic experiences.[97] Guo Hongan 郭宏安, a leading Chinese scholar of French literature, discusses three attitudes of French writers toward foreign, exotic cultures like Chinese civilization: some writers put on the mask of hermits and eulo-gize the pastoral atmosphere far away from overly civilized life, such as Jacques-Henri

---

[95] For scholarship of imagology in general, see, for instance, Mark C. Taylor, Esa Saarinen, and Marjaana Virta, *Imagologies: Media Philosophy* (London: Routledge, 1994); Manfred Beller and Joseph Theodoor Leerssen, eds., *Imagology: The Cultural Construction and Literary Representation of National Characters: A Critical Survey* (Amsterdam: Rodopi, 2007).

[96] Victor Segalen, *Paintings*, trans. Andrew Harvey and Iain Watson (London: Quartet Books, 1991), vii.

[97] Tzvetan Todorov, *On Human Diversity: Nationalism, Racism, Exoticism in French Thought* (Cambridge, MA: Harvard University Press, 1993), 323–338.

Bernardin de Saint-Pierre (1737–1814); some writers imitate the conqueror and hunt for exotic pleasures and novelty, such as Pierre Loti (1850–1923); and some writers are insensitive to cultural differences and obsessed with finding the sameness in foreign cultures, such as Paul Claudel (1868–1955).[98] Segalen's exotic imagination differs sharply from all these attitudes. As a matter of fact, he shows more affinity to the sixteenth-century writer Michel de Montaigne (1533–1592), aiming to propagate equal and harmonious relations between the civilized and the barbarians. Guo Hongan observes,

> Victor Segalen is never satisfied with the exotic appearance, but attempts to go into the deep interior of another civilization; he never blindly despises or worships but tenaciously explores a strange civilization; he never assimilates or obliterates but discovers and highlights the differences among civilizations.... The reason he steps into the field of exoticism is not for flight or dominance, but to achieve a new sensibility and recognition, enlarge the maps of human knowledge, and take the understanding of exotic civilization as the path to recognize his own civilization.[99]

To recognize oneself by means of understanding the "other" is to reflect one's own culture by taking "the view from afar." Victor Segalen strives for a two-way communication: to go into the exotic culture, such as the Chinese civilization, using it as a mirror to perceive the French culture; and to take the French culture as the preunderstanding or horizon of expectation from which to scrutinize and imagine Chinese culture.

A much neglected author and thinker, Segalen and his cross-cultural endeavors deserve serious attention and exploration. Victor Segalen entered a navy medical college (École de Sante Navale in Bordeaux) in 1898. Two years later, he began to write poetry and met several important scientists and novelists, including Max Nordau (1849–1923), Joris Karl Huysmans (1848–1907), and Remy de Gourmont (1858–1915). In October 1902, while visiting San Francisco, Segalen fell ill; however, he had a chance to pay a visit to Chinatown. This was a critical moment, in that the accidental encounter with Chinese culture began an obsession that lasted his whole life. He started to study Chinese in 1908 and traveled to China for the first time in 1909. He arrived in Beijing on June 19 and stayed there and in other places as a doctor, scholar, archaeologist, and adventurer (from 1909 to 1914, and on a second

---

[98] Guo Hongan, "Ping *Lenei Laisi*: Zhongyiben daixu" 評<勒內•萊斯> : 中譯本代序 [Comments on *René Leys*: Preface to the Chinese Version], in *Lenei Laisi* 勒內•莱斯, trans. Mei Bin 梅斌, revised by Guo Hongan (Beijing: Sanlian shudian, 1991), 1–2.

[99] Guo, "Ping *Lenei Laisi*," 2.

trip from January 1917 to March 1919). He even paid a formal visit to Puyi, the last Emperor of the Qing Dynasty. This experience was described in his novel *René Leys*. He was also a friend of Yuan Shikai, the late Qing general who had forced the abdication of the last emperor, became the first official President of the Republic of China, and later set out to restore monarchy in China. As early as in 1912, Segalen proposed that the Beijing government should establish a museum of art.[100]

On June 6, 1910, Segalen wrote a letter to Claude Debussy (1862–1918) describing his adventure, impression, and discovery of China. Segalen's journey first passed through Hong Kong, a British-type city, which is not what he wanted to find; then Shanghai, which has a typically American flavor; and then he traveled to Hankou along the Yangtze River. He thought that could be the real China, but the buildings on the banks were still German or British or whatever foreign styles. Eventually he took the train, leaving for Beijing. About thirty hours later, Segalen realized that he had finally reached China. Beijing is purely China, and the whole Chinese land is condensed there. But not everyone can see this.[101] What Segalen was looking for was "a vision of China," a pure "Other," with no similarities to his own homeland and mother-tongue cultural expectations. Therefore, his journey from Paris via San Francisco to Chinese cities was like a pilgrimage on which he hoped to discover a brand-new land, a vision in his heart and mind, and an Oriental Dragon so different from the Occidental Unicorn.[102] Segalen names Beijing "my city," his Chinese courtyard house near Tiananmen "my palace," and his personal library or museum as "my china" (or "my room of Chinese porcelain," in a metaphorical translation). In a poetic way, he describes his everyday life in Beijing. In the early morning, he is awakened by the soft voice of a peddler selling bean curd. At dusk, he appreciates the blue sky right above his Beijing courtyard house. And in the evening, he sleeps in the same direction as the Chinese emperor, oriented north south, and feels that he is engaging with the life of the whole city. He thinks that a courtyard house is comfortable and a convenient way to live. And he calls Beijing the ideal home of which he had always dreamed.[103]

---

[100] Victor Segalen, *Essays on Exoticism: An Aesthetics of Diversity*, trans. and ed. Yaël Rachel Schlick (Durham, NC: Duke University Press, 2002), 7–10. Hua Xinmin 華新民, "Faguo shiren he lao Beijing" 法國詩人和老北京 [French poet and old Beijing], *Renmin ribao* 人民日報 [People's daily], July 8, 2000; Ye Rulian 葉汝璉, "Xie Gelan: Dongfang gulao wenming de tansuozhe" 謝閣蘭——東方古老文明的探索者 [Victor Segalen: An Explorer of Ancient Oriental Civilization], http://blog.sina.cn/s/blog_497851f0010009g7.html.

[101] See Ye, "Xie Gelan." For Segalen's original French letter to Claude Debussy on June 6, 1910, see Annie Joly-Segalen, ed., *Segalen et Debussy. Textes recueillis et présentés par Annie Joly-Segalen et André Schaeffner* (Monaco: Éditions du Rocher, 1962), 113.

[102] See Yue Daiyun and Alan Le Pichion, eds., *Dujiaoshou yu long* 獨角獸與龍 [Unicorn and dragon] (Beijing: Beijing daxue chubanshe, 1995).

[103] Sha Lin 沙林, "Zhuanfang 'Hutong baoweizhe': Beijing haineng yu Sheng Bidebao pimei ma" 專訪"胡同保衛者": 北京還能與聖彼得堡媲美嗎? [A specific interview with "The defender of alleyways": Can Beijing

The picture of the city and related urban life in Segalen's writings are reminiscent of the Englishman Mr. Goodrich's Beijing imagery, depicted in Lao She's novel *Four Generations Under One Roof*:

He rented three rooms and a garden in the southeastern corner of the city which had been part of an old estate. The walls of the three rooms were completely covered with scrolls on which were mounted Chinese paintings and calligraphy, and in the rooms were a variety of Chinese curios. He had asked a Chinese scholar to write the characters for a Board of Honor to hang over his gate. He called his place the "Little Liu Li Chang" after the street in Peiping where books and curios were sold. In the garden were a few great jars for goldfish, several cages with birds, and many kinds of flowers. Just inside the gate he had built a small room for the eunuch he had found to be his gatekeeper, who had been in the service of Emperor Kuang Hsu. During the festivals and at the New Year, he would have the eunuch wear his official red-tasseled hat, and make *chiaotse* for him to eat. He observed Christmas and Easter, and also observed the Fifth Moon Festival and the Moon Festival of the Eighth Moon.[104]

Mr. Goodrich's "Little Liu Li Chang" (Xiao Liulichang 小琉璃廠) was a small museum of Chinese paintings, calligraphy, and historical artifacts, exactly what Segalen passionately collected. The only difference might be that Goodrich needed a native scholar's generous help to assemble his works: "Rey Shuan often helped him collect material for the masterpiece that probably would never be finished, and also helped him translate Chinese poetry and essays that he wanted to use."[105] Segalen was a more qualified collector and connoisseur; as a professional sinologist, he could put into practice a much more profound understanding of the city.

However, in the city composed of circles within circles, walls limiting recognition stand up one after another. The imperial walls of the Forbidden City keep out his views, the city moat underneath the five-fold Bridge of Golden Water (Jinshuiqiao 金水橋) stops his steps, and the interior of the imperial court turns out to be the secret of secrets or "limit of recognition." The Forbidden City constitutes a cultural token, signifying not only the tangible material world but also the unfathomable inner world of this ancient civilization. Meanwhile, the declining empire is the field where he

---

be compared to St. Petersburg?"], *Beijing qingnianbao* 北京青年報 [Beijing youth daily], August 19, 2003. Nevertheless, Segalen betrays a significant ambivalence, shared by other narrators: he actually imagines China at large when he thinks that he narrates Beijing, and vice versa.

[104] Lau Shaw, *The Yellow Storm*, 205.

[105] Ibid., 215.

investigates the relationship between the real and the imagined. Finished around 1913, *René Leys* best represents Segalen's Beijing imagination. The first French edition was published in 1922, about three years after the author's accidental death. In the opening passages, the author reflects on the impossible mission of completing the book. *René Leys*, as the author puts it, would take "a splendid posthumous title— The Book That Never Was!"[106] Like Mr. Goodrich's dream book entitled *Beijing*, Segalen's Beijing narrative remains an incomplete project and defies closure. In his posthumous work *Essays on Exoticism*, Segalen elucidates several types of exoticism:

So, Exoticism in $\left\{\begin{array}{l}\text{Time}\\ \text{Space}\end{array}\right.$

In Time $\left\{\begin{array}{l}\text{Past:}\\ \text{Present:}\\ \text{Future:}\end{array}\right.$

Past: Historical Exoticism, *chronicles above all.*

Present: Does not exist by definition.

Future: Imaginary Exoticism: Wells, for example. His mechanism: the dissociation of ideas, and their subsequent reassociation with a peculiar state of mind. Examine the question of "the Future."

in $\left\{\begin{array}{l}\text{Maeterlink}\\ \text{Wells, his prediction of the future}\end{array}\right.$

In Space: The only one *I will develop.* [107]

Thus *René Leys* can be read as a masterpiece of exoticism in space. It is also a work of metafiction, in that the narrator continuously challenges his own narratives and deals with the process of writing as a main theme. James Clifford suggests, "[T]his brilliant mystery story about the imperial Forbidden City undermines the classic exoticist topography of barriers and thresholds surrounding a 'secret.'"[108] The narrator observes the ancient capital veiled in mystery and seeks to peep behind the imperial walls at the secrets of the "Great Within." The explorer Segalen rode on "the uniformly rectangular courses of this gigantic chessboard" and was aware that his journey through Beijing had the quality of a "knight's progress."[109]

In his seminal work *Orientalism*, Edward W. Said discusses the function of the Orientalist:

To a large extent the Orientalist provides his own society with representations of the Orient (a) that bear his distinctive imprint, (b) that illustrate his conception of what the Orient can or ought to be, (c) that consciously contest someone else's view of the Orient, (d) that provide Orientalist discourse with what, at

---

[106] Victor Segalen, *René Leys: A Novel*, trans. J. A. Underwood (Woodstock, NY: Overlook Press, 1988), 17.

[107] Segalen, *Essays on Exoticism*, 16–17.

[108] See Clifford, *The Predicament of Culture*, 158.

[109] Segalen, *René Leys*, 33.

that moment, it seems most in need of, and (e) that respond to certain cultural, professional, national, political, and economic requirements of the epoch.[110]

Segalen is intrigued by the myth of Beijing and the Orient at large, develops his own "distinctive imprint" of "exoticism in space," and illustrates his unique conception of what Beijing/the Orient "can or ought to be." In a letter to Debussy, he confesses, "In the end, I came here looking for neither Europe nor China but for a vision of China."[111] Yet this adventure is akin to what Georg Simmel defines as "unsettled moments within the arc of an individual life," the "moments of intensity cut off from the sensory experiences of the everyday, islands that rise up from the daily events that wash over us and circulate around us."[112] To borrow Edward Said's words again, Segalen does not care to "respond to certain cultural, professional, national, political, and economic requirements of the epoch." More likely, he would collect visions of and information about Beijing, Chinese, and the Oriental world, to produce a type of knowledge reminiscent of Foucauldian "subjugated knowledges." In his essay "Lecture: 7 January 1976," Michel Foucault calls attention to "subjugated knowledges," which have been buried in the course of history. He distinguishes between two categories: erudite and disqualified knowledges. It is through the resurrection of these very knowledges disguised by well-established knowledge or naïve knowledge, "located low down on the hierarchy," that we are able to excavate "a historical knowledge of struggles."[113] Foucault defines his archaeological research project of mapping the operation of power within the hierarchy of knowledge as "genealogy."

Particularly striking here is the extraordinarily great efforts Foucault takes to differentiate his genealogical research activity from the kind of practice that legitimizes some repressed or oppressed knowledge as "true knowledge" and thus begins a new round of canonization. When he writes, "We are concerned, rather, with the insurrection of knowledges that are opposed primarily not to the contents, methods or concepts of a science, but to the effects of the centralising powers which are linked to the institution and functioning of an organized scientific discourse within a society such as ours,"[114] he is well aware of the danger that excavating "the subjugated knowledges" might fall into the trap of inscribing these "disordered, marginal, disqualified and illegitimate knowledges"[115] in the unitary hierarchical order of power in the name of science.

---

[110] Said, *Orientalism*, 273.

[111] Quoted from Clifford, *The Predicament of Culture*, 155.

[112] Quoted from Michael Robinson's *Time to Eat Dogs*, a blog about science, history, and exploration, http://timetoeatthedogs.com/category/anthropology/.

[113] Michel Foucault, "Lecture: 7 January 1976," in *Twentieth Century Literary Theory*, ed. K. M. Newton (London: Macmillan / New York: St. Martin's Press, 1997), 130.

[114] Ibid. 132.

[115] Ibid. 133.

Indeed, how can we avoid the reemergence of Knowledge A conditioning the repression of Knowledge B? How can we prevent the insurrection of the subjugated knowledge engendering a kind of "displacement of space," a question Spivak raises as a response to Foucault's genealogical efforts in her reading of Mahasweta Devi's novel "Douloti the Bountiful"?[116] In Segalen's construction of a vision of China and his spatial imagination of Beijing, how does he place or displace spaces when producing, restoring, fictionalizing, or subjugating certain categories of knowledge?

Victor Segalen sets his story in two cities: the Forbidden City, and a fictional underground city beneath it. The story unfolds in the eve of the Xinhai Revolution of 1911. The narrator, who has the same name as the author, "headed my horse at a fast trot in the direction of my true objective—the imperial City, which contains the purple-walled Forbidden City, the Within. It is perhaps the twentieth time I have set out thus to lay siege to the place, encompass it, verify its exact contours, circle like the sun about the foot of its eastern, southern, and western walls, and try if possible to complete the circle and come back by way of the north."[117] The narrator Segalen is like a French dandy or flâneur in an exotic city and alien empire: sometimes he lies back in his cane chair and gazes, without thinking of anything in particular, at the concave ceiling of the sky; sometimes he stands up in the stirrups or leans over the ramparts to observe the full palace moat, the blooming palace lotus, the yellow-roofed pavilions, and the teeth of the two-tiered crenellations. Even his house, or his "palace," follows Beijing's cosmological orientation so that he is "living a *parallel existence*, in all the cold and measured rigorousness of the term, to the hidden life of the Palace."[118] In so doing, he transfigures the imperial capital into a space that the narrator can relate to personally, inhabit, and access.

René Leys, the narrator's Chinese-language tutor, is the actual main character who has free passage into and out of the Forbidden City. René is an eighteen- or twenty-year-old Belgian man with passion, impulse, and youth and speaks excellent Chinese. As the story unfolds, he is appointed to the imperial secret police after having saved the Qing emperor several times. Meanwhile, he is also the Empress Dowager Long Yu's secret lover. The romantic relationship between the young European man and the Manchu empress stays a puzzle. The narrator wonders whether it is a childish game, a shameful necessity, a service, an adventure, a fashion, a well-drilled mannerism, or a "ritual governed by chapter and verse of the physiological Bible instilled with the maternal milk in every fecundable female on earth

---

[116] Gayatri Chakravorty Spivak, "Woman in Difference: Mahasweta Devi's 'Douloti the Bountiful,'" in *Nationalisms and Sexualities*, ed. Andrew Parker, Mary Russo, Doris Sommer, and Patricia Yaeger (New York: Routledge, 1992), 98–99.

[117] Segalen, *René Leys*, 29–30.

[118] Ibid., 34, 49.

and in hell"?[119] The narrator himself never has a romantic liaison with a Chinese woman in Beijing. However, he seems to quite enjoy listening to stories of imagined sexual conquests of his young, handsome Belgian friend:

> You have gone further in your penetration of China than any other European known or unknown . . . . You have attained the heart of the center of the Within—nay, better than the heart: the bed!
>
> [René Leys] has laid siege to and vanquished the heart that is imperially sealed, the Triple Person quadruply enclosed, the Inexpugnable, Mother of the Empire, Ancestress of the Ten Thousand Ages![120]

The romantic fantasies not only involve the exoticism of transnational and transracial sexuality but also serve a narrative function that constructs the subjectivity of the "self" through the attainment or fabrication of the body of a female "other."[121] Readers are not certain if the romance, or René's other adventures, actually happen or are pure imaginations. Indeed, the boundary between reality and imagination is constantly blurred and redrawn, just like the vertical juxtaposition of an actual city and its mysterious underground other can be considered as a spatial displacement and a psychological alter ego where desires or illicit activities are housed. Yvonne Y. Hsieh maintains, "although firmly anchored in space and time (Peking, 1911), *René Leys* is neither a novel concerning the Chinese capital nor a documentary work about the Revolution. Its main theme is again the dialectical tension between the Real and the Imaginary."[122] As this young Belgian man narrates his adventures traversing across the secret rooms in imperial Beijing and communicating with the powerful figures inside and outside of the Forbidden City, the fictional narrator Victor Segalen keeps posing questions to him. To respond to Victor's inquiries, René Leys furthers his expeditions into the imperial center, to discover accurate information and produce more knowledge. Intriguingly, the narrator functions as a prophet whose speculations guide and propel René Leys to further investigations and actions. In this collaborative work, Beijing is configured as a magical reality, a spatial, cognitive, and psychological labyrinth replete with unexpected discoveries and unsolved enigma.

---

[119] Ibid., 122.

[120] Ibid., 140–141.

[121] Charles Forsdick, "Sight, Sound, and Synaesthesia: Reading the Senses in Victor Segalen," in *Sensual Reading: New Approaches to Reading in Its Relations to the Senses*, ed. Michael Syrotinski and Ian Maclachlan (London: Associated University Press, 2001), 229–247. See also Charles Forsdick, *Victor Segalen and the Aesthetics of Diversity: Journeys between Cultures* (New York: Oxford University Press, 2000); and Chris Bongie, *Exotic Memories: Literature, Colonialism, and the Fin de Siècle* (Stanford, CA: Stanford University Press, 1991).

[122] Yvonne Y. Hsieh, *Victor Segalen: Literary Encounter with China: Chinese Moulds, Western Thoughts* (Toronto: University of Toronto Press, 1988), 158.

The author writes about the interactions between Victor Segalen the narrator and René Leys the agent:

> He always abided by what he said . . . . I asked him, "*Yes* or *no*—have you . . . . ?"
> But I should have been mortally disappointed had he disowned his (even
> invented) deeds; I trembled more than he did at feeling the whole splendid
> edifice teeter . . . in ruthlessly disabusing me he would have the more bitterly
> deceived me. He kept his word and it may be by my suggestions . . . .
>
> Everything I said, he did, Chinese fashion, for with his death he has just
> given me, Chinese fashion, the best proof—that he preferred to lose his life it
> if meant saving face . . . if it was the only way of not being false either to himself
> or to me, of neither breaking faith or forfeiting my esteem.[123]

René Leys is also like a young version of Victor Segalen, or Segalen might be the elder alter ego of René Leys. I would argue that Segalen plays the role of an anthropologist or ethnographer who conducts experimental fieldwork or an empirical investigation of old Beijing. When playing the role of a handsome secret agent, a fearless adventurer, and a foreign knight tracking dangers, René Leys is also a cross-cultural imperial messenger, or a disguised foreign "native informant" who tirelessly looks for information and yearns for knowledge about the "Great Within." In charting a cognitive map of Beijing, Segalen and René Leys represent two ways of producing knowledge—objective and subjective, by means of scientific investigation and individual experiences respectively. The narrator or thinker drives the protagonist to embark on a series of adventures, which end unavoidably in the abyss of death. How to come to terms with the thin line between the mapping of the imperial inner city and an imaginative construction? In the novel, the real and the imaginary communicate and contest with each other in such a way that they can hardly be differentiated. This corelationship is managed in a harmonious manner until the final moment, when René Leys loses his life in the great maze of Beijing.

A recurring haunting image in the novel depicts the narrator riding a horse through the gigantic and legendary Beijing, and all of a sudden hearing a sound resonating from underground. The deep rumbling frightens him. A stunning fantasy of Beijing unravels in the great space beneath the Forbidden City:

> He let me into the secret—"in depth." Pei-king is not, as one might think, a
> chessboard whose game, fair or foul, is played on the surface. No—there is an
> Underground City complete with its redans, its corner forts, its highways and

---

[123] Segalen, *René Leys*, 219.

byways, its approaches, its threats, its "horizontal wells" even more formidable than the wells of drinking and other water that yawn up at the open sky . . . . He described it all so well that by the time he had finished he had got me trembling myself.[124]

René Leys' introduction of the mysterious, dreamlike palaces inside the Forbidden City along with the fictional underground city unleashes the narrator Segalen's wild, uncontrollable fantasies:

> He has let me into the secret, and I begin to admire him. He comes and goes in his usual way. Yet for me he has suddenly opened up other Palaces of Dreams whose passages I am far from having trodden! None of this was on my plan of the city! It's—and I can't get away from it; I keep coming back to it in spite of myself—it's as mysterious as the Forbidden City itself! All the unknown, thrice immured behind twenty-foot-high walls, has taken on ten times the mystery in being furnished with this vertical abyss at their base—the Profound City with all its subterranean cavitations! Beneath the broad, flat expanse of the capital anything that even nibbles at the dimension of depth is unexpected . . . disturbing.[125]

The "horizontal wells" in the profound abyss are tremendously significant: they not only remind the narrator of chilling images of incarceration at the bottom of a well but also refer to a true historical event: the death and last cry of Concubine Zhen of Emperor Guangxu, who was killed by being thrown into a well inside the Forbidden City. With more knowledge about the "Great Within" accessible, René Leys suffers more and more intensely from sudden fainting spells and recurring nightmares, in which he sees himself drowning at the bottom of a well. The narrator is trapped in the same dilemma. He cannot help obsessing about images of wells, unfathomable vertigo, and the idea of death. At the end of the story, a disenchanting moment, the narrator Segalen laments that Beijing "is no longer the haunt of my dreams . . . . I even begin to doubt that I ever wanted to set foot inside it!"[126] And in front of the inexplicable Forbidden City, with René Leys' enigmatic receipt for his first night of love in the palace, Segalen collapses in schizophrenia—the Chinese characters "represent

---

[124] Ibid., 171. See also Jonathan D. Spence, "Chinese Fictions in the Twentieth Century," in *Asia in Western Fiction*, ed. Robin W. Winks and James R. Rush (Honolulu: University of Hawai'i Press, 1990), 100–116; and his *The Chan's Great Continent: China in Western Minds* (New York and London: Norton, 1998).

[125] Segalen, *René Leys*, 171–172.

[126] Ibid., 210.

a series of the most alarming objects: knives, a barbed spear, eyes placed lengthwise or vertically, flowers, rat's teeth, women hiding their bellies, wells, pits, tombs, the stopped-up holes of some lid . . . a magic crucible . . . an empty mouth . . . a boat."[127] The profound fear of and obsession with physical and symbolic "horizontal wells" signify his profound fear of and obsession with death, and the immeasurable knowledge about the Forbidden City, the imperial capital, and the Orient at large.

In their distinctive manners, these three cosmopolitan writers construct an ideal imperial Beijing traversing the boundaries between fiction and history, the East and the West, the traditional and the modern. Lin Yutang's idealized city-text envisions a pleasant, harmonious fringe surrounding the Manchu inner city. Der Ling's Forbidden City narratives provide access to the "Great Within" of the imperial city, and even to the psychology of the Empress Dowager Cixi. Victor Segalen fabricates and investigates the treacherous "horizontal wells" and the fictional city underneath the Forbidden City. In these cross-cultural cosmopolitan imaginations of an imperial polis par excellence, Beijing is constructed as a Confucian/Taoist fusion of leisure and harmony, a token of Manchu ethnography inflected by a female Western/native informant, a cognitive vertigo, or a horizontal well. In these split and conflicting images, the city is conceived as incomprehensible, defying all attempts to classify and decipher it.

[127] Ibid., 216.

Include me out (把我包括在外).
—SAMUEL GOLDWYN/ZHANG AILING

5

A Displaced City and Postmemory

RELOCATING BEIJING IN SINOPHONE WRITING

THE 1949 DIVIDE in China deepened and complicated the geopolitical and geo-poetic distances among Beijing, Taipei, and Hong Kong. As writers and literary critics relocated or assimilated into new cultural and political environments, the literary topography of modern China went through tremendous transformations. This chapter focuses on post-1949 diasporic and Sinophone writings related to Beijing imaginations, and explores the dialectical and dialogical relationships between language and diasporic experiences, urban narratives, and cultural memories and postmemories.

By raising the question, "Where have all the natives gone?" I inquire how native Beijing writers who were relocated to Taipei after the 1949 division projected poignant cultural and political implications into their reminiscent writings about a lost hometown. Among these writers are Qi Rushan, Liang Shiqiu, Tang Lusun, Xia Yuanyu 夏元瑜 (1909–1995), Ding Bingsui 丁秉鐩 (1916–1980), and Hou Rongsheng 侯榕生 (1926–1990). Liang Shiqiu's and Tang Lusun's emotional culinary depictions of Beijing render food as both nutrition for the body and an art of life, and more important, as a tangible embodiment of nostalgic sentiments. Culinary menus paved foodways for an imaginary return to the inaccessible hometown besieged by Cold War ideology. In this way, these two writers resurrect their lost geographical and spiritual hometown in the republic of letters and in the gourmet world.

During the Republican period, Taiwan writers left their birthplace and resided in Beijing before returning to Taiwan. These Beijing sojourners include Hong Yanqiu 洪炎秋 (1899–1980), Zhang Wojun 張我軍 (1902–1955), Zhang Shenqie 張深切 (1904–1965), Zhong Lihe, and Lin Haiyin, among others, who later described their Beijing experiences in their autobiographies or writings in other literary genres.[1] My discussion focuses on Zhong Lihe and Lin Haiyin and how they constructed contrasting imageries of South Beijing to deal with the intricate relationships between hometown and a strange land, assimilation and dissimilation, as well as dislocation and identity crisis.

The last part of the chapter examines the diasporic writer Jin Yong and his imagined chivalric topography of Beijing. Placing his Beijing imaginations in the Manchu Empire, Jin Yong's martial-arts fantasy endeavors to straddle the borders between intervention and withdrawal, history and fiction, imperial peripheries and the political center. By intertwining historical documents and martial-arts imagination, Jin Yong's popular *wuxia* fiction inscribes post-loyalist attachments and detachments into the imagery of Beijing, the imperial capital, and into Hong Kong, the birthplace of his chivalric work. In his remapping of an imagined imperial Beijing using modern Sinophone articulations, there emerged a category of frustrated yet flexible identity, and a supplementary yet self-sufficient republic of letters. Examining the memoirs and fictional imaginations of Beijing contributed by émigré and native writers in Taiwan and Hong Kong, I trace the trajectories of travel and severance in both personal and national terms, and highlight the dialectic of "lost and found" in their reflections on the nation and the city, dislocation and nostalgia, the application of Chinese language and the formation of cultural identity.

FOOD MEMORY, EMOTIONAL TOPOGRAPHY, AND BITTERSWEET AFTERTASTE

It is no accident that even the purest pleasures, those most purified of any trace of corporeality . . . contain an element which, as in the "crudest" pleasures of the tastes of food, the archetype of all taste, refers directly back to the oldest and deepest experiences, those which determine and over-determine the primitive oppositions—bitter/sweet, flavourful/ insipid, hot/cold, coarse/delicate, austere/bright—which are as essential to gastronomic commentary as to the refined appreciations of aesthetes.

—PIERRE BOURDIEU

---

[1] For a study of Zhong Lihe, Zhang Shenqie, Hong Yanqiu, Zhang Wojun, and their Beijing experiences, see Michelle Yeh, "Taiwan ren zai Beijing" 台灣人在北京 [Taiwan writers in Beijing], in *Beijing: Dushi xiangxiang yu wenhua jiyi* 北京：都市想像與文化記憶 [*Beijing: Urban Imagination and Cultural Memory*], ed. Chen Pingyuan and David Der-wei Wang (Beijing: Beijing daxue chubanshe, 2005), 371–389.

Since the 1970s, a few noteworthy studies about Chinese culinary culture published in English—such as the classical volume *Food in Chinese Culture*, edited by K. C. Chang, E. N. Anderson's *The Food of China*, Gang Yue's 樂鋼 *The Mouth That Begs*, Judith Farquhar's *Appetites*, and Mark Swislocki's *Culinary Nostalgia*,[2] to just name a few—have pointed out that food, eating, drinking, and the appreciation of gastronomy have constituted a significant theme in and projected aesthetical and political implications onto Chinese literature, history, and culture from ancient times to the present era of globalization. Indeed, between necessity and luxury, and between the fundamental five flavors and various tastes and aftertastes, food description and culinary imagination can be related to nutrition, artifacts, customs, habits, ritual, regional features, national character, and human nature. D. C. Lau translates Mencius' *shi se xing ye* 食色性也 as "appetite for food and sex is nature," indicating that, in Mencian thought, desiring food is human nature. "Governing a large state is like boiling a small fish," the famous line in the Taoist classic *Tao Te Ching* 道德經, is a salient example of an analogy between governing and cooking, between political and gastronomical imagination. Culinary experiences have been explicitly incorporated into the linguistic expressions, critical terms, emotional articulations, and even refined lifestyle in the Chinese literati tradition: for example, Su Dongpo's literary self-portrait "Laotao fu" 老饕賦 (A rhymed prose of the epicurean) and gastronomic creation "Dongpo pork"; Yang Shen 楊慎 (1488–1559) and his culinary quest; Cao Xueqin and his encyclopedic presentation of refined cuisine in *The Story of the Stone*; Li Yu 李漁 (1611–1680) and his subtle illustrations of diets and tastes in *Xianqing ouji* 閒情偶寄 (Sketches of idle leisures); as well as Yuan Mei 袁枚 (1716–1797) and his delicate and stylish *Suiyuan shidan* 隨園食單 (Recipes of the Sui garden). All these writers are widely recognized for their sophisticated tastes, erudition, and elegant articulations of Chinese culinary culture.[3]

---

[2] A short list includes Kwang-chih Chang, ed., *Food in Chinese Culture: Anthropological and Historical Perspectives* (New Haven, CT: Yale University Press, 1977); E. N. Anderson, *The Food of China* (New Haven, CT: Yale University Press, 1990); Gang Yue, *The Mouth that Begs: Hunger, Cannibalism, and the Politics of Eating in Modern China* (Durham, NC: Duke University Press, 1999); Judith Farquhar, *Appetites: Food and Sex in Post-Socialist China* (Durham, NC: Duke University Press, 2002); and Mark Swislocki, *Culinary Nostalgia: Regional Food Culture and the Urban Experience in Shanghai* (Stanford, CA: Stanford University Press, 2009). See also Sau-ling Cynthia Wong, *Reading Asian American Literature: From Necessity to Extravagance* (Princeton, NJ: Princeton University Press, 1993), esp. chap. 1, entitled "Big Eaters, Treat Lovers, 'Food Prostitutes,' 'Food Pornographers,' and Doughnut Makers"; and Ping-hui Liao 廖炳惠, *Chi de houxiandai* 吃的後現代 [Ways of eating: Savoring postmodernity] (Taipei: Eryu, 2004).

[3] See David Knechtges, "A Literary Feast: Food in Early Chinese Literature," *Journal of the American Oriental Society* 106, no.1 (1986): 49–63; and "Gradually Entering the Realm of Delight: Food and Drink in Early Medieval China," *Journal of the American Oriental Society* 117, no. 2 (1997): 229–239; Stephen West, "Playing

Modern and contemporary Chinese writers, in particular essayists, are involved in and influenced by this literary tradition. A recent English anthology, *Food and Chinese Culture*, features artistic and tasteful short essays and "descriptions, critiques and memories" of China's sophisticated and splendid cuisines by twenty-six well-known writers, in terms of "the color, smell, and taste of food, its myriad regional styles and flavors and its profound cultural underpinnings."[4] In a different socio-cultural context, when addressing the abundant banquet images—food, drink, and swallowing—in François Rabelais's (1483–1553) novel *La vie de Gargantua et de Pantagruel* (*The Life of Gargantua and of Pantagruel*) and their connections with literary imagination, physiological behavior, and human nature, Bakhtin also pointed out, "the encounter of man with the world, which takes place inside the open, biting, rending, chewing mouth, is one of the most ancient, and most important objects of human thought and imagery."[5] With regard to the diversity of culinary practices, Carolyn Korsmeyer argues in *Making Sense of Taste*, "taste, food and drink, and eating and drinking—the sense, its objects, its activities—are too complex to be considered from any single perspective."[6] Therefore, the reading and understanding of food and foodways in the modern Chinese culinary imagination should be considered within a wide range of texts and contexts, or tours and detours of complicated literary, geographical, philosophical, social, and cultural representations.

---

with Food: Performance, Food, and the Aesthetics of Artificiality in the Sung and Yuan," *Harvard Journal of Asiatic Studies* 57, no. 1 (1997): 67–106; Da'an Pan, "Tasting the Good and the Beautiful: The Aestheticization of Eating and Drinking in Traditional Chinese Culture," *The Cal Poly Pomona Journal of Interdisciplinary Studies* 16 (2003): 67–76. For a concise and comprehensive introduction of Chinese imperial cuisines described by scholars, literati, calligraphers, painters, historians, and even medical specialists, see "The History of Chinese Imperial Food," China Internet Information Center, http://www.china.org.cn/english/imperial/25995.htm.

4 Chen Zishan 陳子善, ed., *Food and Chinese Culture: Essays on Popular Cuisines* (San Francisco: Long River Press, 2005), 7. Noteworthy essays in this anthology include Lin Yutang's "On Diet," Xia Mianzun's 夏丏尊 "On Eating," Yu Dafu's "The Cuisine of Fuzhou," Liang Shiuqiu's "Peking Duck," Ye Shengtao's 葉聖陶 "Lotus Root and Water Shield," Ye Lingfeng's 葉靈鳳 "Wild Herbs South of Yangtze," Zhou Zuoren's "Snacks of South and North China," Wang Zengqi's 汪曾祺 "Foods in My Hometown," Lu Wenfu's 陸文夫 "Man and His Sense of Taste," Tang Zhenchang's 唐振常 "On Sichuan Cuisine," Deng Yunxiang's 鄧云鄉 "Memories of Hangzhou Cuisine," Feng Jicai's 馮驥才 "An Angler's Recipe for Crucian Carp," Wang Meng's 王蒙 "I Love Porridge," and Jia Pingwa's 賈平凹 "A Trivial Record of Shaanxi Snacks." For an insightful and important approach to *xiaopin wen* (little prose pieces) and "literature of leisure," see Charles Laughlin, *The Literature of Leisure and Chinese Modernity* (Honolulu: University of Hawai'i Press, 2008). See also Chen Pingyuan, *Zhongguo sanwen xiaoshuo shi* 中國散文小説史 [History of Chinese proses and novels] (Beijing: Beijing daxue chubanshe, 2010), esp. chap. 6.

5 Mikhail Bakhtin, *Rabelais and His World*, trans. Hélène Iswolsky (Bloomington: Indiana University Press, 1984), 281.

6 Carolyn Korsmeyer, *Making Sense of Taste: Food and Philosophy* (Ithaca, NY: Cornell University Press, 1999), 2.

This section focuses on Liang Shiqiu's affective mapping of the long-lasting flavors of Chinese food and the lingering aroma of his hometown dishes. By using "affective mapping," I investigate the emotional topography, sentimental cartography, imagined geography, performative psychogeography of nostalgia and longing, epiphany and loss, as well as melancholy and hope, as evidenced in Liang's repetitive, reiterative, and regurgitative reminiscences on Chinese tastes and Beijing flavors. Liang's literary notions were inspired by Chinese culinary classics and the ideas of "New Humanism" and "Cultural Renewal" coined by his spiritual mentor, Irving Babbitt (1865–1933). I explore Liang's influential and subtle articulations, affective and emotional topography, and tangible and symbolic embodiments of Chinese culinary culture (in particular the exquisite tastes of Beijing food) as the incarnation of humanity, the authenticity of individual identity, the tokens of collective memory, the traces of diaspora, the souvenirs of nostalgia, and the aftertaste of home in *Yashe xiaopin* 雅舍小品 (From a cottager's sketchbook), his *xiaopin wen* 小品文 (little prose pieces), and his literary criticism and humanist ideas.[7]

As early as the 1920s, Liang Shiqiu was already a representative figure in the prominent literary school *Xinyue she* 新月社 (the Crescent Moon Society), famous for its adaptation of European salon culture, especially the English afternoon tea gathering, as well as for its conscious continuation of the Chinese literati tradition. For the literary minds in the Crescent Moon Society, the ways of tasting food and drinking tea or coffee represented not only a particular lifestyle but also a loosely defined "lyrical philosophy"[8] well substantiated in the writings of Anglo-Saxon trained writers and scholars, including Xu Zhimo, Hu Shi, Chen Xiying 陳西瀅 (1896–1970), Liang Shiqiu, Lin Huiyin, Wen Yiduo, and Ye Gongchao 葉公超 (1904–1981).[9] Liang Shiqiu was one of the most prolific writers in this group. During his mainland Chinese years, particularly from 1940 to 1949, he composed a series of essays in Chongqing and Beijing for *Xingqi pinglun* 星期評論 (Weekly review) and other newspapers. These thirty-four essays formed the original *From a Cottager's Sketchbook*, published after he had resettled in Taiwan in 1949. For the next four decades, Liang continued to produce such little prose pieces, which first appeared in newspapers and periodicals and were subsequently collected and reissued under the same general title: thirty-two essays in volume 2 (1973), thirty-seven in volume 3

[7] Charles Laughlin translates *Yashe xiaopin* 雅舍小品 as "*Xiaopin* from the Elegant Lodging"; see his *The Literature of Leisure and Chinese Modernity*, 41.

[8] Lin, *The Importance of Living*, vii.

[9] Gong Pengcheng 龔鵬程, "Yinzhuan de wenxue shehuixue" 飲饌的文學社會學 [Literary sociology of drinking and eating], in *Liang Shiqiu yu zhongxi wenhua* 梁實秋與中西文化 [Liang Shiqiu in Chinese and Western cultures], ed. Gao Xudong 高旭東 (Beijing: Zhonghua shuju, 2007), 73–94.

(1982), and forty in volume 4 (1986).[10] Moreover, in the 1970s and 1980s, he wrote a substantial number of essays on Chinese food and diet and the ways of eating and drinking, which were collected in the widely circulated anthology *Yashe tanchi* 雅舍談吃 (A cottager's ideas about eating, 1985). Ta-tsun Chen 陳達遵, Liang's disciple, addresses Liang's nostalgia in the introductory essay of his English translation of *From A Cottager's Sketchbook*,

> Although the craftsmanship remains unchanged, a careful observer may discern in the later volumes a steady increase in depth and a subtle shift from poignant sarcasm to benign humor as he mellowed. His nostalgia for his hometown only increased with age.
>
> 雖然他的寫作技巧始終不變,但如細心觀察,卻不難看出作者的態度日趨穩健,後來的幾集逐漸增加深度,又從尖刻的諷刺微妙地轉向謔而不虐的幽默。他的鄉愁卻與歲月俱增。[11]

Beginning in 1949, when both Communist and Nationalist political authoritarianism imposed barriers to cultural and economic exchanges across the Taiwan Strait,[12] Liang compiled and completed a sensational list of food items, everyday eateries, and decent restaurants with the quintessence of Chineseness, colored by a "keen sense of humor" and a sustained mood of nostalgia. In addition to his enduring memory of the unforgettable aftertastes of hometown dishes, which I will address later in this section, *A Cottager's Ideas About Eating* charts the all-directional foodways in China, as well as the traces of tastes from the north to the south, from the east to the west, by using food items as essay titles and telling their stories: "Guoba" 鍋巴 (Crispy rice) was once called "bombing Tokyo" in wartime China; "Baoyu mian" 鮑魚面 (Abalone noodles) reveals Liang's culinary pleasure during a winter visit to Shenyang; "Jiucai lou" 韭菜簍 (Leek dumplings) showcases the flavor of Shandong cuisine; "Caibao" 菜包 (Vegetable bun) in Manchu-style maintained its popularity in north China; "Qiang qingha" 熗青蛤 (Quick-boiled clam), "Laobing/baobing" 烙餅/薄餅 (Pancakes), and "Ban yazhang" 拌鴨掌 (Duck feet with mustard) achieved their fame in Beijing's Shandong-style restaurants; "Liangzuo yu" 兩做魚 (Carp in

---

10 For a study of *Fukan*-based literary culture, middle-class genres, and Liang Shiqiu as a literary guru in Taiwan's post-1949 cultural filed, see Sung-sheng Yvonne Chang, *Literary Culture in Taiwan: Martial Law to Market Law* (New York: Columbia University Press, 2004).

11 Ta-tsun Chen, *From a Cottager's Sketchbook* (Hong Kong: The Chinese University Press, 2005), 1:xxii–xxiii.

12 See, for instance, David Der-wei Wang and Carlos Rojas, eds., *Writing Taiwan: A New Literary History* (Durham, NC: Duke University Press, 2007); David Der-wei Wang, Chen Sihe 陳思和, and Xu Zidong 許子東, eds., *Yijiu sijiu yihou* 一九四九以後 [After 1949] (Hong Kong: Oxford University Press, 2010); and Wang, *Modernity with a Cold War Face*.

two styles), "Shengchao shanyu si" 生炒鱔魚絲 (Fried eel slices), and "Wakuai yu" 瓦塊魚 (Fried fish chunks) are highlights of the Yu cuisine (Henan province). Liang Shiqiu's artistic and affective mapping of these regional flavors continues in the items and essays about *chi zai sifang* 吃在四方 (eating in all regions outside of the hometown) colored by his personal experiences and erudite illustrations: the complimentary "Liuhuang cai" 溜黃菜 (Slided egg yolk) popular in northern restaurants; "Culiu yu" 醋熘魚 (Sweet and sour fish fillets) from the West Lake of Hangzhou; the way of cooking "Shizi tou" 獅子頭 (Lion's head meat balls) in Yangzhou; "Layou" 臘肉 (Preserved meat) in Hunan; the famous Fuzhou dish "Fo tiaoqiang" 佛跳牆 (Assorted meat and vegetables cooked in embers); "Ge" 鴿 (Pigeon) in Cantonese cuisine; "Xishi she" 西施舌 (Orchid tongue) in Qingdao, Fuzhou, and Yu Dafu's frequently anthologized essay "The Cuisine of Fuzhou"; "Sun" 笋 (Bamboo shoots) in Zhejiang and Taiwan; "Huotui" 火腿 (Ham) in Jinhua, Shanghai, Nanjing, and Chongqing, and the difficulty of obtaining the authentic Jinhua ham in Taiwan; "Yuchi" 魚翅 (Shark fin) in Sichuan, Yunnan, Guangdong, and Taiwan; his personal style of cherishing the popular "Doufu" 豆腐 (Bean curd); the different tastes of "Xie" 蟹 (Crab) served in regional restaurants in mainland China, Taiwan, and Hong Kong; and, more importantly and frequently, his persistent and recurrent memories of enjoying (sometimes together with his father) "Haishen" 海參 (Sea cucumber), "Zaozheng yagan" 糟蒸鴨肝 (Steamed duck liver in wine), "Longxu cai" 龍鬚菜 (Asparagus), "Lianzi" 蓮籽 (Refreshing lotus seeds), "Gali ji" 咖喱雞 (Chicken curry), and "Huangyu" 黃魚 (Yellow croaker) in Republican Beijing restaurants, as well as "Ganbei" 干貝 (Scallops), "Yuwan" 魚丸 (Fish balls), and "Zhou" 粥 (Congee) cooked by his mother at home.

Furthermore, Liang makes frequent comparisons and contrasts between Chinese and foreign culinary culture in the following encyclopedic essays and entries: "You xiongzhang shuoqi" 由熊掌說起 (Beginning with bear's paws), one of the eight treasures in Chinese cuisine; eating in Beijing and New York; the use and abuse of "Weijing 味精" (Monosodium glutamate) in China, Japan, and the United States; "Zha huoyu" 炸活魚 (Deep-fried live fish) and the primitive and cruel minds in the Oriental and Occidental worlds; "Babao fan" 八寶飯 (Eight-treasure rice pudding) mixed with Chinese and American ingredients; cross-cultural anecdote "Doufugan fengbo" 豆腐乾風波 (Confusion about dried bean curd) at the Seattle airport; "Ji Riben zhi yinshidian" 記日本之飲食店 (Random thoughts on Japanese restaurants); "Kangnaixin niunai" 康乃馨牛奶 (Carnation milk) in Washington State; culinary memory of "Chi zai meiguo" 吃在美國 (Eating in the United States) and a humorous piece "Maidanglao" 麥當勞 (McDonald's fast food); "Zongzi jie" 粽子節 (The dragon boat festival) in Shanghai and "Dacai" 大菜 (Western-style food); and his delicious illustrations of the constant search for and discoveries of authentic tastes, the pleasures of the gourmet foodscape, as well as the art of Chinese cooking in short essays such as "Du *Yuanshan shipu*" 讀《媛珊食譜》 (Reading *Yuanshan's cookbook*), "*Yinshan zhengyao*" 《飲膳正要》 (*Principles of correct diet*), "Qianli chungeng weixia yangu" 千里蓴羹 未下鹽豉 (Water-lily soup from thousand-li Lake and salted legumes from Weixia),[13] "Du *zhongguochi*" 讀《中國吃》 (Reading *Chinese Eating*), "Zaitan 'zhongguochi'" 再談"中國吃 (More on Chinese eating), and "Du *Pengtiao yuanli*" 讀《烹調原理》 (Reading *Culinary Principles*). Liang Shiqiu's depictions of food and eating provide an affective map or emotional topography of alleyways, streets, courtyard houses, and restaurants in different geographical locations from Beijing to Chongqing, from Taipei to Seattle, and in general, from mainland China to the other Sinophone worlds.

As a Beijing native, Taipei dweller, and sophisticated connoisseur of fine cuisine, Liang envisions and exhibits his passionate recollections of the variety of cooking, eating, and drinking, rendering food as both nutrition for the body and an art of life, and more importantly, as a palpable embodiment of humanity, in his *Yashe* little prose pieces. Food items, culinary stories, and taste discussions appear vividly in the intertextual liaisons between his personal experiences of eating and drinking and his erudite and elegant quotations and illuminations of Chinese classics, such as *The Rites of Zhou Dynasty*, *Shanhaijing* 山海經 (Collection of the mountains and seas), *Shijing* 詩經 (The book of songs), *Chuci* 楚辭 (Songs of the south), *Guyuefu* 古樂府 (Old music bureau poems), *Lüshi chunqiu* 呂氏春秋 (Mister Lü's spring and autumn [annals]), *Wenxuan* 文選 (Selections of refined literature), Yan Zhitui's 顏之推 (531–591) *Yanshi jiaxun* 顏氏家訓 (The family instructions of Master Yan), Shen Kuo's 沈括 (1031–1095) *Mengxi bitan* 夢溪筆談 (Dream pool essays), Hu Sihui's 忽思慧 *Yin Shan zhengyao* 飲膳正要 (Principles of correct diet) in the Yuan dynasty, and many others. The retrospective exhibition of Chinese culinary aesthetics and practices in imperial rituals or daily life are entertaining, enriching, encouraging, and enlightening, and reveal vividly the experiences of tasting food and shaping the mind of China in the long history of Chinese culinary culture.

In the preface to *A Cottager's Ideas about Eating*, Liang Shiqiu disagrees with Zhu Xi about the principle of heaven, human desire, and the enjoyment of food and eating:

The recorded sayings of Master Zhu had it: "Someone asked, 'As for eating and drinking, which are heavenly principles, which is human desire?' [Master

---

[13] The words come from Liu Yiqing's 劉義慶 *Shishuo xinyu* 世說新語. For the only available English translation, see *A New Account of Tales of the World*, 2nd ed., trans. Richard B. Mather (Ann Arbor: Center for Chinese Studies, University of Michigan, 2002). Mather also pointed out that Weixia 未下 should be Moxia 末下.

Zhu] replied: 'Eating and drinking are heavenly principles; the request for delicious tastes is human desire. Scholars must first extinguish human desire, then maintain heavenly principles, which will lead to the beginning of scholarship.' " I hold a different opinion. I think that to request good tastes is indeed human desire, yet how does it ever contradict heavenly principle? If heavenly principle does not include the request for delicious tastes, then why are people born with so many taste buds on their tongues?

朱子語錄:"問:'飲食之間,孰為天理,孰為人慾?'曰:'飲食者,天理也;要求美味,人慾也。學者須是革盡人慾,復盡天理,方始是學。'"我的想法異於是。我以為要求美味固是人慾,然而何曾有背於天理?如果天理不包括美味的要求在內,上天生人,在舌頭上為什麼要生那麼多的味蕾?[14]

For Zhu Xi, eating and drinking are principles of heaven, yet the craving for delicious tastes is human, and should therefore be regulated and exterminated. Liang argues that to enjoy the taste of food is indeed a human desire, yet it does not violate the principle of heaven. The human body needs and demands, physiologically and psychologically, pleasing tastes and palatability. Liang's debate with Zhu Xi reminds us of his consistent literary notions shaped by Irving Babbitt, so much so that for his whole career, Liang regards human life and human nature as the only proper subjects for literature, eloquently and tirelessly addressed in his critical treatises "Wenxue de jilü" 文學的紀律 (The discipline of literature), "Wenxue yu geming" 文學與革命 (Literature and revolution), "Wenxue shi you jiejixing de ma" 文學是有階級性的嗎? (Is there class consciousness in literature?), "Renxing yu jiejixing" 人性與階級性 (Humanity and class), and "Wenxue de mei" 文學的美 (The beauty of literature).[15] For him, humanity is the true value of literature, transcending the limits of social class and political divisions. Food and the ways of eating and drinking constitute a major motif in his persistent and consistent concern with humanity and humanist literary representations. In his famous essay "*Chan* 饞," Liang compellingly articulates his notion of tastes and appetites:

---

[14] Liang Shiqiu, *Yashe tanchi* 雅舍談吃 [A cottager's ideas about eating] (Tianjin: Tianjin jiaoyu chubanshe, 2006), 1. For a revised and enlarged 2009 Taiwan edition of the original 1985 version, see *Yashe tanchi* (Taipei: Jiuge, 2009).

[15] See, for instance, Marián Gálik, "Liang Shih-ch'iu and Chinese New Humanism," in *The Genesis of Modern Chinese Literary Criticism, 1917–1930* (London: Curzon Press, 1980), 285–307; Bai Liping, "Babbitt's Impact in China: The Case of Liang Shiqiu," *Humanitas* 17, nos. 1–2 (2004): 46–68; Liang Kan, "Hu Shi and Liang Shiqiu: Liberalism and Others," *Chinese Studies in History* 39, no. 1 (2005): 3–24. See also *Liang Shiqiu piping wenji* 梁實秋批評文集 [Liang Shiqiu's literary criticism], ed. Xu Jingbo 徐靜波 (Zhuhai: Zhuhai chubanshe, 1998).

The Chinese word *chan* has no exact equivalent in English.... Eating excessively because of one's indulgence in certain foods is gluttony. On the other hand, *chan* attaches importance to the quality of food, and it is the tongue, rather than the stomach, that has the greatest need to be satisfied.... *Chan*, though based on a physiological need, is capable of developing into a quasi-artistic taste.

饞，在英文裏找不到一個十分適當的字。對有某一種食物有所偏好，對於大量的吃，這是貪得無厭。饞，則著重在食物的質，最需要滿足的是品味。饞，基於生理的要求；也可以發展成為近於藝術的趣味。[16]

"A quasi-artistic taste" surpasses the boundaries of class and hierarchy and appeals to the basic human needs and psyche, primary aspects of both primitive and cultivated humanity. The longing and passion for fine foods and dream tastes should not be considered a sin but human instinct and "symptomatic of a good appetite and good health." In a word, "*Chan* has nothing to do with one's social standing."[17]

Among his humanist and universalist illustrations of Chinese culinary aesthetics at large, most striking are Liang Shiqiu's writings on Beijing food culture completed in the 1970s and 1980s in Taiwan. After he left Beijing in 1949 and settled in Taipei, his nostalgia for his native city increased remarkably with age. Liang himself put it as follows: "It is human nature to maintain a nostalgic longing for the distinctive culinary flavor of one's hometown" (人就是這個樣子，對於家鄉風味總是念念不忘).[18] In *A Cottager's Ideas about Eating* and *A Cottager's Sketchbook*, he provides an affective mapping of gastronomic places and spaces in his hometown Beijing, for example, Dongxing Lou Restaurant 東興樓, Zhimei Zhai Restaurant 致美齋, and Hou De Fu Restaurant 厚德福, among many others, where his culinary nostalgia and bittersweet emotional aftertaste loom large in a delicious, enjoyable, and memorable way. Liang recalls scenes of the New Year festival in Beijing in one of the essays in *A Cottager's Sketchbook*:

One must spend the New Year holiday at home in order to really enjoy it. A person who lives away from home tends to feel miserable due to loneliness and, being totally incapable of sharing the festive mood at the approach of the New Year, can only express his feelings in sighs.... Beijing seems far, far away; I can return to it only in dreams.

[16] Liang, *From a Cottager's Sketchbook*, 2:80. Liang regards "piggish," "gluttonous," and "greedy" as inappropriate translations of the Chinese character *chan* 饞, see his *Yashe tanchi*, 171.

[17] Liang, *From a Cottager's Sketchbook*, 2:86, 90; *Yashe tanchi*, 183.

[18] Liang, *From a Cottager's Sketchbook*, 2:84, 85.

過年須要在家鄉裏才有味道。覊旅悽涼，到了年下只有長吁短嘆的分兒，還能有半點歡樂的心情？…. 北平遠在天邊，徒縈夢想.[19]

Inspired by Jacques Derrida and Barbara Johnson's interpretations of Plato's simile of writing, I believe that, in Liang's culinary memory and regurgitative essays, food becomes the *pharmakon*, dealing with both the body and the mind of the diasporic Beijing native when there seems no hope of returning home.[20] The writer's unquenchable nostalgia for his hometown was channeled into his lavish descriptions and verbal exhibitions of local rituals of New Year's sacrifice and ancestral worship, as well as distinctive family gatherings. The most striking presentation is his long list of fine foods and beverages and the idiosyncratic ways of consuming them. A quick glance at the individual titles of the essays shows how deeply Liang invested his sentiments in the local food culture: volume 3 of *A Cottager's Sketchbook* collects the variety of acts of eating, in essays such as "Xiyan" 喜筵 (The wedding banquet), "*Chan*" 饞 (*Chan*, or, craving good food), "Hecha" 喝茶 (Drinking tea), "Yinjiu" 飲酒 (Drinking wines), "Guonian" 過年 (Chinese New Year), and "Fanqian qidao" 飯前祈禱 (Grace before meals). Volume 3 includes pieces such as "Beiping de dongtian" 北平的冬天 (Winter in Beiping) and "Wotou" 窩頭 (Wotou, or Chinese cornbread) to continue his imagined journey back to his remote hometown at the heart of China. Most significantly in this regard, Liang described in an amusing and seductive way fifty-seven kinds of Beijing daily dishes and drinks in his *A Cottager's Ideas about Eating*, to satisfy his starving stomach as well as his longing for a bygone age and a lost home. The tasteful entries with the lingering flavors of his hometown dishes appear as the essay titles, including "Kao yangrou" 烤羊肉 (Roast lamb), "Shaoya" 燒鴨 (Roast duck), "Jiangcai" 醬菜 (Preserved vegetable in soy), "Shuijing xiabing" 水晶蝦餅 (Sautéed shrimp cake), "Tangbao" 湯包 (Steamed bun stuffed with juicy pork), "Hetao lao" 核桃酪 (Sweet walnut soup), "Tieguo dan" 鐵鍋蛋 (Egg cooked in an iron pan), "Suanmei tang yu tang hulu" 酸梅湯與糖葫蘆 (Syrup of plum and crispy sugar-coated hawthorns on a stick), "Guoshao ji" 鍋燒雞 (Fried chicken), "Jian hundun" 煎餛飩 (Fried dumplings), "Hetao yao" 核桃腰 (Walnuts), "Douzhi'er" 豆汁兒 (Fermented bean drink), "Furong jipian" 芙蓉雞片 (Sautéed chicken slices in egg white), "Wuyuqian" 烏魚錢 (Cuttlefish), "Zha wanzi" 炸丸子 (Deep-fried meatballs), "Lizi" 栗子 (Chestnuts), "Manhan xidian" 滿漢細點 (Manchu-Han refined pastry and beautiful dessert), "Qiezi" 茄子 (eggplant), "Bairou" 白肉 (Pork), "Bao shuangcui" 爆雙脆 (Fried two crispy ingredients),

[19] Ibid., 1:346–347.

[20] See Jacques Derrida, *Dissemination*, trans. Barbara Johnson (New York: Continuum, 2004), 98–118; Barbara Johnson, "Writing," in Lentricchia and McLaughlin, *Critical Terms for Literary Study*, 39–49.

"Jiaozi" 餃子 (Dumplings), "Shao yangrou" 燒羊肉 (Braised lamb in brown sauce), "Bocai" 菠菜 (Spinach), "Beiping de lingshi xiaofan" 北平的零食小販 (Peking peddlers), "Lao" 酪 (Cheese), and "Miantiao" 面條 (noodles). A closer culinary and cultural look at the variety of food and drinks in this volume is truly intriguing: Beijing's "suanmei tang" 酸梅湯, the black sweet-and-sour drink that is a favorite for people in all classes and social ranks, like the rickshaw puller, the protagonist in Beijing writer Lao She's novel *Luotuo xiangzi* (*Rickshaw Boy*); "tang hulu" 糖葫蘆, made of sweet red hawthorns, is depicted as Beijing's signature snack food "unafraid of New Times' dust"[21] by Lin Huiyin, one of the most talented women writers of modern China and Liang Shiqiu's fellow member of the Crescent Moon Society in the 1930s; the versatile chestnut nourishing both body and soul, which reminds Liang Shiqiu of the lovely chestnut tree in his Beijing house.[22] Citing Hu Jinquan's 胡金銓 (1932–1997) famous proposal about douzhi'er 豆汁兒, a typical Beijing breakfast fermented bean drink, "One who can not enjoy *douzhi'er* should not be regarded as a true Beijinger" (不能喝豆汁兒的人算不得是真正的北平人), Liang attempts to depict and define diversified regions, local identities, and urban characteristics by Chinese people's habits of eating and drinking.[23] The emotional topography of Beijing's dishes charts the geographical and affective traces of his increasing nostalgia: he craved Beijing's "baodu'er" 爆肚兒 (quick-fried tripe) when he pursued his advanced degrees in the United States; he missed Beijing's "kao yangrou" 烤羊肉 (roast lamb) when he stayed in Qingdao; and he missed desperately the authentic *douzhi'er* while he lived in Taipei.

Rather than directly approaching "the order of things," Liang Shiqiu prefers random reflections and idle talk (隨便談談，既無章法，亦無次序) about fine cuisine in Beijing and beyond.[24] Yet in a ruminatory and repetitive way, he blends his personal experiences, food memory, and diasporic nostalgia in his depictions and recollections of the long-lasting flavors of Chinese food and the lingering aroma of Beijing dishes during his Taipei years. In "*Chan*" 饞, he confesses that "a person tends to feel the strongest craving for a particular food at a time when it is not available."[25] Liang's essays on food and eating make the unavailable accessible, thus conveying his strong craving for the delicacies from his hometown. For instance, he was dying for a dish of "yangtou rou" 羊頭肉 (lamb's head meat) for seven or eight years

---

[21] Liang, *Lin Huiyin wenji-wenxue juan*, 212.

[22] Liang Shiqiu, *Yashe tanchi* 雅舍談吃 [A cottager's ideas about eating] (Beijing: Wenhua yishu chubanshe, 1998), 40, 57, 64. A short English introduction of Beijing snacks in celebration of the 2008 Olympic Games, see Song Weizhong et al., *Beijing Local Delicacies*, trans. Wang Yufan (Beijing: China Pictorial Publishing House, 2006).

[23] Liang, *Yashe tanchi*, 26.

[24] Liang, *Yashe tanchi*, 1.

[25] Liang, *From a Cottager's Sketchbook*, 2:82.

in a government-controlled area outside Beijing during his Sino-Japanese wartime exile, but eventually satisfied his body and mind when he returned to his hometown after the announcement of Japan's surrender in mid-August 1945:

> I held the dish of meat on my palm, crawled back into the bed, and began to feed myself, one slice after another, until I fell asleep with a feeling of total gratification.
>
> 我托着一盤羊頭肉，重複鑽進被窩，在枕上一片一片的羊頭肉放進嘴裏，不知不覺的進入了睡鄉，十分滿足的解了饞癮。[26]

And later in Taiwan, he hoped that he could go back again to fulfill his desire for this particular Beijing gourmet dish, as he could not have until a winter midnight months after V-J Day.

In modern Chinese literature, an array of writers have dealt with the poetics and politics of metabolic and metaphysical desire for food. Examples that come readily to mind are Lu Xun's allegory of cannibalism at the inception of modern Chinese literature and Zhang Ailing's hunger aesthetics in her novel *Rice-sprout Song*. In the short story "Lust, Caution," Zhang quotes an English saying that "the way to a man's heart is through his stomach" to characterize men as different from women.[27] Ang Lee's 李安 cinematic elaboration of the analogy of culinary and family contradiction and harmony in *Yinshi nanü* 飲食男女 (Eat drink man woman) reveals the male protagonist's story of losing and regaining his appetite, a compelling example of "food fetishism."[28] In Liang Shiqiu's culinary aesthetics and essay writing, food serves as both a mainstay of material existence and a cultural trope. It seems that Liang never lost his strong appetite for local Beijing cuisine. Since authentic Beijing foods are not easy to obtain in Taipei, Liang seeks to satisfy his yearning and longing for home through exquisite writings about food, flavor, and aftertaste. This verbal consumption points to the double functions of orality: taking in sustenance and speaking out. And his repetitive, regurgitative, and compulsive writings on Chinese cuisine, in particular Beijing food, reveal an intriguing dialectic between starvation and satisfaction, necessity and extravagance: the absent authentic hometown flavors

---

[26] Ibid., 84–85.

[27] Eileen Chang et al., *Lust, Caution: The Story, the Screenplay, and the Making of the Film*, trans. Julia Lovell (New York: Pantheon, 2007), 36.

[28] See Shih, *Visuality and Identity*, 53; Wei Ming Dariotis and Eileen Fung, "Breaking the Soy Sauce Jar: Diaspora and Displacement in the Films of Ang Lee," in *Transnational Chinese Cinemas: Identity, Nationhood, Gender*, ed. Sheldon Lu (Honolulu: University of Hawai'i Press, 1997), 207–213; for the meaning of food, see also Rey Chow, "We Endure, Therefore We Are: Survival, Governance, and Zhang Yimou's *To Live*," in her *Ethics After Idealism: Theory-Culture-Ethnicity-Reading* (Bloomington: Indiana University Press, 1998), 113–132.

can be symbolically replaced, yet also displaced by verbal composition and exhibition of the cuisine; the yearning for a lost hometown can be gratified by spiritual consumption and emotional mapping of the lingering flavor and bittersweet aftertaste of "authentic" homeland food. Therefore, his culinary "little prose pieces" are presented to feed not only the starving body but also the diasporic mind craving an imagined homecoming to a distanced and idealized Beijing.

Liang Shiqiu's long list of foods and beverages mainly covers "xiaochi" 小吃 (snack food) or "shijingcai" 市井菜 (street dishes), which are popular food for the masses and are related mostly to daily scenes. In contrast, Tang Lusun, another and even more provocative food writer called "chanren" 饞人 (the man with a craving for fine food), provides depictions of Beijing cuisine that not only pay attention to the genealogy of food and customs of eating and drinking but also focus more on the gourmet culture of the imperial courts and palaces, the grand aristocratic families, and the upscale restaurants.[29] Tang Lusun's sophisticated introductions to ways of eating are meant to entertain himself, his overseas readers, and, thanks to the publication of the PRC edition, the global Chinese community. In his twelve-volume anthology on ways of life, 70 percent of the essays focus on food, eating, and drinking. Describing enchanting dishes in Chinese-speaking communities in various geographical locations, Tang dedicates a large part of his writing to Beijing cuisine. Through recollecting Beijing's food culture, he conveys his nostalgia for his hometown in books including *Tang Lusun on Eating, Guyuan qing* 故園情 (Feeling for hometown), *Zhongguo chi* 中國吃 (Chinese eating), *Zhongguo chi de gushi* 中國吃的故事 (Stories about Chinese eating), and *Suan tian ku la xian* 酸甜苦辣鹹 (Sour, sweet, bitter, spicy, and salty), a fusion of essays with unparalleled elegance and nostalgia. Tang remembers food and eating in Beijing's past in his encyclopedic essays, such as "Taiwan mei jianzhao de Beiping xiaochi lingshi" 台灣沒見着的北平小吃零食 (Beijing snack foods unavailable in Taiwan), "Gudu de naipin xiaochi" 故都的奶品小吃 (Milky snacks in my hometown), "Chi zai Beiping" 吃在北平 (Eating in Beijing) (I, II), "Beiping de dute shipin" 北平的獨特食品 (Unique Foods in Beijing) (I, II), "Beiping de tianshi" 北平的甜食 (Desserts in Beijing), "Gudu de zaodian" 故都的早點 (Breakfast in Beijing), "Beiping shang fanguan de jueqiao" 北平上飯館的訣竅 (Secrets of Beijing restaurants), and many others.[30] And the most exquisitely written essays are depictions of the rare gourmet dishes in imperial

29 David Der-wei Wang, "Beijing menhua lu" 北京夢華錄 [Beijing dreams], in his *Ruci fanhua* , 41–53. After all, Tang's distinguished family background and Manchu Imperial blood greatly shaped his appetites and cultivated his gourmet taste. See also Wang, *Hou yimin xiezuo*, esp. 23–70.

30 Tang Lusun, *Zhongguo chi* 中國吃 [Chinese eating] (Taipei: Dadi chubanshe, 1976), 7–82.

courts, gardens, and even palaces. Some examples are "Huangjia yinzhuan" 皇家飲饌 (Imperial drinking and eating), "Manhan quanxi" 滿漢全席 (Qing Dynasty palace food and the full Manchu-Han banquet), and "Shanzhen haiwei" 山珍海味 (Delicacies from land and sea).[31] Tang shares the forbidden secrets of imperial cuisine with its mythical ingredients and recipes, thus stirring up readers' curiosity and nostalgia about a bygone imperial era and enabling them to embark on an imagined journey in time and place. Tang believes in his tongue and his linguistic ability so deeply that he records his stomach/mind and tastes/experiences with his hands and with his words. He never attempted to eliminate his Beijing accent in his writings. Rather, his distinctive Beijing dialect, tone, style, manner, and taste constitute a unique part of his diasporic memories from the 1970s and 1980s. Tang's collections and recollections of authentic Beijing food and beverages are warm to touch, delicious to taste, pure to drink, and subtle to appreciate.

To borrow a few concepts developed by Michel de Certeau, Luce Giard, and Pierre Mayol, I would argue that while the "art of living" reveals the possibility of designing and revising people's lifeworlds, the "art of talking" signifies ordinary people's ways of appropriating and reappropriating the dominant language for their own purposes, and the "art of cooking" transforms physical nutrition into verbal utterances regarding body language and body memory.[32] Liang Shiqiu's and Tang Lusun's "art of eating" and "art of writing" indicate the dialectic of hunger and indulgence, starvation and satisfaction, in which remembrance of food and eating in the past and exhibition of the endless passion for and obsession with authentic hometown dishes help quench the urges of hungry diasporic Beijing natives.

Liang's literary notion of humanity, as well as his aesthetic consciousness, is vividly manifested in his depictions of the Chinese gastropolis, especially his native city. Furthermore, there is a poignant relationship between the gastronomic and political implications in Liang's reminiscent writings. His nostalgic sentiments aim not only at the flavor and taste of the lost hometown cuisine but also at an irretrievable mode of life and culture that has disappeared along with a historical epoch defined by political antagonism between the Communist and the Nationalist regimes, as well as by the changes wrought by Chinese modernization. In Taiwan in the 1970s

---

[31] See Tang Lusun, *Zhongguo chi de gushi* 中國吃的故事 [Stories about Chinese eating] (Taipei: Hanguang wenhua, 1983), 11–61. In 2007, Guangxi Normal University Press 廣西師範大學出版社 released a three-volume hardcover anthology of Tang's essays entitled *Tang Lusun tanchi* 唐魯孫談吃 [Tang Lusun on eating], indicating a canonization of Tang's food notebooks and culinary memory. An English translation of Tang Lusun's essay is entitled "Spring Festival Cuisine," in Chen, *Food and Chinese Culture*, 41–51.

[32] See Michel de Certeau, *The Practice of Everyday Life*, trans. Steven Rendall (Berkeley: University of California Press, 1988); Michel de Certeau, Luce Giard, and Pierre Mayol, *The Practice of Everyday Life*, vol. 2, *Living & Cooking*, trans. Timothy J. Tomasik (Minneapolis: University of Minnesota Press, 1998).

and 1980s, when Liang wrote his little prose pieces, the hope of recovering the lost land was becoming ever dimmer. With the blossoming of Taiwanese nativist literature, the image of a new homeland emerged, and for mainland immigrants, the island might well become their new native soil. At such a turning point, recollecting his Beijing experiences through writing its food culture, Liang registered not only nostalgia for the native city but also anxiety about the shifting notion of China and Chinese tradition. When the concepts of China and Chinese cultural authenticity were undergoing serious dispute and redefinition, what could be more bitter tasting and untimely than recollecting and mourning the culinary and cultural authenticity of a lost "homeland"?

In these randomly collected essays about food and gastronomic practices, readers can start from and end at any piece, with the major theme remaining the same: nostalgic passion and longing fueled by a ceaseless flow of Chinese gourmet food and catering. By repeating various stories of eating and drinking, Liang describes an intriguing relationship between necessity and extravagance: on the one hand, his culinary writings depict a rich and vivid Chinese food culture with its culinary wisdom and secret recipes; on the other hand, this literary luxury is informed and reinforced by a strong sense of loss, which points not only to the lost hometown and old Beijing customs and tastes but also to the awareness of the impossibility of returning to the spiritual home of Chinese culture.

The great novelist Cao Xueqin stated, "All a fool the author hold,/But their zest who can unfold" (都云作者痴，誰解其中味)?[33] How can we decode Liang Shiqiu's zest and (after)taste? I would argue that Liang's culinary essays recollect and remap Beijing and Chinese gourmet dishes in terms of emotional affiliation and spatial rearrangements or "reunion," and make the disappeared reappear in the gourmet kingdom and the "republic of letters." His culinary aesthetics in little prose pieces about food and diet, taste and aftertaste, constitute a symbolic trope of and an imaginary solution to the fundamental human hunger, the subtle and universal "*chan*" or craving, as well as the everlasting homesickness and spiritual starvation.

---

[33] Cao Xueqin, *The Dream of the Red Chamber*, trans. H. Bencraft Joly (North Clarendon, VT: Tuttle Publishing, 2010), 6. The introductory quatrain regarding the origin of *Honglou meng* 紅樓夢 has two more lines of verse (trans. H. Bencraft Joly): "滿紙荒唐言，一把辛酸淚" (Pages full of silly litter, Tears a handful sour and bitter). David Hawkes's translation of the quatrain is "Pages full of idle words / Penned with hot and bitter tears: All men call the author fool; None his secret message hears," in *The Story of the Stone: A Chinese Novel in Five Volumes* (Harmondsworth, NY: Penguin, 1973–1986), 1:51. Yang Xianyi 楊憲益 and Gladys Yang's 戴乃迭 translation is "Pages full of fantastic talk, Penned with bitter tears; All men call the author mad, None his message hears," in *A Dream of Red Mansions* (Peking: Foreign Languages Press, 1978–1980), 1:6.

BEIJING SOJOURN: BETWEEN ALLERGY AND EULOGY

The god of writing is thus also a god of medicine. Of "medicine": both a science and an occult
drug. Of the remedy and the poison. The god of writing is the god of the *pharmakon*.
—JACQUES DERRIDA

In this section, I consider the ways Zhong Lihe and Lin Haiyin, two original Taiwan
writers, projected their different diasporic "states of mind" onto their traveling and
sojourning experiences in Republican Beijing. During his six-year stay in Beijing
between 1941 and 1946, Zhong Lihe completed a dystopian novella, "Jiazhutao"
夾竹桃 (Oleander), on July 7, 1944, which was collected in the eponymous anthology together with another novella and other two short stories. "Oleander" was first
published by the journal *Taiwan wenhua* 台灣文化 (Taiwan culture) and later
by Beijing's Ma Dezeng 馬德增 bookstore in 1945 under the pen name Jiang Liu
江流. *Oleander* is the only book that Zhong published during his lifetime.[34] The
leading piece, "Oleander," portrays a bleak city image, and launched cynical criticism
of the hygienic morass and moral decline in Beijing's lower-class society on the south
side of the city. While Zhong's work is shot through with profound disillusionment
about the old capital, Lin Haiyin, with her twenty-five-year sojourn in Beijing from
1923 to 1948, presents a beautiful and encouraging image of oleander and warm and
nostalgic imagery of Beijing in her novel *Chengnan jiushi* 城南舊事 (*Memories of
Peking: South Side Stories*, 1960), which eulogizes her bittersweet childhood memory, lived and imagined, of the south side of Republican Beijing.

Zhong Lihe's literary recognition as a renowned Hakka writer and father of
Taiwan nativist literature (Taiwan xiangtu wenxue zhi fu 台灣鄉土文學之父) came
rather late, after his death from tuberculosis and poverty. Zhong was born in 1915
into a big and wealthy landowning family in south Taiwan. He received thorough
Chinese training in private (Chinese) school and solid Japanese training in a public
(Japanese and colonial) elementary school in the rural environment. Zhong Lihe
fell in love and married Zhong Taimei (1911–2008), yet the dominant taboo against
same-surname marriage in the local Hakka community forced the couple to leave
their native hometown. They traveled from Taiwan via Japan and Korea to China,
first to Mukden or Shenyang of Manchukuo, which was then a Japanese puppet
state. Later they chose to relocate to Beijing (Beiping) from 1941 to 1946.[35]

---

[34] Zhong Lihe, "Jiazhutao," reprinted in Liu Yatie 劉亞鐵 ed., *Zhong Lihe daibiaozuo* 鍾理和代表作 [Selected
writings of Zhong Lihe] (Beijing: Huaxia chubanshe, 1999), 145–185. See Fenghuang Ying, "The Literary
Development of Zhong Lihe and Postcolonial Discourse in Taiwan," in Wang and Rojas, *Writing Taiwan*, 140–
155. See also an online database about Zhong Lihe: http://cls.hs.yzu.edu.tw/ZHONGLIHE/01/main_01.htm.
[35] See http://paper-republic.org/authors/zhong-lihe/, a biography of Zhong Lihe contributed by T. M.
McClellan, a scholar and English translator of Zhong Lihe's major works. For a comprehensive English

Mukden/Shenyang in Manchukuo mixes elements of Chinese and Japanese culture, which may have met Zhong's cultural expectations—his bilingual education in Taiwan under the Japanese colonial rule probably helped him feel comfortable in a strange yet acceptable urban milieu. On the other hand, his strong *yuangxiang* complex, or his longing for an ancestral hometown, a native land, or an old country of his cultural origin, was intensely triggered by his second elder brother's passionate words and mainland souvenirs, and Zhong may have been satisfied in his bold and adventurous journey to the vast land of China. Yet Mukden and Manchukuo become his nightmare and living hell. In Zhong's diary-style story "Gates" (Men 門), the first-person narrator sees Mukden and Manchukuo as "desolate city in ruins" (huangliang de huangcheng feixu 荒涼的荒城廢墟) and "a disheartened and dead place" (hui yu si de difang 灰與死的地方).[36] And the narrator confesses that at heart, he feels a strong sentiment of loneliness, like a stranger in a remote and alienated foreign country.[37] Mr. Yuan, an aged guard of a Manchurian timber storage facility who came from Tianjin, provides a sharp contrast between Mukden and Beijing, and suggests that the narrator should abandon colonial and dying Mukden/Manchuria for Beijing, a warm and welcoming city in the authentic China.[38] Zhong envisioned Beijing, the capital of early Republican China and the center of Chinese culture, as the symbolic "old country," "original hometown," or Chinese motherland in terms of cultural origin and political identification. Yet a deeper crisis emerged from his sojourn in Beijing, which pushed Zhong to reorient and redefine his geopolitical imagination of home and homeland, as well as his cultural identity and authenticity, in his border-crossing travels and literary praxis against the tumultuous backdrop of the second Sino-Japanese War, the Chinese Civil War, and the high Cold War years until 1960. T. M. McClellan's English translation of Zhong Lihe's major works organizes Zhong's stories and sketches composed in Taiwan and mainland China into "formative years," "stories from old country," and "homeland" (in particular Meinong township, the "remote, impoverished hill-country villages and farms of Zhong Lihe's native Hakka district").[39]

---

biography of Zhong Lihe, see Terence Russell, "Zhong Lihe," in *Chinese Fiction Writers, 1950–2000*, ed. Thomas Moran and Ye (Dianna) Xu (Detroit: Gale, Cengage Learning, 2013), 311–318. See also Peng Ruijin 彭瑞金, *Zhong Lihe zhuan* 鍾理和傳 [Biography of Zhong Lihe] (Nantou: Taiwan sheng wenxian weiyuanhui, 1994).

[36] Zhong Lihe, "Men," repr. in *Zhong Lihe daibiaozuo*, 113, 117.

[37] Zhong, "Men," 116.

[38] Ibid., 92.

[39] In his famous "From the Old Country," Zhong confesses, "As I gradually gained in years, I learned from my father's conversation that 'the Old Country' meant China and that 'Old Country people' were the Chinese; China had eighteen provinces, and we had come from Jiaying in Canton province . . . . In the fifth grade of Japanese school I started geography lessons. Here I found that China had become 'Shina' and Chinese people had become 'Shina jin.'. . . All these phrases had specific implications: 'Shina' meant 'decrepit' and

During his stay there in the 1940s, Zhong depicted his Beijing nightmare in his demonstrative novella "Oleander," a mix of loosely structured story and philosophical prose. Through the eyes of Zeng Simian 曾思勉, a cynical intellectual "from the South" (a subtle indicator of Taiwan), Zhong Lihe describes Beijing as a filthy, stinking, diseased, and demoralized city. He concentrates on a crowded and impoverished residential compound in a slum neighborhood, regarding it as a microcosm of the city, as well as a laboratory to explore Chinese national character from the perspectives of a *lüxingjia* 旅行家 (traveler) and/or a *shehuixue zhe* 社會學者 (sociologist) from a foreign land: "The tenement yard corroborated various studies that had been written on the living landscape of Peking people. In other words, this compound was a typical representative of all the courtyard dwellings of the city of Peking."[40] Throughout "Oleander," Zhong reveals a shocking image of modern Beijing in the mid-1940s: the lower-class residents are trapped in modern darkness: "And so they lived—amid smog and dust, filth and anemia, scarcity and bedbugs, poor light and forbearance. No matter how hard they worked, no matter how small and how low— unhealthily how—their hopes for security and material comfort, their lives never improved. On the contrary, life's menace and cruelty toward them only grew."[41]

"Canopy, fish basin, pomegranate" remain three typical urban objects decorating Beijing courtyard houses. Yet in Zhong Lihe's novella, oleander becomes the poverty-stricken household's alternative to pomegranate, symbolizing the misery of a Beijing residential compound occupied by many households. My examination focuses on three complex characteristics of oleander. First, oleander has both toxic and beneficial effects on the heart, and is primarily a poisonous plant, containing compounds that can be lethal to people. I argue that Zhong Lihe intentionally highlights the toxicity of oleander and regards it as the "flower of evil," growing from and shining above the filth of this hygienic and moral hell. As Zhong Lihe underlines in "Oleander," blooming flowers are usually connected with health and bonhomie. Yet in his dystopian portrait, oleander witnesses and accompanies the injustice, misery, ugliness, and sadness in a tiny yet crowded courtyard, the dark side of human society. This Beijing slum is not only glutted with domestic and disgusting garbage like wild pigs' "dark, filthy, damp nests,"[42] but is also marked by crime and prostitution, selfishness and malicious pleasure at other people's misfortune.

'broken-down'; 'Shina jin' meant 'opium addicts' and a 'shameless, filthy race'; 'Shina hei' represented craven cowardice, lack of discipline, and so on." Zhong Lihe, *From the Old Country: Stories and Sketches of China and Taiwan*, trans. T. M. McClellan (New York: Columbia University Press, 2014), 35–36.

[40] Zhong Lihe, "Jiazhutao," 145; Zhong, *From the Old Country*, 63.

[41] Zhong, "Jiazhutao," 171; Zhong, *From the Old Country*, 91.

[42] Zhong, "Jiazhutao," 146; Zhong, *From the Old Country*, 65.

Second, oleander is an evergreen shrub and small tree, and blooms throughout spring, summer, and autumn. It indicates a strong will to live and the capability to survive tough and rough surroundings. While these dishonored Beijing inhabitants in the south side residential compound are depicted as barbarians who enjoy the filthy environment of their pigsty, Zhong Lihe also betrays his surprise at these people's resilient and nonchalant ways of living and surviving, like oleander that is immune from the threats of malnutrition and disease.[43]

Last but not least, oleander is also a fruitless flower, which presents and symbolizes the hopeless future of the underprivileged ghetto in 1940s Beijing. The author Lin Yutang intentionally exhibits the happiness and joy of ordinary Beijing inhabitants and chooses to ignore the pain and misery in the city's impoverished everyday life. In a diary entry, Zhong expresses strong opposition to Lin Yutang's performance of pleasure: "I've read Lin Yutang's *My Country and My People, Between Tears and Laughter* and am currently reading *The Importance of Living* for the second time. It strikes me very strongly that Lin Yutang is just this kind of person, the kind who often misunderstands; who, on seeing a person hanging himself, thinks that person is swinging on a swing." [44] From Zhong's cynical and pessimistic viewpoint, there is no way for these people to be released from the hygienic and moral morass of the counterutopian living hell. They are forever trapped in the prison house of the urban slum. At the end of the novella, Li Jirong, a philosophy student and a doppelgänger of Zeng Simian in this compound, has degenerated from a "warm-hearted humanitarian" to "a melancholic, gloomy" pessimist.[45] Zeng Simian saw two beggars, one old lady "who now seemed almost totally blind," and one young man "without any expression on his face," on West Chang'an Street. Zeng "looked at them with deep sorrow in his heart, ... his feelings were akin to loathing and contempt."[46]

Ying Fenghuang points out the double ignorance of "Oleander" in both Taiwan and mainland China:

The time period in which he wrote it is critical. In 1944, the Second Sino-Japanese War was not yet over, and Beijing was under Japanese government. Although Zhong was an important postwar writer in 1950s Taiwan, this is the only work we have of his predating the end of the war. Moreover, in it he

---

[43] Zhong praises "the yielding but tough adaptability of wild grass" with an ironic tone; see "Jiazhutao," 147; Zhong, *From the Old Country*, 65.

[44] *Zhong Lihe riji* 鍾理和日記 [Zhong Lihe's diary], in *Zhong Lihe quanji* 鍾理和全集 [The complete works of Zhong Lihe], ed. Zhang Liangze 張良澤 (Taipei: Yuanxing chubanshe, 1976), 6:177, quoted in Ying, "The Literary Development of Zhong Lihe and Postcolonial Discourse in Taiwan," 146.

[45] Zhong, "Jiazhutao," 184; Zhong, *From the Old Country*, 106.

[46] Zhong, "Jiazhutao," 185; Zhong, *From the Old Country*, 106.

wrote of his experience of life in occupied Beijing. After the rise of "nativist consciousness" in Taiwan, very few critics looked at *Jiazhutao*. And most literary histories (especially those written in mainland China) simply gloss over it as early and technically immature—if they mention it at all. [47]

Chen Yingzhen 陳映真, a leftist intellectual with a consistent and fervent "Chinese consciousness," conducted the earliest serious study of Zhong's "Oleander." In his pioneering yet cynical article "Yuanxiang de shiluo" (The loss of old homeland), published in 1977, Chen regards Zhong Lihe's Beijing/China image as a distorted and belittled caricature, and argues that Zhong's dystopias of Beijing and China indicates a loss of *yuanxiang* (old homeland) complex, a shortage of positive belief in China as a cultural entity, and a spiritual/identity crisis in his destructive imagination. [48] Fenghuang Ying forcefully challenges Chen Yingzhen's pride and prejudice, and regards Chen's arguments as "an excellent example of how, in the 1970s, the notion of a Chinese ethnic consciousness was turned into an ideology and became a tool with which to criticize literature." [49] Responding to Chen Yingzhen's "Chinese ethic consciousness" as well, Cheng Hsiu-ting highlights "the found" over the "the lost" in Zhong's border-crossing travel—the discovery of a new cultural identification and the affirmation of Taiwan as Zhong's spiritual and physical hometown after he ended his disillusioned and disenchanted journey to Beijing and China. [50] As a scholar and biographer of Zhong Lihe, T. M. McClelland argues that Zhong developed his literary criteria under the influence of the May Fourth writers, particularly Lu Xun, and formed his influential notions on old home and native land from his border-crossing travel. [51] Zhang Chongyang, a mainland scholar, also addresses Zhong's acceptance of the May Fourth stimulus, and points out the perplexity and paradox in his literary writing and cultural identification: as a Taiwanese, Zhong is obsessed with China and embarks on an imagined journey back to his ancestral homeland, but in reality he is shocked and disillusioned by the political and cultural

[47] Ying, "The Literary Development of Zhong Lihe and Postcolonial Discourse in Taiwan," 149.

[48] Chen Yingzhen, "Yuanxiang de shiluo: Shiping *Jiazhutao*" 原鄉的失落：試評《夾竹桃》 [The loss of old homeland: Comments on *Jiazhutao*], *Xiandai wenxue* 現代文學 [Modern literature], literary supplement, no. 1 (July 1977), repr. in Chen Yingzhen, *Gu'er de lishi, lishi de gu'er* 孤兒的歷史，歷史的孤兒 [Orphans' history, and history's orphans] (Taipei: Yuanjing chuban shiye gongsi, 1984), 97–109.

[49] Ying, "The Literary Development of Zhong Lihe and Postcolonial Discourse in Taiwan," 150.

[50] Cheng Hsiu-ting, "Shui de yuanxiang? Shui de shiluo?—Ping Chen Yinzheng dui Zhong Lihe minzu rentong de qujie" 誰的原鄉？誰的失落？──評陳映真對鍾理和民族認同的曲解 [Whose native land? Whose loss?—On Chen Yingzhen's misunderstanding of Zhong Lihe's national identification], *Taiwan wenxue pinglun* 台灣文學評論 [Taiwan literary review] 4 (2005): 160–185.

[51] T. M. McClelland, "Home and the Land: The 'Native' Fiction of Zhong Lihe," *Journal of Modern Literature in Chinese* 9, no. 2 (December 2009): 154–182.

backwardness and depravity in local Beijing and China at large.[52] From the perspectives of guest and host, and hospitality and hostility, Chien-hsin Tsai understands "Oleander" as an illuminating case of a "stranger in his homeland" and the paradoxical struggle between leaving home and returning.[53]

Indeed, Zhong Lihe famously stated about the relation between a native son and his native land, "I am not a patriot, but Old Country blood must flow back to the Old Country before it can stop seething!"[54] Therefore, it is a continuous and crucial issue to locate Zhong's *yuanxiang*, his ancestral homeland, Old Country, and spiritual hometown. The first generation of Beijing sojourners with Taiwan origins and background, including Hong Yanqiu, Zhang Wojun, and Zhang Shenqie, called themselves "fanshu ren" 番薯人 (sweet potato people), and fanshu 番薯 indicates both the geographical shape of Taiwan and the representative, sometime stereotyped, local specialty of Formosa (the beautiful island). During the fifty years of Japanese colonial control, *"fanshu ren"* expressed the bitterness and humiliation of local Taiwanese. And "sweet potato" not only reminds Zhong Lihe of his Taiwan origin and life under Japanese rule but also brings to light new meanings in Republican China—doubly marginal status as a Japanese colonized citizen and a stranger in Beijing. Zhong uses *baishu* instead of *fanshu* to tell his unpleasant and frustrating story in China. In "Baishu de beiai" 白薯的悲哀 (The sadness of sweet potato), Zhong exposes a strong sense of being abandoned by both Beijing and China after Japan surrendered in 1945. When living on Beijing's south side, he repositioned himself as an outsider and sojourner in an alienated city called Beijing. Chien-hsin Tsai states,

> Life in Beijing grew more disconcerting as the Japanese surrendered in 1945. Before, Zhong Lihe was considered Japanese, and now he was Taiwanese—still not Chinese. In fact, the Beijing natives started to refer to people from colonial Taiwan as "sweet potato" with Japan's defeat. The nicknaming was indicative of a problematic redirection of anti-Japanese sentiments to people from Taiwan. The distinction between colonial victimizer and the victimized was willfully

---

[52] Zhang Chonggang 張重崗, "Yuanxiang tiyan yu Zhong Lihe de Beiping xushi" 原鄉體驗與鍾理和的北平敘事 [Zhong Lihe's motherland experience and Beiping narration], in *Zhongguo xiandai wenxue luncong* 中國現代文學論叢 [Forum of modern Chinese literature] 1 (2008): 117–129, repr. in *Zhongyuan lunjian: Dierjie shijie huawen wenxue luntan wenji* 中原論劍：第二屆世界華文文學論壇文集 [China forum: Selected articles from the second Chinese-language literature conference], ed. Zou Youfeng 鄒友峰, Mao Jianhua 冒建華, and Mu Naitang 穆乃堂 (Lanzhou: Gansu renmin meishu chubanshe, 2008), 210–222.

[53] Chien-hsin Tsai, "Of Guest and Host: Zhong Lihe, Hakka, and Sinophone Hospitality," in Shih, Tsai, and Bernards, *Sinophone Studies*, 276–277.

[54] Zhong Lihe, "Yuanxiang ren" 原鄉人, repr. in *Zhong Lihe daibiaozuo*, 13; Zhong, *From the Old Country*, 43.

overlooked to help the restoration of order of Beijing. Trapped in an ongoing political swirl and identity shuffle, it is no wonder that Zhong puzzles over the meaning of being a guest in China whose ancestors came from China.[55]

Zhong uses "the sadness of sweet potato" to indicate the loss of identity for Taiwan sojourners in post-World War II China. The longing to return to the original and eternal *yuanxiang* has been displaced by abjection and lack of belonging in Zhong's literary perception, urban imagination, and cultural memory of 1940s Beijing.

Intriguingly, Lin Haiyin also called herself, and the sojourners in Republic Beijing, the generation of "fanshu zai" 番薯仔 (sweet potato guys).[56] Lin was even called by Zhang Guangzheng 張光正, Zhang Wojun's son, "lao Beijing de 'fanshu zai'" 老北京的 "番薯仔" (sweet potato guy of old Beijing). Yet when she returned to Taiwan, Lin immediately regarded the beautiful island as her first and primary hometown, although she "has often been classified as a writer of Mainland origin, owing partly to the towering success of *Memories of Peking: South Side Stories*, with its genuine flavor of the old capital, and partly to her own perfect Peking accent."[57] The dual hometowns, or the double identity, would not produce a schizophrenic dilemma for Lin Haiyin; Chi Pan-yuan 齊邦媛, a literary scholar, exile writer, and one of the English translators of Lin's representative novel, portrays Lin's mental picture as follows: "Full of memories of the old China of the south side of Peking, she came to Taiwan without any experience of war or being a refugee. It seems that her life had no shadows of desolation. It might be difficult for her to understand the symbolic and omen-like feeling of severance I had felt."[58] Residing in Taiwan for the rest of her life, Lin took Beijing and Taipei as her dual hometowns.

Lin Haiyin was born in Osaka, Japan, and moved with her parents to Beijing in 1923. Her affectionate father, a wealthy and educated Hakka Taiwanese, hated Japanese colonial dominance and relocated his entire family to Beijing, where he died in 1931. Lin graduated from Beiping xinwen zhuanke xuexiao (The Beiping

---

[55] Tsai, "Of Guest and Host," 276–277.

[56] Zhang Guangzheng 張光正, son of Zhang Wojun, contributes an essay, "Lao Beijing de 'fanshu zai': Ji Lin Haiyin qingshaonian shidai de ren he shi" 老北京的 "番薯仔" : 記林海音青少年時代的人和事 [Sweet potato guys: Records of people and stories during Lin Haiyin's youth], in *Lin Haiyin yanjiu lunwenji* 林海音研究論文集 [Collected essays on Lin Haiyin], ed. Shu Yi 舒乙 and Fu Guangming 傅光明 (Beijing: Taihai chubanshe, 2001), 60–71. Zhang Wojun wrote a poem, "Luandu zhilian" 亂都之戀 [Love in a chaotic city] in 1924 to record his love and loss during his Beijing sojourn in warlord China.

[57] Hsiao-yen Peng, "Introduction: Lin Hai-yin's *Memories of Peking: South Side Stories*," trans. Steven K. Luk, in Lin Hai-yin, *Memories of Peking: South Side Stories*, trans. Nancy C. Ing and Chi Pang-yuan (Hong Kong: The Chinese University Press, 2002), xiv.

[58] Chi Pang-yuan, "Severance—for Hai-yin," trans. Nicholas Koss, *The Chinese Pen: Contemporary Chinese Literature from Taiwan* 30 (Spring 2002): 12–13.

School of Journalism, founded by Cheng Shewo in 1933) and became a journalist for *Shijie ribao* (World daily news). Lin returned to Taiwan in 1948, together with her husband He Fan 何凡 (Xia Chengying 夏承楹, 1910–2002) and three children. From 1951 to 1962, she was the editor-in-chief of *Lianfu,* the literary supplementary of *Lianhe bao* (United daily news), and made significant contributions to the localization of Taiwan literature: "At a time when anti-Communist propaganda was a dominant ideological force in literary creation, the *Literary Supplement* under Lin's editorship created a new space where the autonomy of literature was valued,"[59] and it became a greenhouse of nonpolitical literature. Lin was also the founder of the famous literary journal *Chunwenxu* (Pure literature), launched in 1967, and established her own publishing house, Chunwenxue chubanshe, in 1968. In the field of literary culture in Taiwan, Lin is a giant of *fukan* (supplement-based) literature; she discovered representative Taiwan writers including Zhong Lihe, Huang Chunming, Zheng Qingwen, Lin Huiming, and Qideng Sheng, among others, and therefore reshaped the landscape and ecology of contemporary Taiwanese literature. [60]

While "oleander" serves as the title, the keyword, and the leading image of Zhong Lihe's 35,000-word novella about his disheartened memory of south side Beijing, Lin Haiyin, in *Memories of Peking*, depicts a completely different imagery of oleander, a robust flower with a fresh, radiant, and optimistic outlook and a magic remedy for mental illness. Whereas Zhong takes oleander as the flower of evil in dystopian Beijing, Lin foregrounds its colorful blooming and its healing power. Evidently, oleander grows fast, expands quickly, and smoothly adjusts to the specific geographical environment in Beijing. Its red, pink, yellow, or white flowers and bamboolike leaves add unrefined yet bright colors to the shabby south side. Oleander also has a medical use in treating congestive heart disease, thus strengthening and stimulating the heart. In *Memories of Peking*, the oleander is identified as Papa's favorite flower, and Ying-tzu, the innocent, passionate, sincere, and engaging heroine of the novel, wears it to her graduation ceremony, which concludes Lin's bittersweet nostalgia about Republican Beijing. The daughter provides a remedy or cure to her family members and to her traumatized neighbors on the south side.

---

[59] Peng, introduction to *Memories of Peking*, xii.

[60] Chang, *Literary Culture in Taiwan*. Lin Haiyin's other Beijing narratives, from short stories to novellas and essays, include *Hunyin de gushi* 婚姻的故事 [Marriage stories, 1963], *Zhuxin* 燭芯 [Candlewick, 1965], *Liangdi* 兩地 [Two regions, 1966] and *Jiazhu shufang bian* 家住書坊邊 [I lived by Liulichang, 1980]. See also Chi Pang-yuan, "Chaoyue beihuan de tongnian" 超越悲歡的童年 [Beyond joyous and sorrowful childhood], repr. in Shu and Fu, eds., *Lin Haiyin yanjiu lunwenji*, 92–97.

In *Memories of Peking*, Lin Haiyin, a "Taiwan Girl in Beijing" who views Beijing as her second hometown, contributes a teenager's *bildungsroman*, which develops and flourishes in a vague and ambiguous context of the New Cultural Movement and historical events thereafter. In the opening chapter, "Winter Sun, Childhood Years, the Camel Caravan," Lin Haiyin sets the basic tone for her memories of Beijing:

Summer had gone, autumn was over, winter had arrived and the camel caravan was back again; but childhood had passed away, never to return. And I would never again be so silly as to imitate the camel's chewing under the winter sun. But how I miss the people and places of those childhood years spent in the south side of the city of Peking! I said to myself, go ahead and write it all down. Let the reality of childhood days pass away, but keep the spirit of childhood forever alive.[61]

Camels serve as an eye-catching and memorable image of old Beijing in the Republican era. For Shen Congwen, camels indicate the urban spectacle and ethos of humanity in everyday life. A sojourner in Beijing, Shen Congwen vividly describes his impression of the camel caravan, a significant form of public transportation in 1920s Beijing, from which he discovers and decodes the quintessence of the city: "When first arriving in the metropolis, one can always catch sight of camels in the streets. These animals are full of experiences of wind and dust, and their eyes are brimming with sorrows and worries, but their steps are extremely firm and steady."[62] Tsurumi Yūsuke (1885–1973), a Japanese politician, orator, author, playwright, and international traveler, foregrounds the majestic manners of Beijing camels and is shocked and amazed by the harmonic coexistence of animals and human beings in urban scenes hardly to be seen in Japanese city life. Beijing street camels give him an unforgettable impression of nobility and Platonic elitism.[63] However, what Ying-tzu, the little girl from Taiwan, captures and remembers is the camels' ugly faces and long teeth, and their funny way of eating and chewing. Only with time can she gradually understand and appreciate that camels suggest the composed and tranquil lifestyle and the calm attitude of Beijing inhabitants. It is also the camels, an unforgettable token of Lin's Beijing experience, that inspired her to compose *Memories of Peking* with a strong sentiment of nostalgia: "Silently I reminisce, slowly I begin to

---

[61] Lin, *Memories of Peking*, 6.

[62] Shen Congwen, *Congwen zizhuan* 從文自傳 [My autobiography], in *Shen Congwen quanji* [Complete works of Shen Congwen] (Taiyuan: Beiyue wenyi chubanshe, 2002), 13:365.

[63] Tsurumi Yūsuke 鶴見祐輔, "Beijing de meili" 北京的魅力 [Beijing charms], trans. Lu Xun, in Tsurumi Yūsuke, *Sixiang, shanshui, renwu* 思想，山水，人物 [Thoughts, landscape, figures], trans. Lu Xun (Shanghai: Beixin shuju, 1929), 245–265.

write. I see the caravan of camels approaching under the winter sun, I hear the pleasing tinkle of the bells, and childhood days return once again into my heart."[64]

Memories of Peking consists of five episodes: "Hui-an Hostel," "Let Us Go and See the Sea," "Lan I-niang," "Donkey Rolls," and "Papa's Flowers Have Fallen." Lin Haiyin adopts the form of a female Bildungsroman to configure a female image of Beijing. The imagery of the city is crystallized in a series of female characters: the madwoman Hsiu-chen, the abandoned little girl Niu-erh, the educated and modern lady Lan I-niang, who is the ex-concubine of Ying-tzu's father's friend, and the diligent yet unfortunate servant Sung Ma. With limited first-person perspective, Ying-tzu observes her lifeworld, from Hui-an Hostel to Xinlianzi alleyway and to Hufangqiao district, all on the south side of the city. She grows up from seven to thirteen years old, remaining an innocent girl with healing powers: she befriends and remedies the madness of Hsiu-chen, and enables the family reunion of Hsiu-chen and Niu-erh; she communicates with the kindhearted thief who sacrifices himself to support his young brother's schooling; she balances the tricky triangular relationship among her father, her mother, and the lady Lan I-niang, and solves the crisis among the adults; she discovers servant Sung Ma's sadness and sorrows, and consoles and helps her through grief over the loss of her beloved children.

For a moment, the south side of the city is a happy retreat for Ying-tzu and Niu-erh.[65] As an innocent girl relocating to a new place, Ying-tzu is not homesick, but vaguely recalls her homeland Taiwan: "I remembered Mama had said that we had come from our homeland far, faraway; an island surrounded by water. We came by a large steamship, then by train, before arriving in Peking. I once asked Mama when we would be going back and she said not for a long time. It was so difficult coming over so we would have to stay for some years."[66] When Zhong Lihe sojourned in Beijing from age twenty-six to thirty-two, he became a disappointed and angry young man, if not a "madman" in Lu Xun's sense, and his heart and mind were haunted and tortured by the enormous tensions, contradictions, and confrontations between his *yuanxiang* fantasy and Mukden-Beijing disenchantment. In sharp contrast, Ying-tzu, a little girl with "a heart of gold," does not feel the pain of homesickness or suffer from the prejudice of estrangement in her initial years on the south side. Soon the happiness is challenged, and eventually it is gone. Hsiu-chen and Niu-erh make a plan to flee from Beijing to Tianjin to start a new life, but the two are killed in a train accident. The young thief hides himself in a haunted place after successfully stealing treasures from a rich family, but is eventually arrested and executed by the local police. Lan I-niang marries an aged yet rich businessman and leaves the south side of

---

[64] Lin, *Memories of Peking*, 6.

[65] Ibid., 46.

[66] Ibid., 34.

Beijing. Sung Ma loses her two kids in the countryside and eventually goes back to her home village. At the end of *Memories of Peking*, Ying-tzu attends her graduation ceremony held in the newly built school auditorium.

> On the left lapel of my uniform jacket was a pink oleander which Mama had plucked from our courtyard and pinned on for me before I left for school. She said, "The oleander was planted by your papa. Wearing it will be as if Papa were watching you on the stage."[67]

While her papa is ill in the hospital, Ying-tzu wears a pink oleander from the oleander tree he planted, represents the graduating class to receive the diplomas, and delivers the farewell speech in the graduation ceremony. Lin ends her Beijing memoirs with the following remarks: "Walking through the courtyard, I looked at the drooping oleander plant and said silently to myself,

> Papa's flowers have fallen
> And I am no longer a child."[68]

The fall of the oleander is a turning point, indicating the father's death, the loss of fatherly love. When Ying-tzu wears the oleander to her graduation ceremony, the flower not only signifies the closure of her innocent childhood in the city but also marks the painful rite of passage into adolescence: "I am no longer a child." The ending is laden with nostalgia, sadness, uncertainty, and a poignant sense of loss.

Mei Chia-ling interprets Lin's *Memories of Peking* as a diasporic and sojourning Bildungsroman narrated from an innocent girl's point of view.[69] Lin Zheng regards Lin Haiyin as an immigrant and an outsider in Beijing, and focuses on her cartographical eyes and conscious remapping of the south side with the help of maps, street names, historical locations, and geographical sites.[70] *Chengnan jiushi* was also adapted into a film (English title: *My Memories of Old Beijing*) by Wu Yigong 吳貽弓, a mainland director based in Shanghai, in 1982. The film was a sensation,

---

[67] Ibid., 288.

[68] Ibid., 302.

[69] Mei Chia-ling 梅家玲 approaches both Lin Haiyin and Ling Shuhua in "Nüxing xiaoshuo de dushi xiangxiang yu wenhua jiyi" 女性小說的都市想象與文化記憶 [Urban imagination and cultural memory in female novels], in Chen and Wang, *Beijing*, 390–409. See also her *Xingbie, haishi jiaguo? Wuling yu bajiuling niandai Taiwan xiaoshuolun* 性別，還是家國？五〇與八、九〇年代台灣小說論 [Gender or nation? Criticism of contemporary Taiwan fiction] (Taipei: Maitian, 2004), 127–155.

[70] Lin Zheng 林崢, "Cong *Jiujing suoji* dao *Chengnan jiushi*" 從《舊京瑣記》到《城南舊事》 [From *Trivial records of old capital* to *Memories of Peking*], *Zhongguo xiandai wenxue yanjiu congkan* 中國現代文學研究叢刊 [Modern Chinese literature studies] 1 (2012): 122–136.

triggered a nationwide nostalgia for Republican Beijing, and won the Best Director Prize at the third annual Golden Rooster Awards, as well as the Golden Eagle Prize (Best Feature Film) at the Manila International Film Festival in 1983. In 1999, *Asia Weekly* selected *My Memories of Old Beijing* as one of the one hundred best Chinese-language films of the twentieth century. Fenghuang Ying makes a detailed comparison between the literary and filmic texts and their intertextual liaison in terms of gender, politics, and the "lost and found" in the film adaptation: the construction of the old Beijing residential compound in a Shanghai film studio, the political criticism of the Nationalist government in Republican China, the loss of Taiwan dialects, and the female consciousness developed in the south side neighborhood and the plebian community.[71] Examining the film adaptation of *Chengnan jiushi*, Jerome Silbergeld takes Lin's south side of Beijing as an

> impoverished stage on which Ying-tzu's tales of innocent friendships and human ruin are set. These remembered relics of a distant past are retained only in the mind of the Taiwanese narrator, for whom time and distance provide a perspective on original events as a material ruin does of an original monument: what were once mere artifacts to the innocent child become the design of cultural history to the adult.[72]

I argue that this allegorical and artistic understanding of the material things and objects in a young Taiwan sojourner's mind as a belated representation of "human ruin" or a material form of cultural history and nostalgic memory displays and exhibits a rich spectrum of human feelings and warm sympathy, evidenced in Ying-tzu's oleander-type medical treatment and cardinal strength. I would even suggest that Ying-tzu, the childhood double of Lin Haiyin in *Memories of Peking*, can be symbolically understood as an oleander flower, which blooms on the plebian south side, functions as a warm and colorful ornament amid a miserable life, and disseminates seeds of vitality in the neighborhood and Beijing at large.

In *Dissemination*, Jacques Derrida rereads Plato's *Phaedrus* and focuses particularly on the Greek keyword *pharmakon*. Barbara Johnson points out in her translator's note that "the word *pharmakon* . . . in Greek can mean both 'remedy' and 'poison.' "[73] Derrida further renders *pharmakon* as "remedy," "recipe," "poison,"

---

71 Fenghuang Ying 應鳳凰, "Bijiao Lin Haiyin *Chengnan jiushi* de xiaoshuo yu dianying" 比較林海音《城南舊事》的小說與電影 [A comparison of the novel and the film of Lin Haiyin's *My Memories of Beijing*], *Taiwanxue yanjiu* 台灣學研究 (Taiwan studies) 3 (1996): 1–15.

72 Silbergeld, *China into Film*, 69.

73 Derrida, *Dissemination*, xxv. Christopher Norris discuss Derrida's understanding of Plato in his chapter "Derrida on Plato: Writing as Remedy and Cure," in *Derrida* (Cambridge, MA: Harvard University Press, 1987), 28–62.

"drug," "philter," and so forth.[74] Oleander may well indicate the double function of poison and remedy, respectively evidenced in Zhong's and Lin's leading Beijing imagery. Zhong Lihe detects the poisons disseminated into all corners of the residential compound, reveals the poisonous nature of the filthy and demoralized urban life, and launches severe criticisms of the negative national characteristics in his "old country" China. In contrast, Lin Haiyin captures Ying-tzu's tireless efforts in providing physical and mental remedies, which leave traces in a part of Beijing colored by Lin's bittersweet nostalgia.

The imagery of oleander on the south side of Beijing functions like a reflexive mirror, a lasting trope, or a penetrating metaphor to envision and manifest the tension and relation of the "Taiwan complex" and the "China complex," as well as the identity crisis and identity formation in Zhong's and Lin's literary praxis, urban observations, and cultural reflections. Oleander, a signifier of *pharmakon*/writing, witnesses and reveals the affective traces in Zhong's and Lin's atlas of emotions, and the dialectic of sojourning mind and *yuanxiang* heart that centers around confusion and obsession, alienation and assimilation, detachment and attachment, and dislocation and relocation.

IN(EX)CLUSION AND CHIVALRIC GEOGRAPHY

Exception and example constitute the two modes by which a set tries to find and maintain its own coherence. But while the exception is, as we saw, an inclusive exclusion (which thus serves to include what is excluded), the example instead functions as an exclusive inclusion.

—GIORGIO AGAMBEN

Jin Yong may well be the most widely read novelist in the Sinophone world since the 1950s. His fifteen martial-arts novels, originally serialized in newspapers, later revised and compiled in thirty-six volumes, have remained popular across the geopolitical territories of Hong Kong, Taiwan, mainland China, Southeast Asia, and other Sinophone regions from the high Cold War years to the post-Cold War era. Regarded as "quanshijie huaren de gongtong yuyan" 全世界華人的共同語言 (the common language of global Chinese communities), Jin Yong's novels have been continually republished and

---

[74] Derrida, *Dissemination*, 77. Derrida also notices and addresses the ambivalence of *pharmakon*: "If the *pharmakon* is 'ambivalent,' it is because it constitutes the medium in which opposites are opposed, the movement and the play that links them among themselves, reverses them or makes one side cross over into the other (soul/body, good/evil, inside/outside, memory/forgetfulness, speech/writing, etc.) . . . . The *pharmakon* is the movement, the locus, and the play: (the production of) difference" (127).

adapted for films, television series, stage performances, comic books, animations, video games, and theme parks.[75]

This section considers Jin Yong's three martial-arts novels, *Shujian enchou lu* 書劍恩仇錄 (*The Book and the Sword*, serialized in 1955–1956, revised in 1975, newly revised in 2002), *Bixue jian* 碧血劍 (The sword stained with royal blood, serialized in 1956–1957, revised in 1975, newly revised in 2004) and *Lujing ji* 鹿鼎記 (*The Deer and the Cauldron*, serialized in 1969–1972, revised in 1981, newly revised in 2006)[76] to examine his diasporic, chivalric remapping of imperial Beijing and how it addresses some key issues in the Sinophone discourse. Created in the British Crown Colony in the Cold War era,[77] Jin Yong's fiction employs the narrative strategies of inclusion and exclusion to traverse the real and the imagined, supplementary and subversive histories, and the imperial center and its peripheries. Set against the backdrop of the Ming-Qing dynastic transformation, Jin Yong's three novels chart the topography of the imperial capital, in particular the Forbidden City (the "Great Within"), in relation to other locations, including the Gobi in the Xinjiang Uygur region, Manchuria, the Russian Empire, the Jiangnan region, Taiwan, and islands in the southern seas (Brunei in Southeast Asia). Beijing as the imperial capital and political center is defined by its geopolitical and geopoetic relationships with other

---

[75] See Chen Pingyuan, *Qiangu wenren xiake meng: Wuxia xiaoshuo leixing yanjiu* 千古文人俠客夢：武俠小說類型研究 [Chivalric dreams of the literati: A generic study of martial arts fiction] (Beijing: Renmin wenxue chubanshe, 1992); Yan Jiayan, *Jin Yong xiaoshuo lun gao* 金庸小說論稿 [Treatises on Jin Yong's fiction], rev. ed. (Beijing: Beijing daxue chubanshe, 2007); Weijie Song 宋偉杰, *Cong yule xingwei dao wutobang chongdong: Jin Yong xiaoshuo zai jiedu* 從娛樂行為到烏托邦衝動：金庸小說再解讀 [From entertainment activity to utopian impulse: Rereading Jin Yong's novels] (Nanjing: Jiangsu renmin chubanshe, 1999); John C. Hamm, *Paper Swordsmen: Jin Yong and the Modern Chinese Martial Arts Novel* (Honolulu: University of Hawai'i Press, 2005); Ann Huss and Jianmei Liu, eds., *The Jin Yong Phenomenon: Chinese Martial Arts Fiction and Modern Chinese Literary History* (Youngstown, NY: Cambria Press, 2007); and Petrus Liu, *Stateless Subjects: Chinese Martial Arts Literature and Postcolonial History* (Ithaca, NY: Cornell East Asia Program, 2011).

[76] Jin Yong's serialized martial-arts novels are collectively known as the *jiuban* (old or original versions). Between 1970 and 1980, he thoroughly revised the *jiuban*, and the novels were republished in book form in Hong Kong, Taibei, and Beijing in what is called the *xinban* (new edition) or *xiuding ban* (revised edition). According to Jin Yong's secretary, Li Yijian, "While Jin Yong's own intellectual cultivation, artistic genius, and creative drive have received considerable attention, what is often ignored is that the success of his *wuxia* novels is ultimately a result of the author's having spent a full ten years revising his novels *after* they came out in serialized form, painstakingly rereading, adding, deleting, revising, and polishing them. The Jin Yong texts which contemporary readers browse and which critics study, are precisely those editions which are the product of ten years of revision and have undergone a canonical literary 'rewriting.'" See Li Yijian, "'Rewriting' Jin Yong's Novels into the Canon: A Consideration of Jin Yong Novels as Serialized Fiction," in Ann and Liu, eds., *The Jin Yong Phenomenon*, 74.

[77] See Liu Yichang 劉以鬯, "Wushi niandai chuqi de xianggang wenxue" 五十年代初期的香港文學 [Hong Kong literature in the early 1950s], in *Liu Yichang juan* 劉以鬯卷 [Volume of Liu Yichang] (Hong Kong: Sanlian shudian, 1991), 361–370; William Tay 鄭樹森 (Zheng Shusen), "Tan sishi nian lai xianggang wenxue de

discursive and geographic locations such as *zhongyuan* 中原 (Central plains), *jiangnan* 江南 (the Jiangnan region), its borderlands, and the vast seas.

Born in Haining, Zhejiang Province, in 1924, Jin Yong, the pen name of Zha Liangyong, also known as Louis Cha Leung Yung and Louis Cha, came to this British colony in 1948 as an international telex editor for the Hong Kong office of the newspaper *Ta Kung Pao* (formerly *L'Impartial*). In 1950, he traveled to Beijing to be interviewed by the Ministry of Foreign Affairs of the People's Republic, but his dream of becoming a diplomat was shattered that year when his father was labeled a counterrevolutionary landlord and executed. In 1952 he moved to *Xin wanbao* 新晚報 (The new evening post), and, invited by his friend and colleague Liang Yusheng 梁羽生 (pen name of Chen Wentong 陳文統, 1924–2009), he used the pen name Jin Yong to start his literary career with serialized chivalric fiction, *Shujian enchou lu* (The book and the sword), in 1955.[78] With *Longhu dou jinghua* (Dragon and tiger vie in the capital), a chivalric story that Liang himself had started serializing in *Xin wanbao* a year earlier, this martial-arts fantasy launched the formation of the New School of martial-arts fiction, which soon kindled the flame of passion among readers in Hong Kong, Singapore, and other Sinophone communities in Southeast Asia, and, in the years that followed, Taiwan and eventually the PRC. In her study of Cold War Hong Kong culture, Xiaojue Wang examines the antagonistic yet mutually dependent relationship between the cultural left and right and points out that the rise of New School martial-arts fiction directly resulted from the promotion of the leading leftist newspaper, *Xin wanbao*.[79] During the heyday of the Cold War, when the martial-arts genre was censored in both the Communist and the Nationalist regimes, the British Crown Colony became the unexpected birthplace of this new fiction. New School martial-arts narrative not only bespeaks the intricate relationship between literature

---

shengcun zhuangtai: Zhimin zhuyi, lengzhan niandai yu bianyuan kongjian" 談四十年來香港文學的生存狀態——殖民主義、冷戰年代與邊緣空間 [The ecology of Hong Kong literature, 1950s–1990s: Colonialism, Cold War era, and marginal space], in *Sishi nian lai de zhongguo wenxue* 四十年來中國文學 [Chinese literature, 1950s–1990s], ed. Zhang Baoqin 張寶琴, Shao Yuming 邵玉銘, and Ya Xian 瘂弦 (Taipei: Lianhe wenxue, 1995), 50–58; Wang Gungwu 王賡武, ed., *Xianggang shi xinbian* 香港史新編 [New Hong Kong history] (Hong Kong: Sanlian shudian, 1997); Wang Hongzhi 王宏志, Li Xiaoliang 李小良, and Chen Qingqiao 陳清僑, *Fouxiang xianggang* 否想香港 [Negating Hong Kong] (Taipei: Maitian, 1997); Wang Hongzhi 王宏志, *Lishi de chenzhong* 歷史的沈重 [Burdens of history] (Hong Kong: Oxford University Press, 2000); Zhao Xifang 趙稀方, *Xiaoshuo xianggang* 小說香港 [Narrating Hong Kong] (Beijing: Sanlian shudian, 2003); and Wang, *Ruci fanhua*.

[78] In 1932 Zha started to read Pingjiang Buxiaosheng's *Jianghu qi xia zhuan* [Stories of amazing knights-errant in the world of adventure, 1924–1930], a pioneering masterpiece of old-school martial-arts fiction; Gu Mingdao's *Jindai xiayi yingxiong zhuan* [Stories of chivalric heroes from the recent era, 1926–1929], which depicts such historical figures as Huo Yuanjia, the founder of the Jingwu Athletic Association, and Gu's *Huangjiang nüxia* (The swordswoman of Huangjiang, 1929).

[79] Wang, *Modernity with a Cold War Face*, 271–274.

and politics, but more importantly, attests to the special geopolitical and geopoetic conjunctions in which Jin Yong's literary imaginations of Beijing are imbedded.

Serialized in *Xin wanbao* from February 8, 1955, to September 5, 1956, Jin Yong's first tour de force, *The Book and the Sword*, was an instant success. It depicts the quest of the secret society, *Honghua hui* 紅花會 (Red Flower Society), in alliance with an Islamic tribe in northwestern China, to overthrow the Manchu Qing dynasty and restore Han Chinese rule. Chen Jialuo 陳家洛, helmsman of the Red Flower Society, becomes involved in a love triangle with two Islamic sisters. Chen struggles between the anti-Manchu mission and his personal romantic liaisons. Later Chen learns that Emperor Qianlong is not a Manchu but a Han Chinese; even more shockingly, Qianlong is actually his older brother, who was switched at birth with Emperor Yongzheng's 雍正 (1678–1735) daughter. Chen and his companions take Qianlong hostage to persuade him to acknowledge his ethnicity and assist the anti-Manchu cause. Qianlong is forced to take an oath of alliance, which he later renounces. After a second defeat by the Red Flower Society, Qianlong agrees to a truce. Chen and his friends retreat to the Islamic western regions of the Qing Empire. Jin Yong's debut establishes the basic features of his chivalric geographic map of the Chinese Empire. In *The Book and the Sword*, Beijing and the imperial frontier are mutually constructed and defined in ethnic, familial, political, and romantic terms.

Jin Yong's second martial-arts novel, *Bixue jian,* was serialized in *Xianggang shangbao* 香港商報 (*Hong Kong Commercial Daily*) from January 1 to December 31, 1956. It is set at the time of the fall of the Ming dynasty in 1644 and centers on the adventures of Yuan Chengzhi 袁承志, the fictional son of Yuan Chonghuan 袁崇煥 (1584–1630), the famous Ming general who defeated Nurhaci 努爾哈赤 (1559–1626) and was later wronged and executed by the Emperor Chongzhen 崇禎 (1611–1644). Tutored by the martial-arts master Mu Renqing 穆仁清, Yuan Chengzhi grows up an able martial artist and joins forces with the rebel leader Li Zicheng 李自成 (1606–1645) to overthrow the corrupt Ming regime and avenge his father. In his journey of adventure, he attempts to assassinate the ruler of the Manchu invaders and later the Emperor Chongzhen, sabotages a battery of cannons supplied to the Ming army by foreigners, and finances the rebellion with a treasure he discovers in Nanjing. The Ming Empire collapses and falls to the Manchus, and Li Zicheng's army turns out to be equally corrupt and brutal. Disappointed with the situation, Yuan Chengzhi leaves China and sails to Brunei with his lover and friends. Traversing the boundaries between the Ming, the peasant rebellion force, and the Manchu Qing, between Chinese territory, the West (represented by the Portuguese artillery), and the southern isle, *The Sword Stained with Royal Blood* continues exploring and expanding the geopolitical imaginations unfolded around Beijing.

Hailed as his most important work, Jin Yong's final book, the anti-martial-arts novel *Luding ji* (translated as *The Deer and the Cauldron: A Martial Arts Novel*,

1997–2002) was serialized in *Ming Pao* from October 24, 1969, to September 23, 1972. The illiterate but sly and witty teenager Wei Xiaobao 韋小寶 (Trinket) was born to a prostitute in a Yangzhou brothel during the Qing dynasty. He makes his way to Beijing and develops a close friendship with the young Emperor Kangxi 康熙 (1654–1722). The antihero Wei has a series of turbulent adventures involving court politics, the martial-arts world, secret societies, the Lamaist section of the Wutai Mountains, the Koxinga (Zheng Chenggong 鄭成功, 1624–1662) court in Taiwan, the satrap Wu Sangui's 吳三桂 (1612–1678) ambitions in Yunnan, and the border negotiations with Russia leading to the Treaty of Nerchinsk of 1689. For his accomplishments, Wei is rewarded with wealth and titles of nobility; he also gains respect from the anti-Manchu secret societies for eliminating tyrannical officials and defending China from foreign invaders. When his conflicting loyalties become too uncomfortable, Wei returns to Yangzhou and later Dali City in northwester Yunnan Province and leads a reclusive life with his seven wives.

Lin Yiliang 林以亮 describes *The Deer and the Cauldron* as "a roller-coaster of a novel, packed with thrills, with fun, rage, humour, and abuse, written in a style that flows and flashes like quicksilver."[80] While *The Book and the Sword* and *The Sword Stained with Royal Blood* map out a connection between Han and non-Han Chinese, between the center and the periphery of the Chinese Empire, Jin Yong's final work greatly complicates this imperial geography. Whereas Chen Jialuo and Yuan Chengzhi often hesitate and suffer from ethnic confrontations and conflicting notions of political, romantic, and cultural loyalty, Wei Xiaobao, who is similarly placed at the front line of such contestations, is rarely concerned about these ambiguities. Or, Wei's identity is precisely defined by his adept yet arbitrary movement between ambivalent positions. Since his mother had Han, Manchu, Mongolian, Muslim, and even Tibetan clients when he was conceived, Wei's ethnic identity remains a mystery. The author goes to great lengths to depict Wei's mixed and often distorted ethical values, historical memories, and cultural imaginations, which mainly derived from listening to the storytellers in the teahouses. The English translator of the novel, John Minford, notes that "Wei Xiaobao's ignorant misuses of idioms and allusions are common, and he is completely unperturbed."[81] Wei's poor knowledge of idioms and his distortions of their meanings remind the reader of the hybrid coexistence and hierarchical use of English, Cantonese, and Chinese in Hong Kong. Wei's messy fund of knowledge is symptomatic of the disorderly historical experience of colonized people.[82]

---

[80] Lin Yiliang (Lin I-Liang, or Stephen Soong 宋淇), *Wuge fangwen* 五個訪問 [Five interviews] (Xianggang: Wenyi shuwu, 1972).

[81] Ibid.

[82] Lam Ling Hon 林凌瀚, "Wenhua gongye yu wenhua rentong" 文化工業與文化認同 [Cultural industry and cultural identity], in *Wenhua xiangxiang yu yishi xingtai* 文化想像與意識形態 [Cultural imagination and ideology],

In his two letters to Jin Yong respectively in 1966 and 1970, Shixiang Chen 陳世驤 (Shih-hsiang Chen) shared how he and his colleagues (including T. A. Hsia, Lien-sheng Yang 楊聯陞, and Shiing-Shen Chern 陳省身) enjoyed reading Jin Yong's works, and stated that his martial-arts novels "jiguan tiancai, yibiao shiyun" 既闚天才, 亦表世運 (manifest the author's own genius and speak to the conditions of the age).[83] Hsiao-hung Chang 張小虹 remarks that Jin Yong skillfully inserts the romantic "affairs of the heart into the violent fury of swords and daggers, with the result being that martial arts and romance become equally perilous and soul-stirring narrative paradigms, which mutually reinforce each other in his work."[84] John Christopher Hamm notes that "gradually extricating itself from the dynastic and territorial concerns that govern the early works," the vision of an essentialized and celebratory Chinese cultural identity "locates itself within a timeless, mandala-like mythic geography; simultaneously, it asserts the priority of *individual emotional experience*—expressed above all in romantic relationships—over political and ethnic allegiances."[85] From the perspective of the Cold War ideology and identity politics, Petrus Liu states that Jin Yong "develops a unique theory of the subject," "stateless subjects . . . in the beginning years of the Cold War when Mao's China descends into a permanent arms economy."[86]

How to map out the imperial geography in ethnic, linguistic, political, and romantic terms constitutes the central focus of all three novels. With Beijing placed as the geographical, symbolic, and political center of the empire, these works set out to chart its relations to other places, including its borderlands, which in turn redefine Beijing's position. The making, assembling, uncovering, or possessing of maps constitute crucial themes in the process of illustrating the geographic parameters. In *The Sword Stained with Royal Blood*, seeing no hope in the Central Plains that have been taken over by the Manchu, Yuan Chengzhi leads his followers to an island in the South Seas. On his maritime expedition, he follows a map, which the Portuguese captain he once defeated presents him. Yuan's sailing off to a southern island is reminiscent of both Li Jun's 李俊 island refuge in Siam 暹羅 in Ming loyalist Chen Chen's 陳忱 (1615–1670) *Shuihu houzhuan* 水滸後傳 (Sequel to the water margin) as well

ed. Chen Qingqiao (Hong Kong: Oxford University Press, 1997): 229–253; Song, *Cong yule xingwei dao wutobang chongdong*, 138–184.

[83] Chen Shixiang (Chen Shih-hsing) 陳世驤, "Chen Shixiang xiansheng shuhan" 陳世驤先生書函 [Letters to Jin Yong], April 22, 1966, and November 20, 1970, repr. in *Tianlong babu* [The demigods and semidevils] (Beijing: Sanlian shudian, 1994), 1975.

[84] Hsiao-hung Chang, "'What Sort of Thing Is Sentiment?' Gifts, Love Tokens, and Material Evidence in Jin Yong's Novels," in *Rethinking Chinese Popular Culture*, ed. Carlos Rojas and Eileen Cheng-yin Chow (New York: Routledge, 2009), 235–261.

[85] Hamm, *Paper Swordsmen*, 79.

[86] Petrus Liu, *Stateless Subjects*, 107–200.

as Zheng He's 鄭和 (1371–1433) leading the Ming treasure fleet to the western sea to explore new territories for the Ming Empire. There have been many interpretations that associate Yuan's dislocation with the 1949 KMT retreat to Taiwan.[87] John Christopher Hamm points out that, although the novel is set in contemporary social historical contexts, the significance of Yuan's departure for the island lies "less in any specific representation of contemporary politics than in its expression of the 'Central Plains Syndrome' and its mapping of the relationship between the discursive territory of the martial-arts novel and that of life in contemporary Hong Kong."[88] The cartography of imperial territory also plays a key role in *The Deer and the Cauldron*, as Wei Xiaobao gets involved in the border negotiations between the Qing and Russian empires and assembling the map to locate the buried treasure that will help force the Manchu out of the Central Plains and restore Han Chinese domination.

Just as the imperial borderlands need to be investigated and recharted, the center of the empire defies a definite spatial or political mapping. In Jin Yong's martial-arts world, the Forbidden City is an intricate maze that can hardly be navigated even with the help of a map. In *The Sword Stained with Royal Blood*, after the chivalric hero, Yuan Chengzhi, enters the Forbidden City, his sense of orientation attained from the martial-arts space of *jianghu* 江湖 (rivers and lakes) is totally in vain, and he gets lost. In his mission to assassinate the emperor, Yuan finds himself trapped deep in the labyrinth of the Forbidden City. Rather than locating Emperor Chongzhen in Qianqing Palace 乾清宮, he ended up in Ningshou Palace 寧壽宮 of the Princess Changping 長平公主 (1629–1646). As a result of his disorientation, the chivalric endeavor to seek poetic justice for the common people takes an unexpected turn to the development of a romantic relationship between the hero and the princess.

In *The Deer and the Cauldron*, as Wei Xiaobao is forced to lead the way to the Forbidden City to help the swordsmen assassinate the Emperor Kangxi, he warns them that even if they manage to enter the heavily guarded imperial palace, they will by no means find the exact location of the emperor among the multitude of buildings. When asked to offer a map of the "Great Within," Wei does not refuse:

This Trinket (Wei Xiaobao) proceeded to do, blinding them with another (but much longer) series of names of buildings and compounds as he took

[87] See, for instance, Wang Qiugui 王秋桂, ed., *Jin Yong xiaoshuo guoji xueshu yantaohui lunwenji* 金庸小說國際學術研討會論文集 [Proceedings of the international conference on Jin Yong's novels] (Taibei: Yuanliu, 1999); Sylvia Li-chun Lin 林麗君, ed., *Jin Yong xiaoshuo yu ershi shiji zhongguo wenxue* 金庸小說與二十世紀中國文學國際研討會論文集 [Jin Yong's novel and the twentieth-century Chinese literature] (Hong Kong: Ming He she, 2000); Wu Xiaodong 吳曉東 and Ji Birui 計璧瑞, eds., *2000 Beijing Jin Yong xiaoshuo guoji yantaohui lunwenji* 2000 北京金庸小說國際研討會論文集 [Proceedings of the international conference on Jin Yong's novels in Beijing 2000] (Beijing: Beijing daxue chubanshe, 2002).

[88] Hamm, *Paper Swordsmen*, 66.

them on a "guided tour" of the Forbidden City. After all, he couldn't see how it could really do any harm. He started with the Meridian Gate, directly behind the Gate of Heavenly Peace, then led them over the five-fold Bridge of Golden Water, and on through the three Great Halls—of Supreme Harmony, Middle Harmony, and Harmony Protected—then through the Gate of the Imperial Ancestors, and on to the Imperial Kitchens (in his former identity as Laurel Goong-goong he had been attached to these kitchens); then through the Palace of Heavenly Purity, and into the women's apartments, the Place of Female Repose and the Palace of Maternal Tranquility; thence into the Imperial Gardens; and northward to the Hall of Nurturing the Mind; and on, and on.

Lady Gui did her utmost to commit all of this to memory.[89]

The impenetrability of the imperial center and the difficulty of locating the sovereign do not present a mere spatial challenge for these knights-errant who are used to a different set of rules of navigation. Their disorientation occurs in affective, ethnic, and political terms. Following the noble codes of chivalry, the pair of Gui swordsmen strive to kill the Emperor Kangxi for his non-Han ethnic identity and thus his lack of political legitimacy as Emperor of China proper. The Central Plains should be ruled and governed by Han Chinese, whether by a benevolent emperor or not. Wei Xiaobao, however, attempts to hinder the assassination plot for the sake of his friendship with Kangxi and his belief that the emperor treats his people well. His protection of the emperor is based less on ethnic and political than private, affective criteria.

The ambivalent discursive mapping of a legitimate empire on the Central Plains is represented in a compelling way in the episode of Yuan Chengzhi's plan to assassinate the Manchu ruler Hong Taiji 皇太極 (Abahai, 1592–1643), fourth son of Nurhaci, before the Manchu troops entered the Shanhai Pass and occupied the entire Central Plains. In chapter 13 of *The Sword Stained with Royal Blood*, after Yuan breaks into Hong Taiji's palace during the assassination mission, he eavesdrops on Hong's conversations with his ministers and is deeply impressed by the latter's knowledge of Chinese language and history and capacity as a statesman. Hong Taiji shows sincere care for the livelihood of Han people and says, "[I]n a word, the reason that the southern court gave rise to so many bandits is only because that the

---

[89] The English translation is an abridged edition of the original Chinese version, which lists more names of palaces, pavilions, and porches, making Lady Gui, the female assassin, sense the difficulty of their assassination yet feel grateful for Trinket's map and guidance. See *The Deer and the Cauldron: The Third Book*, translated by John Minford and Rachel May (Hong Kong: Oxford University Press, 2002), 330.

common people have no food. If we succeed in overthrowing the Ming Empire, the first important matter will be to feed the common people." Hearing these words, Yuan Chengzhi, the son of an anti-Manchu general, "only felt that every sentence was reasonable and totally forgot his mission to assassinate him."[90] At this moment of hesitation, Yuan, who is committed to avenge his father's death or the patriotic mission to impede the invasion of non-Chinese, for the first time is exposed to an alternative political legitimacy based on benevolent sovereignty instead of ethnic distinction.

Embedded in Jin Yong's chivalric imaginations of Chinese imperial geography are not just his deep interest in Chinese history but also his awareness of the geographical and discursive separation of Chinese terrains during the Cold War. How to come to terms with the division and boundaries in the British Colony of Hong Kong? How to preserve a historical and cultural consciousness in the peripheral Hong Kong without being subject to any dominant ideological restraints, Communist in Beijing or Nationalist in Taipei? Jin Yong's martial-arts stories complicate the ideological binary confrontation during the Cold War time, and are to be considered in a Sinophone context.

Jin Yong's literary remapping of imperial Beijing, in a multilayered and decentralized fashion, addresses and enriches what Shu-mei Shih calls "geopolitical situatedness, a place-based practice," and the Sinophone areas as places of cultural production.[91] Imperial Beijing is continuously localized and situated in the image gallery and literary landscape of colonial Hong Kong, and the tale of two cities—visible Beijing and invisible Hong Kong—highlights the intriguing dialectic of absence and presence, or more precisely, "absent presence" and "present absence" in Jin Yong's martial-arts fiction. Giorgio Agamben uses "exception" and "example" to inquire into the coherent relation between "inclusive exclusion" and "exclusive inclusion": "Exception" functions as an "inclusive exclusion" (including what is excluded), and "example" serves as an "exclusive inclusion" (excluding what is included).[92] In this sense, Jin Yong's Hong Kong Sinophone articulation and his chivalric topography of imperial Beijing can also be situated in the categories of "example" and "exception" among manifold Sinophone articulations:[93] imperial Beijing

[90] Jin Yong, *Bixue jian* 碧血劍 [The sword stained with royal blood] (Beijing: Sanlian shudian, 1994), 468–469.

[91] Shu-mei Shih, "The Concept of the Sinophone," *PMLA* 126.3 (2011): 717; see also her "Global Literature and the Technologies of Recognition," *PMLA* 119.1 (2004): 16–30; *Visuality and Identity*.

[92] Giorgio Agamben, *Homo Sacer: Sovereign Power and Bare Life*, trans. Daniel Heller-Roazen (Stanford, CA: Stanford University Press, 1998), 21–22.

[93] Jin Yong's position in Hong Kong, Chinese, and Sinophone literary history is yet another significant case of "inclusion" and "exclusion," "exception" and "example": he is incorporated into the literary history compiled by mainland Chinese scholars; his martial-arts fiction is regarded as a model example of Hong Kong and overseas

is an "example" or an "exclusive inclusion" because Beijing is included in Jin Yong's chivalric geography but excluded from the British colony; Hong Kong turns out to be an "exception" or an "inclusive exclusion" in that it is excluded from Jin Yong's Beijing narrative but included in Jin Yong's mechanism of Cold War remapping of the imperial capital.

When examining the literary travels and global imagination of Sinophone literature under the shadow of culturally dominant and geographically remote mainland and homeland, David Der-wei Wang borrows Zhang Ailing's famous proposal, confession, or paradox of "include me out" [94] to call attention to the complex entanglement between the genealogy of Sinophone writing and the geopolitical dissemination of mainland Chinese literary tradition. He further redefines the Sinophone connection with mainland Chinese literature as a possibility of "including China out."[95] I would go further and argue that Jin Yong's Hong Kong Sinophone chivalric remapping of imperial Beijing "includes Beijing out" and "excludes Hong Kong in."

"Absent presence" and "present absence," "exclusive inclusion" and "inclusive exclusion," as well as "including Beijing out" and "excluding Hong Kong in," present and display Jin Yong's writing strategy, covering the topography of the Manchu imperial capital from his modern perspectives of ethnicity and race, Han and non-Han liaisons, as well as imperial, national, and colonial questions. Beijing is geopolitically absent and far away from Hong Kong, yet appears as a significant literary place, and it is represented and dramatized as a core urban setting constantly violated by imagined intervention and bodily transgression in Jin Yong's three martial-arts fictions. Hong Kong is absent in the Beijing narratives, yet the colonial experiences in the British colony stimulate Jin Yong to showcase the utopian impulse of paying imagined face-to-face visits to the (Manchu) emperors in the Forbidden City and getting involved in the critical moments of grand historical events in China, although this chivalric manifestation is fictional and fabricated emplotment, and Beijing appears as a phantom in the paper world of literary imagination rather than as a tangible or accessible material place. In *The Book and the Sword*, Master Yu, Chen Jialuo's mentor, breaks into the Forbidden City, meets with Emperor Qianlong for two

---

literature, and even labeled as a canon of Chinese-language literature. But on the other hand, Jin Yong's literary praxis is also understood as an exception in terms of content, language, genre, and literary categorizations of popular and elite writings.

[94] Zhang Ailing borrowed and interpret Samuel Goldwyn's words "include me out" in her 1979 essay "Bawo baokuo zaiwai" 把我包括在外 [Include me out], in Zhang Ailing 張愛玲, *Wangran ji* 惘然記 (Taipei: Huangguan wenhua chuban gongsi, 2010), 123–124.

[95] David Der-wei Wang, "Zhongwen xiezuo de yuejie yu huigui: Tan huayu yuxi wenxue" 中文寫作的越界與回歸：談華語語系文學 [The transboundary and return of Chinese-language writing: On Sinophone literature], *Shanghai wenxue* 上海文學 [Shanghai literature] 9 (2006): 91–93.

hours, reveals the secret that Emperor Qianlong is Chinese, and urges Qianlong to overthrow the Manchus and restore the throne of China to the Chinese while remaining as emperor himself.[96] In *The Sword Stained with Royal Blood*, Yuan Chengzhi accidentally ventures into Princess Changping's palace, meets and talks with Emperor Chongzhen, reveals his identity as the son of the wronged and framed Yuan Chonghuan, and witnesses the decline of the Ming Empire.[97] In *The Deer and the Cauldron*, Wei Xiaobao lives and grows in the Forbidden City, situated amid court politics, martial-arts assassinations, sexual affairs with imperial princess, and the ongoing alliances and grudges between Han people and Manchu rulers, which connect and displace the complex colonial situation in Hong Kong.[98]

Richard Hughes describes Hong Kong and its many faces as a "borrowed place" and "borrowed time."[99] If Cold War Hong Kong lives on "borrowed time," then Jin Yong's chivalric Beijing romance borrows time—premodern Manchu sagas and Chinese legends—and on "borrowed time," reconstructs a collective memory and imagined history for Hong Kong and Sinophone readers and audiences. If Hong Kong is a "borrowed place," a city on lease from China to Britain for ninety-nine years, then Jin Yong's chivalric topography borrows spaces—the vast Chinese lands from the center to the peripheries—and situates factual and fictional literary spaces in the "borrowed place," or more precisely, not to rent Hong Kong but to reverse its status as a British colony by virtue of imagined chivalric intervention in the imperial capital, the Forbidden City, the frontiers and borders, and the adjacent foreign territories; to claim an imagined takeover of the Central Plains, the ethnic regions, and the areas occupied by foreign powers.

David Der-wei Wang coins the term "post-loyalism" to detect and diagnose the poetics and politics of disenchantment and enchantment, memory and amnesia, hometown and foreign land, and argues that "[i]f loyalist consciousness always implies the disappearance and dislocation of time and space, substitution and evolution, then post-loyalist consciousness further intensifies the trend, would rather displace the dislocated time and space, remember and reflect an orthodoxy that may never have been orthodox."[100] With regard to political orthodoxy, Han and

---

[96] Jin Yong, *Shujian enchou lu* 書劍恩仇錄 [*The Book and the Sword*], trans. Graham Earnshaw, ed. Rachel May and John Minford (Hong Kong: Oxford University Press, 2004), 85, 231.

[97] Jin, *Bixue jian*, chapters 17–19.

[98] Jin, *Ludeng ji* 鹿鼎記 [*The Deer and the Cauldron*] (Beijing: Sanlian shudian, 1994), chaps. 4, 5, 6, 7, 10, 11, 12, 21, 25, 37, 43.

[99] Richard Hughes, *Hong Kong: Borrowed Place, Borrowed Time* (1968; rev., London: Deutsch, 1976). See also Kwok Kou Leonard Chan, *Ganshang de lücheng: Zai Xianggang du wenxue* 感傷的旅程：在香港讀文學 [Sentimental journey: Reading literature in Hong Kong] (Taipei: Xuesheng shuju, 2003).

[100] Wang, *Hou yimin xiezuo*, 6. The English translation is mine. An abridged rendition of the paragraph is as follows: "the *post* in *post-loyalist* therefore suggests liberation from existing confinements of loyalist discourse . . . .

non-Han gratitude and revenge, the loss and gain of romantic love, Chen Jialuo's vacillation and melancholia, Yuan Chengzhi's hesitation about assassination, and Wei Xiaobao's hybrid identification and multiparty negotiations exemplify the dislocation and relocation of post-loyalist mentality/identity, as well as the ambivalence and ambiguity of post-loyalist narration and representation in Jin Yong's martial-arts fantasy. In light of home and exile, the remote Islamic district in Western Regions, the overseas kingdom Brunei in Southeast Asia, the unknown hiding places in Qing Yangzhou and Dali, all suggest that post-loyalist positions cannot be predicted, traced, navigated, or confirmed. The post-loyalist specter wanders in Jin Yong's Cold War Hong Kong Sinophone chivalric topography of imperial Beijing, which invokes the city's dramatic past in the Ming-Qing dynastic crisis and transformation, dislocates the already displaced time and space, performs the ritual of evocation and resurrection, reappears in the British Colony, and travels in and haunts the Sinophone world.

In sum, by emplotting political, ethnic, and cultural crises in dynastic transitions, Jin Yong explores a wide range of topics, including gratitude and revenge between Han and non-Han peoples, loyalty and betrayal, and imagined cultural memory against the great backdrop of the 1949 Chinese division and migrations that reshaped the Sinophone world. And by intertwining martial intervention and escapist hermitage, historical rewriting and martial-arts fantasy, Jin Yong inscribes the "post-loyalist" ethos and emotional attachment into the imagery of Beijing as the imperial capital, as well as that of Hong Kong as the colony at the imperial margin. In his chivalric cartography produced in the interstices of the British Colony and the two antagonistic regimes across the Taiwan Strait, he creates an ambiguous yet flexible identity to respond to the included/excluded zone of contact between the center and the margin, Chinese and non-Chinese, literature and history in modern Sinophone articulations.

The loyalist consciousness perpetually hints at a vanished space in time, fixating on a political orthodoxy that may have never been orthodox." See Shih, Tsai, and Bernards, eds., *Sinophone Studies*, 101. For the "post" in "postmemories" in Marianne Hirsch's discussions of traumatic and generational memories, see Marianne Hirsch, "The Generation of Postmemory," *Poetics Today* 29, no. 1 (2008): 103–128.

It was the best of times, it was the worst of times, it was the age of wisdom, it was the age of foolishness, it was the epoch of belief, it was the epoch of incredulity, it was the season of Light, it was the season of Darkness, it was the spring of hope, it was the winter of despair, we had everything before us, we had nothing before us, we were all going direct to heaven, we were all going direct the other way.

—CHARLES DICKENS

Epilogue
BEIJING AND BEYOND

GOING TO RETURN. Returning to go. This chapter situates Beijing in a larger context of modern Chinese urban literature, and charts the trajectories of affective mapping of major cities in the Chinese-speaking world from the late nineteenth century to the present. I seek to sketch modern Chinese literary trajectories of urban awareness, historical consciousness, individual/collective memories, and nationalist perceptions regarding the old and new capital, Beijing; the semicolonial metropolis and socialist Shanghai and its remnants; the traumatized and aloof Nanjing; the abandoned capital, Xi'an; Taipei under Japanese colonial rule and the subsequent Nationalist Party's dominance; and Hong Kong from a British Crown Colony to a Special Administrative Region of China.

URBAN LITERATURE IN LATE QING AND REPUBLICAN CHINA

In this age, old things are crumbling and new things are growing. People feel that things in their daily lives are just not right—even to the point of terror. They live in this age, but this age is sinking like a shadow, and people feel abandoned. In order to confirm our own existence, we need to take hold of something real, or something most fundamental, and to that end, we seek the help of an ancient memory.

—ZHANG AILING

Since the Opium War, the opening and growth of Chinese treaty ports to foreign trade brought to light the contacts, confrontations, and juxtapositions of indigenous and foreign cultures in cities such as Shanghai, Ningbo 寧波, Hankou (Hankow) 漢口, Guangzhou (Canton) 廣州, Shantou (Swatow) 汕頭, Fuzhou (Foochow) 福州, Xiamen (Amoy) 廈門, Tianjin 天津, and Harbin 哈爾濱. Shanghai has become the foremost "modern" city and has provided a dynamic context for the development of urban narratives. Han Bangqing's *Haishanghua liezhuan* (*The Sing-Song Girls of Shanghai*, 1892–1894) may well manifest the early achievements of depicting and envisioning a modernized Chinese city in terms of persons and things, emotions and morality, amusement and edification, and regional linguistic consciousness (Wu dialect) in the fin-de-siècle Shanghai. David Der-wei Wang observes that Han's urban narrative provides a panoramic portrait of lust, desire, romantic liaisons, and moral dilemmas among two dozen courtesans and their male patrons in different social positions in the Shanghai pleasure quarters during the last decades of the nineteenth century, and inquires into the ethical and psychological realities in its pioneering infusion of modernist sensibilities into the traditional genre of courtesan novels.[1]

If Han's tedious and repetitive representation of life and desire in the courtesan house demonstrates an internalized view of the human bondage and the everlasting emotions in the urban milieu, then a grand and transnational "China Dream," or a prolonged fantasy that haunts the Chinese mind, focuses on an imagined World Expo to be held in Shanghai in the paper world. Liang Qichao's *Xin Zhongguo weilai ji* 新中國未來記 (The future of new China, 1902), Wu Jianren's *Xin shitou ji* 新石頭記 (The new story of the stone, 1905), and Lu Shi'e's 陸士諤 (1878–1944) *Xin Zhongguo* 新中國 (New China, 1910) imagine and invent scenes about national exhibitions and the World Expo, envisioning a modern Shanghai and a strong China standing proudly in the ranks of nation-states. Yet, Lu's utopian narrative suddenly comes to an end when the protagonist wakes up from his daydreaming.

Shili yangchang 十里洋場 (the ten miles of foreign zone) and the greater Shanghai glamour and lure provide a fertile land for literary production and consumption, in which popular literature, particularly the butterfly school, emerged and prevailed, and extended from Shanghai and its nearby cities to Beijing and Tianjin. Authors such as Bao Tianxiao 包天笑 (1896–1973), Xu Zhenya 徐枕亞 (1889–1937) , Zhou Shoujuan 周瘦鵑 (1859–1968), Chen Dieyi 陳蝶衣 (1907–2007), and Qin Shouou capture daily scenes, write sentimental stories, and produce popular romances in the changing urban environment. One outstanding writer in this group is Zhang Henshui, arguably the most prolific and popular writer in the first half of the twentieth century, who contributed a genealogy of

---

[1] Wang, *Fin-de-siècle Splendor*, 89–90.

literary mappings of Shanghai, Nanjing, Xi'an, Chongqing, and, most significantly, Republican Beijing. Zhang's literary topography of modern Beijing—mostly fiction serialized in literature supplements of newspapers and later published as best sellers in book form—captures the fleeting and ephemeral moments in Beijing's everyday life, on the one hand, and seizes the everlasting joys and griefs in the transitional city, on the other hand. Zhang's popular, romantic, and melancholic imaginations— *Unofficial History of Beijing, Grand Old Family,* and *Fate in Tears and Laughter*— provide a sentimental journey in and an amorous psychogeography of Republican Beijing.

The 1930s witnessed a peak decade of urban literature in Republican China. Ba Jin's *Jia (Family,* serialized in 1931–1932) sets the city of Chengdu as the battle-field between the feudalist authority and the young rebel generation, and launches a severe attack on the "cannibalistic" nature of the Confucian family ethics and hierarchy by presenting a "revolution of the heart." Mao Dun's magnum opus, *Ziye (Midnight),* an ambitious and naturalist/realist Shanghai epic, depicts the finan-cial and social crisis, the defeat of Chinese nationalist industries by foreign capi-talist exploitation, the struggles of the working class, and the labyrinth of money and desire. A milestone in leftist and revolutionary literature, *Midnight* constructs a profound connection between modern history and class-consciousness in terms of Chinese revolution and urban modernity. Cao Yu, a leading dramatist hailed as "China's Ibsen,"[2] chooses Tianjin, Shanghai, and Beijing, respectively, for his *Leiyu* 雷雨 *(Thunderstorm,* 1933), *Richu* 日出 *(Sunrise,* 1936), and *Beijing ren,* to cope with the moral degeneration, the corruption of patriarchy, and the destruction of family in the hostile and semicolonial, semifeudalist cities.

The fierce debates between the Beijing School and the Shanghai School in the 1930s highlight the contradictory and competitive understanding of Chinese urban culture. The Shanghai writers include Shi Zhecun, Liu Na'ou, Mu Shiying (all three also known as New Sensationalists), Shao Xunmei, Ye Lingfeng (1905–1975), Zhang Ziping, and Du Heng 杜衡 (1916–1980). The Beijing writers consist of Shen Congwen, Zhou Zuoren, Fei Ming, Li Jianwu, Zhang Tianyi, Zhu Guanqian, Xiao Qian, Lu Fen (Shi Tuo), Ling Shuhua, Yang Jiang, and Lin Huiyin. Shanghai moder-nity is measured by speed, height, and brightness, as conveyed by the neon sign "light, heat, power," which starts Mao Dun's tour de force of Shanghai, *Midnight.* The imagery of Beijing, however, is dominated by ancient city walls, gate towers, the imperial palaces, historical relics, idyllic scenes, and slow yet steady camels, all enhancing a landscape of harmony and tranquility unfolding in a timeless capital.

---

[2] Chen, *The Columbia Anthology of Modern Chinese Drama with a Critical Introduction,* 14.

Beijing is eulogized as authentically Chinese, profoundly cultural and aesthetic, rooted in tradition, elegant, serene, and grand. In contrast, Shanghai is stereotyped as a demonic metropolis (*modu* 魔都), an antithesis of Beijing, as well as an antiurban noncity.

On the eve of the Second Sino-Japanese War, Lao She, a pre-eminent Beijing native writer and Manchu bannerman, presented a set of city-texts witnessing the charming legacy of old Beijing and the problematic encroachment of modernity. His critically acclaimed novel *Rickshaw Boy* portrays the fate and failure of rickshaw puller Xiangzi, an orphan of Beijing, and demonstrates the metamorphosis of the symbolically homeless orphan who encounters a complete process of dream-making and dream-waking irony in Lao She's literary topography of Xiangzi's urban desires.

During the Second Sino-Japanese war and the Chinese civil war, Zhang Ailing appeared as a phenomenal literary legend in wartime Shanghai. Her urban narratives locate at the nexus of a "contrast in de-cadence" (*cenci de duizhao* 參差的對照), a technique of popular fiction, an aesthetics of desolation, as well as a strategy of romancing the ordinary in tumultuous times.[3] Zhang's "Fengsuo" 封鎖 (Sealed off, 1943) captures the ambivalent amorous encounter between a female English instructor and a married male accountant trapped in a tramcar in Shanghai during the Japanese occupation. Her novella "Jinsuo ji" 金鎖記 (The golden cangue, 1943), hailed as a masterpiece for all time, portrays the abnormal state of mind of a woman, Cao Qiqiao, who is desperately confined in the hostile and stressful family hierarchy within a transitional modern Shanghai. Her "Hong meigui yu bai meigui" 紅玫瑰 與白玫瑰 (Red rose and white rose, 1944) provides a nuanced portrait of subtle feelings, confusing romances, economic calculation, and emotional cynicism firmly situated in an indifferent urban milieu.[4] "Qingcheng zhilian" 傾城之戀 (Love in a fallen city, 1943), one of Chang's most popular and representative works, tells a tale of twin cities—Shanghai and Hong Kong—by famously exemplifying the uneven contrast of romance and warfare, twisted love and (re)marriage, and unexpected destruction and catastrophe in her urban imagination, which is at times enchanting and at times disenchanting.

Other major urban literature in the 1940s includes Qin Shouou's *Qiuhaitang* 秋海棠 (Begonia, serialized in 1941–1942, the book in 1943), arguably the most popular and sentimental Shanghai comedy–tragedy about the fate

---

[3] Lee, *Shanghai Modern*, 283.

[4] Rey Chow, "Seminal Dispersal, Fecal Retention, and Related Narrative Matters: Eileen Chang's Tale of Roses in the Problematic of Modern Writing," *differences: A Journal of Feminist Cultural Studies* 11, no. 2 (1999): 153–176.

of local opera singers, which established Qin as a leading butterfly writer during the war. Ba Jin's *Hanye* 寒夜 (*Cold Nights*, 1947) captures the melancholia and depression of humble Chinese intellectuals in Chongqing against the great backdrop of the Japanese invasion of China. Lao She also contributes a wartime epic, *Four Generations under One Roof*, which discloses an affective mapping of a wounded Beijing under Japanese rule and its rebirth through war baptism.

MAPPING MAINLAND CITIES AFTER 1949

If there are still men who really want to live in this world, they should first dare to speak out, to laugh, to cry, to be angry, to accuse, to fight-that they may at least cleanse this accursed place of its accursed atmosphere!

—LU XUN

When I look at contemporary China, I see a nation that is thriving yet distorted, developing yet mutated. I see corruption, absurdity, disorder and chaos. Every day, something occurs that lies outside ordinary reason and logic.

—YAN LIANKE

During the Maoist era from the seventeen-year period to the Cultural Revolution, the antiurban bias of Mao's peasant-based Communist revolution "tended to relegate urban history to a subordinate role in the grand narrative of modern China."[5] In the landscape of mainstream socialist realist literature, urban writings were sporadic, marginal, and mainly centered on industrial themes. The cities had to undergo a socialist remodeling and reconstruction. Xiao Yemu's 蕭也牧 (1918–1970) short story "Women fufu zhijian" 我們夫婦之間 (Between husband and wife, 1950) touches upon the sensitive gap between the country and the city: the wife, from a worker–farmer background, feels discomfort and distress after she is settled in Beijing to reunite with her husband, an intellectual cadre with urban petit bourgeois viewpoints and tastes. The severe contemporary ideological attack on Xiao's Beijing story set the basic tone for the Maoist urban writing: literature and art should serve workers, peasants, soldiers—rather than exploiters and oppressors—after Mao's Yan'an spirit entered Chinese cities.

Lao She's *Dragon Beard Ditch* presents an intriguing and intervening case of the production of socialist space: changing a notorious, filthy slum into a purified residential community, and cultivating the insulted and harmed proletarians into new citizens with advanced class consciousness. His three-act play *Teahouse* masterfully

---

[5] Esherick, *Remaking the Chinese City*, ix.

condenses the fifty-year social-political change into a warping teahouse and captures related emotional variations (nostalgia, loss, melancholia, and self-mourning) from the late Qing to the Chinese Civil War.

Shanghai is depicted in socialist literature as a bygone capitalist center of decadence and appropriation, and a newly established socialist city inhabited by citizens with new class-consciousness. Zhou Erfu's 周而復 (1914–2004) four-volume *Shanghai de zaochen* 上海的早晨 (Morning in Shanghai, 1958, 1980), "a successor to Mao Dun's *Midnight*,"[6] reveals the disappearance of capitalist forces, the prolonged process of socialist reconfiguration of body and mind, and the urban planning of new communities for model workers. Ouyang Shan's 歐陽山 (1908–2004) five-volume *Yidai fengliu* 一代風流 (Romance of a generation, 1959, 1964, 1981, 1983, and 1985)—in particular, the first volume, *Sanjia xiang* 三家巷 (Three-family lane) set in a span from the May Fourth Movement to the "Great Revolution" period—chooses Guangzhou as the geographical site for revolutionary and romantic Bildungsroman centering on three families respectively with capitalist, landlord– bureaucrat, and working-class backgrounds.[7] In the field of drama and theater, revolutionary plays such as Shen Ximeng's 沈西蒙 (1919–2006) *Nihong dengxia de shaobing* 霓虹燈下的哨兵 (Sentinel under the neon lights, 1963), Chen Yun's 陳耘 (1923–1999) *Nianqing de yidai* 年青的一代 (*The Young Generation*, 1963), and Cong Shen's 叢深 (1928–2007) *Qianwan buyao wangji* 千萬不要忘記 (Never forget, 1964) reflect urban life in Shanghai and Harbin to showcase the ongoing class struggle, the formation of proletarian consciousness, and the critique of bourgeois entertainment and fetishism.

From the post-Mao period to the present, urban literature has rejuvenated in the 1980s, proliferated in the 1990s, and flourished in the twenty-first century. Lu Wenfu's (1928–2005) "Xiaofan shijia" 小販世家 (The man from a peddler's family, 1980) depicts a Suzhou wonton peddler's frustration, pride, and affection for his beloved hometown. Lu's acclaimed "Meishijia" 美食家 (The gourmet, 1983) incorporates distinctive culinary experiences, vanishing and re-emerging refined lifestyles, and the appreciation of gastronomy into his subtle illustrations of Suzhou. Liu Xinwu 劉心武 (1942–), a representative of scar literature, published his Mao Dun Prize–winning novel *Zhong gu lou* 鐘鼓樓 (The bell tower and drum tower) in 1985. This Beijing saga colorfully depicts how many Beijingers suffered and survived the catastrophic Cultural Revolution and eventually obtained their urban identity and historical consciousness when they happened to stand in front of the

[6] McDougall and Louie, *The Literature of China in the Twentieth Century*, 241.

[7] Jianmei Liu, *Revolution Plus Love: Literary History, Women's Bodies, and Thematic Repetition in Twentieth-Century Chinese Fiction* (Honolulu: University of Hawai'i Press 2003), 178.

Bell Tower and Drum Tower, the obsolete time-telling center that lost its original function in 1924, the year the last emperor of the Qing Dynasty was forced to leave the Forbidden City. Feng Jicai (1942–), a native of Tianjin and a passionate defender and tireless advocate of the indigenous culture of his hometown, contributed his Tianjin-flavor works, including his aesthetic and grotesque representations of martial arts and queue culture in his "Shenbian" 神鞭 (Magic braid, 1984), and of foot-binding tradition in his *Sancun jinlian* 三寸金蓮 (*The Three-Inch Golden Lotus*, 1986). Other authors labeled as urban writers include Deng Youmei 鄧友梅 (1931–), Wang Zengqi 汪曾祺 (1920–1997), Chen Jiangong 陳建功 (1949–), Su Shuyang 蘇叔陽 (1938–), Han Shaohua 韓少華 (1933–2010), Liu Suola 劉索拉 (1955–), and Xu Xing 徐星 (1956–).

Wang Shuo 王朔 (1958–) was a major urban author in the late 1980s and early 1990s, a leading figure of hooligan literature. Considered a contemporary successor of Lao She,[8] Wang's poignant Beijing stories include "Wanzhu" 頑主 (The troubleshooters, 1987), *Wande jiushi xintiao* 玩的就是心跳 (Playing for thrills, 1989), *Qingchun wuhui* 青春無悔 (No regrets about youth, 1991), and "Dongwu xiongmeng" 動物凶猛 (Wild beasts, 1991), among many others. Rebellious youth culture and resistance against authorities as well as perplexing configurations of individuality, collectivity, sexual imagination, and political fantasy constitute the major themes of Wang's urban adventures from the military compound to the mean streets, from leisure parks to the political monuments. Wang's Beijing writing is characterized by strong cynicism and dark humor, and is disguised by a fearless use and abuse of Maoist propaganda, ideological cliché, and revolutionary emotions.

Another wave of urban literature emerged and intensified in the 1990s and has continued to flourish since then. Shanghai has been configured as a feminine city by female writers such as Cheng Naishan 程乃珊 (1946–2013), Chen Danyan 陳丹燕 (1958–), Wei Hui 衛慧 (1973–), Mian Mian 棉棉 (1970–), Xu Lan 須蘭 (1969–), Ren Xiaowen 任小雯 (1978–),[9] and, the most prolific and significant writer among them, Wang Anyi (1954–). Wang's representative Shanghai narratives include *Changhen ge* 長恨歌 (*The Song of Everlasting Sorrow*, 1995), *Biandi xiaoxiong* 遍地梟雄 (Fierce heroes everywhere, 2005), *Qimeng shidai* 啟蒙時代 (The era of enlightenment, 2007), and *Tianxiang* 天香 (Heavenly fragrance, 2011). Despite Wang's vehement disavowal, she is often compared with Zhang Ailing because both writers reflect and obsess about Shanghai, and their urban narratives

---

[8] Geremie R. Barmé, *In the Red: On Contemporary Chinese Culture* (New York: Columbia University Press, 1999), 72.

[9] Shi Zhanjun 施戰軍, "Lun Zhongguo shide chengshi wenxue de shengcheng" 論中國式的城市文學的生成 [The birth of Chinese-style urban literature], *Wenyi yanjiu* 文藝研究 1 (2006): 4–11.

are characterized by meticulously elaborate and nuanced feminine description of the city. *The Song of Everlasting Sorrow*, which narrates the capitalist, Maoist, and (post) socialist romance and accidental death of a former beauty pageant winner of Republican Shanghai, is widely hailed as an instant classic in modern Chinese literature. For Xudong Zhang, the novel is "a saga of modern Shanghai told ruthlessly and meticulously from the viewpoint of a class living in the heart of the dreams, fantasies, and everyday rituals of a Shanghai that ceased to exist after 1949."[10] Jin Yucheng's 金宇澄 (1952–) *Fanhua* 繁花 (Blossoms, 2012), first released online and narrated in Shanghai dialect, features an encyclopedic exhibition of memories, emotions, and material life in post-1949 Shanghai. It resurrects the charms of traditional Chinese storytelling and combines it with modern, Faulknerian narrative skills so as to exhibit the authentic Shanghai life represented by male characters, which is different from the overwhelming female voices and *petits récits* conceived successfully by woman writers.

Although literature in Shanghai and Shanghai in literature have been mainly determined by female writers and feminine imagination and representation, other literary writings of mainland Chinese cities are mostly defined by male writers and male points of view—for example, the historical memory and "evening glow" of a derelict Xi'an 西安 configured by Jia Pingwa (1952–); the romance and nostalgia of a traumatized Nanjing presented by Ye Zhaoyan (1957–) and Ge Liang 葛亮 (1978–); Suzhou in Zhu Wenying's 朱文穎 (1970–) subtle portraits of the local charms; Chengdu, China's fifth most populous city, in Murong Xuecun's 慕容雪村 (1974–) ironic and comic–tragic urban romance, *Chengdu, jinye qing jiangwo yiwang* 成都，今夜請將我遺忘 (*Leave Me Alone: A Novel of Chengdu*); Shenzhen, the Special Economic Zone (SEZ) adjacent to Hong Kong, in Ding Li's 丁力 (1958–) business and workplace novels; and Beijing in Liu Zhenyun's 劉震雲 (1958–) neorealist representations, Qiu Huadong's 邱華棟 (1969–) up-to-date urban records and romances, and Xu Zechen's 徐則臣 (1978–) youth Bildungsroman. The only exception to such male dominance occurs to Wuhan, as two of its major writers are female (Chi Li 池莉 [1957–] and Fang Fang 方方 [1955–]).

Jia Pingwa's *Feidu* 廢都 (*Ruined City*, 1993), *Lao Xi'an* 老西安 (*Old Xi'an*, 1999), and *Gaoxing* 高興 (The king of trash, 2007) reiterate the historical privilege and geographical disadvantage of Xi'an in its dialects, habits, customs, and infrastructure. *Ruined City*, which had been banned since 1994 and only recently reissued in 2009, displays the early post-Maoist urban life and its moral corruption, exotic obsession, and everlasting unorthodox beliefs and superstitions. *Old Xi'an* calls attention to the

---

[10] Xudong Zhang, "Shanghai Nostalgia: Postrevolutionary Allegories in Wang Anyi's Literary Production in the 1990s," *Positions: east asia cultures critiques* 8, no. 2 (2000): 369.

glorious legacy of Xi'an and its reluctant transformation in modern times. Through filters of confusion and chaos brought by the maelstrom of modernization, Jia seeks to exhibit a superstable Xi'an preserved in words, dialects, images, and memories. The spontaneous but erudite essays in *Old Xi'an* demonstrate Jia's impressive familiarity with Xi'an not only as a physical city but as an ancient capital in personal and collective memories that are vital in the establishment of its cultural identity.

Along with Beijing, Xi'an, and Luoyang, Nanjing is one of the top four ancient cultural capitals, and has suffered but survived historical calamities and dynastic transformation. Ye Zhaoyan's *Yijiusanqi nian de aiqing* 一九三七年的愛情 (*Nanjing 1937: A Love Story*, 1996) represents the catastrophic Nanjing Massacre colored by a sentimental romance permeated with mourning and nostalgia by an omnipresent and omnipotent witness and survivor of this calamity, who looks backward at the ruins of a magnificent city, sighing in regret and grief. For Michael Berry, this recollection of the traumatized city constitutes "both a longing for the grandeur and decadence of old Nanjing and a nostalgic gesture of remembering (and re-creating) Republican-era literary texts and traditions."[11] Ye's *Lao Nanjing: Jiuying qinhuai* 老南京：舊影秦淮 (*Old Nanjing: Reflections of Scenes on the Qinhuai River*, 1999) attempts to invoke the power of photography and the charms of old photos to exhibit the breath and heartbeat of the city's history. Similarly, Ge Liang's *Zhuque* 朱雀 (Scarlet finch, 2009) demonstrates an obsessive nostalgia for Nanjing. He blends family histories and fictional stories (three generations), blurs the boundaries between tradition and modernity, and thus unfolds the multilayered mysteries and discoveries of Nanjing around the 1920s, 1930s, and 1950s.

When examining the rise of urban literature in the twenty-first century, Chen Xiaoming 陳曉明 points out that urban literature in a strict sense should present the existence of the city, its objective images, the authors' reflections on urban life, and the spiritual contradictions between literary characters and the city.[12] Meng Fanhua 孟繁華 observes that urban literature in the twenty-first century does not lack in writers, works, stories, or social issues, but the re-emerging genre has not yet provided representative literary characters for the times and therefore remains an ongoing and incomplete project.[13]

---

[11] Michael Berry, *A History of Pain: Trauma in Modern Chinese Literature and Film* (New York: Columbia University Press, 2008), 163.

[12] Chen Xiaoming, "Chengshi wenxue—wufa xianshen de 'tazhe'" 城市文學—無法現身的"他者" [Urban literature: An invisible "other"], *Wenyi yanjiu* 文藝研究 [Literature and art studies] 1: (2006): 12–25.

[13] Meng Fanhua, "Jiangou shiqi de Zhongguo chengshi wenxue—dangxia Zhongguo wenxue zhuangkuang de yige fangmian" 建構時期的中國城市文學——當下中國文學狀況的一個方面 [Chinese urban literature in construction: One aspect of current Chinese literature], *Wenyi yanjiu* 文藝研究 [Literature and art studies] 2 (2014): 5–14.

IMAGINING TAIPEI, HONG KONG, AND BEYOND

This is an affective mapping that ultimately puts us in touch with mental landscapes and inner world.

—GIULIANA BRUNO

To live in a floating city, however, you need more than courage; you need will-power and faith as well.

—XI XI

If we extend our scope of investigation from mainland Chinese cities to Taipei and Hong Kong, then the year 1949 would serve as a key point of departure. For writers of mainland origins who migrated to Taiwan, Hong Kong, and other Sinophone regions outside of the newly established socialist China, literary writings of cities have to counter the memories of recent experiences of a severed nation, as well as rethink, restructure, and reframe their memories—individual, urban, and national—in order to provide their affective mappings of cities, detached and reconnected, near and afar. Some writers attempt to balance and bridge their new urban experiences in Taipei or Hong Kong, and their memories about mainland cities ranging from their old hometowns to their sojourning cities are shaped by unforgettable recollections and creative reinventions. Other writers born after 1949 cannot easily claim themselves as the legitimate native sons or daughters of Taipei or Hong Kong and have engaged and developed sustained dialogues with earlier generations and the legacy of diversified and complicated urban narratives.

I have examined in details how native Beijing writers like Liang Shiqiu and Tang Lusun relocate to Taiwan and envision an imagined return to a lost hometown in their culinary writing and symptomatic nostalgia. I have also explored Taiwan sojourners in China, in particular Zhang Lihe and Lin Haiyin, and their distinct representations and reflections of their urban experiences. Moreover, Bai Xianyong 白先勇 (Pai Hsien-yung, 1937–) contributes the well-crafted, psychologically profound *Taibei ren* 台北人 (*Taipei People*, 1971), a collection of fourteen short stories that describes not only a bleak Taipei image but also its entangled links with Nanjing, Shanghai, Guilin, Kunming, Beijing, and other mainland cities against the great backdrop of the 1949 divide and the diasporic experiences across the Taiwan Strait. *Taipei People* provides vivid portraitures of melancholic mainland émigrés—including schizophrenic scholars ("Winter Night," 1970), the never-aged high-ranked courtesan lady from Shanghai's Paramount Dance Hall to Taipei's fashionable district ("Yongyuan de Yin Xueyan" 永遠的尹雪艷 [Eternal Yin Xueyan], 1965), and depressed Nationalist officials and disheartened social ladies

("Youyuan jingmeng" 遊園驚夢 [Wandering in the garden, waking from a dream], 1966), among many others—in terms of diaspora and exile, as well as physical and psychological deterioration and reorientation.[14] Later, Bai shifts his focus to a local Taipei story in his *Niezi* 孽子 (*Crystal Boys*, 1983), a pioneering gay novel that deals with the sounds, furies, frustrations, and desires of rebel youths in a local homosexual community.

During the peak Cold War years in the 1960s–1970s, Wang Wenxing's 王文興 (1939–) modernist and avant-garde novel *Jiabian* 家變 (*Family Catastrophe*, 1973) presented Taipei as the new home for mainland emigrants as well as a battlefield for an ongoing father/son contradiction and an imagined solution to generational, familial, and geopolitical dilemma. Huang Chunming's 黃春明 (1935–) literary Taipei, a city of sadness, emerges from his early stories "Erzi de da wanou" 兒子的大玩偶 (My son's big doll, 1968), "Xiaoqi de na yiding maozi" 小琪的那一頂帽子 (Xiaoqi's cap, 1974), and, in particular, "Pingguo de ziwei" 蘋果的滋味 (Taste of apples, 1972), which captures the tensions between the country and the city, Taiwan and the United States, in a Taipei morning car accident and its unexpected and bittersweet consequences.[15]

Since the 1980s, urban writing has been flourishing in the landscape of Taiwan literature, thanks to native-born writers and Malaysian émigrés, such as Huang Fan 黃凡 (1950–), Zhang Dachun 張大春 (1957–), Lin Yaode 林耀德 (1962–1996), Ping Lu 平路 (1953–), Yang Zhao 楊照 (1963–), Zhu Tianwen (Chu T'ien-wen, 1956–), Zhu Tianxin (Chu T'ien-hsin 朱天心, 1958–), Su Weizhen 蘇偉貞 (1954–), Yuan Qiongqiong 袁瓊瓊 (1950–), Li Yongping 李永平 (1947–), Wu He 舞鶴 (1951–), Li Zishu 黎紫書 (1971–), Ng Kim Chew 黃錦樹 (Huang Jinshu, 1967–), and Luo Yijun 駱以軍 (1967–), to just name a few. Zhang Dachun's *Da shuohuang jia* 大說謊家 (The great liar, 1988–1989), first serialized in newspapers and later published as a book, combines different genres such as news reportage, detective story, political exposé, and historical fiction, thereby forcefully presenting an absurd urban reality. Widely regarded as a leading novelist and scriptwriter, Zhu Tianwen reads Taipei as follows: "It is utterly chaotic, but it has a tremendous energy, with every kind of potential."[16] Her "Shijimo de huali" 世紀末的華麗 (Fin-de-siècle Splendor, 1990) sees the unseen, presents the unpresentable, and provides a feminist declaration, a redefinition of smell and visuality, and an alternative utopia

---

[14] Ko Ching-ming 柯慶明, *Taiwan xiandai wenxue de shiye* 臺灣現代文學的視野 [Perspectives on Taiwan literature] (Taipei: Maitian, 2006), 199–244.

[15] Chen Fang-ming 陳芳明, *Taiwan xin wenxue shi* 台灣新文學史 [A history of modern Taiwanese literature] (Taipei: Lianjing, 2011), 540–545.

[16] Margaret Hillenbrand, *Literature, Modernity, and the Practice of Resistance: Japanese and Taiwanese Fiction, 1960–1990* (Leiden: Brill, 2007), 288.

for redemption. Yvonne Chang states that the novella "envisions a hollow existential condition that has resulted from the unbridled development of materialist urban culture."[17] Zhu's acclaimed queer novel *Huangren shouji* 荒人手記 (*Notes of a Desolate Man*, 1994) inherits Zhang Ailing's legacy of desolation and cynicism, and contributes an erotics and aesthetics of decadence in a new fin de siècle. Her *Wuyan* 巫言 (Words of a witch, 2007) reflects the meaning of writing and femininity from the perspective of a solitary woman. Zhu Tianxin, Zhu Tianwen's younger sister and another leading writer in contemporary Taiwan, contributes a vaguely defined but critically acclaimed Taipei trilogy. "Xiang wo juancun de xiongdimen" 想我眷村 的兄弟們 (In Remembrance of my Buddies from the Military Compound, 1992) touches upon friendship, nostalgia, anxiety, and cultural consciousness among the mainlander military retirees and their second-generation children, cultivated within the unique urban milieu and sociopolitical communities. Her *Gudu* 古都 (*The Old Capital: A Novel of Taipei*, 1997) and *Manyouzhe* 漫遊者 (The wanderer, 2000) highlight an old soul, or an urban wanderer who relies on imaginary maps, invokes literary geography and cartography,[18] and observes and participates in the great urban transformation with a post-loyalist complex.

Beginning in 1949, while political conflicts between socialist and capitalist blocs loomed large and enhanced the ideological confrontations across the Taiwan Strait, "Hong Kong has become a unique urban space where forces of politics and commerce, colonialism and nationalism, and modernity and historicity converge. Ever since the early 1950s, Hong Kong has been a haven for émigré writers, dissident critics, and exiled scholars whose voices would otherwise have been muffled by either the Nationalist or the Communist regime. The colony also became an arena where different political forces contested to gain the upper hand in the propaganda war."[19] Huang Guliu's 黃谷柳 (1908–1977) *Xiaqiu zhuan* 蝦球傳 (The tale of a shrimpball, 1947–1948) features Hong Kong, Guangzhou, and the guerrilla war zone of South China to tell how a proletarian boy is cultivated into a revolutionary hero. Zhao Zifan's 趙滋蕃 (1924–1986) *Banxialiu shehui* 半下流社會 (Semi-lower-class society, 1953) depicts the misery of unfortunate refugees and diasporic sentiments in the post-1949 Hong Kong ghetto-like resettlement sites and the hostile urban environment at large. Cao Juren's 曹聚仁 (1900–1972) *Jiudian* 酒店 (Hotel, 1954) touches upon the calamity of mainland emigrants in Hong Kong, in particular the madness

[17] Sung-sheng Yvonne Chang, *Modernism and the Nativist Resistance: Contemporary Chinese Fiction from Taiwan* (Durham, NC: Duke University Press, 1993), 78.

[18] Lingchei Letty Chen, "Mapping Identity in a Postcolonial City: Intertextuality and Cultural Hybridity in Zhu Tianxin's *Ancient Capital*," in Wang and Rojas, *Writing Taiwan*, 301–323.

[19] Pang-yuan Chi and David Der-wei Wang, eds., *Chinese Literature in the Second Half of a Modern Century: A Critical Survey* (Bloomington: Indiana University Press, 2000), xxi–xxii.

of the female protagonist trapped in a decadent and immoral nightlife. Liu Yichang's 劉以鬯 (1918–) *Jiutu* 酒徒 (The drunkard, 1963), a stream-of-consciousness novel, exhibits an urban professional writer's suffering and pain when he is forced to abandon his beloved serious literature and obliged to write popular literature driven by the urban market and commercial forces (martial-arts and even erotic works). Liu's *Duidao* 對倒 (Intersection, 1972) delineates the confusion and intersection of Hong Kong time and space, silence and articulation, and Chinese and British/Western cultural influences.

If Liu Yichang adopts a critical attitude toward Hong Kong popular literature, arguably the mainstream of colonial Hong Kong, then Jin Yong, the most widely read novelist in the Sinophone world since the 1950s, constructs an alternative urban narrative from the 1950s to 1980s by writing about mainland cities in imperial dynasties—Beijing, Hangzhou, Haining, Suzhou, Yangzhou, Nanjing, Luoyang, Kaifeng, Dali, Kunming, Fuzhou, Foshan, and so on—in his Cold War martial arts novels to register an illuminating historical, cultural, and colonial (Hong Kong/Sinophone) consciousness.

Richard Hughes once described Hong Kong and its many faces as a "borrowed place" and "borrowed time." Indeed, located in between motherland China and colonizer Britain, Hong Kong literature faces the in-betweenness, and configures its historical consciousness and urban awareness, which bring to light the identity crisis and symbolic resolution starting from the 1970s, a time of rapid economic growth and, more significantly, of growth in self-confidence and the forging of a local identity. Xi Xi's (1938–) representative works weave female consciousness, everyday life, and the mood of the city, and contribute a genealogy of Hong Kong images and urban emotions ranging from fear and anxiety to hope, which are vividly demonstrated in her *Wocheng* 我城 (*My City*, 1979), the collection of short stories *Xiangwo zheyang de yige nüzi* 像我這樣的一個女子 (A girl like me, 1982), the series of allegorical stories of "The Fertile Town" (*Feituzhen* 肥土鎮), *Fucheng zhiyi* 浮城誌異 (*Marvels of a Floating City*, 1988), and *Meili dasha* 美麗大廈 (The beautiful mansion, 1977). As Stephen C. K. Chan (Chen Qingqiao) puts it, for Xi Xi, "the city offers a unique display of space, with distinct structures, specific postures, particular orientations, and possibilities for boundless imagination."[20]

Other famous Hong Kong narratives in the 1980s–1990s include the talented female writer Zhong Xiaoyang's 鍾曉陽 (1962–) *Tingche zan jiewen* 停車暫借問 (Stopping by the roadside, 1982); Yi Shu's 亦舒 (1946–) dozens of popular urban romances; and prolific and popular writer Li Bihua's 李碧華 (Lillian Lee, 1959–)

---

[20] Stephen C. K. Chan, "The Cultural Imaginary of a City: Reading Hong Kong Through Xi Xi," in Chi and Wang, *Chinese Literature in the Second Half of a Modern Century*, 181.

sensational *Yanzhi kou* 胭脂扣 (*Rouge*, 1985), *Bawang bieji* 霸王別姬 (*Farewell My Concubine*, 1988), and many others. *Rouge* was adapted into a critically acclaimed box-office hit film in 1987 by Stanley Kwan (Guan Jinpeng 關錦鵬), marking a crucial moment in Hong Kong literature, cinema, history, and a global trend of Hong Kong nostalgia.[21]

Taiwanese female writer and Hong Kong sojourner Shi Shuqing (Shih Shu-ch'ing 施叔青, 1945–) has composed a Hong Kong trilogy—*Ta mingjiao Hudie* 她名叫蝴蝶 (Her name is butterfly, 1993), *Bianshan yang zijing* 遍山洋紫荊 (Bauhinia are everywhere, 1995), and *Jimo yunyuan* 寂寞雲園 (The lonely garden, 1997). The trilogy (abridged English, *City of the Queen: A Novel of Colonial Hong Kong*, 2005) describes Hong Kong as a city of commerce, colonialism, sex, and adventure. The legend of the British Crown Colony is firmly tied with the story of the heroine—a beautiful rural girl who is kidnapped and sold as a prostitute in Hong Kong, but who eventually becomes a rich landowner and grandmother of the first Chinese judge on the Hong Kong Supreme Court.

As a poet, essayist, novelist, translator, cultural critic, and film scholar, Leung Ping-kwan 梁秉鈞 (1948–2013) shows a consistent and critical obsession with Hong Kong in his creative and scholarly works. His collections of short stories, *Dao yu dalu* 島與大陸 (Islands and continents, 1987), *Jiyi de chengshi, xugou de chengshi* 記憶的城市, 虛構的城市 (A city of memories, a city of fictions, 1994), and *Houzhimin shiwu yu aiqing* 後殖民食物與愛情 (Postcolonial food and love, 2012), together with his anthologies of poems and essays, display a sophisticated Hong Kong preceding and following the 1997 handover in terms of the poetics and politics of daily objects, and mundane urban spaces and places as well as "old ends" and "new ends" in "a city of transition."[22]

The new trendsetters in literary Hong Kong are Wong Bik-wan 黃碧雲 (1961–) and Dung Kai-cheung (1967–). Wong, a unique voice in Hong Kong literature, is usually compared to Lu Xun, Zhang Ailing, or Wang Anyi. Her *Wenrou yu baolie* 溫柔與暴烈 (Tenderness and violence, 1994), *Lienü tu* 烈女圖 (Portraits of pious women, 1999), and *Lielao zhuan* 烈佬傳 (Biographies of martyred men, 2012) introduce inscrutable nightmares, unbearable loss and melancholia, abrupt familial and urban violence, unexpected cruelty and ferocity in striking, and depressing metropolitan settings before and after the 1997 handover

---

[21] Kwok Kou Leonard Chan ed., *Wenxue xianggang yu Li Bihua* 文學香港與李碧華 ["Literary Hong Kong" and Lilian Lee] (Taipei: Maitian, 2000).

[22] Esther M. K. Cheung, "Introduction to the New Edition: New Ends in a City of Transition," in Leung Ping-kwan, *City at the End of Time*, trans. Gordon T. Osing and Leung Ping-kwan (Hong Kong: Hong Kong University Press, 2012), 1.

of Hong Kong. Dung Kai-cheung compellingly challenges the stereotyped images of Hong Kong:

> There are enough fictitious Hong Kongs circulating around the world. It does-n't matter so much how real or false these fictions are but how they are made up. The Hong Kong of Tai-Pan and Suzie Wong, a mixture of economic adven-tures, political intrigues, sexual encounters, and romances; the Hong Kong of Bruce Lee, Jackie Chan, and Jet Li kung-fu-fighting their way through to the international scene; the Hong Kong of John Woo's gangster heroes shooting double-handed and Stephen Chow's underdog antiheroes making nonsensical jokes. And yet, in spite of these eye-catching exposures, Hong Kong remains invisible. A large part of the reality of life here is unrepresented, unrevealed, and ignored.[23]

Dung's early novels, *Mingzi de meigui* 名字的玫瑰 (The rose of the name, 1997) and a series of *V cheng* V 城 (Visible cities), including *Dituji: Yige xiangxiang de chengshi de kaoguxue* 地圖集：一個想像的城市的考古學 (*Atlas: The Archaeology of an Imaginary City*, 1997), *V cheng fansheng lu* V 城繁盛錄 (Visible cities, 1998), *Menghua lu* 夢華錄 (The catalog, 1999), *Bowu zhi* 博物誌 (Unnatural recollec-tions, 1999–2000), acknowledge Umberto Eco, Italo Calvino, Jorge Luis Borges, Roland Barthes, Walter Benjamin, Charles Baudelaire, as well as classical Chinese urban narratives by Meng Yuanlao, Nai Deweng 耐得翁, Zhou Mi 周密, Xihu Laoren 西湖老人, as his sources of inspiration. His recent ambitious works include a trilogy of natural history, *Tiangong kaiwu* 天工開物 (Works and creation, 2005), *Shijian fanshi* 時間繁史 (Histories of time, 2007), and *Wuzhong yuanshi* 物種源始 (The age of learning, 2010), which blends Visible City/Hong Kong and imagi-nary history, urban objects and family saga, historical events and private letters, and personal feelings and daily minutiae in his creative and distinctive literary narratives.

Dung's avant-garde imaginations/representations of Hong Kong and other (in) visible cities illuminate his unique understanding of urban literature, which is evi-denced in his newly written preface for the 2012 English translation of his 1997 fic-tional account, *Atlas: The Archaeology of an Imaginary City*. In "An Archaeology for the Future," Dung forcefully states, literature "is not just a different way of world-representing but also a different way of world-building, that is, creating conditions for understanding, molding, preserving, and changing the world that we live in.

---

[23] Kai-cheung Dung, *Atlas: The Archaeology of an Imaginary City*, translated by Dung Kai-cheung, Anders Hansson, and Bonnie S. McDougall (New York: Columbia University Press, 2012), xi–xii.

It is the task of literature to make visible the invisible . . . [and] to articulate the unarticulated." [24]

Lost in an urban labyrinth. Found in a literary topography. Emotions serve as a navigation system, although sometimes they dysfunction. Martha Nussbaum quotes Marcel Proust's description of the emotions as "geological upheavals of thought," and contends that "emotions shape the landscape of our mental and social lives."[25] Urban experiences, emotional vicissitudes, and literary topography continue to provide methods of mapping Beijing and beyond.

---

[24] Kai-cheung Dung, *Atlas*, xii.

[25] Martha C. Nussbaum, *Upheavals of Thought: The Intelligence of Emotions* (Cambridge: Cambridge University Press, 2003), 1.

SELECTED BIBLIOGRAPHY

A Ying 阿英 (Qian Xingcun 錢杏邨). *Wanqing xiaoshuo shi* 晚清小說史 [A history of late Qing novel]. Shanghai: Shanghai guji chubanshe, 1985.

Abbas, Ackbar. *Hong Kong: Culture and Politics of Disappearance*. Minneapolis: University of Minnesota Press, 1997.

Agamben, Giorgio. *Homo Sacer: Sovereign Power and Bare Life*. Translated by Daniel Heller-Roazen. Stanford, CA: Stanford University Press, 1998.

Ahmed, Sara. *The Cultural Politics of Emotion*. New York: Routledge, 2004.

Aldridge, A. Owen. "The Empress Dowager CI-XI in Western Fiction: A Stereotype for the Far East?" *Revue de littérature comparée* 1 (2001): 113–122.

———. "Lin Yutang." In *American National Biography Online*, American Council of Learned Societies. New York: Oxford University Press, 2000.

Allen, Joseph. *Taipei: City of Displacements*. Seattle: University of Washington Press, 2012.

Althusser, Louis. *For Marx*. Translated by Ben Brewer. London: Verso, 1979.

Anderson, Benedict. *Imagined Communities: Reflections on the Origin and Spread of Nationalism*. London: Verso, 1991.

Anderson, E. N. *The Food of China*. New Haven, CT: Yale University Press, 1990.

Anderson, Marston. *The Limits of Realism: Chinese Fiction in the Revolutionary Period*. Berkeley: University of California Press, 1990.

Appadurai, Arjun. *Modernity at Large: Cultural Dimensions of Globalization*. Minneapolis: University of Minnesota Press, 1996.

———. "Topographies of the Self: Praise and Emotion in Hindu India." In *Language and the Politics of Emotion*, edited by Catherine Lutz and Lila Abu-Lughod, 92–112. Cambridge: Cambridge University Press, 1990.

Arlington, L. C., and William Lewisohn. *In Search of Old Peking*. New York: Oxford University Press, 1987.

Ashcroft, Bill, Gareth Griffiths, and Helen Tiffin. *The Empire Writes Back: Theory and Practice in Post-Colonial Literatures*. 2nd ed. London: Routledge, 2002.

Auslander, Philip. *Liveness: Performance in a Mediatized Culture*. London: Routledge, 1999.

Ba Jin 巴金. *Suixiang lu* 隨想錄 [Random thoughts]. Beijing: Beijing renmin chubanshe, 1980.

Bachelard, Gaston. *The Poetics of Space: The Classic Look at How We Experience Intimate Places*. Translated by Maria Jolas. Boston: Beacon Press, 1994.

Bachner, Andrea. *Beyond Sinology: Chinese Writing and the Scripts of Cultures*. New York: Columbia University Press, 2014.

Bai, Liping. "Babbitt's Impact in China: The Case of Liang Shiqiu." *Humanitas* 17, nos. 1–2 (2004): 46–68.

Backhouse, Edmund. *Decadence Mandchoue: The China Memoirs of Sir Edmund Trelawny Backhouse*. Hong Kong: Earnshaw Books, 2011.

Bakhtin, Mikhail. *The Dialogic Imagination: Four Essays*. Austin: University of Texas Press, 1981.

———. *Rabelais and His World*. Translated by Hélène Iswolsky. Bloomington: Indiana University Press, 1984.

Barlow, Tani E. *I Myself Am a Woman: Selected Writings of Ding Ling*. Edited with Gary J. Bjorge. Boston: Beacon Press, 1989.

Barmé, Geremie. *The Forbidden City*. Cambridge, MA: Harvard University Press, 2008.

———. *In the Red: On Contemporary Chinese Culture*. New York: Columbia University Press, 1999.

———. "Zhu Qiqian's Silver Shovel." *China Heritage Quarterly* 14 (June 2008): http://www.chinaheritagequarterly.org/.

Barthes, Roland. *A Barthes Reader*. Edited and with an introduction by Susan Sontag. New York: Hill and Wang, 1987.

Baudrillard, Jean. *Simulations*. Translated by Paul Foss, Paul Patton, and Philip Beitchman. New York: Semiotext(e), 1983.

Beijing renmin yishu juyuan *Yishu yanjiu ziliao* bianjizu 北京人民藝朮劇院《藝朮研究資料》編輯組 [Editorial board of *Art Research Archives* at Beijing People's Art Theatre], eds. *Chaguan de wutai yishu* 《茶館》的舞台藝朮 [Stage art of *Teahouse*]. Beijing: Zhongguo xiju chubanshe, 1980.

Beijing shehui kexue yanjiusuo 北京社會科學研究所, eds. *Beijing lishi jinian* 北京歷史紀年 [Chronicle of Beijing history]. Beijing: Beijing chubanshe, 1984.

Beijingshi zhengxie wenshi ziliao yanjiu weiyuanhui deng bian 北京市政協文史資料研究委員會等編. *Huogong jishi: Zhu Qiqian xiansheng shengping jishi* 蠖公紀事：朱啓鈐先生生平紀實 [The life of Zhu Qiqian]. Beijing: Zhongguo wenshi chubanshe, 1991.

Beller, Manfred, and Joseph Theodoor Leerssen, eds. *Imagology: The Cultural Construction and Literary Representation of National Characters: A Critical Survey*. Amsterdam: Rodopi, 2007.

Bellow, Saul. *More Die of Heartbreak*. London: Secker & Warburg, 1987.

Benhabib, Seyla. *The Reluctant Modernism of Hannah Arendt*. Lanham, MD: Rowman & Littlefield, 2003.

Benedict, Barbara M. *Curiosity: A Cultural History of Early Modern Inquiry*. Chicago: University of Chicago Press, 2001.

Benevolo, Leonardo. *The History of the City*. Translated by Geoffrey Culverwell. Cambridge, MA: The MIT Press, 1980.

Benjamin, Walter. *Charles Baudelaire: A Lyric Poet in the Era of High Capitalism*. Translated by Harry Zohn. London: Verso, 1983.

———. "Eduard Fuchs: Collector and Historian." In *The Essential Frankfurt School Reader*, edited by Andrew Arato and Eike Gebhardt, 225–253. New York: Continuum, 1998.

———. *Illuminations: Essays and Reflections*. Edited by Hannah Arendt, translated by Harry Zohn. New York: Schocken Books, 1969.

———. *Reflections: Essays, Aphorisms, Autobiographical Writings*. Translated by Peter Demetz. New York: Schocken Books, 1986.

———. "The Storyteller: Reflections on Nikolai Leskóv." In *Illuminations, Essays and Reflections*. Edited by Hannah Arendt, translated by Harry Zohn, 83–109. New York: Schocken Books, 1969.

———. *Walter Benjamin: Selected Writings*. Vol. 1, *1913–1926*. Edited by Marcus Bullock and Michael W. Jennings. Cambridge, MA: Harvard University Press, 1996.

Ben-Ze'ev, Aaron. *The Subtlety of Emotions*. Cambridge, MA: The MIT Press, 2000.

Berger, Peter. *The Homeless Mind*. New York: Random House, 1973.

Berman, Marshall. *All That Is Solid Melts into Air: The Experience of Modernity*. New York: Penguin, 1982.

Berry, Michael. *A History of Pain: Trauma in Modern Chinese Literature and Film*. New York: Columbia University Press, 2008.

———. *Speaking in Images: Interviews with Contemporary Chinese Filmmakers*. New York: Columbia University Press, 2005.

Bhabha, Homi K. *The Location of Culture*. New York: Routledge, 1994.

Bing Xin 冰心. *Bing Xin quanji* 冰心全集 [Complete writings of Bing Xin]. Fuzhou: Haixia wenyi chubanshe, 1994.

Blanchard, Marc E. *In Search of the City: Engels, Baudelaire, Rimbaud*. Saratoga, CA: Anna Libri, 1985.

Bloom, Harold. "Cities of the Mind." In *New York*, vii–xi. New York: Chelsea House Publishers, 2004.

———. *The Ringers in the Tower: Studies in Romantic Tradition*. Chicago: University of Chicago Press, 1971.

Bongie, Chris. *Exotic Memories: Literature, Colonialism, and the Fin de Siècle*. Stanford, CA: Stanford University Press, 1991.

Bourdieu, Pierre. *Distinction: A Social Critique of the Judgement of Taste*. Translated by Richard Nice. Cambridge, MA: Harvard University Press, 1984.

Boym, Svetlana. *The Future of Nostalgia*. New York: Basic Books, 2001.

———. "Nostalgia and Its Discontents." *Hedgehog Review* 9, no. 2 (2007): 7–18.

———. "Nostalgic Technology." http://www.svetlanaboym.com/main.htm

Bradbury, Malcolm, and James McFarlane, eds. *Modernism: A Guide to European Literature, 1890–1930*. London: Penguin Books, 1991.

Braester, Yomi. *Painting the City Red: Chinese Cinema and the Urban Contract*. Durham, NC: Duke University Press, 2010.

———. *Witness against History: Literature, Film and Public Discourse in Twentieth-Century China*. Stanford, CA: Stanford University Press: 2003.

Braudel, Fernand. *The Mediterranean and the Mediterranean World in the Age of Phillip II*. 2 vols. Translated by Sian Reynolds. New York: Harper and Row, 1972–1974.

———. *On History*. Translated by Sarah Matthews. London: Weidenfeld and Nicolson, 1980.

Bredon, Juliet. *Peking: A Historical and Intimate Description of Its Chief Places of Interest*. Shanghai: Kelly & Walsh, 1922, second edition, revised and enlarged.

Brennan, Teresa. *The Transmission of Affect*. Ithaca, NY: Cornell University Press, 2004.

Brooks, Peter. *The Melodramatic Imagination: Balzac, Henry James, Melodrama, and the Mode of Excess*. New Haven, CT: Yale University Press, 1976.

Brown, Jeremy, and Paul G. Pickowicz, eds. *Dilemmas of Victory: The Early Years of the People's Republic of China*. Cambridge, MA: Harvard University Press, 2007.

Bruno, Giuliana. *Atlas of Emotion: Journeys in Art, Architecture, and Film*. London: Verso, 2002.

Buck-Morss, Susan. *The Dialect of Seeing: Walter Benjamin and the Arcade Project*. Cambridge, MA: The MIT Press, 1993.

Butler, Judith. *Precarious Life: The Powers of Mourning and Violence*. London: Verso, 2006.

Calhoun, Craig, ed. *Habermas and the Public Sphere*. Cambridge, MA: The MIT Press, 1992.

Calinescu, Matei. *Faces of Modernity: Avant-Garde, Decadence, Kitsch*. Bloomington: Indianan University Press, 1977.

Calvino, Italo. *Invisible Cities*. Translated by William Weaver. New York: Harcourt Brace Jovanovich, 1972.

Cameron, Nigel, and Brian Brake. *Peking: A Tale of Three Cities*. Foreword by L. Carrington Goodrich. New York: Harper & Row, 1965.

Cao Xueqin 曹雪芹. *The Dream of the Red Chamber*. Translated by H. Bencraft Joly, with a new foreword by John Minford, and a new introduction by Edwin Lowe. North Clarendon, VT: Tuttle Publishing, 2010.

———. *A Dream of Red Mansions*. Translated by Yang Xianyi 楊憲益 and Gladys Yang 戴乃迭. Peking: Foreign Languages Press, 1978–1980.

———. *The Story of the Stone: A Chinese Novel in Five Volumes*. Translated by David Hawkes. Harmondsworth, NY: Penguin, 1973–1986.

Cao Yu (Ts'ao Yu) 曹禺. *Sunrise: A Play in Four Acts*. Translated by A. C. Barnes. Peking: Foreign Languages Press, 1960.

Cao Zixi 曹子西 and Yu Guangdu 于光度. *Beijing tongshi* 北京通史 [General history of Beijing]. Beijing: Zhongguo shudian, 1994.

Carroll, John M. *Edge of Empires: Chinese Elites and British Colonials in Hong Kong*. Cambridge, MA: Harvard University Press, 2009.

Caws, Mary Ann, ed. *City Image: Perspectives from Literature, Philosophy, and Film*. New York: Gordon & Breach, 1991.

Certeau, Michel de. *The Practice of Everyday Life*. Translated by Steven Rendall. Berkeley, CA: University of California Press, 1984.

———. *The Practice of Everyday Life*. Vol, 2, *Living and Cooking*. Translated by Timothy J. Tomasik. Minneapolis: University of Minnesota Press, 1998.

Chan, Kwok Kou Leonard 陳國球. *Ganshang de lücheng: Zai Xianggang du wenxue* 感傷的旅程：在香港讀文學 [Sentimental journey: reading literature in Hong Kong]. Taipei: Xuesheng shuju, 2003.

———, ed. *Wenxue xianggang yu Li Bihua* 文學香港與李碧華 ["Literary Hong Kong" and Lilian Lee]. Taipei: Maitian, 2000.

Chan, Kwok Kou Leonard and David Der-wei Wang 王德威, eds. *Shuqing zhi xiandaixing* 抒情之現代性 [The modernity of lyricism]. Beijing: Sanlian shudian, 2014.

Chan, Stephen C. K. "The Cultural Imaginary of a City: Reading Hong Kong Through Xi Xi." In *Chinese Literature in the Second Half of a Modern Century*, edited by Pang-yuan Chi and David Der-wei Wang, 180–192. Bloomington: Indiana University Press, 2000.

Chang, Hao. *Liang Ch'I-ch'ao and Intellectual Transition in China*. Cambridge, MA.: Harvard University Press, 1971.

Chang, Hsiao-hung. "'What Sort of Thing Is Sentiment?' Gifts, Love Tokens, and Material Evidence in Jin Yong's Novels." In *Rethinking Chinese Popular Culture*, edited by Carlos Rojas and Eileen Cheng-yin Chow, 235–261. New York: Routledge, 2009.

Chang, Kwang-chih 張光直, ed. *Food in Chinese Culture: Anthropological and Historical Perspectives*. New Haven, CT: Yale University Press, 1977.

Chang, Sung-sheng Yvonne. *Literary Culture in Taiwan: Martial Law to Market Law*. New York: Columbia University Press, 2004.

——. *Modernism and the Nativist Resistance: Contemporary Chinese Fiction from Taiwan*. Durham, NC: Duke University Press, 1993.

Chatterjee, Partha. *The Nation and Its Fragments: Colonial and Postcolonial Histories*. Princeton, NJ: Princeton University Press, 1993.

——. *Nationalist Thought and the Colonial World: A Derivative Discourse*. Minneapolis: University of Minnesota Press, 1993.

Chen Fang-ming 陳芳明. *Taiwan xin wenxue shi* 台灣新文學史 [A history of modern Taiwanese literature]. Taipei: Lianjing, 2011.

——. *Zhimindi modeng: Xiandaixing yu Taiwan shiguan* 殖民地摩登：現代性與台灣史觀 [Colonial modernity: Historical and literary perspectives on Taiwan]. Taipei: Maitian, 2004.

——. *Zuoyi Taiwan: Zhimindi wenxue yundong shilun* 左翼台灣：殖民地文學運動史論 [Leftist Taiwan: A history of literary movements in the colony]. Taipei: Maitian, 1998.

Chen, Jian. *China's Road to the Korean War: The Making of the Sino-American Confrontation*. New York: Columbia University Press, 1997.

Chen Jianzhong 陳建忠. "Bei zuzhou de wenxue? Zhanhou chuqi (1945–1949) Taiwan xiaoshuo de lishi kaocha" 被詛咒的文學？戰後初期 (1945–1949) 台灣小說的歷史考察 [The cursed literature? A historical reflection on Taiwanese fiction of early postwar years 1945–1949]. In *Taiwan xiandai xiaoshuo shi zonglun* 台灣現代小說史綜論 [An anthology of the history of modern Taiwanese fiction], edited by Chen Yizhi 陳義芝, 31–82. Taipei: Lianjing, 1998.

Chen Lirong 陳禮榮. "Shenmi de Princess Der Ling" 神秘的 "德齡公主" [Mythical Princess Der Ling]. *Guangming ribao* 光明日報 [Guangming daily], July 13, 2000.

Chen, Lingchei Letty. *Writing Chinese: Reshaping Chinese Cultural Identity*. New York: Palgrave Macmillan, 2006.

Chen Pingyuan 陳平原. *Beijing jiyi yu jiyi Beijing* 北京記憶與記憶北京 [Beijing memories]. Beijing: Sanlian shudian, 2008.

——. *Dangnian youxia ren* 當年游俠人 [Wandering knight-errants of the past]. Taipei: Eryu, 2003.

——. *Ershi shiji Zhongguo xiaoshuo shi: Diyi juan* 二十世紀中國小說史：第一卷 [A history of twentieth-century Chinese fiction, vol. 1]. Beijing: Beijing daxue chubanshe, 1989.

——. "Literature High and Low: 'Popular Fiction' in Twentieth-Century China." In *The Literary Field of Twentieth-Century China*, edited by Michel Hockx, 113–133. Honolulu: University of Hawai'i Press, 1999.

———. *Qiangu wenren xiake meng: Wuxia xiaoshuo leixing yanjiu* 千古文人俠客夢：武俠小說類型研究 [Chivalric dreams of the literati: A generic study of martial arts fiction]. Beijing: Renmin wenxue chubanshe, 1992.

———. *Zai dongxi wenhua pengzhong zhong* 在東西文化碰撞中 [Between the conflict of Eastern and Western culture]. Hangzhou: Zhejiang wenyi chubanshe, 1987.

———. *Zhongguo sanwen xiaoshuo shi* 中國散文小說史 [History of Chinese proses and novels]. Beijing: Beijing daxue chubanshe, 2010.

———. *Zhongguo xiaoshuo xushi moshi de zhuanbian* 中國小說敘事模式的轉變 [Transformations of narrative modes in Chinese novels]. Shanghai: Shanghai renmin chubanshe, 1988.

———. *Zuowei xueke de wenxue shi* 作為學科的文學史 [Literary history as a discipline]. Beijing: Beijing daxue chubanshe, 2011.

Chen Pingyuan and David Der-wei Wang, eds. *Beijing: dushi xiangxiang yu wenhua jiyi* 北京：都市想像與文化記憶 [Beijing: Urban imaginations and cultural memories]. Beijing: Beijing daxue chubanshe, 2005.

Chen Shixiang (Chen Shih-hsing) 陳世驤. "Chen Shixiang xiansheng shuhan" 陳世驤先生書函 [Letters to Jin Yong], April 22, 1966, and November 20, 1970." Reprinted in *Tianlong babu*, 1975–1978.

Chen Shizeng 陳師曾. *Beijing fengsu* 北京風俗 [Folk life in Beijing]. Beijing: Beijing chubanshe, 2003.

Chen Shunxin 陳順馨. *Shehui zhuyi xianshi zhuyi lilun zai zhongguo de jieshou yu zhuanhuan* 社會主義現實主義理論在中國的接受與轉換 [The reception and modification of the theory of socialist realism in China]. Hefei: Anhui jiaoyu chubanshe, 2000.

Chen, Ta-tsun. *From a Cottager's Sketchbook*. Hong Kong: The Chinese University Press, 2005.

Chen Tushou 陳徒手. "Wumen chengxia de Shen Congwen" 午門城下的沈從文 [Shen Congwen under the Wumen Gate]. In *Ren youbing, tian zhifou: 1949 nianhou zhongguo wentan jishi* 人有病天知否——一九四九年後的中國文壇紀實 [People are sick, is heaven aware? Chronicles of the Chinese literary world after 1949], 13–42. Beijing: Renmin wenxue, 2000.

Chen Wenliang 陳文良, ed. *Beijing chuantong wenhua bianlan* 北京傳統文化便覽 [An encyclopedia of Beijing traditional culture]. Beijing: Yanshan chubanshe, 1992.

Chen, Xiaomei. *Acting the "Right" Part: Political Theater and Popular Drama in Contemporary China*. Honolulu: University of Hawai'i Press, 2002.

———, ed. *The Columbia Anthology of Modern Chinese Drama*. New York: Columbia University Press, 2010.

———. *Occidentalism: A Theory of Counter-Discourse in Post-Mao China*. New York: Oxford University Press, 1995.

———, ed. *Reading the Right Text: An Anthology of Contemporary Chinese Drama*. Honolulu: University of Hawai'i Press, 2003.

Chen Xiaoming 陳曉明. "Chengshi wenxue—wufa xianshen de 'tazhe'" 城市文學一無法現身的"他者" [Urban literature: An invisible "other"]. *Wenyi yanjiu* 文藝研究 [Literature and art studies] 1 (2006): 12–25.

Chen Xueyong 陳學勇. *Cainü de shijie* 才女的世界 [World of a talented lady]. Beijing: Kunlun chubanshe, 2001.

Chen Yixian 陳貽先 and Chen Lengtai 陳冷汰, trans. *Qinggong ernian ji* 清宮二年記 [Two years in the Forbidden City]. Shanghai: Shangwu yinshuguan, 1937.

Chen Yingzhen 陳映真. "Gu'er de lishi, lishi de gu'er: Shiping Yaxiya de gu'er" 孤兒的歷史，歷史的孤兒：試評亞細亞的孤兒 [The history of an orphan, the orphan of the history: Interpreting *Orphan of Asia*]. In *Chen Yingzhen zuopin ji* 陳映真作品集 [Selected works of Chen Yingzhen], vol. 9, *Bianzi yu tideng* 鞭子與提燈 [Lash and lamp]. Taipei: Renjian chubanshe, 1988.

———. "Yuanxiang de shiluo: Shiping *Jiazhutao*" 原鄉的失落：試評《夾竹桃》 [The loss of old homeland: Comments on *Jiazhutao*]. *Xiandai wenxue* 現代文學 [Modern literature], literary supplement, no. 1 (July 1977). Reprinted in Chen Yingzhen, *Gu'er de lishi, lishi de gu'er* 孤兒的歷史，歷史的孤兒 [Orphans' history, and history's orphans], 97–109. Taipei: Yuanjing chuban shiye gongsi, 1984.

Chen Yu 陳宇. "Yilu jiedu Xu Zhimo: Xu Zhimo qinpeng caifang shouji" 一路解讀徐志摩：徐志摩親朋採訪手記 [Reading Xu Zhimo all along: Notes on Interviews with Xu Zhimo's Relatives and Friends]. *Zhuanji wenxue* 傳記文學 [Biographical literature] 12 (1999): http://www.shuku.net/novels/zhuanji/sahqzwrpbj/zlsj14.html.

Chen Zishan 陳子善, ed. *Food and Chinese Culture: Essays on Popular Cuisines*. San Francisco: Long River Press, 2005.

Cheng Hsiu-ting. "Shui de yuanxiang? Shui de shiluo?—Ping Chen Yinzheng dui Zhong Lihe minzu rentong de qujie" 誰的原鄉？誰的失落？——評陳映真對鍾理和民族認同的曲解 [Whose native land? Whose loss?—On Chen Yingzhen's misunderstanding of Zhong Lihe's national identification]. *Taiwan wenxue pinglun* 台灣文學評論 [Taiwan literary review] 4 (2005): 160–185.

Cheng Zhang 成長. "80hou yanyuan jiegou *Chaguan*" 80 後演員解構《茶館》 [The Post-80s generation actors deconstructed *Teahouse*]. *Zhongguo wenhua bao* 中國文化報 [Chinese culture daily], January 29, 2010.

Cheung, Esther M. K. "Introduction to the New Edition: New Ends in a City of Transition." In Leung Ping-kwan, *City at the End of Time*, translated by Gordon T. Osing and Leung Ping-kwan, 1–19. Hong Kong: Hong Kong University Press, 2012.

Chi Pang-yuan 齊邦媛. "Chaoyue beihuan de tongnian" 超越悲歡的童年 [Beyond joyous and sorrowful childhood]. Reprinted in *Lin Haiyin yanjiu lunwenji* 林海音研究論文集 [Selected articles on Lin Haiyin], edited by Shu Yi and Fu Guangming, 92–97. Beijing: Taihai chubanshe, 2001.

———. "Severance—for Hai-yin." Translated by Nicholas Koss. *The Chinese Pen: Contemporary Chinese Literature from Taiwan* 30 (Spring 2002): 5–14.

Chi, Pang-yuan, and David Der-wei Wang, eds. *Chinese Literature in the Second Half of a Modern Century*. Bloomington: Indiana University Press, 2000.

Ching, Leo T. S. *Becoming "Japanese": Colonial Taiwan and the Politics of Identity Formation*. Berkeley: University of California Press, 2001.

Chow, Eileen. "Serial Sightings: News, Novelties, and an *Unofficial History of the Old Capital*." In *Rethinking Chinese Popular Culture*, edited by Carlos Rojas and Eileen Cheng-yin Chow, 54–74. London: Routledge, 2009.

———. "Spectacular Novelties, 'News' Culture, Zhang Henshui, and Practices of Spectatorship in Republican China." PhD diss., Stanford University, 2000.

Chow, Rey. *Ethics after Idealism: Theory-Culture-Ethnicity-Reading*. Bloomington: Indiana University Press, 1998.

———. "Fateful Attachments: On Collecting, Fidelity, and Lao She." *Critical Inquiry* 28, no. 1 (Autumn 2001): 286–304.

———. *Primitive Passions: Visuality, Sexuality, Ethnography, and Contemporary Cinema*. New York: Columbia University Press, 1995.

———. "Seminal Dispersal, Fecal Retention, and Related Narrative Matters: Eileen Chang's Tale of Roses in the Problematic of Modern Writing." *Differences: A Journal of Feminist Cultural Studies* 11, no. 2 (1999): 153–176.

———. *Woman and Chinese Modernity: The Politics of Reading between West and East*. Minneapolis: University of Minnesota Press, 1991.

———. *Writing Diaspora: Tactics of Intervention in Contemporary Cultural Studies*. Bloomington: Indiana University Press, 1993.

Chow, Tse-Tsung. *The May Fourth Movement: Intellectual Revolution in Modern China*. Cambridge, MA: Harvard University Press, 1960.

Chu, T'ien-wen. *Note of a Desolate Man*. Translated by Howard Goldblatt and Sylvia Li-chun Lin. New York: Columbia University Press, 1999.

Clarke, Graham, ed. *The American City: Literary and Cultural Perspectives*. New York: St. Martin's Press, 1988.

Clifford, James. *The Predicament of Culture: Twentieth-Century Ethnography, Literature, and Art*. Cambridge, MA: Harvard University Press, 1988.

Clough, Patricia Ticineto, ed. *The Affective Turn*. Durham, NC: Duke University Press, 2007.

Clunas, Craig. *Superfluous Things: Material Culture and Social Status in Early Modern China*. Urbana: University of Illinois Press, 1991.

Cody, Jeffrey W., Nancy Steinhardt, and Tony Atkin, eds. *Chinese Architecture and the Beaux-Arts*. Honolulu: University of Hawai'i Press; Hong Kong: Hong Kong University Press, 2011.

Cohen, Paul A. *China Unbound: Evolving Perspectives on the Chinese Past*. London: Routledge, 2003.

———. *Discovering History in China: American Historical Writing on the Recent Chinese Past*. New York: Columbia University Press, 1984.

Confucius et al. *The Book of Rites (Li Ji): English-Chinese Version*. Edited by Dai Sheng, translated by James Legge. Beijing: Intercultural Press, 2013.

Dai, Jinhua 戴錦華. *Cinema and Desire: Feminist Marxism and Cultural Politics in the Work of Dai Jinhua*. London: Verso, 2002.

———, ed. *Shuxie wenhua yingxiong: Shiji zhijiao de wenhua yanjiu* 書寫文化英雄：世紀之交的文化研究 [Writing cultural heroes: Cultural studies in the twentieth-century fin-de-siècle]. Nanjing: Jiangsu renmin chubanshe, 2000.

Dariotis, Wei Ming, and Eileen Fung. "Breaking the Soy Sauce Jar: Diaspora and Displacement in the Films of Ang Lee." In *Transnational Chinese Cinemas: Identity, Nationhood, Gender*, edited by Sheldon Lu, 207–213. Honolulu: University of Hawai'i Press, 1997.

Daruvala, Susan. *Zhou Zuoren and an Alternative Chinese Response to Modernity*. Cambridge, MA: Harvard University Asia Center, 2000.

Davis, Mike. *City of Quartz: Excavating the Future in Los Angeles*. London: Verso, 1990.

De Man, Paul. *Blindness and Insight: Essays in the Rhetoric of Contemporary Criticism*. Minneapolis: University of Minnesota Press, 1983.

Deleuze, Gilles, and Felix Guattari. *Anti-Oedipus: Capitalism and Schizophrenia*. Translated by Robert Hurlet, Mark Seem, and Helen R. Lane. Minneapolis: University of Minnesota Press, 1983.

———. *A Thousand Plateaus*. Translated by Brian Massumi. Minneapolis: University of Minnesota Press, 1987.

Denton, Kirk A. *Exhibiting the Past: Historical Memory and the Politics of Museums in Postsocialist China*. Honolulu: University of Hawai'i Press, 2014.

———, ed. *Modern Chinese Literary Thought: Writings on Literature, 1893–1945*. Stanford, CA: Stanford University Press, 1996.

Denton, Kirk A., and Michel Hockx, eds. *Literary Societies of Republican China*. Lanham, MD: Lexington Books, 2008.

Der Ling, Princess. *Imperial Incense*. New York: Dodd, Mead, 1933.

———. *Kowtow*. New York: Dodd, Mead, 1929.

———. *Lotos Petals*. New York: Dodd, Mead, 1930.

———. *Old Buddha*. New York: Dodd, Mead, 1928.

———. *Two Years in the Forbidden City*. 1911. Rpt. New York: Dodd, Mead, 1931.

Derrida, Jacques. *Dissemination*. Translated by Barbara Johnson. New York: Continuum, 2004.

Dirlik, Arif. "The Predicament of Marxist Revolutionary Consciousness: Mao Zedong, Antonio Gramsci, and the Reformulation of Marxist Revolutionary Theory." *Modern China* 9, no. 2 (April 1983): 182–211.

Dong, Madeleine Yue. *Republican Beijing: The City and Its Histories*. Berkeley: University of California Press, 2003.

Dooling, Amy D., and Kristina M. Torgeson, eds. *Writing Women in Modern China: An Anthology of Women's Literature from the Early Twentieth Century*. New York: Columbia University Press, 1998.

Du Xiaozhen 杜小真. *Yaoyuan de muguang* 遙遠的目光 [The views from afar]. Beijing: Sanlian shudian, 2003.

Duara, Prasenjit. *Rescuing History from the Nation: Questioning Narratives of Modern China*. Chicago: University of Chicago Press, 1995.

Dung, Kai-cheung. *Atlas: The Archaeology of an Imaginary City*. Translated by Dung Kai-cheung, Anders Hansson, and Bonnie S. McDougall. New York: Columbia University Press, 2012.

Dutton, Michael, ed. *Streetlife China*. New York: Cambridge University Press, 1998.

Dyer, Richard. "Entertainment and Utopia." In *The Cultural Studies Reader*, 2nd ed., edited by Simon During, 371–381. London: Routledge, 1999.

Elvin, Mark, and G. William Skinner, eds. *The Chinese City between Two Worlds*. Stanford, CA: Stanford University Press, 1974.

Eng, David L., and David Kazanjian, eds. *Loss: The Politics of Mourning*. Berkeley, CA: University of California Press, 2003.

Esherick, Joseph W., ed. *Remaking the Chinese City: Modernity and National Identity, 1900–1950*. Stanford, CA: Stanford University Press, 2000.

Fairbank, John K. *Chinabound: A Fifty-Year Memoir*. New York: Harper & Row, 1982.

Fairbank, Wilma. *Liang and Lin: Partners in Exploring China's Architectural Past*. Philadelphia: University of Pennsylvania Press, 1994.

Farquhar, Judith. *Appetites: Food and Sex in Post-Socialist China*. Durham, NC: Duke University Press, 2002.

Fei Ming 廢名. *Fei Ming xuanji* 廢名選集 [Selected works of Fei Ming]. Chengdu: Sichuan wenyi chubanshe, 1988.

Felman, Shoshana, and Dori Laub. *Testimony: Crises of Witnessing in Literature, Psychoanalysis, and History.* New York: Routledge, 1992.

Fine, Ellen S. "The Absent Memory: The Act of Writing in Post-Holocaust French Literature." *Writing and the Holocaust* (1988): 41–57.

Fiske, John. *Understanding Popular Culture.* London: Routledge, 1991.

Flatley, Jonathan. *Affective Mapping: Melancholia and the Politics of Modernism.* Cambridge, MA: Harvard University Press, 2008.

Fogel, Joshua. *Between China and Japan: The Writings of Joshua Fogel.* Leiden: Brill, 2015.

Forsdick, Charles. "Sight, Sound, and Synaesthesia: Reading the Senses in Victor Segalen." In *Sensual Reading: New Approaches to Reading in Its Relations to the Senses*, edited by Michael Syrotinski and Ian Maclachlan, 229–247. London: Associated University Press, 2001.

———. *Victor Segalen and the Aesthetics of Diversity: Journeys Between Cultures.* New York: Oxford University Press, 2000.

Foucault, Michel. *Language, Counter-Memory, Practice.* Translated by Donald F. Bouchard and Sherry Simon. Ithaca, NY: Cornell University Press, 1977.

———. "Lecture: 7 January 1976." Translated by David Macey. In *Twentieth Century Literary Theory: A Reader*, edited by K. M. Newton, 129–134. New York: St. Martin's Press, 1997.

———. *The Order of Things: An Archaeology of the Human Sciences.* New York: Vintage, 1973.

———. "Of Other Spaces." *Diacritics* 16 (1986): 22–27.

Franco, Jean. *The Decline and Fall of the Lettered City: Latin America in the Cold War.* Cambridge, MA: Harvard University Press, 2002.

Freud, Sigmund. "Family Romance." In *The Freud Reader*, edited by Peter Guy, 297–300. New York: Norton, 1989.

———. "Mourning and Melancholia." In *The Freud Reader*, edited by Peter Gay, 584–589. New York: Norton, 1989.

Fried, Daniel. "A Bloody Absence: Communist Narratology and the Literature of May Thirtieth." *Chinese Literature: Essays, Articles, Reviews* 26 (2004): 23–53.

Fu, Poshek. *Between Shanghai and Hong Kong: The Politics of Chinese Cinemas.* Stanford, CA: Stanford University Press, 2003.

Gálik, Márian. "Liang Shih-ch'iu and Chinese New Humanism." In *The Genesis of Modern Chinese Literary Criticism, 1917–1930*, 285–307. London: Curzon Press, 1980.

Geertz, Clifford. *The Interpretation of Cultures.* New York: Basic Books, 1973.

Gernet, Jacques. *Daily Life of China.* Stanford, CA: Stanford University Press, 1970.

Gilloch, Graeme. *Myth and Metropolis: Walter Benjamin and the City.* Cambridge, UK: Polity Press, 1996.

Gleber, Anke. *The Art of Taking a Walk: Flanerie, Literature, and Film in Weimar Culture.* Princeton, NJ: Princeton University Press, 1999.

Goldman, Andrea. *Opera and the City: The Politics of Culture in Beijing, 1770–1900.* Stanford, CA: Stanford University Press, 2012.

Gong Pengcheng 龔鵬程. "Yinzhuan de wenxue shehuixue" 飲饌的文學社會學 [Literary sociology of drinking and eating]. In *Liang Shiqiu yu zhongxi wenhua* 梁實秋與中西文化 [Liang Shiqiu in Chinese and Western cultures], edited by Gao Xudong 高旭東, 73–94. Beijing: Zhonghua shuju, 2007.

Goodman, Brynna. *Native Place, City, and Nation: Regional Networks and Identities in Shanghai, 1853–1937.* Berkeley: University of California Press, 1995.

Gottdiener, M., and Alexandros Ph. Lagopoulos, eds. *The City and the Sign: An Introduction to Urban Semiotics*. New York: Columbia University Press, 1986.

Gramsci, Antonio. *Selections from the Prison Notebooks*. New York: International Publishers, 1971.

Gregg, Melissa, and Gregory J. Seigworth, eds. *The Affect Theory Reader*. Durham, NC: Duke University Press, 2010.

Gu Qiuxin 顧秋心, trans. *Qinggong ernian ji* 清宮二年記 [Two years in the Forbidden City]. Kunming: Yunnan renmin chubanshe, 1981.

Guan Jixin 關紀新. *Lao She yu manzu wenhua* 老舍與滿族文化 [Lao She and Manchu culture]. Shenyang: Liaoning minzu chubanshe, 2008.

Gunn, Edward. *Rendering the Regional: Local Language in Contemporary Chinese Media*. Honolulu: University of Hawai'i Press, 2006.

———. *Rewriting Chinese: Style and Innovation in Twentieth-Century Chinese Prose*. Stanford, CA: Stanford University Press, 1991.

———. *Unwelcome Muse: Chinese Literature in Shanghai and Peking, 1937–1945*. New York: Columbia University Press, 1980.

Guo Hongan 郭宏安. "Ping *Lenei Laisi*: zhongyiben daixu" 評《勒內•萊斯》：中譯本代序 [Comments on *René Leys*: Preface to the Chinese Version]. In *Lenei Laisi* 勒內•萊斯 [*René Leys*], translated by Mei Bin 梅斌, revised by Guo Hongan, 1–11. Beijing: Sanlian shudian, 1991.

Habermas, Jürgen. *The Structural Transformation of the Public Sphere*. Translated by Thomas Burger. Cambridge, MA: The MIT Press, 1991.

Halbwachs, Maurice. *The Collective Memory*. New York: Harper, 1980.

Hall, Peter. *Cities of Tomorrow: An Intellectual History of Urban Planning and Design in the Twentieth Century*. New York: Basil Blackwell, 1988.

———. *City in Civilization*. New York: Pantheon Books, 1998.

———. *The World Cities*. New York: McGraw-Hill, 1966.

Hamm, John Christopher. *Paper Swordsmen: Jin Yong and the Modern Chinese Martial Arts Novel*. Honolulu: University of Hawai'i Press, 2005.

Han, Bangqing. *The Sing-Song Girls of Shanghai*. First translated by Eileen Chang, revised and edited by Eva Hung. New York: Columbia University Press, 2005.

Han Guanghui 韓光輝. *Beijing lishi renkou dili* 北京歷史人口地理 [A historical demographic geography of Beijing]. Beijing: Beijing daxue chubanshe, 1996.

Han, Shaogong. *A Dictionary of Maoqiao*. Translated by Julia Lovell. New York: Columbia University Press, 2003.

Hanan, Patrick. *The Sea of Regret: Two Turn-of-the-Century Chinese Romantic Novels*. Honolulu: University of Hawai'i Press, 1995.

Handlin, Oscar, and John Burchard. *The Historian and the City*. Cambridge, MA: The MIT Press, 1962.

Hansen, Valerie. "The Mystery of the Qingming Scroll and Its Subject: The Case Against Kaifeng." *The Journal of Sung-Yuan Studies* 26 (1996): 183–200.

Harding, Jennifer, and E. Deidre Pribram, eds. *Emotions: A Cultural Studies Reader*. London: Routledge, 2009.

Hardt, Michael, and Antonio Negri. *Empire*. Cambridge, MA: Harvard University Press, 2000.

Harvey, David. *The Condition of Postmodernity: An Enquiry into the Origins of Cultural Change*. Oxford: Blackwell, 1989.

———. *Consciousness and the Urban Experience: Studies in the History and Theory of Capitalist Urbanization.* Baltimore: Johns Hopkins University Press, 1985.

———. *Paris, Capital of Modernity.* New York: Routledge, 2003.

———. *The Urbanization of Capital.* Baltimore: Johns Hopkins University Press, 1985.

Hayot, Eric. *The Hypothetical Mandarin: Sympathy, Modernity, and Chinese Pain.* New York: Oxford University Press, 2009.

———. *On Literary Worlds.* New York: Oxford University Press, 2012.

Hayot, Eric, Haun Saussy, and Steven Yao, eds. *Sinographies: Writing China.* Minneapolis: University of Minnesota Press, 2007.

Hayter-Menzies, Grant. *Imperial Masquerade: The Legend of Princess Der Ling.* Hong Kong: Hong Kong University Press, 2008.

He Guimei 賀桂梅. *Zhuanzhe de shidai: siwushi niandai zuojia yanjiu* 轉折的時代：四五十年代作家研究 [A time of transition: Studies of writers of the 1940s and 1950s]. Jinan: Shandong jiaoyu chubanshe, 2003.

He Qun 何群. "He Qun fangtan" 何群訪談 [An interview with He Qun]. *Dazhong dianying* 大眾電影 [Popular cinema] 16 (2010): 34–36.

Hershatter, Gail. *Dangerous Pleasures: Prostitution and Modernity in Twentieth-Century Shanghai.* Berkeley: University of California Press, 1997.

Hevia, James. *Cherishing Men from Afar: Qing Guest Ritual and the McCartney Embassy of 1793.* Durham, NC: Duke University Press, 1995.

———. "Cong chaogong tizhi dao zhimin yanjiu" 從朝貢體制到殖民研究 [From tributive system to colonial study]. Translated by Weijie Song. *Dushu* 讀書 [Reading] 8 (1998): 61–69.

———. "Looting Beijing: 1860, 1900." In *Tokens of Exchange: The Problem of Translation in Global Circulations*, edited by Lydia H. Liu, 192–213. Durham, NC: Duke University Press, 1999.

Hillenbrand, Margaret. *Literature, Modernity, and the Practice of Resistance: Japanese and Taiwanese Fiction, 1960–1990.* Leiden: Brill, 2007.

Hirsch, Marianne. "The Generation of Postmemory." *Poetics Today* 29, no. 1 (Spring 2008): 103–128.

Hobsbawn, Eric J. *Primitive Rebels: Studies in Archaic Form of Social Movement in the 19th and 20th Centuries.* New York: W. W. Norton & Company, Inc., 1959.

Hockx, Michel, ed. *The Literary Field of Twentieth Century China.* Honolulu: University of Hawai'i Press, 1999.

Hockx, Michel. *Questions of Style: Literary Societies and Literary Journals in Modern China, 1911–1937.* Leiden: Brill, 2003.

———. *A Snowy Morning: Eight Chinese Poets on the Road to Modernity.* Leiden: CNWS, 1994.

Holdsworth, May, and Caroline Courtauld, rev. ed. *The Forbidden City: The Great Within.* London: Frances Lincoln, 2008.

Hong Zicheng 洪子誠. *Zhongguo dangdai wenxue shi* 中國當代文學史 [History of Chinese contemporary literature]. Beijing: Beijing daxue chubanshe, 1999.

———, ed. *Zhongguo dangdai wenxue shi shiliaoxuan 1945–1999* 中國當代文學史史料選 1945–1999 [Selections of historical materials for contemporary Chinese literary history, 1945–1999]. Wuhan: Changjiang wenyi chubanshe, 2002.

———. *A History of Contemporary Chinese Literature.* Translated by Michael Day. Leiden: Brill, 2007.

———. *Wenti yu fangfa: Zhongguo dangdai wenxue shi yanjiu jianggao* 問題與方法：中國當代文學史研究講稿 [Problems and methods: Manuscripts of study on contemporary Chinese literary history]. Beijing: Beijing daxue chubanshe, 2010.

Hou Renzhi 侯仁之, ed. *Beijing lishi ditu ji* 北京歷史地圖集 [Historical maps of Beijing]. Beijing: Beijing chubanshe, 1988.

Hsia, C. T. *Classical Chinese Novels*. New York: Columbia University Press, 1968.

———. *C. T. Hsia on Chinese Literature*. New York: Columbia University Press, 2004.

———. *A History of Modern Chinese Fiction*. With an introduction by David Der-wei Wang. Bloomington: Indiana University Press, 1999.

———. *Jichuang ji* 雞窗集 [A collection of the study]. Shanghai: Sanlian shudian, 2000.

Hsia, T. A. *The Gate of the Darkness: Studies on the Leftist Literary Movement in China*. Seattle: University of Washington Press, 1968.

Hsieh, Yvonne Y. *From Occupation to Revolution: China through the Eyes of Loti, Claudel, Segalen, and Malraux (1895–1933)*. Birmingham, AL: Summa Publications, 1996.

———. *Victor Segalen: Literary Encounter with China: Chinese Moulds, Western Thoughts*. Toronto: University of Toronto Press, 1988.

Hu Jieqing 胡絜青, ed. *Lao She shenghuo yu chuangzuo zishu* 老舍生活與創作自述 [Lao She's accounts of his life and works]. Hong Kong: Sanlian, 1980.

Hu Jinquan 胡金銓 (King Hu). *Lao She he ta de zuopin* 老舍和他的作品 [Lao She and his works]. Hong Kong: Wenhua shenghuo chubanshe, 1977.

Hu, Shih 胡適. *Chinese Renaissance*. New York: Paragon Book Reprint Corp., 1963.

Huang, Martin W. *Desire and Fictional Narrative in Late Imperial China*. Cambridge, MA: Harvard University Asia Center, 2001.

Huang, Nicole. *Women, War, Domesticity: Shanghai Literature and Popular Culture of the 1940s*. Leiden: Brill, 2005.

Huang Yongyu 黃永玉, ed. *Changhe bujinliu: Huainian Shen Congwen xiansheng* 長河不盡流——懷念沈從文先生 [Long river flows endlessly: Memories of Mr. Shen Congwen]. Changsha: Hunan wenyi chubanshe, 1989.

Huang Ziping 黃子平. *Geming, lishi, xiaoshuo* 革命·歷史·小說 [Revolution, history, and fiction]. Hong Kong: Oxford University Press, 1996.

Huang Ziping, Chen Pingyuan, and Qian Liqun 錢理群. *Ershi shiji Zhongguo wenxue sanren tan* 二十世紀中國文學三人談 [Three critics on twentieth-century Chinese literature]. Beijing: Renmin wenxue chubanshe, 1988.

Hughes, Richard. *Hong Kong: Borrowed Place, Borrowed Time*. Rev. ed. London: Deutsch; revision, 1976.

Hung, Chang-tai. "Revolutionary History in Stone: The Making of a Chinese National Monument." *The China Quarterly* 166 (June 2001): 457–473.

Hunt, Lynn. *The Family Romance of the French Revolution*. Berkeley: University of California Press, 1993.

Huss, Ann, and Jianmei Liu, eds. *The Jin Yong Phenomenon: Chinese Martial Arts Fiction and Modern Chinese Literary History*. Youngstown, NY: Cambria Press, 2007.

Huyssen, Andreas. *After the Great Divide: Modernism, Mass Culture, Postmodernism*. Bloomington: Indiana University Press, 1986.

———. *Present Pasts: Urban Palimpsests and the Politics of Memory*. Stanford, CA: Stanford University Press, 2003.

————. *Twilight Memories: Marking Time in a Culture of Amnesia*. New York: Routledge, 1995.

Jacobs, Jane. *The Death and Life of Great American Cities*. New York: Random House, 1961.

Jameson, Fredric. *The Geopolitical Aesthetic: Cinema and Space in the World System*. Bloomington: Indiana University Press, 1992.

————. *Postmodernism, or the Cultural Logic of Late Capitalism*. Durham, NC: Duke University Press, 1991.

————. "Third-World Literature in the Era of Multinational Capitalism." *Social Text* 15 (Autumn 1986): 65–88.

Jaye, Michael C., and Ann Chalmers Watts, eds. *Literature and the Urban Experience*. New Brunswick, NJ: Rutgers University Press, 1972.

Jensen, Katharine Ann, and Miriam L. Wallace. "Introduction—Facing Emotions." *PMLA* 130, no. 5 (2015): 1249–1268.

Jiang Deming 姜德明, ed. *Beijing hu: xiandai zuojia bixia de Beijing, 1919–1949* 北京乎：現代作家筆下的北京（一九一九—一九四九）[Ah, Beijing: Beijing in modern Chinese writings, 1919–1949]. Beijing: Sanlian shudian, 1992.

Jiao Juyin 焦菊隱. "Lun minzuhua" 論民族化 [On nationalization]. *Xinwenhua shiliao* 新文化史料 [Historical materials of new culture] 2 (1996): 11.

Jiao Juyin 焦菊隱 et al. "Zuotan Lao She de *Chaguan*" 座談老舍的《茶館》[Symposium on Lao She's *Teahouse*]. *Wenyi bao* 文藝報 [Literary Gazette], 1958. Reprinted in *Lao She yanjiu ziliao*, edited by Zeng Guangcan and Wu Huaibin, 788–800. Beijing: Zhishi chanquan chubanshe, 2010.

Jin Shoushen 金壽申. *Lao Beijing de shenghuo* 老北京的生活 [Life in old Beijing]. Beijing: Beijing chubanshe, 1989.

Jin Yong (Louis Cha) 金庸. *Bixue jian* 碧血劍 [The sword stained with royal blood]. Beijing: Sanlian shudian, 1994.

————. *The Book and the Sword*. Translated by Graham Earnshaw, edited by Rachel May and John Minford. Hong Kong: Oxford University Press, 2004.

————. *The Deer and the Cauldron: A Martial Arts Novel*. Translated by John Minford and Rachel May. 3 vols. Hong Kong: Oxford University Press, 1997–2002.

————. *Lujing ji* 鹿鼎記 [The deer and the cauldron]. Beijing: Sanlian shudian, 1994.

————. *Shujian enchou lu* 書劍恩仇錄 [The book and the sword]. Beijing: Sanlian shudian, 1994.

Johnson, Barbara. "Writing." In *Critical Terms for Literary Study*, edited by Frank Lentricchia and Thomas McLaughlin, 39–49. Chicago: University Of Chicago Press, 1995.

Johnson David, Andrew Nathan, and Evelyn Rawski, eds. *Popular Culture in Late Imperial China*. Berkeley: University of California Press, 1985.

Johnston, Reginald F. *Twilight in the Forbidden City*. Cambridge: Cambridge University Press, 1934; reprinted 2011.

Joly-Segalen, Annie, ed. *Segalen et Debussy. Textes recueillis et présentés par Annie Joly-Segalen et André Schaeffner*. Monaco: Éditions du Rocher, 1962.

Jones, Andrew F. "Portable Monuments: Architectural Photography and the 'Forms' of Empire in Modern China." *positions* 18, no. 3 (2010): 599–631.

Kadir, Djelal. *Questing Fictions: Latin America's Family Romance*. Minneapolis: University of Minnesota Press, 1986.

Kafka, Franz. "Building the Great Wall of China." In *Kafka's Selected Stories*, translated and edited by Stanley Corngold, 113–123. New York: W. W. Norton, 2007.

———. "The Great Wall of China." Translated by Edwin Muir and Willa Muir, in *The Metamorphosis and Other Writings*, edited by Helmuth Kiesel, 163–174. New York: Continuum, 2002.

———. "An Imperial Message." Translated by Ian Johnson. http://www.kafka-online.info/an-imperial-message.html.

———. *Kafka's Selected Stories: New Translations, Backgrounds and Contexts, Criticism*. Translated and edited by Stanley Corngold. New York: W. W. Norton, 2007.

———. *The Metamorphosis and Other Writings*. Edited by Helmuth Kiesel. New York: Continuum, 2002.

Kale, Steven. *French Salons: High Society and Political Sociability from the Old Regime to the Revolution of 1848*. Baltimore: John Hopkins University Press, 2006.

Kao, George, ed. *Two Writers and the Cultural Revolutions: Lao She and Chen Jo-hsi*. Hong Kong: Chinese University Press, 1980.

Kaplan, E. Ann. *Trauma Culture: The Politics of Terror and Loss in Media and Literature*. New Brunswick, NJ: Rutgers University Press, 2005.

Karl, Katherine A. *Empress Dowager Cixi: Her Art of Living*. Hong Kong: The Regional Council and the Palace Museum, 1996.

———. *With the Empress Dowager*. New York: The Century, 1905. Rpt. *With the Empress Dowager of China*, London: KPI Limited, 1986.

Karp, Ivan, and Steven D. Lavine, eds. *Exhibiting Cultures: The Poetics and Politics of Museum Display*. Washington, DC: Smithsonian Institution Press, 1991.

Kim, Elaine. *Asian American Literature: An Introduction to the Writings and Their Social Context*. Philadelphia: Temple University Press, 1982.

King, Marjorie. *China's American Daughter: Ida Pruitt (1888–1985)*. Hong Kong: Chinese University Press, 2006.

Kinkley, Jeffrey C. *The Odyssey of Shen Congwen*. Stanford, CA: Stanford University Press, 1987.

Kirby, William C. "Continuity and Change in Modern China: Economic Planning on the Mainland and on Taiwan, 1943–1953." *Australian Journal of Chinese Affairs* 24 (July 1990): 121–141.

Knechtges, David. "Gradually Entering the Realm of Delight: Food and Drink in Early Medieval China." *Journal of the American Oriental Society* 117, no. 2 (1997): 229–239.

———. "A Literary Feast: Food in Early Chinese Literature." *Journal of the American Oriental Society* 106, no. 1 (1986): 49–63.

Ko Ching-ming 柯慶明. *Taiwan xiandai wenxue de shiye* 臺灣現代文學的視野 [Perspectives on Taiwan literature]. Taipei: Maitian, 2006.

Kong, Haili, and John A. Lent, eds. *One Hundred Years of Chinese Cinema: A Generational Dialogue*. Norwalk, CT: EastBridge, 2006.

Konvitz, Josef W. *The Urban Millennium: The City-Building Process from the Early Middle Ages to the Present*. Carbondale: Southern Illinois University Press, 1985.

Korsmeyer, Carolyn. *Making Sense of Taste: Food and Philosophy*. Ithaca, NY: Cornell University Press, 1999.

Kracauer, Siegfried. *The Mass Ornament: Weimar Essays*. Cambridge, MA: Harvard University Press, 1995.

———. *Theory of Film: The Redemption of Physical Reality*. Princeton, NJ: Princeton University Press, 1997.

Kumar, Krishan. *Utopianism*. Milton Keynes: Open University Press, 1991.

Lam Ling Hon 林凌瀚. "Wenhua gongye yu wenhua rentong" 文化工業與文化認同 [Cultural industry and cultural identity]. In *Wenhua xiangxiang yu yishi xingtai* 文化想像與意識形態 [Cultural imagination and ideology], edited by Chen Qingqiao 陳清僑, 229–253. Hong Kong: Oxford University Press, 1997.

Lancashire, Douglas. *Li Po-yuan*. Boston: Twayne Publishers, 1981.

Lao She 老舍. *Beneath the Red Banner*. Translated by Don J. Cohn. Beijing: Panda Books, 1985.

———. *Blades of Grass: The Stories of Lao She*. Translated by William A. Lyell and Sarah Wei-ming Chen. Honolulu: University of Hawai'i Press, 1999.

———. *Camel Xiangzi*. Translated by Shi Xiaoqing. Beijing: Foreign Languages Press, 1981.

———. *Chaguan* 茶館 *Teahouse*. Translated by John Howard-Gibbon. Hong Kong: Chinese University Press, 2004.

———. *Crescent Moon and Other Stories*. Beijing: Chinese Literature, 1985.

———. (Lao Sheh). *Dragon Beard Ditch: A Play in Three Acts*. Translated by Liao Hung-ying. Peking: Foreign Languages Press, 1956.

———. *The Drum Singers*. Translated by Helena Kuo. New York: Harcourt Brace and Co., 1952.

———. *Lao She juzuo quanji* 老舍劇作全集 [Complete dramas of Lao She]. Vol. 2. Beijing: Zhongguo xiju chubanshe, 1982.

———. *Lao She wenyi pinglun ji* 老舍文藝評論集 [Collection of Lao She's literary criticisms]. Hefei: Anhui renmin chubanshe, 1982.

———. (Lau Shaw). *Rickshaw Boy*. Translated by Evan King. New York: Reynal & Hitchcock, Inc., 1945.

———. *Rickshaw: The Novel of Lo-t'o Hsiang Tzu*. Translated by Jean M. James. Honolulu: University of Hawai'i Press, 1979.

———. *Rickshaw Boy*. Translated by Howard Goldblatt. New York: Harper Perennial Modern Chinese Classics, 2010.

———. *Shen Quan* 神拳 [Magical boxers]. Beijing: Zhongguo xiju chubanshe, 1963.

———. *Sishi tongtang* 四世同堂 [Four generations under one roof]. In *Lao She wenji* 老舍文集 [Selected writings of Lao She]. Vol. 4–6. Beijing: Renmin wenxue chubanshe, 1983–1984.

———. *Teahouse*. Translated by John Howard-Gibbon. Beijing: Foreign Languages Press, 1980.

———. *Teahouse*. Translated by Ying Ruocheng. Taipei: Shulin chuban, 2004.

———. *Teahouse: A Play in Three Acts*. Translated by John Howard-Gibbon. Beijing: Foreign Languages Press, 1980.

———. "Xiang Beiping" 想北平 [Missing Beijing]. In *Beijing hu*, edited by Jiang Deming, 408–411. Beijing: Sanlian shudian, 1992.

———. (Lau Shaw [S. Y. Shu]). *The Yellow Storm*. Translated by Ida Pruitt. New York: Harcourt, Brace and Company, 1951.

Larson, Wendy. *Literary Authority and the Modern Chinese Writer*. Durham, NC: Duke University Press, 1993.

———. *Women and Writing in Modern China*. Stanford, CA: Stanford University Press, 1998.

———. *From Ah Q to Lei Feng: Freud and Revolutionary Spirit in 20th Century China*. Stanford, CA: Stanford University Press, 2009.

Lau, Joseph. "Naturalism in Chinese Fiction." *Literature East and West* 2 (1970): 148–160.

Laughlin, Charles A. "The *Analects* Group and the Genre of *Xiaopin*." In *Literary Societies of Republican China*, edited by Kirk A. Denton and Michel Hockx, 207–240. Lanham, MD: Lexington Books, 2008.

———. *The Literature of Leisure and Chinese Modernity*. Honolulu: University of Hawai'i Press, 2008.

Laurence, Patricia. *Lily Briscoe's Chinese Eyes: Bloomsbury, Modernism, and China*. Columbia: University of South Carolina Press, 2003.

Lee, Haiyan. "All the Feelings That Are Fit to Print: The Community of Sentiment and the Literary Public Sphere in China, 1900–1918." *Modern China* 27, no. 3 (2001): 291–327.

———. "The Charisma of Power and the Military Sublime in Tiananmen Square." *Journal of Asian Studies* 70, no. 2 (2011): 397–424.

———. *Revolution of the Heart: A Genealogy of Love in China, 1900–1950*. Stanford, CA: Stanford University Press, 2007.

———. "The Ruins of Yuanmingyuan; Or, How to Enjoy a National Wound." *Modern China* 35, no. 2 (2009): 155–190.

———. "Tears That Crumbled the Great Wall: The Archaeology of Feeling in the May Fourth Folklore Movement." *Journal of Asian Studies* 64, no. 1 (2005): 35–65.

Lee, Leo Ou-fan. "In Search of Modernity: Some Reflections on a New Mode of Consciousness in Twentieth-Century Chinese History and Literature." In *Ideas Across Cultures: Essays on Chinese Thoughts in Honor of Benjamin I. Schwartz*, edited by Paul Cohen and Merle Goldman, 109–135. Cambridge, MA: Harvard University Press, 1990.

———. *Shanghai Modern: The Flowering of a New Urban Culture in China, 1930–1945*. Cambridge, MA: Harvard University Press, 1999.

———. "The Solitary Traveler: Images of the Self in Modern Chinese Literature." In *Expressions of Self in Chinese Literature*, edited by Robert Hegel and Richard Hessney, 282–307. New York: Columbia University Press, 1985.

———. *Voices from the Iron House: A Study of Lu Xun*. Bloomington: Indiana University Press, 1987.

Lees, Andrew. *Cities Perceived: Urban Society in American and European Thought, 1820–1940*. New York: Columbia University Press, 1985.

Lefebvre, Henri. *Critique of Everyday Life*. Vol. 1. Translated by John Moore. London: Verso, 1991.

———. *Critique of Everyday Life*. Vol. 2. Translated by John Moore. London: Verso, 2002.

———. *The Production of Space*. Translated by Donald Nicholson-Smith. Oxford: Blackwell, 1991.

———. *The Urban Revolution*. Minneapolis: University of Minnesota Press, 2003.

———. *Writings on Cities*. Oxford: Blackwell, 1996.

LeGates, Richard T., and Frederic Stout, eds. *City Reader*. New York: Routledge, 2000.

Lehan, Richard. *The City in Literature: An Intellectual and Cultural History*. Berkeley: University of California Press, 1998.

Lentricchia, Frank, and Thomas McLaughlin, eds. *Critical Terms for Literary Studies*. Chicago: University of Chicago Press, 1995, second edition.

Leung, Ping-kwan 梁秉鈞. *City at the End of Time*. Translated by Gordon T. Osing and Leung Ping-kwan. Hong Kong: Hong Kong University Press, 2012.

———. "Zhang Ailing yu Xianggang" 張愛玲與香港 [Eileen Chang and Hong Kong]. In *Zaidu Zhang Ailing* 再讀張愛玲 [Re-reading Eileen Chang], edited by Joseph S. M. Lau, Leung Ping-kwan, and Xu Zidong, 197–206. Jinan: Shandong huabao chubanshe, 2004.

———. "1957 nian, Xianggang" 1957 年, 香港 [1957 Hong Kong]. In *1949 yihou: dangdai wenxue liushi nian* 1949 以後：當代文學六十年 [After 1949: Sixty years of contemporary literature], edited by David Der-wei Wang, Chen Sihe, and Xu Zidong, 199–211. Shanghai: Shanghai wenyi chubanshe, 2011.

Levenson, Joseph R. *Confucian China and Its Modern Fate*. Vol. 1. Berkeley: University of California Press, 1965.

Levi-Strauss, Claude. *The View from Afar*. Translated by Joachim Neugroschel and Phoebe Hoss. New York: Basic Books, 1985.

Li Baozhen 李葆真, trans. *Yuyuan lanxin ji* 御苑蘭馨記 [Old Buddha]. Hong Kong: Baixin shudian, 1954. Rpt. *Cixi lianai jishi* 慈禧戀愛紀實 [Empress Dowager Cixi's romance]. Beijing: Zuojia chubanshe, 1989.

Li Boyuan 李伯元. *Gengzi guobian tanci* 庚子國變彈詞 [Tanci, on the Boxer Rebellion of 1900]. Shanghai: Shijie fanhua bao, 1902.

———. *Officialdom Unmasked*. Translated and abridged by T. L. Yang. Hong Kong: Hong Kong University Press, 2001.

———. *Modern Times: A Brief History of Enlightenment*. Translated by Douglas Lancashire. Hong Kong: Chinese University Press, 1996.

Li Jianwu 李健吾. "Du *Chaguan*" 讀《茶館》[Reading *Teahouse*]. *Renmin wenxue* 人民文學 [People's literature] 1 (1958): 1, 45.

———. "Jiushijiu du zhong—Lin Huiyin nüshi zuo" 《九十九度中》—林徽因女士作 [In Ninety-Nine-Degree Heat—Written by Madam Lin Huiyin]. In *Chuangzi neiwai yi Huiyin*, edited by Liu, 19–22. Beijing: Renmin wenxue chubanshe, 2001.

Li Lei 李蕾. "Jingpai zuojia de juhe xingtai kaojiu: Yi shalong wei lunshu zhongxin" 京派作家的聚合形態考究：以沙龍為論述中心 [Beijing school writers' group gathering: Salon as a distinctive form]. *Jilin daxue shehui kexue xuebao* 吉林大學社會科學學報) [Jilin University journal of social sciences] 4 (2009): 106–110.

Li, Lillian M., Alison Dray-Novey, and Haili Kong. *Beijing: From Imperial Capital to Olympic City*. New York: Palgrave Macmillan, 2007.

Li, Peter. *Tseng Pu*. Boston: Twayne Publishers, 1980.

Li Yijian. "'Rewriting' Jin Yong's Novels into the Canon: A Consideration of Jin Yong Novels as Serialized Fiction." In *The Jin Yong Phenomenon: Chinese Martial Arts Fiction and Modern Chinese Literary History*, edited by Ann Huss and Jianmei Liu, 73–96. Youngstown, NY: Cambria Press, 2007.

Li Zehou 李澤厚 and Liu Zaifu 劉再復. *Gaobie geming* 告別革命 [Farewell to revolution: a critical dialogue]. Taipei: Maitian, 1999.

Lianhe wenxue 聯合文學 [Unitas] 6–7 (2003), special issues on Beijing.

Liang Congjie 梁從誡. "Shuhu renjian siyue tian" 倏忽人間四月天 [Suddenly the Beautiful April on the Earth]. In *Lin Huiyin wenji—Wenxue juan*, edited by Liang Congjie, 415–449. Tianjin: Baihua wenyi chubanshe, 1999.

Liang, Kan. "Hu Shi and Liang Shiqiu: Liberalism and Others." *Chinese Studies in History* 39, no. 1 (2005): 3–24.

Liang Qichao 梁啓超. *Yinbingshi heji* 飲冰室合集 [Collected works of Yinbing Chamber]. Beijing: Zhonghua shuju, 1989.

Liang, Shiqiu 梁實秋. *From A Cottager's Sketchbook*. Translated by Ta-tsun Chen. 2 vols. Hong Kong: The Chinese University Press, 2005.

———. *Liang Shiqiu piping wenji* 梁實秋批評文集 [Liang Shiqiu's Literary Criticism]. Edited by Xu Jingbo 徐靜波. Zhuhai: Zhuhai chubanshe, 1998.

———. *Yashe tanchi* 雅舍談吃 [A cottager's ideas about eating]. Beijing: Wenhua yishu chubanshe, 1998.

———. *Yashe tanchi* 雅舍談吃 [A cottager's ideas about eating]. Tianjin: Tianjin jiaoyu chubanshe, 2006.

———. *Yashe tanchi* 雅舍談吃 [A cottager's ideas about eating]. Taipei: Jiuge, 2009.

Liang Sicheng 梁思成. "Beiping de wenwu bixu zhengli yu baocun" 北平的文物必須整理與保存 [The cultural relics in Beijing must be preserved]. In *Liang Sicheng wenji* 梁思成文集 [Selected writings of Liang Sicheng], 365–371. Beijing: Zhongguo jianzhu chubanshe, 1982.

———. *Liang Sicheng wenji* 梁思成文集 [Collected works of Liang Sicheng]. Beijing: Zhongguo jianzhu gongye chubanshe, 1986.

———. *A Pictorial History of Chinese Architecture: A Study of the Development of Its Structural System and the Evolution of Its Types.* Edited by Wilma Fairbank. Cambridge, MA: The MIT Press, 1985.

———. "Wo weishenme zheyang ai women de dang?" 我為甚麼這樣愛我們的黨 [Why I love our party so much]. In *Renmin ribao* 人民日報 [People's daily], July 14, 1957.

Liao Ping-hui 廖炳惠. *Chi de houxiandai* 吃的後現代 [Ways of eating: Savoring postmodernity]. Taipei: Eryu, 2004.

———. *Linglei xiandaiqing* 另類現代情 [Alternative modernity]. Taipei: Yunchen, 2000.

Liao, Ping-hui, and David Der-wei Wang, eds. *Taiwan under Japanese Colonial Rule.* New York: Columbia University Press, 2006.

Lin Haiyin (Lin Hai-yin) 林海音. *Memories of Peking: South Side Stories.* Translated by Nancy C. Ing and Chi Pang-Yuan. Hong Kong: Chinese University Press, 1992.

———. *Jianying hua wentan* 剪影話文壇 [Profiles in the literary arena]. Taipei: Chunwenxue, 1984.

Lin Huiyin 林徽因, ed. *Dagongbao wenyi congkan xiaoshuo xuan* 大公報文藝叢刊小說選 [Anthology of short stories published in the Literary Supplement of Dagongbao]. Shanghai: Shanghai shudian, 1990.

———. *Heping liwu* 和平禮物 [Presents of peace]. Beijing: Beijing daxue chubanshe, 2009.

———. *Lin Huiyin wenji—Jianzhu juan* 林徽因文集·建築卷 [Selected writings of Lin Huiyin: Volume of architecture]. Edited by Liang Congjie 梁從誡. Tianjin: Baihua wenyi chubanshe, 1999.

———. *Lin Huiyin wenji—Wenxue juan* 林徽因文集·文學卷 [Selected writings of Lin Huiyin: Volume of literature]. Edited by Liang Congjie. Tianjin: Baihua wenyi chubanshe, 1999.

———. "On the Gate Tower." In *Writing Women in Modern China: An Anthology of Women's Literature from the Early Twentieth Century*, edited by Amy Dooling and Kristina Torgeson, 304. New York: Columbia University Press, 1998.

Lin Shan 林杉. *Yidai cainü Lin Huiyin* 一代才女林徽因 [Lin Huiyin the talent lady]. Beijing: Zuojia chubanshe, 2005.

Lin Shu 林紓. *Jinghua bixue lu* 京華碧血錄 [Record of blood shed in righteous death in Beijing]. Beijing: Pingbao she, 1913.

Lin, Sylvia Li-chun 林麗君, ed. *Jin Yong xiaoshuo yu ershi shiji zhongguo wenxue* 金庸小說與二十世紀中國文學國際學術研討會論文集 [Jin Yong's novel and the twentieth-century Chinese literature]. Hong Kong: Ming He she, 2000.

Lin Taiyi 林太乙. *Lin Yutang zhuan* 林語堂傳 [Biography of Lin Yutang]. Taipei: Lianjing, 1989.

Lin Yiliang 林以亮 (Lin I-Liang, or Stephen Soong 宋淇). *Wuge fangwen* 五個訪問 [Five interviews]. Xianggang: Wenyi shuwu, 1972.

Lin, Yu-sheng. *The Crisis of Chinese Consciousness: Radical Antitraditionalism in the May Fourth Era*. Madison: University of Wisconsin Press, 1979.

Lin Yutang 林語堂. *The Gay Genius: The Life and Times of Su Tungpo*. New York: The John Day Company, 1947.

———. *Imperial Peking: Seven Centuries of China*. London: Elek Books Limited, 1961.

———. *The Importance of Living*. New York: The John Day Company, 1937.

———. *Juniper Loa*. New York: Dell, 1963.

———. *Lin Yutang wenxuan* 林語堂文選 [Selected writings of Lin Yutang]. Beijing: Zhongguo guangbo dianshi chubanshe, 1990.

———. *Looking Beyond*. New York: Prentice-Hall, 1955.

———. "*Miren de Beiping*" 迷人的北平 [Amazing Peiping]. In Lu Xun, Zhou Zuoren, Lin Yutang, et al., *Beijing ren, Shanghai ren*, 73–76. Hong Kong: Sanlian shudian, 2001.

———. *Moment in Peking: A Novel of Contemporary Chinese Life*. New York: The John Day Company, 1939.

———. "*Shuo Beiping*" 說北平 [On Peiping]. In *Lin Yutang sanwen jingdian quanbian* 林語堂散文經典全編 [Complete prose of Lin Yutang] (Beijing: Jiuzhou tushu chubanshe, 1997), 4:409–413.

———. *The Vermillion Gate*. New York: The John Day Company, 1953.

———. *The Wisdom of Confucius*. New York: The Modern Library, 1938.

———. *With Love and Irony*. New York: The John Day Company, 1940.

Lin Zhaohua 林兆華. "*Chaguan* buhui yuegai yueliang" 《茶館》不會越改越涼 [Adaptation of *Teahouse* cannot be getting worse]. *Beijing Youth Daily* 北京青年報, September 30, 2005.

———. "Lin Zhaohua fangtanlu" 林兆華訪談錄 [An interview with Lin Zhaohua]. *Xiju wenxue* 戲劇文學 [Drama and literature] 8 (2003): 4–14, 38.

Lin Zheng 林崝. "Cong *Jiujing suoji* dao *Chengnan jiushi*" 從《舊京瑣記》到《城南舊事》 [From *Trivial records of old capital* to *Memories of Peking*]. *Zhongguo xiandai wenxue yanjiu congkan* 中國現代文學研究叢刊 [Studies on modern Chinese literature] 1 (2012): 122–136.

Lin Zhu 林洙. *Kunhuo de dajiang: Liang Sicheng* 困惑的大匠：梁思成 [The confused master Liang Sicheng]. Jinan: Shangdong huabao chubanshe, 1997.

Ling, Shuhua, *Ancient Melodies*. New York: Universe Books, 1988.

Link, Perry. *Mandarin Ducks and Butterflies: Popular Fiction in Early Twentieth Century Chinese Cities*. Berkeley: University of California Press, 1981.

Lippit, Seiji M. *Topographies of Japanese Modernism*. New York: Columbia University Press, 2002.

Liu, E. *The Travels of Lao Ts'an*. Translated by Harold Shadick. Ithaca, NY: Cornell University Press, 1966.

Liu, James J. Y. *The Chinese Knight-errant*. Chicago: University of Chicago Press, 1967.

Liu, Jianmei. *Revolution Plus Love: Literary History, Women's Bodies, and Thematic Repetition in Twentieth-Century Chinese Fiction*. Honolulu: University of Hawai'i Press, 2003.

———. *Zhuangzi de xiandai mingyun* 莊子的現代命運 [The fate of Zhuangzi in modern China]. Beijing: Shangwu yinshuguan, 2012.

Liu, Kang, and Xiaobing Tang, eds. *Politics, Ideology and Chinese Literature: Theoretical Interventions and Cultural Critique*. Durham, NC: Asian/Pacific Studies Institute, Duke University, 1993.

Liu, Lydia H. *The Clash of Empires: The Invention of China in Modern World Making*. Cambridge, MA: Harvard University Press, 2004.

———. *Tokens of Exchange: The Problem of Translation in Global Circulation*. Durham, NC: Duke University Press, 1999.

———. *Translingual Practice: Literature, National Culture, and Translated Modernity—China, 1900–1937*. Stanford, CA: Stanford University Press, 1995.

Liu, Petrus. *Stateless Subjects: Chinese Martial Arts Literature and Postcolonial History*. Ithaca, NY: Cornell East Asian Series, 2011.

Liu, Ts'un-yan, ed. *Chinese Middlebrow Fiction: From the Ch'ing and Early Republican Eras*. Hong Kong: Chinese University Press, 1984.

Liu Xiaoqin 劉小沁, ed. *Chuangzi neiwai yi Huiyin* 窗子內外憶徽因 [In memory of Huiyin inside and outside of the window]. Beijing: Renmin wenxue chubanshe, 2001.

Liu Yansheng 劉炎生. *Lin Yutang pingzhuan* 林語堂評傳 [Annotated biography of Lin Yutang]. Nanchang: Baihuazhou wenyi chubanshe, 1994.

Liu Xinwu 劉心武. *Zhong gu lou* 鐘鼓樓 [Bell tower and drum tower]. Beijing: Renmin wenxue chubanshe, 1985.

Liu Yichang 劉以鬯. *Liu Yichang juan* 劉以鬯卷 [Volume of Liu Yichang]. Hong Kong: Sanlian shudian, 1991.

———. "Wushi niandai chuqi de xianggang wenxue" 五十年代初期的香港文學 [Hong Kong literature in the early 1950s]. In *Liu Yichang juan*, 361–370. Hong Kong: Sanlian shudian, 1991.

Liu, Yiqing. *A New Account of Tales of the World*. 2nd ed. Translated with introduction and notes by Richard B. Mather. Ann Arbor: Center for Chinese Studies, University of Michigan, 2002.

Lombardo, Patrizia. *Cities, Words and Images: From Poe to Scorsese*. New York: Palgrave Macmillan, 2003.

Lowenthal, David. *The Past Is a Foreign Country*. New York: Cambridge University Press, 1985.

Louie, Kam, ed. *Eileen Chang: Romancing Languages, Cultures, and Genres*. Hong Kong: Hong Kong University Press, 2011.

Love, Heather. *Feeling Backward*. Cambridge, MA: Harvard University Press, 2009.

Lu, Hanchao. *Beyond the Neon Lights: Everyday Shanghai in the Early Twentieth Century*. Berkeley, CA: University of California Press, 1999.

Lu, Sheldon. *China, Transnational Visuality, Global Postmodernity*. Stanford, CA: Stanford University Press, 2001.

———. *Chinese Modernity and Global Biopolitics: Studies in Literature and Visual Culture*. Honolulu: University of Hawai'i Press, 2007

Lu Xun 魯迅. *A Brief History of Chinese Fiction*. Translated by Yang Hsien-yi and Gladys Yang. Beijing: Foreign Languages Press, 1976.

———. *Diary of a Madman and Other Stories*. Translated by William Lyell. Honolulu: University of Hawai'i Press, 1990.

———. *Lu Xun quanji* 魯迅全集 [Complete works of Lu Xun]. 16 vols. Beijing: Renmin wenxue chubanshe, 1981.

———. *Selected Stories of Lu Hsun*. Translated by Yang Hsien-yi and Gladys Yang. New York: Norton, 1972.

———. *Selected Works of Lu Hsun*. Translated by Yang Hsien-yi and Gladys Yang. Peking: Foreign Languages Press, 1957.

Lu Xun, Zhou Zuoren, Lin Yutang, et al. *Beijing ren, Shanghai ren* 北京人，上海人 [Beijingers, Shanghaines]. Hong Kong: Sanlian shudian, 2001.

Lukács, Georg. *History and Class Consciousness: Studies in Marxist Dialectics*. Translated by Rodney Livingstone. Cambridge, MA: The MIT Press, 1971.

———. *The Theory of the Novel: A Historico-Philosophical Essay on the Forms of Great Epic Literature*. Translated by Anna Bostock. Cambridge, MA: The MIT Press, 1971.

Lü Chao 呂超. *Dongfang didu: Xifang wenhua shiye zhong de Beijing xingxiang* 東方帝都：西方文化視野中的北京形象 [Oriental imperial capital: The image of Beijing in Western cultures]. Jinan: Shandong huabao chubanshe, 2008.

Lü Zhenghui 呂正惠. *Zhanhou Taiwan wenxue jingyan* 戰後台灣文學經驗 [Literary experiences in postwar Taiwan]. Taipei: Xindi wenxue, 1992.

Luo Gang 羅崗. *Xiangxiang chengshi de fangshi* 想像城市的方式 [Ways of imagining cities]. Nanjing: Jiangsu renmin chubanshe, 2006.

Lynch, Kevin. *The Image of the City*. Cambridge, MA: The MIT Press, 1960.

———. *A Theory of the Good City*. Cambridge, MA: The MIT Press, 1970.

Ma Fengyang 馬逢洋, ed. *Shanghai* 上海. Shanghai: Wenhui chubanshe, 1996.

Ma Zhixiang 馬芷庠. *Beiping lüxing zhinan* 北平旅行指南 [A travel guide to Beijing]. Beiping: Jingji xinwen she, 1935.

Mao, Dun 茅盾. *Midnight*. Translated by A. C. Barnes. Beijing: Foreign Languages Press, 1957.

———. *Rainbow*. Translated by Madeline Zelin. Berkeley: University of California Press, 1992.

Marx, Leo. *The Machine in the Garden: Technology and the Pastoral Ideal in America*. New York: Oxford University Press, 1981.

Massumi, Brian. *Parables for the Virtual: Movement, Affect, Sensation*. Durham, NC: Duke University Press, 2002.

———. *A User's Guide to Capitalism and Schizophrenia*. Cambridge, MA: The MIT Press, 1992.

McClellan, T. M. "Change and Continuity in the Fiction of Zhang Henshui (1895–1967)." *Modern Chinese Literature* 10, nos. 1–2 (1998): 113–134.

———. "Home and the Land: The 'Native' Fiction of Zhong Lihe." *Journal of Modern Literature in Chinese* 9, no. 2 (December 2009): 154–182.

———. *Zhang Henshui and Popular Chinese Fiction, 1919–1949*. Lewiston: Edwin Mellen Press, 2005.

McDougall, Bonnie S., and Kam Louie. *The Literature of China in the Twentieth Century*. New York: Columbia University Press, 1997.

McMahon, Keith. *Polygamy and Sublime Passion: Sexuality in China on the Verge of Modernity*. Honolulu: University of Hawai'i Press, 2010.

Mei Jialing 梅家玲. "Nüxing xiaoshuo de dushi xiangxiang yu wenhua jiyi" 女性小說的都市想象與文化記憶 [Urban imagination and cultural memory in female novels]. In *Beijing*, edited by Chen Pingyuan and David Der-wei Wang, 390–409. Beijing: Beijing daxue chubanshe, 2005.

———. *Wenhua qimeng yu zhishi shengchan* 文化啟蒙與知識生產 [Cultural enlightenment and the production of knowledge]. Taipei: Maitian, 2006.

———. *Xingbie, haishi jiaguo? Wushi yu bajiushi niandai Taiwan xiaoshuo lun* 性別，還是家國？五十與八九十年代台灣小說論 [Gender or nation? Criticism of contemporary Taiwah fiction]. Taipei: Maitian, 2004.

Meisner, Maurice. *Mao's China and After: A History of the People's Republic*. New York: Free Press, 1986.

Meng Fanhua 孟繁華. "Jiangou shiqi de Zhongguo chengshi wenxue—dangxia Zhongguo wenxue zhuangkuang de yige fangmian" 建構時期的中國城市文學——當下中國文學狀況的一個方面 [Chinese urban literature in construction: One aspect of current Chinese literature]. *Wenyi yanjiu* 文藝研究 2 (2014): 5–14.

Meng Guanglai 孟廣來 et al., eds. *Lao She yanjiu lunwen ji* 老舍研究論文集 [Selected essays on Lao She]. Ji'nan: Shandong renmin chubanshe, 1983.

Meng Hua 孟華. *Bijiao wenxue xingxiangxue* 比較文學形象學 [Imagology in comparative literature]. Beijing: Beijing daxue chubanshe, 2001.

Meng Yue 孟悦 and Dai Jinhua 戴錦華. *Fuchu lishi dibiao* 浮出歷史地表 [Emerging out from the horizon of history]. Zhengzhou: Henan renmin chubanshe, 1990.

Meng Yuanlao 孟元老. *Dongjing menghua lu* 東京夢華錄 [The eastern capital: A dream of splendor]. Beijing: Zhonghua shuju, 1982.

Meyer, Jeffrey F. *The Dragons of Tiananmen: Beijing as a Sacred City*. Columbia: University of South Carolina Press, 1991.

Mi, Jiayan. *Self-Fashioning and Reflexive Modernity in Modern Chinese Poetry*. Lewiston, NY: Edwin Mellen, 2004.

Mitchell, William. *City of Bits*. Cambridge: The MIT Press, 1995.

Miller, J. Hillis. *Topographies*. Stanford, CA: Stanford University Press, 1995.

Morrison, Hedda. *A Photographer in Old Peking*. New York: Oxford University Press, 1985.

Moretti, Franco. *Atlas of the European Novel, 1800–1900*. London: Verso, 1998.

Mumford, Lewis. *The City in History: Its Origins, Its Transformations, and Its Prospects*. New York: Harcourt Brace Jovanovich, 1961.

———. *The Culture of Cities*. New York: Harcourt, Brace, Jovanovich, 1970.

Murphy, Rhoads. "The City as a Center of Change: Western Europe and China." *Annals of the Association of American Geographers* 44 (1954): 349–362.

———. *The Fading of the Maoist Vision: City and Country in China's Development*. New York: Methuen, 1980.

———. "The Treaty Ports and China's Modernization." In *The Chinese City Between Two Worlds*, edited by Mark Elvin and William Skinner, 17–72. Stanford, CA: Stanford University Press, 1974.

Myer, Jeffrey F. *The Dragons of Tiananmen: Beijing as a Sacred City*. Columbia: University of South Carolina Press, 1991.

Naquin, Susan. *Peking: Temples and City Life, 1400–1900*. Berkeley: University of California Press, 2000.

Nathan, Andrew. *Peking Politics, 1918–1923: Factionalism and the Failure of Constitutionalism*. Berkeley: University of California Press, 1976.

Ng, On Cho, and Q. Edward Wang. *Mirroring the Past: The Writing and Use of History in Imperial China*. Honolulu: University of Hawai'i Press, 2005.

Nietzsche, Friedrich. *On the Advantage and Disadvantage of History for Life*. Translated by Peter Preuss. Indianapolis: Hackett, 1980.

Nora, Pierre. *Realms of Memory*. New York: Columbia University Press, 1996–1998.

Norris, Christopher. "Derrida on Plato: Writing as Remedy and Cure." In *Derrida*, 28–62. Cambridge, MA: Harvard University Press, 1987.

Nussbaum, Martha C. *Upheavals of Thought: The Intelligence of Emotions.* Cambridge: Cambridge University Press, 2003.

Olsen, Donald. *The City as a Work of Art: London, Paris, Vienna.* New Haven, CT: Yale University Press, 1986.

Ong, Aihwa. *Flexible Citizenship: The Cultural Logics of Transnationality.* Durham, NC: Duke University Press, 1999.

Owen, Stephen. *Remembrances: The Experience of the Past in Classical Chinese Literature.* Cambridge, MA: Harvard University Press, 1986.

Pan, Da'an. "Tasting the Good and the Beautiful: The Aestheticization of Eating and Drinking in Traditional Chinese Culture." *The Cal Poly Pomona Journal of Interdisciplinary Studies* 16 (2003): 67–76.

Park, Robert, and Ernest Burgess. *The City: Suggestions for Investigation of Human Behavior in the Urban Environment.* Chicago: University of Chicago Press, 1925.

Parker, Andrew, Mary Russo, Doris Sommer, and Patricia Yaeger, eds. *Nationalisms and Sexualities.* New York: Routledge, 1992.

Peng, Hsiao-yen. "Introduction: Lin Hai-yin's *Memories of Peking: South Side Stories.*" Translated by Steven K. Luk, in Lin Hai-yin, *Memories of Peking: South Side Stories*, translated by Nancy C. Ing and Chi Pang-yuan, ix–xxxi. Hong Kong: The Chinese University Press, 2002.

Peng Ruijin 彭瑞金. *Miaozhun Taiwan zuojia: Peng Ruijin wenxue pinglun* 瞄準台灣作家：彭瑞金文學評論 [Aiming at Taiwan writers: Literary critiques by Peng Ruijin]. Gaoxiong: Paise wenhua, 1992.

———. *Taiwan xinwenxue yundong sishi nian* 台灣新文學運動四十年 [Forty years of new literature movement in Taiwan]. Taipei: Zili wanbao, 1991.

———. *Zhong Lihe zhuan* 鍾理和傳 [Biography of Zhong Lihe]. Nantou: Taiwan sheng wenxian weiyuanhui, 1994.

Perry, Elizabeth J. *Shanghai on Strike: The Politics of Chinese Labor.* Stanford, CA: Stanford University Press, 1993.

Pike, Burton. *The Image of the City in Modern Literature.* Princeton, NJ: Princeton University Press, 1981.

Plaks, Andrew. "Toward a Critical Theory of Chinese Narrative." In *Chinese Narrative: Critical and Theoretical Essays*, edited by Andrew Plaks, 309–352. Princeton, NJ: Princeton University Press, 1977.

Pollard, David. *A Chinese Look at Literature: The Literary Values of Zhou Zuoren in Relation to the Tradition.* London: Hurst, 1973.

Prado-Fonts, Carles. "Beneath Two Red Banners: Lao She as a Manchu Writer in Modern China." In *Sinophone Studies: A Critical Reader*, edited by Shu-mei Shih, Chien-hsin Tsai, and Brian Bernards, 353–363. New York: Columbia University Press, 2013.

———. "Fragmented Encounters, Social Slippages: Lin Huiyin's 'In Ninety-Nine Degree Heat.'" *Lectora: Revista de Dones i Textualitat* 16 (2010): 125–141.

Pratt, Mary Louis. *Imperial Eyes: Travel Writing and Transculturalism.* New York: Routledge, 1992.

Preston, Peter, and Paul Simpson-Housley. *Writing the City: Eden, Babylon and the New Jerusalem.* London: Routledge, 2002.

Prusek, Jaroslav. *The Lyrical and the Epic: Studies of Modern Chinese Literature.* Bloomington: Indiana University Press, 1980.

Qi Rushan 齊如山. *Gudu sanbai liushi hang* 古都三百六十行 [360 professions in the ancient capital]. Beijing: Shumu wenxian chubanshe, 1993.

Qian Liqun 錢理群. *1948 Tiandi xuanhuang* 1948 天地玄黃 [1948: World in-between]. Jinan: Shandong jiaoyu chubanshe, 1998.

———. *Duihua yu manyou: Sishi niandai xiaoshuo yandu* 對話與漫遊：四十年代小說研讀 [Dialogues and rambles: Studies of fiction in the 1940s]. Shanghai: Shanghai wenyi chubanshe, 1999.

———. *Jujue yiwang: Qian Liqun wenxuan* 拒絕遺忘：錢理群文選 [Rejection to forget: Selected writings of Qian Liqun]. Shantou: Shantou daxue chubanshe, 1999.

Qian Liqun, Wu Fuhui 吳福輝, Wen Rumin 溫儒敏, and Wang Chaobing 王超冰. *Zhongguo xiandai wenxue sanshinian* 中國現代文學三十年 [Thirty years of modern Chinese literature]. Shanghai: Shanghai wenyi chubanshe, 1987.

Qian, Suoqiao. *Liberal Cosmopolitanism: Lin Yutang and Middling Chinese Modernity*. Leiden: Brill, 2011.

Qian Zhongshu 錢鐘書. *Ren, Shou, Gui* 人，獸，鬼 [Human beings, animals, and ghosts]. Shanghai: Kaiming, 1946.

Qin Shouou 秦瘦鷗, trans. *Yuxiang piaomiao lu* 御香縹緲錄 [*Imperial Incense*]. Shanghai: Shenbao guan, 1936.

Rancière, Jacques. *Dissensus: On Politics and Aesthetics*. Edited by Steven Corcoran. London: Continuum, 2010.

———. "From Politics to Aesthetics?" *Paragraph* 28, no. 1 (2005): 13–25.

Resina, Joan Ramon, and Dieter Ingenschay, eds. *After-Images of the City*. Ithaca, NY: Cornell University Press, 2003.

Ricoeur, Paul. "Ideology and Utopia." In *From Text to Action*, translated by Kathleen Blamey and John B. Thompson, 308–324. Evanston, IL: Northwestern University Press, 1991.

———. *Lectures on Ideology and Utopia*. Edited by George H. Taylor. New York: Columbia University Press, 1986.

Rojas, Carlos. *The Great Wall: A Cultural History*. Cambridge, MA: Harvard University Press, 2010.

———. *The Naked Gaze: Reflections on Chinese Modernity*. Cambridge, MA: Harvard University Asia Center, 2008.

Rojas, Carlos, and Eileen Chow, eds. *Rethinking Modern Chinese Popular Culture: Cannibalizations of the Canon*. London: Routledge, 2009.

Rolston, David. *Traditional Chinese Fiction and Fiction Commentary: Reading and Writing between the Line*. Stanford, CA: Stanford University Press, 1997.

Ross, Kristin, and Alain Badiou. *Jacques Rancière: History, Politics, Aesthetics*. Edited by Gabriel Rockhill and Philip Watt. Durham, NC: Duke University Press, 2009.

Rowe, William T. *Hankow: Commerce and Society in a Chinese City, 1796–1889*. Stanford, CA: Stanford University Press, 1984.

———. *Hankow: Conflict and Community in a Chinese City, 1796–1895*. Stanford, CA: Stanford University Press, 1989.

Run Hua 潤華 "Chuangzao she de lixiang shehui" 創造社的理想社會 [Creation Society's Ideal Society]. *Ershiyi shiji* 二十一世紀 [The 21st century] 8 (1999): 85–91.

Rupprecht, Xiaowei Wang. *Departure and Return: Chang Hen-shui and the Chinese Narrative Tradition*. Hong Kong: Joint Publishing Co., 1987.

Russell, Terence. "Zhong Lihe." In *Chinese Fiction Writers, 1950–2000*, edited by Thomas Moran and Ye (Dianna) Xu, 311–318. Detroit: Gale, Cengage Learning, 2013.

Said, Edward W. *Culture and Imperialism*. New York: Vintage Books, 1993.

———. *Humanism and Democratic Criticism*. New York: Columbia University Press, 2004.

———. *Orientalism*. New York: Vintage, 1978.

———. *Reflections on Exile and Other Essays*. Cambridge, MA: Harvard University Press, 2000.

———. *The World, the Text, and the Critic*. Cambridge, MA: Harvard University Press, 1983.

Sang, Tze-lan. "Romancing Rhetoricity and Historicity: The Representational Politics and Poetics of *Little Reunion*." In *Eileen Chang: Romancing Languages, Cultures, and Genres*, edited by Kam Louie, 193–214. Hong Kong: Hong Kong University Press, 2012.

Santangelo, Paolo. "The Cult of Love in Some Texts of Ming and Qing Literature." *East and West* 50 (2000): 439–499.

———. *Sentimental Education in Chinese History: An Interdisciplinary Textual Research on Ming and Qing Sources*. Leiden: Brill, 2013.

———. "Some Conclusive Remarks on the Examination of Different Sources: The Analysis of Non-literary Documents (Moralistic and Judicial Materials)." In *Love, Hatred, and Other Passions*, edited by Santangelo and Guida, 404–408. London: Brill, 2006.

Santangelo, Paolo, and Donatella Guida, eds. *Love, Hatred, and Other Passions: Questions and Themes on Emotions in Chinese Civilization*. London: Brill, 2006.

Sargent, Lyman Tower. *Utopianism: A Very Short Introduction*. New York: Oxford University Press, 2010.

Saunders, Frances Stonor. *The Cultural Cold War: The CIA and the World of Arts and Letters*. New York: The New Press, 1999.

Saussy, Haun. *Great Walls of Discourse and Other Adventures in Cultural China*. Cambridge, MA: Harvard University Asia Center, 2001.

Schaer, Roland, Gregory Claeys, and Lyman Tower Sargent, eds. *Utopia: The Search for Ideal Society in Western World*. New York: Oxford University Press and Smithsonian, 2000.

Scheff, Thomas J. *Bloody Revenge: Emotions, Nationalism, and War*. Boulder, CO: Westview Press, 1994.

Schivelbusch, Wolfgang. *Disenchanted Night: The Industrialization of Light in the Nineteenth Century*. Berkeley: University of California Press, 1991.

———. *The Railway Journey: The Industrialization of Time and Space in the Nineteenth Century*. Berkeley: University of California Press, 1986.

Schorske, Carl. *Fin-de-Siècle Vienna: Politics and Culture*. New York: Knopf, 1980.

———. "The Idea of the City in European Thought: Voltaire to Spengler." In *The Historian and the City*, edited by Oscar Handlin and John Burchard, 95–114. Cambridge, MA: The MIT Press, 1963.

Schwarcz, Vera. *The Chinese Enlightenment: Intellectual and the Legacy of the May Fourth Movement of 1919*. Berkeley: University of California Press, 1986.

Schwartz, Benjamin. *In Search of Wealth and Power: Yen Fu and the West*. Cambridge, MA: Harvard University Press, 1964.

Seagrave, Sterling. *Dragon Lady: The Life and Legend of the Last Empress of China*. New York: Knopf, 1992.

Segalen, Victor. *Essays on Exoticism: An Aesthetics of Diversity*. Translated and edited by Yaël Rachel Schlick. Durham, NC.: Duke University Press, 2002.

———. *Paintings*. Translated by Andrew Harvey and Iain Watson. London: Quartet Books, 1991.

———. *René Leys: A Novel*. Translated by J. A. Underwood. Woodstock, NY: Overlook Press, 1988.

Sennett, Richard, ed. *Classical Essays on the Culture of Cities*. Englewood Cliffs, NJ: Prentice Hall, 1969.

———. *The Conscience of the Eye: The Design and Social Life of Cities*. New York: Knopf, 1990.

———. *The Fall of Public Man*. New York: W.W. Norton, 1976.

———. *Flesh and Stone: The Body and the City in Western Civilization*. New York: W. W. Norton, 1994.

Shan Dexing 單德興. *Mingke yu zaixian: Huayi meiguo wenxue yu wenhua lunji* 銘刻與再現：華裔美國文學與文化論集 [Inscriptions and representations: Chinese American literary and cultural studies]. Taipei: Maitian, 2000.

Shang, Wei. *Rulin waishi and Cultural Transformation in Late Imperial China*. Cambridge, MA: Harvard University Press, 2003.

Sharpe, William, and Leonard Wallock, eds. *Visions of the Modern City: Essays in History, Art, and Literature*. Baltimore, MD: Johns Hopkins University Press, 1987.

Shen Congwen 沈從文. *Shen Congwen quanji* 沈從文全集 [Complete works of Shen Congwen]. Edited by Zhang Zhaohe 張兆和. 32 vols. Taiyuan: Beiyue wenyi chubanshe, 2002.

———. "Sugeladi tan Beiping suoxu" 蘇格拉底談北平所需 [Socrates talks about what Beijing needs]. In *Shen Congwen quanji* 沈從文全集 [Complete works of Shen Congwen], edited by Zhang Zhaohe, 14:370–381. Taiyuan: Beiyue wenyi chubanshe, 2002.

Shen, Shuang. *Cosmopolitan Publics: Anglophone Print Culture in Semi-Colonial Shanghai*. Piscataway, NJ: Rutgers University Press, 2009.

Shi Changyu. "Wang Yangming's Neo-Confucian School of Mind and the Growth of Ancient Chinese Popular Novel." Translated by Yao Zhenjun. *Frontiers of Literary Studies in China* 2, no. 3 (2009): 195–217.

Shi Jianwei 施建偉. *Lin Yutang zai dalu* 林語堂在大陸 [Lin Yutang in mainland China]. Beijing: Beijing shiyue wenyi chubanshe, 1991.

———. *Lin Yutang zai haiwai* 林語堂在海外 [Lin Yutang overseas]. Tianjin: Baihua wenyi chubanshe, 1992.

Shi, Mingzheng. "Beijing Transforms: Urban Infrastructure, Public Works, and Social Change in the Chinese Capital, 1900–1928." PhD diss., Columbia University, 1993.

Shi Zhanjun 施戰軍. "Lun Zhongguo shide chengshi wenxue de shengcheng" 論中國式的城市文學的生成 [The birth of Chinese-style urban literature]. *Wenyi yanjiu* 文藝研究 1 (2006): 4–11.

Shih, Shu-mei. "The Concept of the Sinophone." *PMLA* 126.3 (2011): 709–718.

———. "Global Literature and the Technologies of Recognition." *PMLA* 119.1 (2004): 16–30.

———. *The Lure of Modern: Writing Modernism in Semicolonial China, 1917–1937*. Berkeley: University of California Press, 2001.

———. *Visuality and Identity: Sinophone Articulations across the Pacific*. Berkeley: University of California Press, 2007.

Shih, Shu-mei, Chien-hsin Tsai, and Brian Bernards, eds. *Sinophone Studies: A Critical Reader*. New York: Columbia University Press, 2013.

Shouse, Eric. "Feeling, Emotion, Affect." *M/c journal* 8, no. 6 (2005): http://journal.media-culture.org.au/0512/03-shouse.php.

Shu Yi 舒乙, ed. *Lao She de guankan he aihao* 老舍的關坎和愛好 [Lao She's troubles and hobbies]. Beijing: Zhongguo jianshe chubanshe, 1988.

——. *Lao She zhisi* 老舍之死 [The death of Lao She]. Beijing: Guoji wenhua chuban gongsi, 1987.

Shu Yi and Fu Guangming 傅光明, eds. *Lin Haiyin yanjiu lunwenji* 林海音研究論文集 [Collected essays on Lin Haiyin]. Beijing: Taihai chubanshe, 2001.

Silbergeld, Jerome. *China into Film: Frames of Reference in Contemporary Chinese Cinema.* London: Reaktion Books, 1999.

Simmel, Georg. "The Metropolis and Mental Life." In *On Individuality and Social Forms*, 324–339. Chicago: University of Chicago Press, 1971.

Siren, Oswald. *The Walls and Gates of Peking.* London: Lane, 1924.

Skinner, G. William, ed. *The City in Late Imperial China.* Stanford, CA: Stanford University Press, 1977.

Smith, Gary, ed. *On Walter Benjamin: Critical Essays and Recollections.* Cambridge, MA: The MIT Press, 1991.

Soja, Edward. *Postmodern Geography: The Reassertion of Space in Critical Social Theory.* New York: Verso, 1989.

Song, Weijie 宋偉杰. "The Aesthetic versus the Political: Lin Huiyin and Modern Beijing." *Chinese Literature: Essays, Articles, Reviews (CLEAR)* 36 (2014): 61–94.

——. *Cong yule xingwei dao wutuobang chongdong: Jin Yong xiaoshuo zai jiedu* 從娛樂行為到烏托邦衝動：金庸小說再解讀 [From entertainment activity to utopian impulse: Rereading Jin Yong's martial arts fiction]. Nanjing: Jiangsu renmin chubanshe, 1999.

——. "Emotional Topography, Food Memory, and Bittersweet Aftertaste: Liang Shiqiu and the Lingering Flavor of Home." *Journal of Oriental Studies* 45, nos. 1–2 (2012): 89–105.

——. "Jin Yong." In *Chinese Fiction Writers, 1950–2000*, edited by Thomas Moran and Ye (Dianna) Xu, 121–133. Detroit: Gale, Cengage Learning, 2013.

——. "Nation-State, Individual Identity, and Historical Memory: Conflicts Between Han and Non-Han Peoples in Jin Yong's Novels." In *The Jin Yong Phenomenon: Chinese Martial Arts Fiction and Modern Chinese Literary History*, edited by Ann Huss and Jianmei Liu, 121–154. Youngstown, NY: Cambria Press, 2007.

——. "Positions of Sinophone Representations." *CLCWeb: Comparative Literature and Culture* 17, no. 1 (2015). http://docs.lib.purdue.edu/clcweb/vol17/iss1/.

——. "Space, Swordsmen, and Utopia: The Dualistic Imagination in Jin Yong's Narratives." In *The Jin Yong Phenomenon: Chinese Martial Arts Fiction and Modern Chinese Literary History*, edited by Ann Huss and Jianmei Liu, 155–178. Youngstown, NY: Cambria Press, 2007.

——. "Writing Cities." In *A Companion to Modern Chinese Literature*, edited by Yingjin Zhang, 326–342. Oxford: Wiley-Blackwell, 2015.

——. *Zhongguo wenxue, meiguo: meiguo xiaoshuo xiju zhong de zhongguo xingxiang* 中國•文學•美國：美國小說戲劇中的中國形像 [Images of China in American and Chinese-American novels and dramas]. Guangzhou: Huacheng Press, 2003.

Song, Weizhong, Wang Jiayan, and Zhou Shuo. *Beijing Local Delicacies.* Translated by Wang Yufan. Beijing: China Pictorial Publishing House, 2006.

Song Yongyi 宋永毅. *Lao She yu Zhongguo wenhua guannian* 老舍與中國文化觀念 [Lao She and Chinese notions of culture]. Shanghai: Xuelin chubanshe, 1988.

Spence, Jonathan D. *The Chan's Great Continent: China in Western Minds.* New York: Norton, 1998.

———. "Chinese Fictions in the Twentieth Century." In *Asia in Western Fiction*, edited by Robin W. Winks and James R. Rush, 100–116. Honolulu: University of Hawai'i Press, 1990.

———. *The Gate of Heavenly Peace: The Chinese and Their Revolution, 1895–1980*. New York: Viking, 1981.

Spengler, Oswald. *The Decline of the West*. Authorized translation with notes by Charles Francis Atkinson. New York: A. A. Knopf, 1926.

Spivak, Gayatri Chakravorty. *A Critique of Postcolonial Reason: Toward a History of the Vanishing Present*. Cambridge, MA: Harvard University Press, 1999.

———. "Woman in Difference: Mahasweta Devi's 'Douloti the Bountiful.'" In *Nationalisms and Sexualities*, edited by Andrew Parker, Mary Russo, Doris Sommer, and Patricia Yaeger, 96–118. New York: Routledge, 1992.

Stallybrass, Peter, and Allon White. *The Politics and Poetics of Transgression*. Ithaca, NY: Cornell University Press, 1986.

Stam, Robert. *Subversive Pleasures: Bakhtin, Cultural Criticism, and Film*. Baltimore: Johns Hopkins University Press, 1989.

Strand, David. *"Civil Society" and "Public Sphere" in Modern China: A Perspective on Popular Movements in Beijing, 1919–1989*. Durham, NC: Asian/Pacific Studies Institute, Duke University, 1990.

———. *Rickshaw Beijing: City People and Politics in the 1920s*. Berkeley, CA: University of California Press, 1989.

Swislocki, Mark. *Culinary Nostalgia: Regional Food Culture and the Urban Experience in Shanghai*. Stanford, CA: Stanford University Press, 2009.

Syrotinski, Michael, and Ian Maclachlan, eds. *Sensual Reading: New Approaches to Reading in Its Relations to the Senses*. London: Associated University Press, 2001.

Szondi, Peter. "Walter Benjamin's City Portraits." In *On Walter Benjamin: Critical Essays and Recollections*, edited by Gary Smith, 18–31. Cambridge, MA: MIT Press, 1988.

Tam, Kwok-kan. "Introduction to *Chaguan* 茶館 *Teahouse*." Translated by Yan Liu, in Lao She, *Chaguan* 茶館 *Teahouse*, translated by John Howard-Gibbon, xxxii–xxxvi. Hong Kong: Chinese University Press, 2004.

Tang Lusun 唐魯孫. *Zhongguo chi* 中國吃 [Chinese eating]. Taipei: Dadi chubanshe, 1976.

———. *Zhongguo chi de gushi* 中國吃的故事 [Stories about Chinese eating]. Taipei: Hanguang wenhua, 1983.

———. *Tang Lusun tanchi* 唐魯孫談吃 [Tang Lusun on eating]. 3 vols. Guilin: Guangxi shifan daxue chubanshe 廣西師範大學出版社, 2007.

Tang, Xiaobing 唐小兵. *Chinese Modern: The Heroic and Quotidian*. Durham, NC: Duke University Press, 2000.

———. *Global Space and the Nationalist Discourse of Modernity: The Historical Thinking of Liang Qichao*. Stanford, CA: Stanford University Press, 1996.

———. "Sanshi niandai Beiping de liangdao fengjingxian" 三十年代北平的兩道風景線 [Two landscapes in 1930s Beijing]. *Shuwu* 書屋 [House of books] 9 (2007): 61–64.

Tang Yijie. *Confucianism, Buddhism, Daoism, Christianity, and Chinese Culture*. Beijing: Foreign Language Teaching and Research Publishing Co., Ltd; Berlin: Springer-Verlag, 2015.

Tay, William 鄭樹森 (Zheng Shusen). "Colonialism, the Cold War, and Marginal Space: The Existential Condition of Five Decades of Hong Kong Literature." In *Chinese Literature in the Second Half of a Modern Century: A Critical Survey*, edited by Pang-yuan Chi and David Der-wei Wang, 31–38. Bloomington: Indiana University Press, 2000.

————. "Tan sishi nian lai xianggang wenxue de shengcun zhuangtai: zhimin zhuyi, lengzhan niandai yu bianyuan kongjian" 談四十年來香港文學的生存狀態：殖民主義，冷戰年代 與邊緣空間 [The ecology of Hong Kong literature, 1950s–1990s: Colonialism, Cold War era, and marginal space]. In *Sishi nian lai de zhongguo wenxue* 四十年來的中國文學 (Chinese literature, 1950s–1990s), edited by Zhang Baoqin 張寶琴, Shao Yuming 邵玉銘, and Ya Xian 瘂弦, 50–58. Taipei: Lianhe wenxue, 1995.

Taylor, Mark C., and Esa Saarinen. *Imagologies: Media Philosophy*. London: Routledge, 1994.

Timms, Edward, and David Kelley, eds. *Unreal City: Urban Experience in Modern European Literature and Art*. Manchester: Manchester University Press, 1985.

Todorov, Tzvetan. *On Human Diversity: Nationalism, Racism, Exoticism in French Thought*. Cambridge, MA: Harvard University Press, 1993.

Tomlinson, John. *Globalization and Culture*. Chicago: University of Chicago Press, 1999.

Towery, Britt. *Lao She, China's Master Storyteller*. Waco, TX: The Tao Foundation, 1999.

Trigg, Stephanie. "Introduction: Emotional Histories—Beyond the Personalization of the Past and the Abstraction of Affect Theory." *Exemplaria* 26, no. 1 (2014): 3–15.

Tsai, Chien-hsin. "Of Guest and Host: Zhong Lihe, Hakka, and Sinophone Hospitality." In *Sinophone Studies: A Critical Reader*, edited by Shu-mei Shih, Chien-hsin Tsai, and Brian Bernards, 276–277. New York: Columbia University Press, 2013.

Tsin, Michael. *Nation, Governance, and Modernity in China: Canton, 1900–1927*. Stanford, CA: Stanford University Press, 1999.

Tsu, Jing. *Failure, Nationalism, and Literature: The Making of Modern Chinese Identity, 1895–1937*. Stanford, CA: Stanford University Press, 2005.

————. *Sound and Script in Chinese Diaspora*. Cambridge, MA: Harvard University Press, 2010.

Tsu, Jing, and David Der-wei Wang, eds. *Global Chinese Literature: Critical Essays*. Leiden: Brill, 2010.

Tsurumi Yūsuke 鶴見祐輔. "Beijing de meili" 北京的魅力 [Beijing charms]. Translated from Japanese into Chinese by Lu Xun, in Tsurumi Yūsuke, *Sixiang, shanshui, renwu* 思想，山水，人物 [Thoughts, landscape, figures], 245–265. Shanghai: Beixin shuju, 1929.

Tu, Wei-ming. "Cultural China: The Periphery as the Center." *Daedalus* 120, no. 2 (Spring 1991): 1–32.

Vidler, Anthony. *Warped Space: Art, Architecture, and Anxiety in Modern Culture*. Cambridge, MA: The MIT Press, 2002.

Visser, Robin. *Cities Surround the Countryside: Urban Aesthetics in Post-Socialist China*. Durham, NC: Duke University Press, 2010.

Viswanathan, Gauri. *Masks of Conquest: Literary Study and British Rule in India*. New York: Columbia University Press, 1989.

Vohra, Ranbir. *Lao She and the Chinese Revolution*. Cambridge, MA: Harvard University Press, 1974.

Wagner, Rudolf G. *Inside a Service Trade: Studies in Contemporary Chinese Prose*. Cambridge, MA: Harvard University Asia Center, 1992.

Wakeman, Fredric. *Policing Shanghai, 1927–1937*. Berkeley: University of California Press, 1995.

Wakeman, Fredric, and Wen-hsin Yeh, eds. *Shanghai Sojourners*. Berkeley: University of California Press, 1992.

Wan Pingjin 萬平近. *Lin Yutang lun* 林語堂論 [On Lin Yutang]. Xi'an: Shanxi renmin chu-banshe, 1987.

Wang Anyi 王安憶. *Xunzhao Shanghai* 尋找上海 [In search of Shanghai]. Shanghai: Xuelin chubanshe, 2001.

Wang, Ban. *Illuminations from the Past: Trauma, Memory, and History in Modern China*. Stanford, CA: Stanford University Press, 2004.

———. *The Sublime Figure of History: Aesthetics and Politics in Twentieth-Century China*. Stanford, CA: Stanford University Press, 1997.

Wang, Cheng-hua. *Empress Dowager Cixi: Her Art of Living*. Hong Kong: The Regional Council and the Palace Museum, 1996

———. "Going Public: Portraits of the Empress Dowager Cixi, Circa 1904." *Nannü* 14, no. 1 (2012): 119–176.

Wang, David Der-wei (Wang Dewei) 王德威. "Beijing menhua lu" 北京夢華錄 [Beijing dreams]. In *Ruci fanhua* 如此繁华 [Urban splendor], 41–53. Shanghai: Shanghai shudian, 2006.

———. *Fictional Realism in 20th Century China: Mao Dun, Lao She, Shen Congwen*. New York: Columbia University Press, 1992.

———. *Fin-de-siècle Splendor: Repressed Modernities of Late Qing Fiction, 1849–1911*. Stanford, CA: Stanford University Press, 1997.

———. *Hou yimin xiezuo: Shijian yu jiyi de zhengzhi xue* 後遺民寫作：時間與記憶的政治學 [Post-loyalist writing: The politics of time and memory]. Taipei: Maitian, 2007.

———. *The Lyrical in Epic Time: Modern Chinese Intellectuals and Artists through the 1949 Crisis*. New York: Columbia University Press, 2015.

———. *The Monster That Is History: History, Violence, and Fictional Writing in Twentieth-Century China*. Berkeley: University of California Press, 2004.

———. "Reinventing National History: Communist and Anti-Communist Fiction of the Mid-Twentieth Century." In *Chinese Literature in the Second Half of a Modern Century: A Critical Survey*, edited by Pang-yuan Chi and David Der-wei Wang, 39–64. Bloomington: Indiana University Press, 2000.

———. *Ruci fanhua* 如此繁華 [Urban splendor]. Shanghai: Shanghai shudian, 2006.

———. *Xiaoshuo Zhongguo: Wan Qing dao dangdai de zhongwen xiaoshuo* 小說中國：晚清到當代的中文小說 [Narrating China: Chinese fiction from the late Qing to the contemporary era]. Taipei: Maitian, 1993.

———. "Zhongwen xiezuo de yuejie yu huigui: Tan huayu yuxi wenxue" 中文寫作的越界與回歸：談華語語系文學 [The transboundary and return of Chinese-language writing: On Sinophone literature], *Shanghai wenxue* 上海文學 [Shanghai literature] 9 (2006): 91–93.

Wang, David Der-wei, and Carlos Rojas, eds. *Writing Taiwan: A New Literary History*. Durham, NC: Duke University Press, 2007.

Wang, David Der-wei, Chen Sihe, and Xu Zidong, eds. *1949 yihou: dangdai wenxue liushi nian* 1949 以後：當代文學六十年 [After 1949: Sixty years of contemporary literature]. Shanghai: Shanghai wenyi chubanshe, 2011.

Wang Gungwu 王賡武, ed. *Xianggang shi xinbian* 香港史新編 [New Hong Kong history]. Hong Kong: Sanlian shudian, 1997.

Wang Hongzhi 王宏志. *Lishi de chenzhong* 歷史的沈重 [Burdens of history]. Hong Kong: Oxford University Press, 2000.

Wang Hongzhi 王宏志, Li Xiaoliang 李小良, and Chen Qingqiao 陳清僑. *Fouxiang xianggang* 否想香港 [Negating Hong Kong]. Taipei: Maitian, 1997.

Wang, Hui 汪暉. *China's New Order: Society, Politics, and Economy in Transition*. Cambridge, MA: Harvard University Press, 2003.

——. "Contemporary Chinese Thought and the Question of Modernity." Translated by Rebecca E. Karl. *Social Text* 55 (Summer 1998): 9–44.

——. "The Politics of Imagining Asia." Translated by Matthew A. Hale. In *The Politics of Imagining Asia*, edited by Theodore Huters, 10–62. Cambridge, MA: Harvard University Press, 2011.

——. *Xiandai zhongguo sixiang de xingqi* 現代中國思想的興起 [The rise of modern Chinese thoughts]. Beijing: Sanlian shudian, 2004.

Wang Jun 王軍. *Beijing Record: A Physical and Political History of Planning Modern Beijing*. Translated by Li Zhurun, Jin Shaoqing, and Xiong Lei. Singapore: World Scientific, 2011.

——. *Chengji* 城記 [Beijing record]. Beijing: Sanlian shudian, 2003.

Wang Qiugui 王秋桂, ed. *Jin Yong xiaoshuo guoji xueshu yantaohui lunwenji* 金庸小說國際學術研討會論文集 [Proceedings of the international conference on Jin Yong's novels]. Taibei: Yuanliu, 1999.

Wang Runhua 王潤華. *Lao She xiaoshuo xinlun* 老舍小說新論 [A new treatise on Lao She's novel]. Taipei: Dongda tushu gonsi, 1995.

Wang Shiren 王世仁 and Zhang Fuhe 張復合. *Zhongguo jindai jianzhu zonglan: Beijing pian* 中國近代建築總覽：北京篇 [A review of modern architecture in China: The section of Beijing]. Beijing: Zhongguo jianzhu gongye chubanshe, 1993.

Wang, Shuo. "Der Ling: Manchu Princess, Cultural Advisor, and Author." In *The Human Tradition in Modern China*, edited by Kenneth James Hammond and Kristin Eileen Stapleton, 73–92. Lanham, MD: Rowman & Littlefield, 2008.

Wang Shuo 王朔. *Playing for Thrills*. Translated by Howard Goldblatt. New York: William Morrow, 1997.

Wang, Xiaojue 王曉珏. "Memory, Photographic Seduction, and Allegorical Correspondence: Eileen Chang's *Mutual Reflections*." In *Rethinking Modern Chinese Popular Culture: Cannibalizations of the Canon*, edited by Carlos Rojas and Eileen Chow, 190–206. London: Routledge, 2009.

——. *Modernity with a Cold War Face: Reimagining the Nation in Chinese Literature across the 1949 Divide*. Cambridge, MA: Harvard University Asia Center, 2013.

——. "*Stone* in Modern China: Literature, Politics, and Culture." In *Approaches to Teaching the Story of the Stone (Dream of the Red Chamber)*, edited by Andrew Schonebaum and Tina Lu, 662–691. New York: Modern Language Association, 2013.

Wang Yao 王瑤. *Zhongguo xin wenxue shi gao* 中國新文學史稿 [A history of Chinese new literature]. Vol. 1: Beijing: Kaiming, 1951; Vol. 2: Beijing: Xin wenyi, 1958.

Wang Zhaosheng 王兆勝. *Lin Yutang de wenhua qinghuai* 林語堂的文化情懷 [Lin Yutang's cultural complex]. Beijing: Zhongguo shehui kexue chubanshe, 1998.

Wasserstrom, Jeffrey N. *Student Protest in Twentieth-Century China: The View from Shanghai*. Stanford, CA: Stanford University Press, 1991.

Watt, Ian. *The Rise of the Novel*. Berkeley: University of California Press, 1957.

Weber, Max. *The City*. Translated and edited by Don Martindale and Gertrud Neuwirth. Glencoe, IL: The Free Press, 1958.

———. *The Religion of China: Confucianism and Taoism*. Translated and edited by Hans H. Gerth. Glencoe, IL: The Free Press, 1951.

Wei Shaochang 魏紹昌, ed. *Yuanyang hudie pai yanjiu ziliao* 鴛鴦蝴蝶派研究資料 [Research materials on the school of Mandarin Ducks and Butterflies]. Shanghai: Shanghai wenyi chubanshe, 1962.

Wei Zi'an 魏子安. *Huayue hen* 花月痕 [Traces of the flower and the moon]. Shanghai: Shanghai guji chubanshe, 1994.

Wen Renjun 聞人軍. *Zhouli: Kaogong ji yizhu* 周禮考工記譯注 [The rites of Zhou dynasty: On craftsmanship. An annotated translation]. Shanghai: Shanghai guji chubanshe, 1993.

Weng Li 翁立. *Beijing de hutong* 北京的胡同 [Beijing's hutong]. Beijing: Yanshan chubanshe, 1992.

Wheatley, Paul. *The Pivot of the Four Quarters: A Preliminary Enquiry into the Origins and Character of the Ancient Chinese City*. Chicago: Aldine, 1971.

West, Stephen. "Playing with Food: Performance, Food, and the Aesthetics of Artificiality in the Sung and Yuan." *Harvard Journal of Asiatic Studies* 57, no. 1 (1997): 67–106.

Widmer, Ellen, and David Der-wei Wang, eds. *From May Fourth to June Fourth: Fiction and Film in Twentieth-Century China*. Cambridge, MA: Harvard University Press, 1993.

Williams, Raymond. *The Country and the City*. New York: Oxford University Press, 1973.

———. *The Long Revolution*. London: Chatto & Windus, 1961.

———. *Marxism and Literature*. Oxford: Oxford University Press, 1977.

Wirth-Nesher, Hana. *City Codes: Reading the Modern Urban Novel*. Cambridge: Cambridge University Press, 1996.

Wong, Sau-ling Cynthia. *Reading Asian American Literature: From Necessity to Extravagance*. Princeton, NJ: Princeton University Press, 1993.

Wong Wang-chi 王宏志. *Lishi de ouran: Cong Xianggang kan zhongguo xiandai wenxue shi* 歷史的偶然：從香港看中國現代文學史 [Historical coincidences: Reflections on history of modern Chinese literature from Hong Kong]. Hong Kong: Oxford University Press, 1997.

Wu Fuhui 吳福輝. *Dushi xuanliu zhong de haipai xiaoshuo* 都市漩流中的海派小說 [Fiction of Shanghai school in urban vortex]. Changsha: Hunan jiaoyu chubanshe, 1995.

Wu, Hung. *The Double Screen: Medium and Representation in Chinese Painting*. Chicago: University of Chicago Press, 1996.

———. *Remaking Beijing: Tiananmen Square and the Creation of a Political Space*. Chicago: University of Chicago Press, 2005.

Wu Jianren 吳趼人. *Ershinian mudu zhi guai xianzhuang* 二十年目睹之怪現狀 [Strange things observed over the past twenty years]. Beijing: Renmin wenxue chubanshe, 1959 (2006 reprint).

———. *Henhai* 恨海 [*The Sea of Regret*]. Shanghai: Guangzhi shuju, 1906.

Wu, Liangyong. *Rehabilitating the Old City of Beijing: A Project in the Ju'er Hutong Neighbourhood*. Vancouver: UBC Press, 1999

Wu Xiaodong 吳曉東 and Ji Birui 計璧瑞, eds. *2000' Jin Yong xiaoshuo guoji huiyi lunwenji* 2000' 金庸小說國際研討會論文集 [Proceedings of the international conference on Jin Yong's novels in Beijing 2000]. Beijing: Beijing daxue chubanshe, 2002.

Wu Zhuoliu 吳濁流. *Yaxiya de gu'er* 亞細亞的孤兒 [Orphan of Asia]. Taipei: Caogen, 1995.

Xia Chun 夏淳. "Jiao Juyin he tade 'Zhongguo Xuepai'" 焦菊隱和他的"中國學派" [Jiao Juyin and his "Chinese School"]. *Xinwenhua shiliao* 新文化史料 [Historical materials of new culture] 2 (1996):14–16.

Xu Zhimo 徐志摩. "Number 7, Stone Tiger Lane." In Jonathan Spence, *The Gate of Heavenly Peace: The Chinese and Their Revolution, 1895–1980*, 16. New York: Viking, 1981.

Xue, Fengxuan. *Beijing: The Nature and Planning of a Chinese Capital City*. Chichester, New York: Wiley, 1995.

——. *China's Regional Disparities: Issues and Policies*. Huntington, NY: Nova Science Publishers, 2001.

——, ed. *Chinese Cities: The Growth of the Metropolis since 1949*. Oxford: Oxford University Press, 1985.

Yan Jiayan 嚴家炎. *Jin Yong xiaoshuo lun gao* 金庸小說論稿 [Treatises on Jin Yong's fiction]. Rev. ed. Beijing: Beijing daxue chubanshe, 2007.

——. *Zhongguo xiandai xiaoshuo liupai shi* 中國現代小說流派史 [A history of the schools of modern Chinese novel]. Beijing: Renmin wenxue chubanshe, 1989.

Yang Jianlong 楊劍龍. "Lun Zhongguo dushi wenxue yu dushi wenxue yanjiu" 論中國都市文學與都市文學研究 [On Chinese urban literature and urban literary studies]. *Jianghan luntan* 江漢論壇 [Jianghan forum] 3 (2013): 11–16.

Yang, Mayfair Mei-hui, ed. *Spaces of Their Own: Women's Public Sphere in Transnational China*. Minneapolis: University of Minnesota Press, 1999.

Yang, Mo. *The Song of Youth*. Translated by Nan Ying. Beijing: Foreign Languages Press, 1964.

Yang Yi 楊義. *Jingpai haipai zonglun* 京派海派綜論 [Beijing school and Shanghai school]. Beijing: Zhongguo shehui kexue chubanshe, 2003.

——. *Zhongguo xiandai xiaoshuo shi* 中國現代小說史 [A history of modern Chinese fiction]. 3 vols. Beijing: renmin wenxue chubanshe, 1986–1991.

Ye Hongsheng 葉洪生. *Ye Hongsheng lunjian* 葉洪生論劍 [Ye Hongsheng on swords]. Taibei: Lianjing, 1994.

Ye Shitao 葉石濤. *Taiwan wenxue shigang* 台灣文學史綱 [An outline of the history of Taiwanese literature]. Gaoxiong: Wenxuejie, 1987.

Ye, Zhaoyan 葉兆言. *Nanjing, 1937*. Translated by Michael Berry. New York: Columbia University Press, 2002.

Yeh, Catherine Vance. "Zeng Pu's Niehaihua as a Political Novel: A World Genre in a Chinese Form." PhD diss., Harvard University, 1990.

Yeh, Michelle (Xi Mi) 奚密. *Modern Chinese Poetry: Theory and Practice Since 1917*. New Haven, CT: Yale University Press, 1991.

——. "'On Our Destitute Dinner Table': Modern Poetry Quarterly in the 1950s." In *Writing Taiwan: A New Literary History*, edited by David Der-wei Wang and Carlos Rojas, 113–139. Durham, NC: Duke University Press, 2007.

——. "Taiwanren zai Beijing" 台灣人在北京 [The Taiwanese in Beijing]. In *Beijing*, edited by Chen and Wang, 371–389.

——, ed. and trans. *Anthology of Modern Chinese Poetry*. New Haven, CT: Yale University Press, 1992.

Yeh, Wen-hsin, ed. *Becoming Chinese: Passages to Modernity and Beyond*. Berkeley: University of California Press, 2000.

Ying Fenghuang 應鳳凰. "Bijiao Lin Haiyin *Chengnan jiushi* de xiaoshuo yu dianying" 比較林海音《城南舊事》的小說與電影 [A comparison of the novel and the film of Lin Haiyin's *My Memories of Beijing*]. *Taiwanxue yanjiu* 台灣學研究 [Taiwan studies] 3 (1996): 1–15.

———. "Fangong+xiandai: Youyi ziyou zhuyi sichao wenxue ban" 反共＋現代：右翼自由主義思潮文學版 [Anti-communism and modernity: The literary version of the Rightist liberalism]. In *Taiwan xiaoshuo shilun* 台灣小說史論 [Essays on Taiwan literary history], edited by Chen Jianzhong 陳建忠, Ying Fenghuang 應鳳凰, Qiu Guifen 邱貴芬, Zhang Songsheng 張誦聖, and Liu Liangya 劉亮雅, 111–196. Taipei: Maitian, 2007.

———. "The Literary Development of Zhong Lihe and Postcolonial Discourse in Taiwan." In *Writing Taiwan: A New Literary History*, edited by David Der-wei Wang and Carlos Rojas, 140–155. Duham, NC: Duke University Press, 2007.

Young, James. *The Texture of Memory: Holocaust Memorials and Meaning.* New Haven, CT: Yale University Press, 1993.

Yu, Anthony C. *Rereading the Dream: Desire and the Making of Fiction in* Dream of the Red Chamber. Princeton, NJ: Princeton University Press, 1997.

Yu Xiaoxia 俞曉霞. "Lin Huiyin xiaoshuo changzuo zhong de wuerfu yinsu" 林徽因小說創作中的伍爾夫因素 [Virginia Woolf Elements in Lin Huiyin's Short Stories]. *Zhongguo xiandai wenxue yanjiu congkan* 中國現代文學研究叢刊 [Modern Chinese literature studies] 6 (2012): 59–67.

Yuan Jin 袁進. *Xiaoshuo qicai Zhang Henshui zhuan* 小說奇才張恨水傳 [Zhang Henshui, A Talented Fiction Writer]. Taipei: Yeqiang chubanshe, 1992.

Yue Daiyun 樂黛雲, and Alan Le Pichion, eds. *Dujiaoshou yu long* 獨角獸與龍 [Unicorn and dragon]. Beijing: Beijing daxue chubanshe, 1995.

Yue Daiyun 樂黛雲. "Dangdai zhongguo bijiao wenxue fazhan zhong de jige wenti" 當代中國比較文學發展中的幾個問題 [Issues in the development of contemporary Chinese comparative literature], *Beijing daxue xuebao* 北京大學學報 [Journal of Peking University] 4 (2009): 15–20.

———. "Hudong renzhi: Bijiao wenxue de renshilun he fangfalun" 互動認知：比較文學的認識論和方法論 [Reciprocal cognition: Epistemology and methodology in comparative literature], *Zhongguo bijiao wenxue* 中國比較文學 [Chinese comparative literature], 1 (2001): 1–7.

Yue, Gang. *The Mouth That Begs: Hunger, Cannibalism, and the Politics of Eating in Modern China.* Durham, NC: Duke University Press, 1999.

Zeng Guangcan 曾廣燦 and Wu Huaibin 吳懷斌, eds. *Lao She yanjiu ziliao* 老舍研究資料 [Research materials on Lao She]. Beijing: Zhishi chanquan chubanshe, 2010.

Zeng Lingcun 曾令存. "Zai jiedu: *Chaguan* wenben de shenceng jiegou" 再解讀：《茶館》文本的深層結構 [Reinterpretation: The text structure of *Teahouse*]. *Xiju xuekan* 戲劇學刊 [Taipei theatre journal] 11 (2010): 251–267.

Zha, Jianying. *China Pop: How Soap Operas, Tabloids and Bestsellers Are Transforming a Culture.* New York: The New Press, 1996.

Zhang, Ailing (Eileen Chang) 張愛玲. *Bansheng yuan* 半生緣 (Half a lifelong romance, 1951). Taipei: Huangguan, 1991.

———. *Haishang huakai, haishang hualuo* 海上花開，海上花落 [Mandarin translation of Han Bangqing's *Sing-song Girls of Shanghai*]. Taipei: Huangguan, 1983.

———. *Liuyan* 流言 [Written on water]. Taipei: Huangguan, 1991.

———. *Love in a Fallen City.* Translated by Karen S. Kingsbury. New York: New York Review of Books, 2007.

———. *Lust, Caution: The Story, the Screenplay, and the Making of the Film.* Translated by Julia Lovell. New York: Pantheon, 2007.

———. *Qingcheng zhilian* 傾城之戀 [Love in a fallen city]. Taipei: Huangguan, 1991.

———. *Wangran ji* 惘然集 [Regrets]. Taipei: Huangguan, 2010.

———. *Written on Water*. Translated by Andrew F. Jones, coedited with an introduction by Nicole Huang. New York: Columbia University Press, 2005.

———. "Yi Hu Shizhi" 憶胡適之 [Remembering Hu Shizhi]. In *Zhang kan*, edited by Ailing Zhang, 142–154. Taipei: Huangguan, 1991.

———. *Zhang kan* 張看 [Chang'sobservations]. Taipei: Huangguan, 1991.

Zhang Chonggang 張重崗. "Yuanxiang tiyan yu Zhong Lihe de Beiping xushi" 原鄉體驗與鍾理和的北平敘事 [Zhong Lihe's motherland experience and Beiping narration]. In *Zhongguo xiandai wenxue luncong* 中國現代文學論叢 [Forum of modern Chinese literature] 1 (2008): 117–129. Reprinted in *Zhongyuan lunjian: Dierjie shijie huawen wenxue luntan wenji* 中原論劍：第二屆世界華文文學論壇文集 [China forum: Selected articles from the second Chinese-language literature conference], edited by Zou Youfeng 鄒友峰, Mao Jianhua 冒建華, and Mu Naitang 穆乃堂, 210–222. Lanzhou: Gansu renmin meishu chubanshe, 2008.

Zhang Geng 張庚. "*Chaguan* mantan" 《茶館》漫談 [Random thoughts on *Teahouse*]. *Renmin ribao* 人民日報 [People's Daily], May 27, 1958. Reprinted in *Lao She yanjiu ziliao*, edited by Zeng Guangcan and Wu Huaibin, 800–804. Beijing: Zhishi chanquan chubanshe, 2010.

Zhang Guangzheng 張光正. "Lao Beijing de 'fanshu zai': Ji Lin Haiyin qingshaonian shidai de ren he shi" 老北京的"番薯仔"：記林海音青少年時代的人和事 [Sweet potato guys in old Beijing: Records of people and stories during Lin Haiyin's youth]. In *Lin Haiyin yanjiu lunwenji* 林海音研究論文集 [Collected essays on Lin Haiyin], edited by Shu Yi 舒乙 and Fu Guangming 傅光明, 60–71. Beijing: Taihai chubanshe, 2001.

Zhang Guiyang 張圭陽. *Jin Yong yu* Ming bao *chuanqi* 金庸與明報傳奇 [Jin Yong and *Ming bao*]. Taipei: Yunchen wenhua, 2005.

Zhang Henshui 張恨水. *Chunming waishi* 春明外史 [Unofficial history of Beijing]. 1934. Taiyuan: Beiyue wenyi chubanshe, 2000, reprint.

———. *Jinfen shijia* 金粉世家 [Grand old family]. 1930. Taiyuan: Beiyue wenyi chubanshe, 2000, reprint.

———. *Shanghai Express: A Thirties Novel*. Translated by William A. Lyell. Honolulu: University of Hawai'i Press, 1997.

———. *Tixiao yinyuan* 啼笑因緣 [Fate in tears and laughter]. 1929–1930. Taiyuan: Beiyue wenyi chubanshe, 2000, reprint.

———. "Weilai de Beijing" 未來的北京 [Beijing in the future]. *Shijie wanbao* 世界日報 [World daily news]. September 27, 1926 to October 7, 1926.

———. *Ye shenchen* 夜深沈 [Deep darkness of the night]. 1937–1938. Taiyuan: Beiyue wenyi chubanshe, 2000, reprint.

———. *Xiezuo shengya huiyi* 寫作生涯回憶 [Memoirs of my writing career]. In *Zhang Henshui yanjiu ziliao* 張恨水研究資料 [Research materials on Zhang Henshui], edited by Zhang Zhanguo 張佔國 and Wei Shouzhong 魏守忠, 7–73. Beijing: Zhishi chanquan chubanshe, 2009.

Zhang Hongsheng 張鴻聲. "'Wenxue zhong de chengshi' yu 'chengshi xiangxiang' yanjiu" "文學中的城市"與"城市想象"研究 ["The city in literature" and research of "urban imagination"]. *Wenxue pinglun* 文學評論 1 (2007): 116–122.

Zhang, Jingyuan. *Psychoanalysis in China: Literary Transformations, 1919–1949*. Ithaca, NY: Cornell East Asia Program, 1992.

Zhang Peng 張鵬. "Jicheng yu fazhan" 繼承與發展 [Inheritance and development], *Zhongguo dianshi* 中國電視 [Chinese television], 10 (2008): 66–68.

Zhang Qingping 張清平. *Lin Huiyin* 林徽因. Tianjin: Baihua wenyi chubanshe, 2002.

Zhang Wu 張伍. *Wo de fuqin Zhang Henshui* 我的父親張恨水 [My father Zhang Henshui]. Shenyang: Chunfeng wenyi chubanshe, 2002.

Zhang Xinying 張新穎. *Ershi shiji shangbanqi zhongguo wenxue de xiandai yishi* 20世紀上半期中國文學的現代意識 [Modern consciousness of Chinese literature in the first half of the twentieth century]. Beijing: Sanlian shudian, 2001.

Zhang, Xudong. *Chinese Modernism in the Era of Reforms: Cultural Fever, Avant-Garde Fiction, and the New Chinese Cinema.* Durham, NC: Duke University Press, 1997.

——. *Postsocialism and Cultural Politics: China in the Last Decade of the Twentieth Century.* Durham, NC: Duke University Press, 2008.

——. "Shanghai Nostalgia: Postrevolutionary Allegories in Wang Anyi's Literary Production in the 1990s." *positions: east asia cultures critiques* 8, no. 2 (2000): 349–387.

Zhang, Yingjin, ed. *China in a Polycentric World: Essays in Chinese Comparative Literature.* Stanford, CA: Stanford University Press, 1998.

——. *Cinema, Space, and Polylocality in a Globalizing China.* Honolulu: University of Hawai'i Press, 2010.

——, ed. *Cinema and Urban Culture in Shanghai, 1922–1943.* Stanford, CA: Stanford University Press, 1999.

——. *The City in Modern Chinese Literature and Film: Configurations of Space, Time, and Gender.* Stanford, CA: Stanford University Press, 1996.

——. *Screening China: Critical Interventions, Cinematic Reconfigurations, and the Transnational Imaginary in Contemporary Chinese Cinema.* Ann Arbor: Center for Chinese Studies, University of Michigan, 2002.

Zhang Wojun 張我軍. *Zhang Wojun shiwen ji* 張我軍詩文集 [Collected poems and essays of Zhang Wojun]. Edited by Zhang Guangzhi 張光直. Taipei: Chunwenxue, 1989.

Zhang Zhanguo 張佔國 and Wei Shouzhong 魏守忠, eds. *Zhang Henshui yanjiu ziliao* 張恨水研究資料 [Research materials on Zhang Henshui]. Beijing: Zhishi chanquan chubanshe, 2009.

Zhang Zhaoji 張肇基, ed. *Beijing siheyuan* 北京四合院 [Courtyard houses in Beijing]. Beijing: Beijing meishu sheying chubanshe, 1995.

Zhao Chen 趙辰. "Zuowei zhongguo jianzhu xueshu xianxingzhe de Lin Huiyin" 作為中國建築學術先行者的林徽因 [Lin Huiyin as a pioneer of Chinese architecture]. *Jianzhu shi* 建築史 [History of architecture] 21 (2005): 1–12.

Zhao Xiaoxuan 趙孝萱. *Zhang Henshui xiaoshuo xinlun* 張恨水小說新論 [New thesis on Zhang Henshui's novels]. Taipei: Xuesheng shuju, 2002.

Zhao Xifang 趙稀方. *Xiaoshuo xianggang* 小說香港 [Narrating Hong Kong]. Beijing: Sanlian shudian, 2003.

Zhao Yuan 趙園. *Beijing: Cheng yu ren* 北京：城與人 [Beijing: The city and its residents]. Shanghai: Shanghai renmin chubanshe, 1991.

Zhong Lihe 鍾理和. "Baishu de bei'ai" 白薯的悲哀 [The sadness of the yam]. In *Zhong Lihe ji* 鍾理和集 [Selected writings of Zhong Lihe], 93–102. Taipei: Qianwei chubanshe, 1991.

——. *From the Old Country: Stories and Sketches of China and Taiwan.* Translated by T. M. McClellan. New York: Columbia University Press, 2014.

————. "Jiazhutao" 夾竹桃 [Oleander]. In *Zhong Lihe daibiaozuo*, edited by Liu Yatie 劉亞鐵, 145–185. Beijing: Huaxia chubanshe, 1999.

————. "Oleander." In *From the Old Country: Stories and Sketches of China and Taiwan*, translated by T. M. McClellan, 63–106. New York: Columbia University Press, 2014.

————. "Yuanxiang ren" 原鄉人 [People of the native land]. In *Yuanxiangren: Zhong Lihe zhong-duanpian xiaoshuo xuan* 原鄉人：鍾理和中短篇小說選 [People of the native land: A selection of novellas and short stories by Zhong Lihe], 2–12. Beijing: Renmin wenxue chubanshe, 1983.

————. *Zhong Lihe daibiaozuo* 鍾理和代表作 [Selected writings of Zhong Lihe]. Edited by Liu Yatie 劉亞鐵. Beijing: Huaxia chubanshe, 1999.

————. *Zhong Lihe quanji* 鍾理和全集 [The complete works of Zhong Lihe]. Edited by Zhang Liangze 張良澤. Taipei: Yuanxing chubanshe, 1976.

Zhou Ning 周寧, ed. *Zhongguo xingxiang: xifang de xueshuo yu chuanshuo* 中國形象：西方的學說與傳說 [Images of China: Western theories and stories]. Beijing: Xueyuan chubanshe, 2004.

Zhou Zuoren 周作人. "Shanghai qi" 上海氣 [Shanghai spirit, 1927]. In *Shanghai* 上海, edited by Ma Fengyang 馬逢洋, 61–62. Shanghai: Wenhui chubanshe, 1996.

Zhu, Jianfei. *Chinese Spatial Strategies: Imperial Beijing, 1420–1911*. London: Routledge, 2003.

Žižek, Slavoj, ed. *Mapping Ideology*. London: Verso, 1994.

INDEX

293

Printed in the USA/Agawam, MA
March 30, 2018

672424.006